D0622409

AUTOMATA THEORY

# AUTOMATA THEORY

Edited by
E. R. CAIANIELLO
*Istituto di Fisica Teorica*
*Università di Napoli, Naples, Italy*

1966

*New York* ACADEMIC PRESS *London*

ACADEMIC PRESS INC.
111 Fifth Avenue, New York, New York 10003

*United Kingdom Edition published by*
ACADEMIC PRESS INC. (LONDON) LTD.
Berkeley Square House, London W. 1

LIBRARY OF CONGRESS CATALOG CARD NUMBER: 65-22775.

PRINTED IN THE UNITED STATES OF AMERICA

## Contributors

Numbers in parentheses indicate the pages on which the authors' contributions begin.

V. Amar, *L.R.E. Olivetti, Pregnana Milanese, Milan, Italy* (1)

Michael A. Arbib,* *Imperial College of Science and Technology, London, England* (6)

Claude Berge, *International Computation Centre, Rome, E.U.R., Italy* (25)

Corrado Böhm, *I.N.A.C.-C.N.R., Piazzale delle Scienze, Rome, Italy* (35)

Mario Borillo, *EURATOM, Ispra, Italy* (66)

J. Richard Büchi, *Department of Mathematics, Ohio State University, Columbus, Ohio* (70)

P. Camion,† *EURATOM-CETIS, Ispra, Italy* (102)

Jack D. Cowan, *Department of Electrical Engineering, Imperial College of Science and Technology, London, England* (131)

Martin Davis, *Belfer Graduate School of Science, Yeshiva University, New York, New York* (146, 153)

Alfonso Caracciolo di Forino, *Centro Studi Calcolatrici Elettroniche del C.N.R., Pisa, Italy* (107, 115)

Arthur Gill, *Department of Electrical Engineering, University of California, Berkeley, California* (164, 176)

Maurice Gross,‡ *Centre National de la Recherche Scientifique, Institut Blaise Pascal, Paris, France* (181)

Wolf Gross, *I.N.A.C.-C.N.R., Piazzale delle Scienze, Rome, Italy* (35)

Erich M. Harth, *Department of Physics, Syracuse University, Syracuse, New York* (201)

John H. Holland, *Department of Communication Sciences, The University of Michigan, Ann Arbor, Michigan* (218)

* *Present address:* Stanford University, Stanford, California.

† *Present address:* Faculté des Sciences, Université de Toulouse, France.

‡ *Present address:* Linguistic Department, University of Pennsylvania, Philadelphia, Pennsylvania.

WILLIAM L. KILMER, *Research Laboratory of Electronics, Massachusetts Institute of Technology, Cambridge, Massachusetts* (269)

H. KOREZLIOGLU,* *Istituto di Fisica Teorica, Naples, Italy* (231)

J. LARISSE, *CETIS-EURATOM, Ispra, Italy* (239)

LARS LÖFGREN, *Lund Institute of Technology, Lund, Sweden* (251)

WARREN S. MCCULLOCH, *Research Laboratory of Electronics, Massachusetts Institute of Technology, Cambridge, Massachusetts* (269)

MAURICE NIVAT, *Centre National de la Recherche Scientifique, Institut Blaise Pascal, Paris, France* (278)

L. NOLIN, *Institut Blaise Pascal, Paris, France* (295)

G. PUTZOLU, *L.R.E. Olivetti, Pregnana Milanese, Milan, Italy* (1)

MICHAEL O. RABIN, *Department of Mathematics, Hebrew University, Jerusalem, Israel* (304)

M. P. SCHÜTZENBERGER, *Institut Blaise Pascal, Paris, France* (239, 314, 320)

L. A. M. VERBEEK, *EURATOM-CETIS, Ispra, Italy* (325)

* *Present address:* Institut Henri Poincaré, Paris, France.

# Preface

In recent years the study of automata has been acquiring increasing importance for a large class of scientists, from the pure logician to the practical programmer, with overtures on fields such as linguistics and neurophysiology. There are several concrete reasons for this arousal of interest, aside from the feeling which seems to characterize our civilization that social and economical phenomena could and should, through quantitative analyses, be understood and brought under control as behaviors of gigantic robot-like organisms.

Many of the automata which are objects of study represent steps toward the ideal Turing machine; what they can do, computation-wise, is of the greatest interest to logicians and mathematicians, including some modern linguists who search for models of the as yet mysterious structures and properties of the human languages.

From the point of view of electronic computation, automata theory has offered the means for studying the functions and potentialities of phenomena *in depth*; from a crude piece of engineering, the computer becomes an organism whose organizational principles can be discovered and put to useful purpose, much in the same way as physiology explains anatomy. There is, in fact, a growing tendency toward the study of automata whose behaviors may come near to those of living organisms; attempts in this direction are, for instance, the "probabilistic automata" of recent invention. This view is encouraged by the modern attempts at a schematization of the brain as a logical network, first among which is the classical one of McCulloch and Pitts: thinkers like N. Wiener and J. von Neumann saw in this the most important challenge with which modern science is confronted.

It has seemed therefore appropriate to dedicate to automata theory a course of our International School of Physics; we were fortunate in having among our lecturers some of the people who have contributed most to its progress. In particular, I am indebted to Professor M. Schutzenberger, whose advice and help have been extremely valuable at all stages of this endeavour, and to Dr. H. Korezlioglu, who has been of great assistance throughout the preparation and organization of the School.

Thanks are due to NATO, whose generous support through their Advanced Study Institute Program made this 6th International School at Ravello (June 14-June 30, 1964) possible; thanks are also due to Academic Press for their courteous and efficient cooperation.

E. R. Caianiello

*December, 1965*

# Contents

# Generalizations of Regular Events

V. AMAR and G. PUTZOLU

*L. R. E. Olivetti*
*Pregnana Milanese, Milan, Italy*

In the theory of formal languages, regular events play a key role, since they exhibit particularly interesting mathematical properties. Many families of languages have been introduced which are more general than regular events, for example, context-free languages, Chomsky 1-languages [1], and so on. Most of these families do not have an interesting mathematical structure, so that their algebraic properties are quite weak. Some trials have been done to obtain families of languages more general than regular events, families which exhibit strong algebraic properties. This was done by M. P. Schützenberger [2]. We have just studied a different approach to the problem of generalizing regular sets. In the following many proofs will be sketched or omitted; more details may be found in references [3] and [4].

Let us now give some definitions: Let $\Sigma = (\sigma_1, \ldots, \sigma_r)$ be a finite alphabet, and $T_\Sigma = (x, y, \ldots)$ the free semigroup with unity $\lambda$ on $\Sigma$. A particular family of subsets of $T_\Sigma$ is the family of regular events. We summarize briefly the fundamental properties of this family [5], which we shall denote by $R$:

1. Regular sets are the sets recognizable by finite automata.
2. To each regular event we may associate a right-invariant equivalence relation of finite index which saturates it and conversely (theorem of Nerode).
3. Regular sets are the minimal family of sets which contains finite sets and which is closed under the operation $+$ (union), $\cdot$ (concatenation), and $^\dagger$, where $A^\dagger = \lambda + A + A \cdot A + A \cdot A \cdot A + \cdots$.

The key point, which is the reason for the pleasant properties of regular events, is, in our opinion, the second one; i.e., regular events are strictly connected with equivalence relations of finite index which are right-invariant with respect to concatenation. Our starting point, then, has been to introduce other abstract products on the set of tapes and to define new families of languages by means of a theorem analogous to the theorem of Nerode. For example, consider the following abstract product on $T_\Sigma$:

$$x \circ y = y' x y''$$

where we have decomposed $y$ in this standard way[1]:

$$y = y' \omega_y y'' \qquad \begin{cases} |y'| = |y''| \\ |\omega_y| \leqslant 1 \end{cases}$$

It is easy to see that "$\circ$" is associative, so that it induces a semigroup structure on the set of tapes, which we shall call $T^{(1)}$.

Now let $R_1$ be the family of all languages saturated by right-invariant equivalence relations on $T^{(1)}$ of finite index. We shall show that $R_1$ is a particular subclass of context-free languages.

Let us recall the definition of context-free grammars. A context-free grammar $G$ is a 4-tuple $G = (\Sigma, \Delta, \delta_0, P)$, where $\Sigma$ is the terminal alphabet, $\Delta$ is the nonterminal alphabet, $\delta_0 \in \Delta$ is the initial symbol, and $P$ is a finite set of productions of the form $\delta \to \varphi$ (where $\delta \in \Delta$ and $\varphi$ is a word on the alphabet $\Sigma \cup \Delta$).

**Definition.** A 1-linear grammar (1LG) is a context-free grammar having only productions of the form

$$\left.\begin{array}{l} \delta \to x\delta' y \\ \delta \to z \\ \delta \to \delta' \end{array}\right\} \qquad \text{where } x, y, z \in T_\Sigma \text{ and } |x| = |y|$$

These grammars are clearly a subclass of linear grammars, which have the condition $|x| = |y|$ relaxed.

Let $L_1$ denote the family of languages generated by 1-linear grammars; the following theorem then holds:

**Theorem 1.** $L_1 = R_1$.

*Proof.* We show first that $R_1 \subset L_1$. Let $r \in R_1$; then by hypothesis there exists a right-invariant equivalence relation $C$ of finite index which saturates $r$. Let $C_1 \cdots C_n$ be the classes of $C$. We associate to each $C_i$ a symbol $\delta_i$, and

[1] $|x|$ denotes the length of the word $x$.

we construct the following $G=(\Sigma,\Delta,\delta_0,P)$, where $\Delta=(\delta_0,\delta_1,\ldots,\delta_n)$ $\delta_0 \in \Delta$ is a new symbol, and $P$ has the productions

$$\begin{array}{ll} \delta_i \to \sigma_\alpha \delta_j \sigma_\beta & \text{iff } C_i \supset \sigma_\alpha C_j \sigma_\beta \\ \delta_i \to \lambda & \text{iff } C_i \ni \lambda \\ \delta_i \to \sigma_\alpha & \text{iff } C_i \ni \sigma_\alpha \\ \delta_0 \to \delta_i & \text{iff } C_i \subset r \end{array}$$

$G$ is obviously a 1-linear grammar and we shall show that $L(G)=r$.

*Case* (*a*). $r \subset L(G)$. Let $x \in r$, $x=\sigma'_p\sigma'_{p-1}\cdots\sigma'_1\omega_x\sigma''_1\cdots\sigma''_{p-1}\sigma''_p$, where $|\omega_x| \leqslant 1$. Let $C_1 \cdots C_{p+1}$ be the classes of $C$ such that

$$C_{i+1} \ni \sigma'_i\sigma'_{i-1}\cdots\sigma'_1\omega_x\sigma''_1\cdots\sigma''_{i-1}\sigma''_i \qquad [i=0,1,\ldots,p]$$

In particular, $C_1 \ni \omega_x$, $C_{p+1} \ni x$; then $C_{p+1} \subset r$. From the right invariance of $C$, $C_{i+1} \supset \sigma'_i C_i \sigma''_i$ $[i=1,\ldots,p]$, so that $G$ has the productions $\delta_1 \to \omega_x$, $\delta_{i+1} \to \sigma'_i\delta_i\sigma''_i$ $[i=1,\ldots,p]$, $\delta_0 \to \delta_{p+1}$. This tells us that $x \in L(G)$.

*Case* (*b*). $L(G) \subset r$. Let $x=\sigma'_p\sigma'_{p-1}\cdots\sigma'_1\omega_x\sigma''_1\cdots\sigma''_{p-1}\sigma''_p \in L(G)$. Then there exists a sequence $\delta_1,\delta_2,\ldots,\delta_{p+1}$ with $\delta_1 \to \omega_x$, $\delta_{i+1} \to \sigma'_i\delta_i\sigma''_i$ $[i=1,\ldots,p]$, $\delta_0 \to \delta_{p+1}$. This means that there exists a sequence $C_1,C_2,\ldots,C_{p+1}$ such that $C_1 \ni \omega_x$, $C_{i+1} \supset \sigma'_i C_i \sigma''_i$ $[i=1,\ldots,p]$, $C_{p+1} \subset r$, i.e., $x \in r$.

Q.E.D.

To prove now that $L_1 \subset R_1$, we observe that each production of the form $\delta \to x'\bar{\delta}x''$ of a (1LG) can be formally written $\delta \to \bar{\delta} \circ (x'x'')$. A technique analogous to the one which shows that the family of one-sided linear languages coincides with regular events gives the desired result [3].

Theorem 1 and the definition of the family $R_1$ tells then that for $L_1$ languages a theorem of Nerode holds.

We observe now that every congruence $C$ is also a right-invariant equivalent relation with respect to "$\circ$."

In fact, if $xCy$ then $\forall(t_1,t_2)$ $t_1xt_2Ct_1yt_2$ and in particular for $\forall(z_1,z_2)$ with $|z_1|=|z_2|$ $z_1xz_2Cz_1yz_2$, from which $x \circ (z_1z_2)Cy \circ (z_1z_2)$; consequently $\forall z$ $x \circ zCy \circ z$. Q.E.D.

Remembering the theorem of Myhill [5], which asserts that regular events are saturated by congruences of finite index, we obtain the following surprising result:

**Theorem 2.** $L_1 \supset R$; i.e., given a regular set, it is always possible to find a (1LG) which generates it. Furthermore, it can be shown that a theorem of Kleene holds for the family $L_1$; i.e., $L_1$ is the minimal family of sets containing finite sets and closed under $+$, $\circ$, and ${}^{\dagger\circ}$:

$$A^{\dagger\circ}=\lambda+A+A\circ A+A\circ A\circ A+\cdots$$

We shall not give the proof of this theorem but note only that the key point of the question is to show that a formal equation on sets of the form

$$X = X \circ A + B$$

where $A$ does not contain any right unity of $T^{(1)}$, can be uniquely solved and gives the result $X = B \circ A^{\dagger\circ}$.

*Example.*

$$G = (\Sigma, \Delta, \delta_0, p) \qquad \Sigma = \{0, 1\}, \Delta = \{\delta_0\}$$

$$P\begin{cases}\delta_0 \to 1\\ \delta_0 \to 0\delta_0 0 = \delta_0 \circ (00)\end{cases}$$

These productions are equivalent to the formal equation

$$\delta_0 = \delta_0 \circ (00) + 1,$$

whose solution is

$$L(G) = 1 \circ (00)^{\dagger\circ} = \sum_{n=0}^{\infty} 0^n 1 0^n$$

This example also tells us that the family $L_1$ properly contains $R$ because, as is well known, $\Sigma_{n=0}^{\infty} 0^n 1 0^n$ is not a regular set.

We now give the generalization of the preceding results. Let $k = k'/k''$ be a rational number ($k'$, $k''$ relatively prime); we decompose each $x \in T_\Sigma$ in the following way:

$$x = x' \omega_x x'' \qquad |x'|/|x''| = k, \ |\omega_x| < k' + k''$$

This decomposition is obviously unique.

Then define an abstract product "$\circ_k$" as follows:

$$x \circ_k y = x \circ_k (y' \omega_y y'') = y' x y'' \qquad |y'|/|y''| = k, \ |\omega_y| < k' + k''$$

"$\circ_k$" turns out to be associative and induces on the set of tapes a semigroup structure which we shall call $T^{(k)}$.

Let $R_k$ be the family of languages saturated by right-invariant equivalence relations of finite index on $T^{(k)}$. It can be shown that $R_k$ coincides with the family of languages $L_k$ generated by the following grammars, which we call $k$-linear grammars (KLG).

**Definition.** A (KLG) is a context-free grammar whose productions are of the form

$$\left.\begin{array}{l}\delta \to x\delta' y\\ \delta \to z\\ \delta \to \delta'\end{array}\right\} \qquad x, y, z \in T_\Sigma; \ |x|/|y| = k$$

It may be seen that the family $L_k$ exhibits analogous properties of the family $L_1$; i.e.,

1. $L_k \supset R$.
2. A Nerode theorem holds for the family $L_k$.
3. A Kleene theorem holds for the family $L_k$.

Finally some remarks are worthwhile when these considerations are applied to regular events [6].

Let $r \in R$ and let $G = (\Sigma, \Delta, \delta_0, P)$ be a (KLG) which generates $r$. Consider the grammar $G^\alpha = (\Sigma, \Delta^\alpha, \delta_0^\alpha, P^\alpha)$, where $\Delta^\alpha = \Delta$, $\delta_0^\alpha = \delta_0$, and $P^\alpha$ is constructed in the following way:

$$(\delta \to x\bar{\delta}) \in P^\alpha \quad \text{iff} \quad (\delta \to x\bar{\delta}y) \in P$$

$$(\delta \to z') \in P^\alpha \quad \text{iff} \quad (\delta \to z'\,\omega_z z'') \in P, \text{ with } |z'|/|z''| = k,$$
$$|\omega_z| = \alpha < k' + k''$$

$G^\alpha$ is a one-sided linear grammar and it generates the set of words $r_\alpha$ so defined:

$$r_\alpha = \{x' \mid \exists x \in r\ [x = x'\,\omega_x x''] \text{ with } |x'|/|x''| = k,\ |\omega_x| = \alpha < k' + k''\}$$

The regular sets come out to be closed under this very complicated and curious operation of fractionalization.

To conclude we shall point out an interesting question, which we were not able to answer: Each $R_k$ (or $L_k$) contains $R$; then $R \subset \bigcap_k R_k$ (the range of $k$ is the set of rationals). Does $R$ exhaust this intersection?

## REFERENCES


1. N. Chomsky, On certain formal properties of grammars, *Inform. and Control* **2**, 137–167 (1959).
2. M. P. Schützenberger, On the definition of a family of automata, *Inform. and Control* **4**, 245–270 (1961).
3. V. Amar and G. Putzolu, On a family of linear grammars (to appear in *Inform. and Control*).
4. V. Amar and G. Putzolu, Generalizations of regular events (to appear in *Inform. and Control*).
5. M. O. Rabin and D. Scott, Finite automata and their decision problems, *IBM J. Res. Develop.* **3**, 115–125 (1959).
6. R. E. Stearns and J. Hartmanis, Regularity preserving modifications of regular expressions, *Inform. and Control* **6**, 55–69 (1963).

# Speed-Up Theorems and Incompleteness Theorems

MICHAEL A. ARBIB[1]

*Imperial College of Science and Technology*
*London, England*

## I. The Speed-Up Theorem[2]

Let us view Turing machines as programmed computers as follows: A Turing machine is a device equipped with a container for cards, a tape scanner-printer-mover, and a tape that is infinite in both directions. The tape is divided into squares along its length, and the scanner can look at one square at a time. The device can print the blank, or one of a finite set $\Sigma$ of symbols, on the square it is examining and shift the tape one square to right or left. The container can hold an arbitrarily large but finite number of cards, together called the program. On each card is printed a single 5-tuple $q_i S_j S_k M q_l$. The $q_i$ denotes internal states of the device; the $S_j$ are tape symbols; and $M$ is a move $L$ (left), $R$ (right), or $N$ (none). When the device is in state $q_i$ and scans the symbol $S_j$, it prints the symbol $S_k$, moves the tape $M$, and changes its internal state to $q_l$. If there is no card starting with $q_i S_j$ in the container when the machine is in state $q_i$ and scanning the symbol $S_j$, then the machine stops. Any program is allowed, subject to the condition that any two cards must differ in the initial pair $q_i S_j$.

We can associate with each program a partial recursive function $\phi$ as follows: The program is placed in the container, an input integer $x$ is written in some suitably encoded form as a finite string of symbols on the tape, the scanner is placed over the rightmost digit of this string, and the device is put in state $q_0$. The device then operates in accordance with the instructions printed in the program. If it never stops, we say $\phi(x)$ diverges. If it does stop, we let $\phi(x)$ be the integer obtained from the string of symbols on the tape by some standard decoding.

[1] *Present address:* Stanford University, Stanford, California.

[2] This section is mainly an exposition of a theorem, discovered by Manuel Blum, which was the stimulus for this paper. My warm thanks to Manuel for this, and for many enjoyable and useful conversations on the subject of difficulty of computation.

Note that we thus obtain many different such machines, one for each choice of $\Sigma$ and of the encoding and decoding functions. A Turing machine, as we usually know it, is any such machine equipped with a suitable program.

Let us pick some particular $\Sigma$ and some simple encoding and decoding functions, e.g., binary notation, and let $M$ be the machine so specified. Just as we usually enumerate the Turing machines $Z_1, Z_2, \ldots$, so may we now effectively enumerate the programs $P_1, P_2, P_3, \ldots$ of our machine $M$. Let $\phi_i$ be the partial recursive function computed by $M$ when supplied with program $P_i$. The theory of recursive functions immediately yields (cf., e.g., [6]).

1. *The Recursion Theorem*

For any recursive function $h$, there exists an integer $y$ such that

$$\phi_y = \phi_{h(y)}$$

i.e., $\phi_y$ is a fixed point of the functional $\phi_i \to \phi_{h(i)}$.

2. *The Iteration Theorem*

For each partial recursive function $f$ of $m + 1$ variables, there is a total recursive function $s(y_1, \ldots, y_m)$ such that

$$f(y_1, \ldots, y_m, x) = \phi_{s(y_1, \ldots, y_m)}(x)$$

Now let

$$\Phi_i(x) = \begin{cases} \text{number of steps which } M \text{ takes to compute } \phi_i(x) \\ \text{when supplied with program } P_i, \text{ if } \phi_i(x) \\ \text{converges; diverges if } \phi_i(x) \text{ diverges} \end{cases}$$

We call $\Phi_i(x)$ a *measure function*. Immediately we obtain

3. *The Measure-Function Theorem*

The functions $\Phi_i(x)$ are partial-recursive and satisfy:

(a) For all $i$ and $x$, $\phi_i(x)$ converges if and only if $\Phi_i(x)$ converges.
(b) There exists a total recursive function $\alpha$ such that for all $i$ and $x$,

$$\alpha(i, x, y) = \begin{cases} 1 & \text{if } \Phi_i(x) = y \\ 0 & \text{otherwise} \end{cases}$$

To see (b), we use Turing's hypothesis, after noting that we may find $\alpha(i, x, y)$ effectively by supplying $M$ with program $P_i$ and input $x$, and letting it run for $y$ steps.

The above discussion leads us to the following very abstract formulation of a computer:

**Definition.** An $M$-computer $C$ is an effective enumeration of pairs of partial-recursive functions

$$(\phi_1, \Phi_1), (\phi_2, \Phi_2), (\phi_3, \Phi_3), \ldots$$

such that every partial-recursive function $f$ is a $\phi_i$ for some $i$, the $\phi_i$ satisfy the recursion theorem and the iteration theorem, and the $\Phi_i$ and $\phi_i$ satisfy the measure-function theorem. We say that $C$ computes $\phi_i$ (with measure function $\Phi_i$) when supplied with program $P_i$. The idea of a program is purely an intuitive device here.

Given a partial recursive function $f$, there may well be many $\phi_i$ which equal $f$ (in our intuitive version: many programs $P_i$ which compute $f$): for such an $i$, we may well find it convenient to write $f_i$ for $\phi_i$, $F_i$ for $\Phi_i$, and to refer to $i$ as an *index* for $f$.

Suppose $P_i$ and $P_j$ are two programs. What shall we mean by $P_j$ is no faster than $P_i$? It will be

(a) $d(\phi_i) \supseteq d(\phi_j)$ $\quad$ $(d(\phi_j) = \{x \mid \phi_j(x) \text{ is defined}\})$
(b) $\Phi_i(x) \leqslant \Phi_j(x)$ $\quad$ for almost all $x \in d(\phi_j)$

(In the context of integers, "almost all $x$" means "for all but finitely many $x$.") The "almost all" phrase in (b) merely ensures that our comparison is not vitiated by any purely transient advantage that $P_j$ may have, e.g., in ordinary computer terminology, owing to a table look-up which allows the machine to obtain the $\phi_j(x)$ very quickly for the finitely many $x$ in the table.

One question that immediately arises is: Does every partial recursive function $f$ have a fastest program; i.e., is there an index $i$ for $f$ such that if $j$ is any other index for $f$, then $P_j$ is no faster than $P_i$? The answer to this question is negative—there are very many functions with no fastest program. In fact, the speed-up theorem below says much more:

Let $i$ and $j$ be two indexes for $f$; and let $r(x,y)$ be any total recursive function. We shall say that program $P_i$ is an $r$ speed-up of program $P_j$ if

$$r(x, F_i(x)) < F_j(x) \qquad \text{for almost all } x$$

Thus $P_i$ is faster than $P_j$ if it is an $e$ speed-up of $P_j$, where $e(x,y) = y$. Since we may choose $r(x,y)$ to grow very quickly indeed, e.g.,

$$r(x,y) = 2^{2^{2^{2^{x+y}}}}$$

we see that an $r$ speed-up of $P_j$ may be very much faster indeed than $P_j$!

The speed-up theorem tells us that no matter how large we choose $r$ to be, we may find then a 0–1 valued characteristic function $f$ such that *any* program $P_j$ for $f$ has an $r$ speed-up $P_i$ which computes $f$—and this means that $P_i$, in turn, has an $r$ speed-up $P_k$ which computes $f$, and so on ad infinitum! This is a most surprising result, and the proof is a long one. Before we turn to it, we must discourage the reader who wishes to treat this as a theorem about real computers, rather than partial recursive functions—the $r$ speed-up fails for finitely many $x$ and this finitude may well contain all those integers (e.g., $0 \leqslant x \leqslant 2^{32} - 1$) that we consider in a real computer. And yet the theorem is not without interest!

4. *The Speed-up Theorem*

Let $r$ be a total recursive function of two variables. Then there exists a total recursive function $f$ taking values 0 or 1, such that to every index $i$ for $f$, there corresponds another index $j$ for $f$ such that

$$F_i(x) > r(x, F_j(x)) \qquad \text{for almost all } x$$

We give here an outline of Blum's proof—for details see [1]. He defines a crucial function $t(u,v,i)$ such that $\phi_{i_0}$ total recursive implies $\phi_{t(u,v,i_0)}$ total recursive and takes only the values 0 or 1; and then proves

**Lemma 1.** If $\phi_{i_0}$ is total recursive, then for all $u$ there exists a $v$ such that

$$\phi_{t(u,v,i_0)} = \phi_{t(0,0,i_0)}$$

**Lemma 2.** If $\phi_{i_0}$ is total recursive, and if

$$f(x) = \phi_{t(0,0,i_0)}(x) \qquad \text{by definition}$$

then for each index $i$ for $f$

$$\phi_{i_0}(x - i) < F_i(x) \qquad \text{for almost all } x$$

Lemma 2 tells us that the theorem will be proved if we can find a total recursive function $\phi_{i_0}$ such that

$$\phi_{i_0}(x - i) \geqslant r[x, \Phi_{j(i)}(x)] \quad \text{for almost all } x, \text{ where } f = \phi_{j(i)} \text{ and } j \textit{ depends on } i \tag{1}$$

This leads to

**Lemma 3.** There exists a total recursive function $\phi_{i_0}$ such that given any $u$ and $v$ we have

$$r[x, \Phi_{t(u,v,i_0)}(x)] \leqslant \phi_{i_0}(x - u + 1) \tag{2}$$

for almost all $x$.

Setting $j(i, v) = t(i + 1, v, i_0)$ (2) becomes

$$r[x, \Phi_{j(i,v)}(x)] \leqslant \phi_{i_0}(x - i) \tag{3}$$

By Lemma 1, we may choose $v(i)$ such that

$$\phi_{t(i+1, v(i), i)} = \phi_{t(0,0,i_0)}$$

But then, setting $j(i) = j(i, v(i))$, (3) reduces to (1), and the theorem follows. The hard work (see [1]) is, of course, the construction of $t$, and the proofs of the three lemmas.

We conclude this section with the definition of a degree of difficulty ordering induced by the $M$-computer $C$.

**Definition.** Let $f$ and $g$ be two partial recursive functions. We say that $f$ is no more difficult to compute than $g(f \preccurlyeq g)$ if for *each* index $i$ for $g$, there exists an index $j$ for $f$ such that

(a) $d(f) \supseteq d(g)$.
(b) $F_j(x) \leqslant G_i(x)$ for almost all $x \in d(g)$.

This is in distinction to the relation on recursive functions introduced by Rabin [2], which in the present terminology takes the form:

(i) $f \prec g$ if there is an index $j$ for $f$, such that if $i$ is *any* index for $g$,

$$F_j(x) < G_i(x) \qquad \text{for almost all } x.$$

(ii) $f \preccurlyeq g \Leftrightarrow f \prec g$ or $f = g$.

We introduce the new definition since Rabin's definition contains a flavor of the assumption that the index $j$ for $f$ is that of the fastest program for $f$—and the speed-up theorem vitiates any such assumption in the present framework. Second, we would hope that many functions would have the same degree of difficulty (cf. [10]).

## II. Speed-Up Theorems and Incompleteness Theorems

The speed-up theorem for $M$-computers bears a resemblance to another speed-up theorem, stated by Gödel [3], and given, in slightly modified form, a proof by Mostowski in his exposition of Gödel's incompleteness theory [4]. (The $M$-computer theorem was proved without knowledge of the Gödel-Mostowski theorem—the mild resemblance was later pointed out to me by both John Holland and Martin Davis.)

Let us briefly recall the setup in Mostowski's monograph. The basic notions of addition, equality, and ordering of the natural numbers are formalized in first-order logic to yield a system **S**. It is shown that **S** is undecidable, and in fact an actual statement, call it $\phi$, is exhibited such that neither $\phi$ nor its negation are provable within **S** if **S** is consistent. A new system $\mathbf{S}_1$ is then formed, essentially by adjoining to **S** the axioms of second-order quantification, in which $\phi$ is provable. However, more turns out to be true.

If $\vdash_{\mathbf{S}}\phi$ (i.e., $\phi$ is provable in **S**), let $p(\phi)$ denote the length of the shortest proof of $\phi$ in **S**. Define $p_1(\phi)$ similarly for $\phi$ provable in $\mathbf{S}_1$.

Since $\mathbf{S}_1$ is an extension of **S**, any **S**-proof of $\phi$ is an $\mathbf{S}_1$-proof of $\phi$, and so we immediately conclude that $p_1(\phi) \leqslant p(\phi)$ for every $\phi$ provable in **S**. But we even have (see [4, pp. 112–115])

### 1. *The Gödel Speed-up Theorem*

For every recursive function $F$ there exists a sentence $\varphi$ of **S** such that $\vdash_{\mathbf{S}}\varphi$ and $\vdash_{\mathbf{S}_1}\varphi$ and such that the minimal $\mathbf{S}_0$- and $\mathbf{S}_1$-proofs of $\varphi$ satisfy the inequality $p(\varphi) \geqslant F(p_1(\varphi))$.

The proof is based on a study of specific properties of the two systems (all the axioms of which are known), and uses results obtained in proving the incompleteness of **S**.

We became interested in studying the incompleteness of logics and speed-up theorems for logics as close as possible to the $M$-computer formulation of the Blum speed-up theorem.

## III. Proof-Measure Systems

Let us capture the most abstract properties of a recursive logic for which we have some measure on the difficulty of proofs:

**Definition.** A PM-system (proof-measure system) on the alphabet $\Sigma$ is a quadruple $L = (G, \phi, p, t)$, where

1. $G$ is a recursive set of words on the alphabet $\Sigma$, the members of which are called well-formed formulas (wff).

2. A recursive enumeration $(\phi_1,p_1), (\phi_2,p_2), (\phi_3,p_3),\ldots$. $\phi_n \in G$ is called the $n$th proof, and $p_n \in N$ is called the measure of the $n$th proof.

$$T_L = \{\phi_n | n = 1, 2, 3, \ldots\}$$

We say $\phi$ is a theorem of $L$, $\vdash_L \phi$, if and only if $\phi \in T_L$. By definition, $p(\phi) = \min\{p_n | \phi = \phi_n\}$, and this is defined only on $T_L$. $p(\phi)$ is the minimal proof measure of $\phi$, and is called the difficulty of $\phi$ (in $L$).

3. $t$ is an increasing total recursive function $t$ such that

$$n > t(m) \Rightarrow p_n > m$$

*N.B.*: (3) implies that if $m = p(\phi)$, then $\phi = \phi_n$ for some $n \leqslant t(m)$. In particular, $\min\{n | \phi = \phi_n\} \leqslant t(p(\phi))$ if $\phi \in T_L$.

We then define the relationship between PM-systems of major interest to us.

**Definition.** Let $L$ and $L_1$ be two PM-systems, with sets of wff's $G$ and $G_1$ and difficulties $p$ and $p_1$, respectively. We say that $L_1$ is a speed-up of $L$ if

(a) $T_L \subseteq T_{L_1}$.

(b) For every total recursive function $r$, $L_1$ is an $r$ speed-up of $L$; i.e., there exists $\phi^r \in T_L$ such that $p(\phi^r) \geqslant r(p_1(\phi^r))$.

**Lemma.** Let $L$ be a PM-system, and let $H$ be any infinite recursive subset of $\Sigma^*$. Then $L|H \underset{\text{def}}{=} (G \cap H, \psi, q, t)$ is a PM-system, where

(a) $\psi_n = \phi_{\alpha(n)}$, where $\alpha(0) = 0$, $\alpha(m+1) = \min\{n > \alpha(m) | \phi_n \in H\}$.

(b) $q_n = p_{\alpha(n)}$.

*Proof.* We have only to verify (3) of the definition. But

$$n > t(m) \Rightarrow \alpha(n) > t(m) \Rightarrow p_{\alpha(n)} > m \Rightarrow q_n > m \qquad \text{Q.E.D.}$$

We now easily obtain a theorem which, roughly speaking, says that if a system $L_1$ can do some things arbitrarily quicker than $L$ can, then $L_1$ can do some things that $L$ cannot do at all.

**Theorem.** Let $L_1$ be a speed-up of $L$. Then there is a $\theta \in G \cap G_1$ such that

$$\theta \in T_{L_1} - T_L$$

*Proof.* Let $\hat{L}_1 = L_1 | G = (G \cap G_1, \psi^1, q^1, t^1)$:

$$\hat{L} = L | G_1 = (G \cap G_1, \psi, q, t)$$

Clearly, $\hat{L}_1$ is a speed-up of $\hat{L}$.

Let us assume, by way of contradiction, that $T_{L_1} \subseteq T_L$. Then we may define the total recursive function $g$ by $g(n) = q_{s(n)}$, where

$$s(n) = \min\{m | \psi_n^1 = \psi_m\}.$$

Now set $\bar{g}(m) = \max\{g(n) | n \leqslant t^1(m)\}$. Since $\hat{L}_1$ is a speed-up of $\hat{L}$, we may pick $\phi \in T_L$ such that

$$\bar{g}(q^1(\phi)) < q(\phi)$$

Let $m_0 = \min\{m | \phi = \psi_m\}$, $n_0 = \min\{n | \phi = \psi_n^1\}$, so that $q_{m_0} = g(n_0)$. But

$$\begin{aligned} q_{m_0} &\geqslant q(\phi) \\ &> \bar{g}(q^1(\phi)) && \text{by choice of } \phi \\ &> g(n_0) && \text{by definition of } \bar{g} \end{aligned}$$

A contradiction! Thus there exists $\theta \in T_{\hat{L}_1} - T_{\hat{L}}$, whence $\theta \in T_{L_1} - T_L$.

Q.E.D.

The remainder of this section is devoted to extremely weak forms of consistency, completeness, and adequacy, and the proof of correspondingly abstract (and insanely general) incompleteness theorems. For much of this work we do not need the proof measures, and consider *weak systems.*

**Definition.** A weak system on the alphabet $\Sigma$ is a pair $L = (G, T_L)$, where

1. $G$ is a recursive subset of $\Sigma^*$.

2. $T_L$ is a recursively enumerable subset of $G$. We say $\phi$ is a theorem of $L$, $\vdash_L \phi$, if and only if $\phi \in T_L$.

*N.B.*: Each PM-system "is" a weak system.

**Definition.** A bi-recursive function $f: A \to B$ is a total recursive function $f: A \to B$ such that

1. $f(A)$ is a recursive subset of $B$.

2. There is a total recursive function $f^{-1}: f(A) \to A$ such that $f^{-1}(f(a)) = a$ for all $a \in A$.

**Definition.** Let $L=(G,T_L)$ be a weak system and $\sim:G\to G$ a bi-recursive function. We say that $L$ is consistent w.r.t. $\sim$ if for no $\theta\in G$ are both $\theta$ and $\sim\theta$ in $T_L$.

**Definition.** Let $L=(G,T_L)$ be a weak system consistent w.r.t. $\sim$, and let $C$ be a recursive subset of $G$ for which $\sim(C)\subseteq C$. We say $L$ is *complete* (w.r.t. $\sim$ and $C$) if, for every $\theta\in C$, *either* $\theta$ *or* $\sim\theta$ is in $T_L$.

*N.B.*: If $L$ were formalized in first-order logic, we would take $\sim$ as negation and $C$ as the collection of closed wff's, i.e., wff's with no free variables.

Our next theorem may be regarded as a generalized converse of the Gödel speed-up theorem.

**Theorem.** Let $S$ be a PM-system consistent w.r.t. $\sim$, and let $S$ possess a speed-up $S_1$, also consistent w.r.t. $\sim$. Then $S$ is complete w.r.t. to *no* nonempty recursive subset $C$ of $G$, for which $\hat{S}_1=S_1|C$ is a speed-up of $\hat{S}=S|C$.

*Proof.* By the last theorem, there exists $\theta\in C$ such that

$$\theta\in T_{\hat{S}_1}-T_{\hat{S}}$$

$S_1$ consistent $\Rightarrow\ \sim\theta\notin T_{S_1}\Rightarrow\ \sim\theta\notin T_S$. Thus neither $\theta$ nor $\sim\theta$ is in $T_S$, and so $S$ is incomplete w.r.t. $C$. Q.E.D.

To represent a set of integers in a weak system $L$, we want to generate a sequence of words $W_1, W_2, W_3,\ldots$ such that $W_n$ may be interpreted "$n\in U$," and with the property that if $n$ actually belongs to $U$, then $W_n$ is provable in $L$.

**Definition.** Let $L=(G,T_L)$ be a weak system, with $C$ a recursive subset of $G$. We say $L$ represents a set $U$ in $C$ if there exists a bi-recursive function $W:N\to C$ [we write $W_n$ for $W(n)$] such that

$$U=\{n|\vdash_L W_n\}$$

*N.B.*: We can take $C=G$ if desired.

**Theorem.** If $L$ represents $U$ in $C$, then $U$ is recursively enumerable.

*Proof.* Since $T_L$ is recursive enumerable,

$$U=\{n|\,W_n\in[\{W_1, W_2,\ldots\}\cap T_L]\}$$

is recursively enumerable. Q.E.D.

Thus, given $L$ and $C$, the most we can expect is that $L$ represents all recursively enumerable sets in $C$. This motivates

**Definition.** Let $L=(G,T_L)$ be a weak system, with $C$ a recursive subset of $G$. We say $L$ is *adequate* through $C$ if $L$ represents every recursively enumerable subset of $N$ in $C$. [If $L$ is consistent, we also demand $\sim(C)\subseteq C$.]

We now have our abstract Gödel-type incompleteness theorem:

**Theorem.** If a system $L$ is consistent and adequate through $C$, then $L$ is incomplete w.r.t. $C$.

*Proof.* Let $L$ be consistent w.r.t. $\sim$.

Let $U$ be a recursively enumerable subset of $N$ which is *not* recursive; so that $\bar{U}=N-U$ is not recursively enumerable. By adequacy, there is a bi-recursive function $W:N\to C$ such that

$$U=\{n \mid \vdash_L W_n\}$$

Since $\sim$ is recursive, and $\sim(C)\subseteq C$,

$$\tilde{U}=\{n \mid \vdash_L \sim W_n\}$$

is represented by $L$ in $C$, and is thus recursively enumerable. Since $L$ is consistent w.r.t. $\sim$,

$$\vdash_L \sim W_n \Rightarrow W_n \text{ is } \textit{not} \text{ a theorem of } L \Rightarrow n \notin U$$

Thus $\tilde{U}\subseteq\bar{U}$, but $\tilde{U}\neq\bar{U}$ since $\tilde{U}$ is recursively enumerable, while $\bar{U}$ is not. Pick any $m\in\bar{U}-\tilde{U}$. Then neither $W_m$ nor $\sim W_m$ is a theorem of $L$, even though both are in $C$. Thus $L$ is incomplete w.r.t. $C$. Q.E.D.

Our treatment was arrived at by a process of abstraction from that we gave in Chapter 5 of [5], which was in turn based on Chapter 8 of [6].

*N.B.*: If $L$ is a recursive logic whose axioms include the usual ones of propositional logic, then $L$ is consistent $\Leftrightarrow G\neq T_L$. Thus every such system is consistent if it is adequate. For if $G=T_L$, then only $N$ and $\phi$ are representable in $L$.

**Definition.** A weak system $(G,T_L)$ is said to be *decidable* if $T_L$ is recursive.

**Theorem.** If $L$ is adequate through $C$, then $L$ is undecidable.

*Proof.* Suppose $L$ is decidable. Let $W:N\to C$ be a bi-recursive function with $U=\{n \mid \vdash_L W_n\}$. Given $n$, we generate $W_n$. Since $T_L$ is recursive, we can tell effectively whether or not $W_n\in T_L$, and thus whether or not $n\in U$. Hence $U$ is recursive, and so $L$ is not adequate. Q.E.D.

## IV. Computation Difficulty in Terms of Proof Difficulty

We started with a discussion of difficulty of computation and then found ourselves, via the Gödel speed-up theorem, discussing the difficulty of proofs in PM-systems. It is thus interesting to recall that Rabin [2] defined a difficulty of computation in terms of a measure on proofs in Post logics. Let us recall some of his work, and then generalize it in our framework of PM-systems and $M$-computers.

He defined a function $m(L,P)$, defined for pairs $L,P$, where $L$ is a Post system and $P$ is a proof in $L$, as a *measure on proofs* if it assumes integral values, and satisfies

(a) $m$ is primitive-recursive.

(b) Given a system $L$ and a number $n$, there is only a finite number $\nu(L,n)$ of proofs $P$ of $L$ such that $m(L,P) \leqslant n$.

(c) The function $\nu(L,n)$ is primitive-recursive.

Pick some standard enumeration $P_1, P_2, \ldots$ of the proofs of the Post logic $L$, let $\phi_n$ be the theorem of which $P_n$ is the proof, and let us define $p_n$ to be $m(L,P_n)$. (a), (b), and (c) imply that $\{P | m(L,P) = n\}$ may be found effectively, and we must generate $P_1, P_2, \ldots$ until $\nu(L,n) - \nu(L,n-1)$ proofs have been found with $m(L,P) = n$. Let $P_{h(n)}$ be the last proof of $\{P | m(L,P) = n\}$ generated by the above process. Then $h(n)$ is total-recursive, and so is

$$\bar{h}(n) = \max_{1 \leqslant i \leqslant n} h(i).$$

Call $\bar{h}$ the $t$-function induced by $m$ on $L$.

We immediately have

**Theorem.** If $L$ is a Post logic, with wff's $G$ and measure on proofs $m(L,P)$, then

$$L_{PM} = (G, \phi, p, \bar{h}) \text{ is a PM-system}$$

where $\phi_n$ and $p_n$ are as above, and $\bar{h}$ is the $t$-function induced by $m(L,P)$.

Assume that all Post logics under consideration contain the stroke $|$ and equality sign $=$ in their alphabet. The word $||\cdots|$, consisting of $n+1$ strokes, will be referred to as the numeral $\bar{n}$ of $n$. Given a Post system $L$ and a word $w$ on the alphabet of $L$, Rabin says that the pair $(L, w)$ computes the function $f$ if for all integers $n, m$

$$\vdash_L w\bar{n} = \bar{m} \Leftrightarrow f(n) = m$$

He then defines the *length of computation* function $F_L(n)$ (which depends on both $L$ and $w$) by

$$F_L(n) = \min\{m(L,P) | P \text{ is a proof of } w\bar{n} = \bar{m} \text{ in } L\}$$

Actually $F_L(n)$ is better called the length of *verification*, for we cannot prove $w\bar{n} = \bar{m}$ unless we already know that $f(n) = m$. To associate a length of *computation* with a logical system, we would prefer to associate with a function $f$ a schema $S(f)$ which, for each integer $n$, allows us to generate a sequence of theorems, guaranteed to terminate with the generation of the theorem $w\bar{n} = \overline{f(n)}$, the sequence then constituting a proof $P_n^f$ of $w\bar{n} = \overline{f(n)}$. The measure $G_{S(f)}(n) = m(L, P_n^f)$ would then represent a *computation* measure rather than a *verification* measure. Note, however, that the verification measure is still useful in establishing lower bounds, since clearly

$$F_L(n) \leqslant G_{S(f)}(n) \qquad \text{for all } n$$

A Post system corresponds to a computer in that its productions may be thought of as basic computer operations. The choice of $w$ is then merely a criterion for telling when the computation has finished. Now, look at a proof of $w\bar{n} = \bar{m}$. It is a finite sequence of applications of productions, and thus corresponds to a sequence of instructions, i.e., a program. In computing $F_L(n)$ we choose the proof, i.e., program, giving the minimal "length" of computation; i.e., for each $n$ our measure is the best possible. But this means that we may choose a different program for each $n$. However, a single program with its loopings and branching corresponds rather to our idea of a proof schema.

We now extend the ideas of computation, and of verification functions from Post systems to our PM-systems.

**Definition.** Let $L = (G, \phi, p, t)$ be a PM-system. We call a bi-recursive function $W: N \times N \to G$ (we write $W_{m,n}$ for $W(m,n)$) an *L-definer*, and we say that it $L$-defines the function $f_W$, where we obtain $f_W(m)$ by generating $\phi_1, \phi_2, \ldots$ until first obtaining one of the form $W_{m,k}$ and taking $f_W(m)$ to be that $k$.

*N.B.*: $f_W$ is clearly (partial) recursive.

**Definition.** Let $L = (G, \phi, p, t)$ be a PM-system, and let $W$ $L$-define $f$. The length of verification function $F_{(L,W)}(n)$ is defined by

$$F_{(L,W)}(n) = p(W_{n,f(n)})$$

and thus is defined if and only if $f$ is defined.

**Definition.** We shall say that the collection of PM-systems $L_\alpha$ forms an array if there is a recursive enumeration

$$\{(L, W)\} = \{(L^1, W^1), (L^2, W^2), \ldots\}$$

of all pairs $(L, W)$, where $L$ is an $L_\alpha$ and $W$ is an $L_\alpha$-definer (perhaps of a restricted set $D_\alpha$). [We sometimes refer to $(L, W)$ as the array.]

We say that the array is universal if every partial-recursive function is $L^m$-defined by $W^m$ for at least one $m$.

Rabin's proof of his theorem 3 shows that Post logics form an array—and if we restrict $W_{m,n}$ to be of the form $w\bar{m} = \bar{n}$, the enumeration is even primitive-recursive. It is, of course, a basic fact of the theory of recursive functions and post logics that the array of Post logics is universal.

We are now in a position to embed Rabin's work in our framework of $M$-computers.

**Definition.** A *weak M-computer* $\{(\phi_n, \Phi_n)\}$ is a recursive enumeration $(\phi_n, \Phi_n)$ $(n = 1, 2, 3, \ldots)$ of partial-recursive functions such that:

1. Every partial-recursive function is a $\phi_n$ for at least one $n$.
2. $\{\Phi_n\}$ is a *measure sequence* for $\{\phi_n\}$, i.e.,

   (a) $\Phi_n(x)$ is defined $\Leftrightarrow$ $\phi_n(x)$ is defined.

   (b) There is a total recursive function $\alpha(i, x, y)$ such that

$$\alpha(i, x, y) = \begin{cases} 1 & \text{if } \Phi_i(x) = y \\ 0 & \text{otherwise} \end{cases}$$

**Theorem.** Let $\{(L, W)\}$ be a universal array, such that $f_m$ is the function $L^m$-defined by $W^m$, and $F_m$ is the verification function

$$F_{(L^m, W^m)}$$

Then $\{(f_m, W_m)\}$ is a weak $M$-computer.

*Proof.* We only have to verify the recursiveness of the $\alpha$-function. But given $m, x$, and $y$ we need only generate the first $t^m(y)$ theorems of $L^m$ and examine those of the form $W^m_{x,k}$ to determine effectively whether or not

$$F_m(x) = y \qquad \text{Q.E.D.}$$

**Theorem.** Let $C = \{(f_n, F_n)\}$ be a weak $M$-computer. Let $h$ be a partial-recursive function. There exists a partial-recursive function $f$, $d(f) = d(h)$, assuming only the values 0 or 1, and such that for any index $m$ for $f$ we have

$$h(n) < F_m(n) \qquad \text{for almost all } n \in d(h)$$

*Proof.* We define by induction both the function $f(n)$ and an auxiliary sequence of finite sets. Set $I = H = H_0 = \varnothing$. The set $I$ may increase, at each stage of the induction. Pick an index $\#$ for $h$, and leave it fixed throughout.

*Stage n.* For each $k \notin H_{n-1}$, $k \leqslant n-1$, compute $\alpha(\#, k, n)$. If it is 1, we adjoin $k$ to $H$ and compute $h(k)$. Then check $\alpha(\#, n, i)$ for $1 \leqslant i \leqslant n$. If any of these is 1, adjoin $n$ to $H$ and compute $h(n)$. Let $H_n$ be the elements in $H$ at this stage. If $H_n - H_{n-1}$ is empty, go to stage $n+1$. If $k_1, \ldots, k_r$ $(r \geqslant 1)$ are elements of $H_n - H_{n-1}$ in ascending order, carry out stages $n(k_1), \ldots, n(k_r)$ and then go to stage $n+1$.

*Stage* $n(k)$. Let $m = m(k)$ be the smallest $m \leqslant k$, $m \notin I$ for which $F_m(k) \leqslant h(k)$. If there is no such $m$, set $f(k) = 1$, and do not change $I$. Otherwise, set $f(k) = \max(1 - f_{m(k)}(k), 0)$ and adjoin $m(k)$ to $I$.

Clearly $f$ is partial-recursive, $d(f) = d(h)$, and takes only the values 0, 1.

Assume now that $m$ is an index for $f$. We prove that there are only finitely many integers $k$ such that

$$F_m(k) \leqslant h(k) \qquad \text{and} \qquad h(k) \text{ is defined} \tag{*}$$

Clearly, since $f = f_m$, $m \notin I$. Let $I_k$ comprise those integers which are in $I$ at the end of stage $k$. Since $I_k \subseteq I_{k+1}$ for each $k$, there is an integer $s$ (which we may assume $\geqslant m$) such that if $j < m$ ever enters $I$, it must be in $I_s$.

We now show that no $p > s$ satisfies (*): Assume that $p > s$ does satisfy (*), and that $q = \max(p, F_{\#}(p))$. We note that $m \notin I_{q-1}$ and that $F_m(p) \leqslant h(p)$. Now consider stage $q(p)$. No $j < m$ can qualify for addition to $I_q$ at this stage, since $q > s$. But this means that $m$ must be placed in $I_q$ at stage $q(p)$—a contradiction. Thus $p$ cannot satisfy (*) if $p > s$. Q.E.D.

If we examine the construction of $f$, we see that we have even proved

**Corollary.** There is a partial-recursive function $g$ of two variables such that if $\#$ is an index for $h$, then $f(x)$ in the above theorem may be taken as $g(\#, x)$.

This immediately yields the further

**Corollary.** If the $\{f_k\}$ satisfy the iteration theorem for $n = 1$ [i.e., for each partial-recursive function $g(\#, x)$, there is a total recursive function $\gamma$ such that $f_{\gamma(\#)}(x) = g(\#, x)$], then there is a total-recursive function $\gamma$ such that if $\#$ is an index for $h$, then $f$ in the above theorem may be taken as $\phi_{\gamma(\#)}$.

The $\gamma$-function thus exists if $C$ is an $M$-computer, rather than just a weak $M$-computer. This form of the result first appeared in [1].

Note that for an $M$-computer, the theorem is an immediate corollary of the speed-up theorem on setting $r(x,y) = h(x)$, for then $F_i(x) > r[x, F_j(x)]$ reduces to $F_i(x) > h(x)$—but this proof does not yield the $g$-function of the corollary.

The original form of the above theorem—Theorem 3 of Rabin [2]—takes $C$ as the array of Post logics, and restricts $h$ to being primitive-recursive, in which case it is shown that $f$ may then also be taken to be primitive-recursive. Our proof is based on Rabin's, simplified in some points by our setup, but complicated in other by the nontotality of $h$.

The next two results and their proofs are just "transliterations" of Rabin's Theorems 7 and 8.

**Corollary.** Let $\{(f_m, F_m)\}$ be a weak $M$-computer. Let $p(n,m)$ be a total-recursive function. There exists a recursive function $f$ assuming only the values 0, 1 and such that for each index $m$ for $f$, and each fixed integer, $\bar{m}$,

$$F_m(n) > p(n, \bar{m}) \qquad \text{for almost all } n \qquad (*)$$

*Proof.* Merely apply the theorem to $h(n) = \Sigma_{k,m \leqslant n} p(k,m)$. Q.E.D.

**Theorem.** Let $L$ be a PM-system, and let $W^m$ be a recursive enumeration of $L$-definers, such that for every recursive set $S$ there exists a $W^m$ which $L$-defines the characteristic function $f_S$ of $S$. (Assume $L$ belongs to a universal array—this condition is usually satisfied trivially, e.g., if $L$ is a Post logic.) Then the system $L$ is undecidable.

*Proof.* Assume on the contrary, that $L$ is decidable. This means that $T_L$ is a recursive set. This implies that we can extend $p: T_L \to N$ to a recursive function $p: G \to N$ by setting $p(\sigma) = 0$ for $\sigma \in G - T_L$.

Define

$$p(n,m) = p(W^m_{n,0}) + p(W^m_{n,1})$$

Let $f$ be the computable function of the above corollary. $f$ is then the characteristic function of a recursive set, and so there is an $m_0$ such that $W^{m_0}$ $L$-defines $f$. Then $F_{m_0}(n) = p(W^{m_0}_{n,f(n)}) \leqslant p(n, m_0)$ for all $n$, contrary to (*). Thus $L$ must be undecidable. Q.E.D.

We end this section with one more variation on the above theme.

**Definition.** We say that a PM-system $L$ is *verification-adequate* if there is a recursive enumeration $W^1, W^2, W^3, \ldots$ of $L$-definers such that each partial-recursive function is $L$-defined by at least one $W^m$.

If $L$ is verification-adequate as above, then $\{(L^1, W^1), (L^2, W^2), \ldots\}$ where each $L^m = L$ reveals $L$ as a universal array in its own right. This immediately yields

**Corollary.** If a PM-system $L$ is verification-adequate, and $h$ is a partial-recursive function, there exists a partial-recursive function $f$, $d(f) = d(h)$, assuming only the values 0, 1 and such that no matter what $W^m$ $L$-defines $f$, we have

$$h(n) < F_m(n) \qquad \text{for almost all } n$$

We could ring many changes on the above definition and corollary but refrain from doing so.

**Theorem.** A consistent verification-adequate system is incomplete.

*Proof.* Let, for each recursively enumerable set $U$, $W^U$ be the $W^m$ which $L$-defines

$$f^U(x) = \begin{cases} 1 & \text{if } x \in U \\ \text{undefined} & \text{otherwise} \end{cases}$$

Consider the sequence $W^U_{n,1} : U = \{n \mid \vdash_L W^U_{n,1}\}$. Thus $L$ is adequate, and so incomplete. Q.E.D.

## V. When Does a PM-System Possess a Speed-Up?

**Lemma.** Let $f$ be a partial-recursive function with domain $R$ (which is thus recursively enumerable). Let $S$ be any recursively enumerable subset of $N$. Then $f' = f \mid R \cap S$ is partial-recursive with domain $R \cap S$.

*Proof.* Given $x$, we generate $S$ until we obtain $x$, and then compute $f(x)$, to yield $f'(x)$—which is thus defined if and only if $x \in R \cap S$. Q.E.D.

**Corollary.** There exists partial-recursive functions $f$ and $f'$ such that $f \subseteq f'$ [i.e., $d(f) \subseteq d(f')$ and $f = f' \mid d(f)$] and $d(f') - d(f)$ is *not* recursively enumerable.

*Proof.* Take any total $f'$ and any recursively enumerable nonrecursive set $R$. Then set $f = f' \mid R$. Q.E.D.

**Theorem.** Let $f \subseteq f'$ with $d(f') - d(f)$ not recursively enumerable. Let $\{(\phi_n, \Phi_n)\}$ be any weak $M$-computer. Take any index $i$ for $f$ and any index $j$ for $f'$. Then for any total recursive function $g$ there exists $x \in d(f)$ such that

$$g(F_j'(x)) \leqslant F_i(x)$$

*Proof.* Suppose there exists a $g$ such that for all $x \in d(f)$,

$$F_i(x) < g(F_j'(x))$$

Then

$$d(f') - d(f) = d(f') \cap \{x \mid F_i(x) \geqslant g(F_j'(x))\}$$

and is thus recursively enumerable—a contradiction. Q.E.D.

**Corollary.** Let $\{(L^m, W^m)\}$ be an array of PM-systems such that

(a) $W = W^i = W^j$ is both an $L^i$-definer and $L^j$-definer, $L^i \neq L^j$.

(b) $W$ $L^i$-defines $f$ and $L^j$-defines $f'$, where $f \subseteq f'$, and $d(f') - d(f)$ is not recursively enumerable.

Then $L^j$ is a speed-up of $L^i$.

*Proof.* Pick the index $i$ for $f$ and $j$ for $f'$, and take any recursive function $g$. Then there is an $x$ such that

$$F_i(x) \nless g(F_j'(x))$$

i.e.,

$$p^i(\phi) \nless g(p^j(\phi)) \qquad \text{where } \phi = W_{x,f(x)}$$ Q.E.D.

The trouble with this characterization and the one which follows is that we have not been able to find "real" arrays which satisfy the premises—but we hope that we shall.

**Theorem.** Let $S$ and $S_1$ be two PM-systems for which $T_S \subseteq T_{S_1}$, and there exists a recursively enumerable subset $V_1, V_2, V_3, \ldots$ of $G \cap G_1$ such that

$$V = \{x \mid \vdash_{S_1} V_x\} - \{x \mid \vdash_S V_x\}$$

is not recursively enumerable. Then $S_1$ is a speed-up of $S$.

*Proof.* Suppose there is a recursive $g$ such that for all $\phi \in T_S$

$$g(p_1(\phi)) \geqslant p(\phi)$$

Given $x$, generate $V_x$, and then generate $T_{S_1}$ until first finding $\phi_n^1$ with $\phi_n^1 = V_x$. Then generate the $\phi_m$ with $m \leqslant t(g(p_n))$. Emit $x$ if no such $\phi_m = V_x$. This yields a recursive enumeration of $V$. A contradiction—and no such $g$ exists. Q.E.D.

**Corollary.** If an undecidable PM-system $S$ has a decidable extension $S_1$ (i.e., $T_S \subseteq T_{S_1}$ with $T_{S_1}$ recursive), then $S_1$ is a speed-up of $S$.

*Proof.* $T_{S_1}$ is recursive and $T_S$ is not recursive, whence $T_{S_1} - T_S$ is not recursively enumerable. Simply take $\{V_x\} = T_{S_1}$ and apply the theorem.

Q.E.D.

If $S_1$ is not consistent, this merely reflects the fact that in $S_1$ we can prove *anything* very quickly! For it to be of interest, $S_1$ must be consistent. However, we know [7] that if we take for our array certain systems of elementary formalized arithmetic, this cannot be; such systems are essentially undecidable in that any consistent extension is undecidable.

We conclude, then, with several questions:

1. Can one verify the premises of any of the above speed-up characterizations for a "real" array?
2. Given an array, when we can be sure that consistent extensions of adequate systems are also adequate?[1]
3. How does the set of theorems of an incomplete recursive logic grow as we add new consistent axioms? In particular, when is the set of new theorems obtained by adjoining a single axiom finite, or recursive, or recursively enumerable? One hopes that there are many cases in which the answer to all three parts of the last question are negative. In which hope we end with the conjecture:

**Conjecture.** There are arrays of essentially undecidable systems of formalized arithmetic in which every system possessess a speed-up.

## Appendix

Question 3 above, with its attendant conjecture, is essentially answered by a result due to A. Ehrenfeucht [unpublished; personal communication]. Consider axiomatic systems with negation and implication satisfying the usual axioms of propositional logic. For a theory (i.e., set of theorems) $T$, we denote by $T\{\theta\}$ the set of all theorems deducible from the theorems of $T$ and the additional axiom $\theta$, using propositional logic.

**Theorem** (*Ehrenfeucht*). Let $T$ be a theory and $\varphi$ a sentence, such that the set $T\{\sim\varphi\}$ is undecidable. Then $T\{\varphi\}$ is a speed-up of $T$.

*Proof.* 1. By propositional logic

$$\vdash_{T\{\sim\varphi\}} \theta \Leftrightarrow \vdash_T \sim\varphi \supset \theta \Leftrightarrow \vdash_T \sim\theta \supset \varphi$$

[1] J. C. Shepherdson has pointed out to me one answer to this question ([8] and [9]): All recursively enumerable sets are representable in any consistent theory $S$ whose theorems are recursively enumerable, in which all recursive functions are definable, and which has a formula $x \leqslant y$ satisfying

$$\vdash_S x \leqslant \bar{n} \leftrightarrow x = \bar{0} \vee x = \bar{1} \vee \cdots \vee x = \bar{n}$$

$$\vdash_S x \leqslant \bar{n} \vee \bar{n} \leqslant x$$

Further,

$$\vdash_{T\{\varphi\}} \sim \theta \supset \varphi$$

2. Assume, then, that $T\{\varphi\}$ is not a speed-up of $T$, so that there is a total recursive function $g$ such that if $\vdash_T \psi$ then $p_T(\psi) \leqslant g(p_{T\{\varphi\}}(\psi))$.

Then we may effectively decide whether or not $\vdash_{T\{\sim\varphi\}} \theta$ by searching the theorems of $T$ with the proof measure $\leqslant g(p_{T\{\varphi\}}(\sim \theta \supset \varphi))$ for $\sim \theta \supset \varphi$. This contradicts the undecidability of $T\{\sim \varphi\}$. Q.E.D.

As a corollary to Ehrenfeucht's *proof* we obtain

**Corollary.** Let $T$ be a theory, and $\varphi$ a sentence, such that $T\{\sim \varphi\}$ is undecidable. Then the difference set

$$T\{\varphi\} - T$$

is *not* recursively enumerable.

*Proof.* Bearing in mind (1) of the above proof, assume that $T\{\varphi\} - T$ *is* recursively enumerable. Then we may decide effectively whether or not $\vdash_{T\{\sim\varphi\}} \theta$ by generating $T$ and $T\{\varphi\} - T$ until we encounter $\sim \theta \supset \varphi$. Contradiction! Q.E.D.

## References

1. M. Blum, Measures on the computation speed of partial recursive functions, *Quart. Progr. Rept. 72, Res. Lab. Electronics, M.I.T.*, pp. 237–253, Jan. 1964.
2. M. O. Rabin, *Degree of Difficulty of Computing a Function and a Partial Ordering of Recursive Sets*, Hebrew University, Jerusalem, Israel, April 1960.
3. K. Gödel, Uber die Länge der Beweise, *Ergeb. eines math. Kolloquiums* 7, 23–24 (1936).
4. A. Mostowski, *Sentences Undecidable in Formalized Arithmetic*, North-Holland, Amsterdam, 1957.
5. M. A. Arbib, *Brains, Machines, and Mathematics*, McGraw-Hill, New York, 1964.
6. M. Davis, *Computability and Unsolvability*, McGraw-Hill, New York, 1958.
7. A. Tarski, A. Mostowski, and R. M. Robinson, *Undecidable Theories*, North-Holland, Amsterdam, 1953.
8. A. Ehrenfeucht and S. Feferman, Representability of recursively enumerable sets in formal theories, *Arch. Math. Logik und Grudlagenforschung* **5**, 37–41 (1960).
9. J. C. Shepherdson, Representability of recursively enumerable sets in formal theories, *Arch. Math. Logik und Grudlagenforschung* **5**, 119–127 (1960).
10. M. A. Arbib and M. Blum, Machine Dependence of Degrees of Difficulty, *Proc. Am. Math. Soc.* **16**, 442–447 (1965).

# Une Application de la Théorie des Graphes à un Problème de Codage

CLAUDE BERGE

*Centre National de la Recherche Scientifique*
*Paris, France*[1]

## I. Introduction

Considérons un émetteur qui peut émettre un ensemble $X$ de signaux. Par suite du bruit, chaque signal peut donner plusieurs interprétations à la réception (avec des probabilités variées), et traçons le graphe, dont les points (ou "sommets") représentent les différents signaux, deux points étant liés (par une "arête") si les signaux correspondants peuvent être confondus à la réception.

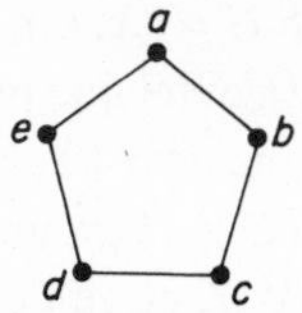

FIG. 1

Considérons, par exemple, le cas où $X=\{a,b,c,d,e\}$ et où le graphe est Fig. 1. Si l'on emploie des signaux d'une seule lettre, on peut adopter, sans risquer de confusion, un code de deux mots: *a* et *c*.

Au lieu de mots d'une seule lettre, on peut aussi utiliser des mots de deux lettres, à condition que ces mots ne se prêtent pas à confusion à la réception. Avec les lettres *a* et *c* qui ne peuvent pas être confondues, on forme le code *aa*, *ac*, *ca*, *cc*.

Mais on peut former un code encore plus riche avec *aa*, *bc*, *ce*, *db*, *ed* (on vérifie immédiatement que deux quelconques de ces mots ne peuvent être confondus à la réception). Shannon a observé que les graphes qui se prêtent à un tel enrichissement sont très rares [6], et a montré que le problème

[1] *Present address:* International Computation Centre, Rome, E.U.R., Italy.

probabilistique (qui consiste à minimiser les chances d'erreur) se ramène directement au problème discret ci-dessus.

La présente étude a pour but de tenter de caractériser les graphes de signaux que l'on peut ainsi enrichir.

## II. Codes Parfaits

Rappelons quelques définitions usuelles en Théorie des Graphes [1].

Etant donné un graphe $G$, dont l'ensemble des sommets est $X$, l'ensemble des arêtes est $U$, on appelle *sous-graphe* un graphe obtenu avec un ensemble $S \subset X$, et avec toutes les arêtes de $U$ qui relient deux points de $S$. L'ensemble $S$ est dit stable (ou "intérieurement stable") si le sous-graphe engendré par $S$ est formé de points isolés. Au contraire, on dit que $S$ est un *clique* si deux quelconques des points de $S$ sont adjacents. Il est d'usage de dénoter par $\alpha(G)$ le nombre maximum de sommets d'un ensemble stable, et par $\theta(G)$ le plus petit nombre de cliques qui partitionnent l'ensemble $X$.

Il est immédiat que $\alpha(G) \leqslant \theta(G)$, et l'on n'a pas toujours l'égalité. Par exemple, dans le graphe de Fig. 1, on a $\alpha(G) = 2$, et $\theta(G) = 3$, donc $\alpha(G) \neq \theta(G)$.

Un graphe tel que $\alpha(G') = \theta(G')$ pour tout sous-graphe $G'$ de $G$ est dit *parfait*. Considérons un graphe $G = (X, U)$, dont l'ensemble des sommets est $X$, l'ensemble des arêtes est $U$, et tel que pour tout $x \in X$, on a $(x, x) \in U$. Considérons de même un graphe $H = (Y, V)$ avec cette même propriété. Par définition, le *graphe produit* $G \times H$ est un graphe dont les sommets sont les couples $(x, y)$, avec $x \in X$, $y \in Y$, et où l'on trace une arête entre $(x, y)$ et $(x', y')$ si et seulement si

$$(x, x') \in U, \qquad (y, y') \in V$$

Si $G$ est un graphe dont les sommets sont des signaux, et si $x$ et $x'$ sont joints lorsque $x = x'$ ou $x$ et $x'$ sont des signaux que l'on peut confondre, le nombre maximum de signaux que l'on peut utiliser sans confusion est $\alpha(G)$; le nombre maximum de mots de $k$ lettres que l'on peut utiliser sans confusion est $\alpha(G \times G \times \cdots \times G) = \alpha(G^k)$.

$\operatorname{Sup}_k \sqrt[k]{\alpha(G^k)}$ est appelé la *capacité* ("zéro-error capacity") de l'ensemble des signaux. La capacité du graphe de Fig. 1 n'est pas connue.

**Lemme 1.** *On a* $\alpha(G \times H) \geq \alpha(G)\, \alpha(H)$.

En effet, si $S$ et $T$ sont des ensembles stables maximaux dans $G$ et $H$, on a

$$|S| = \alpha(G), \qquad |T| = \alpha(H),$$

le produit cartésien $S \times T$ est un ensemble stable de $G \times H$, donc

$$\alpha(G \times H) \geqslant |S \times T| = |S| \times |T| = \alpha(G)\,\alpha(H)$$

**Lemme 2.** *On a* $\theta(G \times H) \leqslant \theta(G)\,\theta(H)$.

En effet, soit $C_1, C_2, \ldots, C_p$ le nombre minimum de cliques qui partitionnent le graphe $G$; soit $D_1, D_2, \ldots, D_q$ le nombre maximum de cliques qui partitionnent le graphe $H$. Pour le graphe produit $G \times H$, l'ensemble $C_i \times D_j$ est une clique (pour $i = 1, 2, \ldots, p$; $j = 1, 2, \ldots, q$). Ces différents produits $C_i \times D_j$ partitionnent le graphe $G \times H$. Donc

$$\theta(G \times H) \leqslant p \cdot q = \theta(G) \cdot \theta(H)$$

**Théorème.** *On a*

$$\alpha(G) \leqslant \sup_k \sqrt[k]{\alpha(G^k)} \leqslant \theta(G)$$

En effet d'après les Lemmes 1 et 2, on a

$$[\alpha(G)]^k \leqslant \alpha(G^k) \leqslant \theta(G^k) \leqslant [\theta(G)]^k$$

En conséquence de ce théorème, on voit que la capacité du graphe de Fig. 1, est compris entre 2 et 3. On voit aussi *que la condition nécessaire et suffisante pour que la capacité du graphe de signaux G soit égale à* $\alpha(G)$ *est que* $\alpha(G) = \theta(G)$. D'où l'intérêt, pour la théorie de l'information, à étudier les graphes parfaits.

Considérons une séquence de sommets $x_1, x_2, \ldots, x_{2k+1}, x_1$ formant un cycle de longueur impair $> 3$; on appelle *corde* de ce cycle toute arête joignant deux sommets nonconsécutifs du cycle.

Si $G$ est un cycle sans cordes de longueur $2k + 1$, on a évidemment $\alpha(G) = k$, $\theta(G) = k + 1$, donc

$$\alpha(G) \neq \theta(G)$$

De même, formons le graphe $\bar{G}$ *complémentaire* de $G$; ($\bar{G}$ a les mêmes sommets que $G$, mais deux sommets sont liés dans $\bar{G}$ si et seulement si ils ne sont pas liés dans $G$); on a $\alpha(G) = 2$, et $\theta(\bar{G}) = 3$, donc

$$\alpha(\bar{G}) \neq \theta(\bar{G})$$

Nous nous sommes proposés de voir si la réciproque était vraie, et sommes arrivés à la conjecture suivante avec P. Gilmore:

**Conjecture.** *Soit G un graphe de signaux; il est parfait si et seulement s'il ne contient pas un cycle impair sans cordes* (*de longueur* $> 3$), *ni le complémentaire d'un cycle impair sans cordes* (*de longueur* $> 3$).

Nous allons maintenant examiner plus en détail différentes catégories de graphes, qui toutes satisfont aux hypothèses de cette conjecture.

## III. Graphes Transitivitables

Un graphe $G$ est dit *transitivitable* s'il est possible d'affecter une orientation à chaque arête de sorte que la relation $a > b$ ("il existe une arête orientée allant du sommet $a$ vers le sommet $b$") soit une relation transitive:

$$a > b, b > c \qquad \text{entraîne } a > c$$

Par exemple, les graphes bichromatiques (ou "bipartites") sont évidemment transitivitables; le sous-graphe d'un graphe transitivitable est aussi transitivitable. Enfin, le lecteur vérifiera sans peine que les graphes transitivitables vérifient l'hypothèse de la conjecture. (cf. [3], [4].)

**Lemme.** *Si $G$ est un graphe transitivitable, il est possible d'affecter à chaque arête une orientation telle que la relation $a > b$ soit à la fois transitive et antisymétrique*:

"$a > b$ et $b > a$ *sont incompatibles*"

Soit $X = \{x_1, x_2, \ldots, x_n\}$ l'ensemble des sommets d'un graphe $G$, que l'on a orienté d'une façon transitive, et considérons l'équivalence

$$x_i \backsim x_j \qquad \text{si } x_i > x_j \text{ et } x_j > x_i \text{ simultanément}$$

Définissons une nouvelle orientation, en posant $x_i \gg x_j$ si:

1. $x_i$ et $x_j$ appartiennent à des classes différentes de l'équivalence $\backsim$, et $x > y$, ou bien:

2. $x_i$ et $x_j$ appartiennent à la même classe d'équivalence mais l'indice $i$ est supérieur à l'indice $j$.

De cette façon on a bien:

$$x \gg y, y \gg z \text{ entraîne } x \gg z$$
$$x \gg y \text{ avec } y \gg x \text{ est impossible}$$

**Théorème 1.** *Un graphe transitivitable est parfait.*

Un théorème célèbre de Dilworth dit que si les orientations des arêtes donnent une relation transitive et antisymétrique, $\alpha(G)$ est égal au plus petit nombre de chemins disjoints qui recouvrent l'ensemble des sommets.

Comme à chaque chemin correspond une clique (par suite de la transitivité), $\alpha(G)$ est égal au plus petit nombre de cliques qui partitionnent les sommets, c'est à-dire $\alpha(G) = \theta(G)$, et $G$ est un graphe parfait.

**Théorème 2.** *Le complémentaire $\bar{G}$ d'un graphe transitivitable $G$ est parfait.*

Ceci sera démontré en appendice.

## IV. Graphes Triangulés

Un graphe est dit *triangulé* si tout cycle de longueur supérieure à 3 possède une corde.

Un *arbre*, par exemple, est un graphe triangulé; un *cactus* (graphe connexe n'ayant de cycles de longueur supérieure à 3) est un graphe triangulé; un graphe représentatif d'une famille d'intervalles sur une droite est un graphe triangulé. Il est à noter que le concept de graphe triangulé et celui de graphe transitivitable sont indépendants.

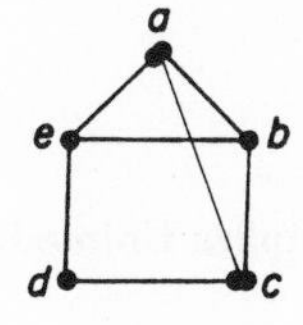


FIG. 2

Considérons par exemple le graphe de Fig. 2. Il est transitivitable, mais nontriangulé (à cause du cycle *ebcd*).

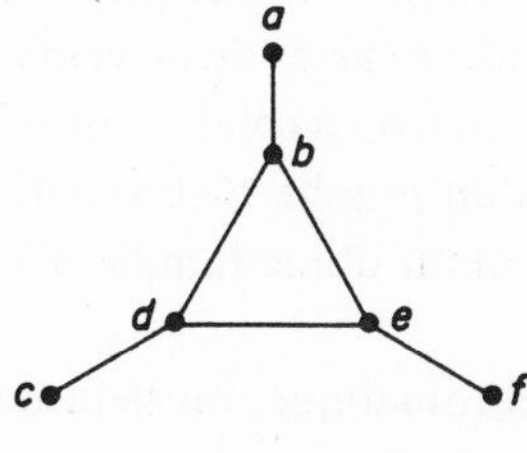


FIG. 3

Considérons maintenant le graphe de Fig. 3. Il est triangulé, mais nontransitivitable (comme on le vérifie aisément en essayant d'orienter les arêtes).

**Théorème 3.** *Un graphe triangulé est parfait.*

Ceci est équivalent à un énoncé de Hajnal et Suranyi [5].

**Théorème 4.** *Le complémentaire $\bar{G}$ d'un graphe triangulé $G$ est parfait.*

Ceci sera démontré en appendice.

*Application au cas d'un ensemble de signaux avec bruit linéaire.* Dans le cas du problème de Shannon, mentionné plus haut, il convient de remarquer que les signaux sont souvent distingués par la longueur d'onde qui leur est propre. Un bruit linéaire se traduit par la substitution sur l'axe des longueurs d'ondes d'un point par un intervalle. Deux signaux peuvent être confondus si leurs intervalles de longueur d'onde intersectent. Autrement dit, le graphe de la confusion pour l'ensemble des signaux est alors le *graphe représentatif d'une famille d'intervalles.*

Il est immédiat que le graphe représentatif d'une famille d'intervalles est triangulé; il est donc parfait.

En d'autres termes, on a montré que dans le cas d'un ensemble de signaux avec bruit linéaire on ne peut pas améliorer la richesse du code en utilisant des mots de plusieurs lettres.

## V. Graphes Unimodulaires

Un graphe $G$ est dit *unimodulaire* si tout sous-graphe $A \subset X$ nonvide peut être partitionné en deux ensembles disjoints $A_1$ et $A_2$ de sorte que toute clique maximale $C$ ayant un nombre pair d'éléments dans $A$, vérifie

$$|C \cap A_1| = |C \cap A_2|$$

Ceci équivaut à dire que la matrice des cliques maximales vs les sommets n'admet que des sous-matrices carrés de déterminant 0, + 1 ou − 1 (et l'on rejoint ainsi la théorie des matrices totalement unimodulaires).

Il est facile de voir qu'un graphe bichromatique est unimodulaire; de même, un graphe représentatif d'une famille d'intervalles sur la droite est unimodulaire.

Si $G$ est un graphe bichromatique, on peut démontrer que son adjoint $G^*$ (représentant les arêtes de $G$) est aussi unimodulaire.

Le concept du graphe unimodulaire est indépendant de celui du graphe triangulé; considérons, par exemple, le graphe de Fig. 4. Il est triangulé, mais il n'est pas unimodulaire (car $A = \{a, e, c\}$ ne peut être divisé en deux classes $A_1$ et $A_2$ conformément à la définition).

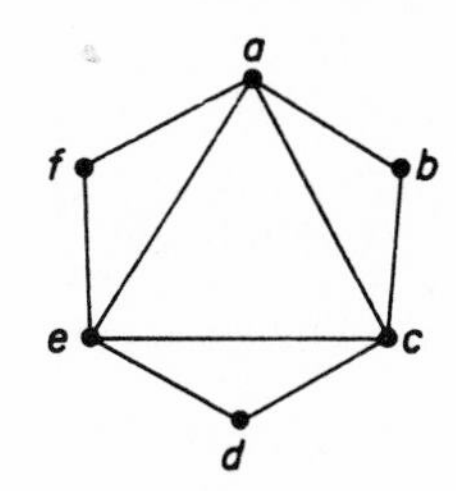


FIG. 4

De même, considérons le graphe de Fig. 5. Il est unimodulaire, mais n'est pas triangulé (à cause du cycle *abfg*), ni même transitivitable (à cause du cycle impair *abcdefg* qui ne contient pas de cordes triangulaires).

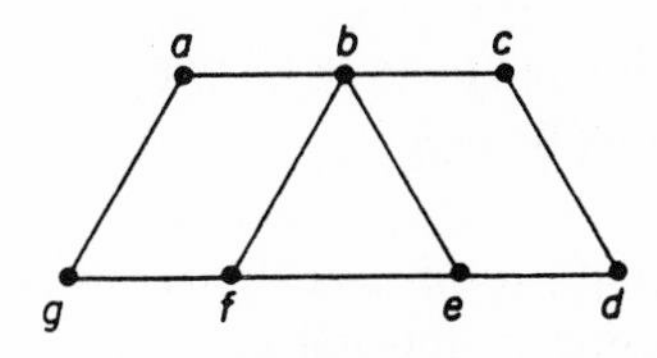


FIG. 5

**Théorème 5.** *Un graphe unimodulaire est parfait.*

Nous avons seulement besoin de démonter que

$$\alpha(G) = \theta(G)$$

On définira un ensemble stable $S$ par un vecteur $z = (z_1, z_2, \ldots, z_n)$, avec $z_i = 1$ si $x_i \subset S$, et $z_i = 0$ sinon.

Considérons enfin la matrice $M = ((m_j^i))$ d'incidence des cliques maximales avec

$$m_j^i = \begin{cases} 1 & \text{si } x_j \in C_i \\ 0 & \text{si } x_j \in C_i \end{cases}$$

Un ensemble stable maximum est donné par un programme linéaire en nombres entiers:

(1) $z \geqslant 0$
(2) $z \leqslant (1, 1, \ldots, 1)$
(3) $Mz \leqslant (1, 1, \ldots, 1)$
(4) maximiser $\Sigma z_j$

La condition (2) peut être supprimée, comme étant contenue dans (3). Le programme dual est

$$(1') \quad t = (t_1, t_2, \ldots, t_m) \geqslant 0$$
$$(2') \quad M^* t \geqslant (1, 1, \ldots, 1)$$
$$(3') \quad \text{minimiser } \Sigma t_i$$

Remarquons que (2′) et (3′) impliquent la condition

$$(4') \quad t \leqslant (1, 1, \ldots, 1)$$

En d'autres termes, le vecteur $t$ que nous cherchons représentera une famille de cliques qui recouvre tous les sommets, ayant un nombre minimum de cliques.

Comme la matrice $M$ est totalement unimodulaire, et d'après le théorème de la dualité, on a

$$\alpha(G) = \max \Sigma z_j = \min \Sigma t_i = \theta(G)$$

(il est à noter que si $G$ est l'adjoint d'un graphe bichromatique, on retrouve ici un fameux théorème de König).

**Théorème 6.** *Si $G$ est un graphe unimodulaire, son complémentaire $\bar{G}$ est parfait.*

Ce résultat sera démontré en appendice.

Outre les six cas mentionnés ci-dessus, il existe d'autre classes de graphes moins importantes, dont nous pouvons démontrer qu'ils sont parfaits; ce qui nous a semblé digne d'être noté, c'est que tous les graphes considérés vérifient l'hypothèse de la conjecture.

Néanmoins, la conjecture elle-même nous a parue très difficile à démontrer, et relève de techniques combinatoires encore mal connues. Les résultats ci-dessus montrent en particulier, comme Shannon [6] l'avait vérifié expérimentalement, qu'il n'y a qu'un seul graphe de moins de six sommets qui puisse représenter un code améliorable.

## Appendice

*Sur la Démonstration de Certains Théorèmes qui Relèvent des Techniques de Coloration.*

Nous avions laissé de côté les démonstrations de certains théorèmes mentionnés, qui sont liés à l'étude du nombre chromatique.

Rappelons que le *nombre chromatique* $\gamma(G)$ d'un graphe $G$ est le plus petit nombre de couleurs nécessaires pour en colorier les sommets, de sorte que deux sommets adjacents ne soient jamais de même couleur; que le *nombre cliquomatique* $\omega(G)$ est le nombre maximum d'éléments d'une clique.

On a toujours $\gamma(G) \geqslant \omega(G)$; si $\bar{G}$ est le complémentaire du graphe $G$ on a aussi,

$$\omega(G) = \alpha(\bar{G})$$
$$\gamma(G) = \theta(\bar{G})$$

Cette remarque va nous permettre de démontrer les résultats suivants.

**Théorème 2.** *Si G est un graphe transitivitable, on a*

$$\gamma(G) = \omega(G)$$

En effet, considérons $G$ avec une orientation transitive et antisymétrique.

Comme $G$ n'a pas de circuits, on peut affecter à chaque sommet $x$ un nombre fini $f(x)$ représentant le plus long chemin commençant par $x$. Si $\max_x f(x) = k - 1$, il existe une clique avec $k$ sommets; il n'existe pas de cliques avec plus de $k$ sommets, puisque, d'après le théorème de König-Redei, une telle clique contiendrait un chemin passant par tous ses sommets, et le plus long chemin contient seulement $k$ sommets. On a donc

$$\omega(G) = k$$

D'autre part, considérons $k$ couleurs $0, 1, \ldots, k-1$, et affectons la couleur $f(x)$ au sommet $x$.

Deux sommets adjacents $x$ et $y$ ne peuvent pas avoir la même couleur, car si l'arête est orientée de $x$ vers $y$, on a $f(x) > f(y)$. Donc

$$\gamma(G) \leqslant k$$

Comme on a toujours $\gamma(G) \geqslant \omega(G) = k$, on a bien

$$\gamma(G) = k = \omega(G)$$

**Théorème 4.** *Si G est un graphe triangulé, on a*

$$\gamma(G) = \omega(G)$$

Ceci a été démontré par nous dans [2].

**Théorème 6.** *Si G est un graphe unimodulaire, on a*

$$\gamma(G) = \omega(G)$$

Si $\omega(G) = k$, cherchons un vecteur $z = (z_1, z_2, \ldots, z_n)$ tel que

$$0 \leqslant z \leqslant (1, 1, \ldots, 1)$$
$$\langle M^i, z\rangle = 1 \quad \text{si la clique } C_i \text{ contient exactement } k \text{ sommets}$$
$$\langle M^i, z\rangle \leqslant 1 \quad \text{si } C_i \text{ contient moins de } k \text{ sommets}$$

$z_0 = (1/k, 1/k, \ldots, 1/k)$ est un point qui satisfait toutes ses inégalités, donc le système est compatible. Mais d'après la propriété unimodulaire de la matrice $M$, il existe une solution en nombre entiers $\bar{z}$.

Considérons l'ensemble $S_1$ des sommets $x_i$ tels que $\bar{z}_i = 1$; il est stable, et rencontre toutes les cliques de $k$ éléments.

Colorons avec une première couleur les sommets de $S_1$; le sous-graphe obtenu en supprimant $S_1$ est aussi unimodulaire, et sa clique maximum contient $k - 1$ éléments.

Colorons avec une deuxième couleur un ensemble stable $S_2$ qui rencontre toutes ces cliques de $k - 1$ éléments, etc....

En continuant ainsi, nous pouvons colorer tous les sommets de $G$ avec $k$ couleurs, donc

$$\gamma(G) = k = \omega(G)$$

(Nous sommes redevables à M. H. McAndrew de cette démonstration, qui est plus courte que notre preuve originale.)

## RÉFÉRENCES

1. C. Berge, *Théorie des graphes et ses applications*, Dunod, Paris, 1958.
2. C. Berge, Les problèmes de coloration en théorie des graphes, I.S.U.P., **9**, 123 (1960).
3. A. Ghouila-Houri, Caractérisation des matrices totalement unimodulaires, *Compt. Rend.* **254**, 1192 (1962).
4. P. C. Gilmore and A. J. Hoffman, Charactêrisation of comparability graphs and of interval graphs (à paraître).
5. A. Hajnal and J. Suranyi, Ueber die Auflösung von Graphen in vollständige Teilgraphen, *Ann. Univ. Budapest* **1**, 153 (1958).
6. C. E. Shannon, The zero-error capacity of a noisy channel, *IRE Trans. Comp. Inform. Theory* **3**, 3 (1956).

# Introduction to the CUCH[1,2]

CORRADO BÖHM

*I.N.A.C.–C.N.R., Piazzale delle Scienze, Rome*
*I.C.C., Palazzo degli Uffici, Rome, Italy*

and WOLF GROSS

*I.N.A.C.–C.N.R., Piazzale delle Science*
*Rome, Italy*

## I. Utility of Introducing Application and Abstraction Operation

It is widely recognized that the notions of abstract machine, program, and algorithm are very near each other and interdependent (see, e.g., Wang [15], Hermes [8a], Shepherdson and Sturgis [12], and Markov [9]).

For example, we can associate a more-or-less formal "description" with each of the preceding entities, i.e., a symbol string from a finite alphabet (possibly the same for all three). On the other hand, each of them can be viewed even in different ways as a partially defined function, of one or more variables, on the set of all strings.

There is something confusing in a notion of a string which denotes both itself and a mapping of strings into strings. Therefore, normally one proceeds with caution, introducing some metalinguistic devices, such as quotation marks "...," some hierarchical level between entities, or by justifying such distinctions by means of explicit operations of "coding," "gödelizing," and so on.

Sometimes the machine itself is supposed to act metalinguistically, as in the universal Turing machines or in the von Neumann computers (provided with a control, an arithmetic unit, and a finite or unlimited number of addressable registers). In the von Neumann computers, there is no difference between a number and an instruction. The same word is interpreted in one

[1] CUCH is a reference mnemonic word for the CUrry combinators system as well as the λ-calculus of CHurch.

[2] Work carried out at the I.N.A.C. in collaboration with the I.C.C. within the Italian Consiglio Nazionale delle Ricerche Research Group No. 22.

way or in another according to the initial computing situation, i.e., essentially according to the will of the programmer. We would like to show that introducing entities which Curry calls *combinators*, and formulas which Church calls *λ-formulas*, is fruitful both to define a very flexible description language for machines, programs, and algorithms, and to define directly an abstract machine with interesting properties.

Let us consider a given machine $M$, two programs $P_1$ and $P_2$, and some information $G$ which must be subjected to processing. If $U$ and $V$ are information for the machine $M$ we will write $(UV)$ for the uniquely determined result, if any, of the processing, taking $U$ as the program and $V$ as the datum. In this case we shall say we have applied $U$ to $V$ with the result $(UV)$, the application being defined as the operation of placing in brackets. More generally, if $f$ is a function of one variable and $a$ is an argument value in its domain we shall write $(fa)$ instead of the more usual $f(a)$.

A repeated use of applications allows us to define more new operations. If, for instance, we give $P_1, P_2, P_3, G$ the following meaning: $P_1$ is a FORTRAN compiler for the machine $M$, $P_2$ is a given object program written in FORTRAN, $P_3$ is the translation of $P_2$ in the code of $M$, and $G$ is a set of input values for $P_2$, then the formula

$$(P_1 P_2) = P_3 \tag{1}$$

has the meaning of a compiled program and

$$((P_1 P_2) G) = (P_3 G) \tag{2}$$

denotes the processing result.

If, on the other hand, $P_1$ denotes the program for the computation of the following function of $y$:

$$\frac{1}{2}\left(y - \frac{1}{y}\right)$$

$P_2$ the program for the computation of $e^x$, $G$ a given real number,

$$(P_1(P_2 G)) = (\sinh G) \tag{3}$$

What happens with the functions of more than one variable? As observed by Schönfinkel [11] they may be considered operators or functionals. This can again be clarified through the interpretation of functions as programs.

If $\Sigma$ is the program for the addition and $n$ and $m$ are numbers, $(\Sigma n)$ can be interpreted as the program of "adding $n$" (to every given number $x$), and then the sum $m + n$ is represented by $((\Sigma n)m)$. In all, $\Sigma$ is the program or the functional that, if applied to a number $n$, transforms it into the program (or function of one argument) of "adding $n$." This reasoning can obviously be enlarged to every other function or program with more than two variables.[1]

We have come to a point where it seems suitable to introduce a new kind of operation, which will be called *abstraction*. Let us, for instance, characterize a program which, as in formula (3), arises from the composition of two given but arbitrary programs, $P_1$ and $P_2$. We do not always have the luck to have as before a name readymade, such as sinh.

We could say "the composition of $P_1$ and $P_2$" but we prefer to say as follows, which is also applicable to other cases (e.g., for $\Sigma$): "the operator that, applied to $x$, gives the result $(P_1(P_2x))$," and after Church [3] we shall write[2]

$$(\lambda x(P_1(P_2x))) \tag{4}$$

We abstracted from the specific value $G$ of $x$ but we can go further, abstracting from the specific program $P_2$ and introducing the idea of "composing with $P_1$," through the formulas

$$(\lambda y(\lambda x(P_1(yx)))) \tag{5}$$

or even of "composing" through a further abstraction, reaching

$$(\lambda z(\lambda y(\lambda x(z(yx))))) \tag{6}$$

We now give another example, taken from the theory of von Neumann's machines.[3] Let $x$ be the initial content of the accumulator, at the instant $y=0$, $y$ being a discrete time variable (an integer), $z$ the address of the generic register of the machine, and 0 the address of the accumulator. The machine is a deterministic device; therefore if we denote by $\gamma(x,y,z)$ the content of $z$ at the instant $y$ [naturally it must be $\gamma(x,0,0)=x$], we know that if the machine stops at the time $y_\dagger$, the result $\gamma(x,y_\dagger,0)$ is uniquely determined by the whole initial situation of the registers.

A proper notation for such a situation is

$$\lambda z\gamma(x,0,z) \tag{7}$$

or, more formally,

$$(\lambda z(((\gamma x)0)z))$$

[1] It is possible to introduce differently a function of $n$ variables, referring to the notion of $n$-tuple (see Sec. III,G). Indeed,

$$((\cdots((fx_1)x_2)\cdots)x_n) = (\langle f\rangle\langle x_1, x_2, \ldots, x_n\rangle).$$

[2] We wish to warn the reader who is meeting this notation for the first time not to read the formula $(\lambda xM)$ "the application of $\lambda x$ to $M$" for reasons to be clarified in the following.

[3] This theory is also to be found in Böhm [1].

Another notation could be the following:

$$\gamma(x,0,0),\ \gamma(x,0,1),\ \gamma(x,0,2),\ \ldots \tag{8}$$

which is equivalent to (7) from an extensional point of view.

*Exercise.* Let us denote by $\Sigma$ and $\Pi$, respectively, the addition and multiplication (between real numbers) operators, with $D$ the differentiation operator. For example, the formula $d(x^2)/dx = 2x$ will be written

$$(D(\lambda x((\Pi x)\,x))) = \lambda x(\Pi 2x)$$

Now try to obtain the differentiation formulas for addition, multiplication, and composition of two functions, $f$ and $g$, of one real variable, using application and the $\lambda$-notation only.

## II. Combinators as an Algebraic System

Let us consider combinators as an algebraic system $[\mathscr{C}, (\cdots), =, \mathbf{S}, \mathbf{K}]$, where $\mathscr{C}$ is a groupoid with respect to the nonassociative binary[1] operation $(\cdots\ \cdots)$ of *application*, $=$ is a congruence relation provided with an extensionality law, and $\mathbf{S}$, $\mathbf{K}$ are two noncongruent generators of the groupoid with special laws of reduction. We shall call every element of $\mathscr{C}$ a *combinator*. More precisely we have[2]:

*Groupoid*

$$a \in \mathscr{C} \wedge b \in \mathscr{C} \rightarrow (a, b) \in \mathscr{C}$$

$$\mathbf{S} \in \mathscr{C} \wedge \mathbf{K} \in \mathscr{C}$$

*Congruence*

$$\left.\begin{array}{l} a = a,\ a = b \rightarrow b = a,\ a = b \wedge b = c \rightarrow a = c \\ a = b \wedge c = d \rightarrow (ac) = (bd) \end{array}\right\} \text{for each } a, b, c, d \in \mathscr{C}$$

*Extensionality*

$$\bigwedge_x [x \in \mathscr{C} \rightarrow (ax) = (bx)] \rightarrow a = b \qquad \text{for each } a, b \in \mathscr{C}$$

*Generator reduction rules*

$$((\mathbf{K}a)\,b) = a \tag{9}$$

$$(((\mathbf{S}a)\,b)\,c) = ((ac)\,(bc)) \qquad \text{for each } a, b, c \in \mathscr{C} \tag{10}$$

[1] A binary operation over a set $S$ is a mapping of $S \times S$ into $S$, where $S \times S$ is the set of all the ordered pairs of $S$.

[2] In the formulas that will follow, $\bigwedge_x$ holds "for all $x$," and $\wedge, \rightarrow$ are the logic marks of conjunction and implication.

Owing to the rule (9), **K** may be interpreted as an operator which transforms an element into a function of one variable which constantly takes this element as a value.

Choosing $\Pi$ for $a$, $(\Sigma 1)$ (successor operator) for $b$, and a number for $c$,[1] because of (10) we have

$$(((\mathbf{S}\Pi)(\Sigma 1))\,c) = ((\Pi c)((\Sigma 1)\,c)) \qquad \text{i.e., } c(c+1) \tag{11}$$

Therefore **S** may be interpreted as a special substitution operator. The extensionality law may be interpreted as follows: If two functions take the same value for every value of the argument, then they are congruent; that is, they may be identified.

Let us now introduce, after Rosenbloom [10], the following definitions of combinators, and let us illustrate the use of the reduction and extensionality rules:

**O** for (**SK**)
**I** for (**OK**)
**B** for ((**S**(**KS**))**K**)
**W** for ((**SS**)**O**)
**C** for ((**S**((**BB**)**S**))(**KK**))

If $a, b, c \in \mathscr{C}$ we have

$$((\mathbf{O}a)\,b) = (((\mathbf{SK})\,a)\,b) = ((\mathbf{K}b)\,(ab)) = b \tag{12}$$

such that

$$\mathbf{I}b = ((\mathbf{OK})\,b) = b \tag{13}$$

proving that I denotes the identity operator:

$$\begin{aligned}(\mathbf{B}a) &= (((\mathbf{S}(\mathbf{KS}))\,\mathbf{K})\,a) = (((\mathbf{KS})\,a)\,(\mathbf{K}a)) \\ &= (\mathbf{S}(\mathbf{K}a))\end{aligned} \tag{14}$$

$$(((\mathbf{B}a)\,b)\,c) = (((\mathbf{S}(\mathbf{K}a))\,b)\,c) = (((\mathbf{K}a)\,c)\,(bc)) = (a(bc)) \tag{15}$$

Using the extensionality law, we obtain, from (12), the following useful relations:

$$(\mathbf{O}a) = \mathbf{I} \qquad \text{for each } a \in \mathscr{C} \tag{16}$$

$$\begin{aligned}((\mathbf{W}a)\,b) &= ((((\mathbf{SS})\,\mathbf{O})\,a)\,b) = (((\mathbf{S}a)\,(\mathbf{O}a))\,b) \\ &= (((\mathbf{S}a)\,\mathbf{I})\,b) = ((ab)\,(\mathbf{I}b)) = ((ab)\,b)\end{aligned} \tag{17}$$

[1] Let us tacitly suppose that the numbers and operators $\Pi, \Sigma$ are representable in $\mathscr{C}$, all of which will be shown in Section IV,D.

$$
\begin{aligned}
(((\mathbf{C}a)\,b)\,c) &= (((((\mathbf{S}((\mathbf{BB})\,\mathbf{S}))\,(\mathbf{KK}))\,a)\,b)\,c) \\
&= ((((((\mathbf{BB})\,\mathbf{S})\,a)\,((\mathbf{KK})\,a))\,b)\,c) \\
&= ((((\mathbf{B}(\mathbf{S}a))\,((\mathbf{KK})\,a))\,b)\,c) \\
&= (((\mathbf{S}a)\,(((\mathbf{KK})\,a)\,b))\,c) \\
&= ((ac)\,((((\mathbf{KK})\,a)\,b)\,c)) = ((ac)\,((\mathbf{K}b)\,c)) \\
&= ((ac)\,b) \qquad (18)
\end{aligned}
$$

So we proved the validity of the following congruences for **I**, **0**, **B**, **W**, **C**:

$$(\mathbf{I}b) = b \tag{19}$$

$$(\mathbf{0}a) = \mathbf{I} \tag{20}$$

$$(((\mathbf{B}a)\,b)\,c) = (a\,(bc)) \tag{21}$$

$$((\mathbf{W}a)\,b) = ((ab)\,b) \tag{22}$$

$$(((\mathbf{C}a)\,b)\,c) = ((ac)\,b) \tag{23}$$

*Exercises.* By means of the reduction rules and of the congruences obtained, reduce $((((\mathbf{SB})(\mathbf{KI}))\,a)\,b)$, $((((\mathbf{BW})\,\mathbf{C})\,a)\,b)$, $(((((\mathbf{BC})\,\mathbf{K})\,a)\,b)\,c)$ and prove, using the extensionality law, that $(\mathbf{KI}) = \mathbf{0}$, $((\mathbf{SB})(\mathbf{KI})) = \mathbf{I}$, $((\mathbf{BW})\,\mathbf{C}) = \mathbf{W}$, $((\mathbf{BC})\,\mathbf{K}) = (\mathbf{BK})$.

## A. Historical Note

Curry [5] and Rosenbloom [10] showed that it is possible to substitute for the extensionality law a finite set of congruence relations between given combinators.

We can derive from Church [3] that $\mathscr{C}$ is a semigroup (with respect to the binary operation **B**), which can be generated by the four combinators $((\mathbf{CI})\,\mathbf{S})$, $((\mathbf{CI})\,\mathbf{K})$, **B**, $(\mathbf{CI})$, and that the "word problem" is unsolvable in $\mathscr{C}$. For sets of basic combinators different from **S** and **K**, see Church [4] and Curry [5].

## B. Combinatory Forms and Completeness Theorems

Let us introduce the notion of combinatory form recursively as follows:

A variable $x, y, \ldots$ is a combinatory form.
**S** and **K** are forms.
If $\alpha$, $\beta$ are forms, then $(\alpha\beta)$ is a form.

In the following, by uniquely determined we mean up to a congruence (i.e., congruence stands here for identity).

It may be observed that a form becomes a combinator when combinators are substituted for all variables occurring in it. If we think of each variable as an unspecified element of $\mathscr{C}$, it is easy to extend to the combinatory forms all the above-mentioned rules defining combinators. Actually this is not necessary, because the following *completeness theorem* holds:

*For each form* $\mathfrak{F}[x]$, *in which the variable x may occur, there is a combinator F uniquely determined such that if* $a \in \mathscr{C}$ *then* $\mathfrak{F}[a] = (Fa)$.

$\mathfrak{F}[a]$ denotes the result of the substitution of $a$ for every occurrence of $x$ in $\mathfrak{F}[x]$.

*Proof.* According to what has been mentioned in Sec. I we use for $F$ the formula $(\lambda x \mathfrak{F}[x])$, which, as we shall see, will not contain $x$, but **S** and **K** only. We build $F$ by means of a recursive algorithm which consists in eliminating or shifting to the right the symbol $\lambda x$ into the form $\mathfrak{F}[x]$, according to cases dependent on the structure of $\mathfrak{F}[x]$.

More precisely, the algorithm is the following:

If $\mathfrak{F}[x]$ does not contain $x$ then $(\lambda x \mathfrak{F}[x])$ is $(\mathbf{K}\,\mathfrak{F}[x])$.
If $\mathfrak{F}[x]$ is $x$ then $(\lambda x \mathfrak{F}[x])$ is **I**.
If $\mathfrak{F}[x]$ is $(\mathscr{A}[x]\mathscr{B}[x])$ then $(\lambda x \mathfrak{F}[x])$ is $((\mathbf{S}(\lambda x \mathscr{A}[x]))(\lambda x \mathscr{B}[x]))$.

For example, applying the algorithm just mentioned to the formula

$$\mathfrak{F}[x] \equiv ((x(\mathbf{K}x))\,\mathbf{S})$$

we obtain

$$\begin{aligned}(\lambda x \mathfrak{F}[x]) &\equiv ((\mathbf{S}(\lambda x(x(\mathbf{K}x))))\,(\lambda x \mathbf{S}))\\ &\equiv ((\mathbf{S}(((\mathbf{S}(\lambda x x))\,(\lambda x(\mathbf{K}x))))\,(\mathbf{KS}))\\ &\equiv ((\mathbf{S}((\mathbf{SI})\,((\mathbf{S}(\lambda x \mathbf{K}))\,(\lambda x x))))\,(\mathbf{KS}))\\ &\equiv ((\mathbf{S}((\mathbf{SI})\,((\mathbf{S}(\mathbf{KK}))\,\mathbf{I})))\,(\mathbf{KS}))\end{aligned}$$

The proof that generally $((\lambda x \mathfrak{F}[x])\,a) = \mathfrak{F}[a]$ is obtained by induction, i.e., over the number of symbols used in a form; in fact, if $\mathfrak{F}[x]$ does not contain $x$, then

$$((\lambda x \mathfrak{F}[x])\,a) = ((\mathbf{K}\,\mathfrak{F}[x])\,a) = \mathfrak{F}[x] = \mathfrak{F}[a]$$

If $\mathfrak{F}[x]$ is $x$, then $((\lambda x \mathfrak{F}[x])\,a) = (\mathbf{I}a) = a = \mathfrak{F}[a]$. Finally, if $\mathfrak{F}[x]$ is $(\mathscr{A}[x]\mathscr{B}[x])$ and the theorem is true for all forms having fewer symbols than $\mathfrak{F}[x]$, then

$$\begin{aligned}((\lambda x(\mathscr{A}[x]\,\mathscr{B}[x]))\,a) &= (((\mathbf{S}(\lambda x \mathscr{A}[x]))\,(\lambda x \mathscr{B}[x]))\,a)\\ &= (((\lambda x \mathscr{A}[x])\,a)\,((\lambda x \mathscr{B}[x])\,a))\\ &= (\mathscr{A}[a]\,\mathscr{B}[a]) = \mathfrak{F}[a] \qquad \text{Q.E.D.}\end{aligned}$$

An equivalent theorem holds for forms having two variables $x$, $y$, *etc.*

$$(((\lambda x(\lambda y\mathfrak{F}[x,y]))\,a)\,b) = \mathfrak{F}[a,b], \text{ etc.}$$

The meaning of the completeness theorem is the following: All functions from $\mathscr{C}$ into $\mathscr{C}$, or from $\mathscr{C} \times \mathscr{C}$ into $\mathscr{C}$, etc., definable by means of the $\lambda$-notation and the application operation (that is, in a determined constructive way), are congruent with elements of $\mathscr{C}$.

## C. Theorems of Nonexistence of Combinators

Let us give two examples:

There exists no $U \in \mathscr{C}$ such that for each $a, b \in \mathscr{C}$, $(U(ab)) = a$.

We shall prove by absurdum that if $U$ exists, then $\mathbf{S} = \mathbf{K}$.

*Proof.* Choose $a = \mathbf{O}$, $b = \mathbf{I}$, and a new combinator $a' = \mathbf{I}$. We have

$$(ab) = (\mathbf{OI}) = \mathbf{I} = (\mathbf{II}) = (a'\,b)$$

If $U$ exists we obtain

$$U(ab) = \mathbf{O} = U(a'\,b) = \mathbf{I}$$

that is, $\mathbf{O} = \mathbf{I}$. So we must have

$$((\mathbf{O}(\mathbf{KS}))\,\mathbf{K}) = (\mathbf{IK}) = \mathbf{K} = ((\mathbf{I}(\mathbf{KS}))\,\mathbf{K}) = ((\mathbf{KS})\,\mathbf{K}) = \mathbf{S}$$

that is, $\mathbf{S} = \mathbf{K}$. As we know that $\mathbf{S} \neq \mathbf{K}$, $U$ does not exist.

There exists no $u \in \mathscr{C}$ such that for any $f, g \in \mathscr{C}$

$$(fu) = (gu)$$

*Proof.* If $u$ exists, choosing $f = (\mathbf{KS})$, $g = (\mathbf{KK})$ we obtain

$$((\mathbf{KS})\,u) = \mathbf{S} = ((\mathbf{KK})\,u) = \mathbf{K}$$

that is, again, $\mathbf{S} = \mathbf{K}$. So $u$ does not exist.

*Exercises.* Below $F$, $X$ are forms, but $F$ does not contain $x$. Prove the following congruences:

(a) $(\lambda x(Fx)) = F$
(b) $(\lambda x(FX)) = ((\mathbf{B}F)(\lambda xX))$
(c) $(\lambda x(XF)) = ((\mathbf{B}(\lambda xX))\,F)$
(d) $(\lambda x(Xx)) = (\mathbf{W}(\lambda xX))$

Eliminate $\lambda$ from the following forms (possibly using the above-mentioned congruences):

(e) $\theta \equiv \lambda x((\mathbf{W}(\mathbf{B}x))(\mathbf{W}(\mathbf{B}x)))$
(f) $\langle \alpha, \beta \rangle \equiv (\lambda x((x\alpha)\beta))$
(g) $(\lambda x((\mathbf{B}(fx))(gx)))$, $(\lambda f(\lambda g(\lambda x((\mathbf{B}(fx))(gx)))))$
(h) $'\mathbf{2} \equiv (\lambda x(\lambda y(x(xy))))$

## D. Remark and Historical Notes

To prove that the system $\mathscr{C}$ is consistent, it is necessary to prove that **K** is not expressible by applications of **S** only, and vice versa. Curry [5] showed all that, and he also proved the complete equivalence existing between the system $\mathscr{C}$ and Church's $\lambda$-**K**-calculus system. The latter will be treated in the next section.

Substantially we can pass from $\lambda$-formulas to combinators applying the completeness theorem to any subform. If we want to follow the inverse procedure it is enough to put

$$\mathbf{S} = (\lambda x(\lambda y(\lambda z((xz)(yz)))))$$
$$\mathbf{K} = (\lambda x(\lambda y x))$$

If the basic combinators are, as in Curry [5], **K**, **B**, **C**, **W**, we may put

$$\mathbf{B} = (\lambda x(\lambda y(\lambda z(x(yz)))))$$
$$\mathbf{C} = (\lambda x(\lambda y(\lambda z((xz)y))))$$
$$\mathbf{W} = (\lambda x(\lambda y((xy)y)))$$

We shall more likely use $\lambda$-formulas instead of combinators because those significant for us are easily reducible to a unique privileged form, which will be called afterward "normal form." This reduction is feasible for combinators, too, as Curry [5] showed, but not in such an easy and natural way. The combinator **2**, seen in Exercise (h), may be expressed by different congruent forms, such as

$$(\mathbf{WB}),\ ((\mathbf{SB})\mathbf{I}),\ ((\mathbf{SB})((\mathbf{CB})\mathbf{I}))$$

# III. Description of the Morphology and Syntax of CUCH

## A. Expressions

The CUCH is a class of *expressions*, that is, of words over an alphabet composed of:

*Variables*, that is, an infinite series of characters... $x, y, z, \ldots$.
*Brackets*, (, ).
*A symbol* $\lambda$.

Possibly a finite number of *constants*, $a, b, c, \ldots$ (which, however, will not be used in this paper).

## B. Formulas

The CUCH formulas are the only following expressions:

*Atomic formulas* consisting of only one *variable* or *constant*.

If $L$, $M$ are formulas, $(LM)$ [or[1] $LM$] is a formula (called *application* of $L$ to $M$).

If $L$ is a formula, $(\lambda xL)$ [or[1] $\lambda xL$] is a formula (operation of *abstraction*).

*Examples*

$$(xy),\ (x(yz)),\ ((xy)\,y),\ ((((ab)\,c)\,d)\,e)$$
$$[\text{or } xy,\ x(yz),\ xyy,\ abcde]$$

are formulas.

$$(\lambda xy),\ (\lambda xx),\ (\lambda x(\lambda yx)),\ (\lambda x(\lambda y(\lambda z(x(yz)))))$$
$$[\text{or } \lambda xy,\ \lambda xx,\ \lambda x\lambda yx,\ \lambda x\lambda y\lambda z(x(yz))]$$

are formulas.

An occurrence of an expression $L$ in an expression $M$ is the partition $(A, L, B)$ when the expression $M$ has the form $ALB$ (where either $A$ or $B$ can be empty).

If we have one or more occurrences of $L$ in $M$, we shall say that $L$ *occurs* in $M$.

## C. Free Variables Occurring in a Formula

We have the following inductive definition:

$x$ is the only free variable occurring in the formula $x$.

If $\Pi$, $\Sigma$ are the sets of the variables occurring in the formulas $P$ and $S$, respectively, the set of free variables occurring in $(PS)$ [that is, in $PS$] is $\Pi \cup \Sigma$.

[1] To save brackets and to ease reading we shall often write:

(a) $ABCD\ldots Z$ instead of $((\ldots(((AB)C)\,D)\ldots)Z)$, where $A, B, \ldots$ are formulas. This means to assume a left association law for brackets.

(b) $\lambda x\lambda y\ldots\lambda zM$ instead of $(\lambda x(\lambda y(\ldots(\lambda zM)\ldots)))$. This means to admit, for each sequence of $\lambda$-operations, a right association law for brackets.

If $\Pi$ is the set of the free variables occurring in the formula $P$, $\Pi - \{x\}$ is the set of the free variables occurring in $(\lambda xP)$ [that is, $\lambda xP$].

Let us observe that the sentence "$x$ does not occur free in formula $M$" may mean:

(a) $x$ does not occur in $M$.

(b) Every occurrence of $x$ occurs in a subformula of $M$ of the form $\lambda xP$.

Every occurrence of $x$ which does not satisfy (b) will be called for short a *free occurrence* of $x$.

The following inductive definition holds:

### D. Subformula of a Formula $F$

$F$ is a subformula of $F$.

If $F$ is $(GH)$ [or $GH$], every subformula of $G$ or $H$ is a subformula of $F$.

If $F$ is $(\lambda xM)$ every subformula of $M$ is a subformula of $F$.

*Examples.* $x$ occurs free in

$$\lambda yx,\ \lambda y\lambda z(xyz),\ ab\lambda z(zb)\,\lambda ux$$

while $y$ does not occur free in the same formulas. In the three formulas, moreover, $x$ is the only variable occurring free.

$\lambda yx$, $x$ are all the subformulas of the first formula.

$\lambda z(xyz)$, $xy$, $y$ are some subformulas of the second formula.

$\lambda ux$, $zb$, $ab$ are some subformulas of the third formula.

### E. Formula Free at the Substitution for a Variable in a Formula[1]

Let $M, E \equiv \mathscr{E}[x]$ be formulas. We write $\mathscr{E}[x]$ (where $x$ may or may not occur in $E$) to mean we are interested in the free occurrences of $x$. We also write $\mathscr{E}[M]$ for the result of the substitution of $M$ for every free occurrence of $x$ in $\mathscr{E}[x]$. (If $x$ does not occur free in $\mathscr{E}[x]$ we have $\mathscr{E}[M] = E$.) We shall say that $M$ is free at the substitution for $x$ if every free occurrence of a variable $z$ in $M$ is free in $\mathscr{E}[M]$, too.

*Examples*

$\lambda x\lambda y(xz)$ is free at the substitution for $u$ in $\lambda xu$.

$xz$ is not free at the substitution in $\lambda xu$, since the free occurrence of $x$ after the substitution is free no more.

[1] Commonly said free for a variable in a formula.

## F. Reduction Rules

The reduction rules will consist of passages denoted by $L \rightarrow M$ from a formula $L$ to a formula $M$. We shall generically call these rules of *immediate reduction.*

These rules will all be of the form $\cdots A \cdots \rightarrow \cdots B \cdots$ and will consist of the substitution of a subformula $A$ for one of its occurrences in the formula $L$ through the formula $B$, obtaining the formula $M$.

The rules $A \rightarrow B$ will be called *elementary rules of reduction*, while the reduction rule $\cdots A \cdots \rightarrow \cdots B \cdots$ will be called the rule of *immediate reduction* of type $A \rightarrow B$.

We shall say that the formula $L$ is reducible to the formula $M$ (by means of certain rules) and we shall write $L \Rightarrow M$ if there exists a succession $L \equiv L_0, L_1, \ldots, L_n \equiv M$ such that for every $0 \leqslant i \leqslant n-1$ we have $L_i \rightarrow L_{i+1}$, i.e., if $L_i$ is immediately reducible to $L_{i+1}$ (by means of the same rules).

Reducibility is obviously a transitive relation. We shall say that $L$ is *convertible* into $M$ (by means of certain rules) and we shall write $L \Leftrightarrow M$ if there exists a sequence as above such that for every $0 \leqslant i \leqslant n-1$ we have $L_i \rightarrow L_{i+1}$ or $L_{i+1} \rightarrow L_i$. Convertibility is a transitive and symmetric relation.

The elementary rules we shall consider in the following will be of three types:

### 1. *Rule α of Redenomination*

Let $A \equiv \lambda x \mathfrak{F}[x]$. Let $y$ be a variable that (a) does not occur free in $\mathfrak{F}[x]$ and (b) is free for $x$ in $\mathfrak{F}[x]$; then the elementary rule

$$\lambda x \mathfrak{F}[x] \rightarrow \lambda y \mathfrak{F}[y] \qquad (\alpha)$$

will be called rule $\alpha$.

It may be seen that the rule is invertible owing to (a) and (b), that the $\alpha$-convertibility coincides with the $\alpha$-reducibility, and that each reduction which contains the rule has the reflexive property while the convertibility becomes an equivalence relation.

Two $\alpha$-reducible formulas (that is, $\alpha$-convertible) in the following will be called *congruent formulas.*

**Effects of Rule α.** We shall call a *bound occurrence* of a variable an occurrence which is not free. Through further applications of rule $\alpha$ it is possible to obtain that the following properties hold:

1. Bound variables are all different from free variables.
2. Bound variables are different from those of a prefixed set.
3. In the formula two $\lambda$ followed by the same variable do not appear.

Let us introduce the following inductive definition:

**Formula without Collisions of Variables**

(a) A formula without $\lambda$ is without collisions.

(b) If $F$ is without collisions and $G$ is without collisions, $FG$ is without collisions.

(c) If $F$ is without collisions and if $F$ does not contain $\lambda x$, then $\lambda xF$ is without collisions.

**Regular Formula.** A formula without collisions and satisfying property 1 is called a regular formula. Because of properties 1, 2, and 3 further applications of rule $\alpha$ allow us to transform every formula into one without collisions and also into a regular formula. Moreover, given two formulas $M$ and $\mathscr{E}(x)$ we can (by means of rule $\alpha$) transform $\mathscr{E}[x]$ into $\mathscr{E}'[x]$ in such a way that $M$ will become free for $x$ in $\mathscr{E}'[x]$.

2. *Rule $\beta$ (Fundamental)*

Let $A \equiv ((\lambda x\mathscr{E}[x])\,M)$ [or $\lambda x\mathscr{E}[x]\,M$] and $M$ be *free for* $x$ in $\mathscr{E}[x]$; then the elementary rule

$$((\lambda x\mathscr{E}[x])\,M) \to \mathscr{E}[M] \quad [\text{or } \lambda x\mathscr{E}[x]\,M \to \mathscr{E}[M]] \qquad (\beta)$$

will be called rule $\beta$.

3. *Rule $\eta$*

Let $A \equiv (\lambda x(Fx))$ [or $\lambda x(Fx)$], where $F$ is a formula and $x$ *does not occur free* in $F$. The elementary rule

$$(\lambda x(Fx)) \to F \; [\text{or } \lambda x(Fx) \to F] \qquad (\eta)$$

will be called rule $\eta$.

4. *Normal Form*

A formula $F$, where no immediate reduction of type $\beta$ or $\eta$ may be executed, is called *normal form.*

5. *Church-Rosser's Theorem*

Church-Rosser's theorem states that if two formulas are convertible one into the other, a third formula exists into which both are reducible.

### 6. *Consequences of Church-Rosser's Theorem*

If a formula is reducible to normal form, then the latter is unique up to some $\alpha$-congruences. In fact, if there were two, one of them would be reducible to the other. If a formula is reducible to the normal form, a procedure exists to obtain it. The existence of such an algorithm enables us to think of the CUCH as an abstract machine, whose input is a formula, and whose output is, if any, the normal form of the same formula.

*Exercises.* Consider the following expressions:

(a) $(\lambda x())$
(a′) $(\lambda x(x))$
(b) $(\lambda xy)$
(c) $(x(\lambda xy))$
(d) $(\lambda x(\lambda y(\lambda z(yz))))$
(e) $(\lambda x(\lambda x(\lambda xy)))$
(f) $(\lambda x((\lambda yx)x))$
(g) $(\lambda x(\lambda t(\lambda zy)))$
(h) $(\lambda x((\lambda xy)x))$
(i) $((\lambda x(\lambda y((xy)y)))(\lambda x(\lambda y(\lambda z(x(yz))))))$

Which of them are formulas? In which of them do free variables occur? Which are subformulas of others? Which can be freely substituted for $x$ in (f) and (g)? Which are $\alpha$-congruent? Which without collisions? Which regular? Which are reducible? (Try to reduce them.) Which are in normal form?

## G. Normal-Form Reduction Algorithm

The condition of having a normal form is not effective for a formula, but if a regular formula has a normal form, Church [3] and Curry [5] showed that there exists the following algorithm to obtain it: Scan the formula from the left to the right searching for the first $\lambda$ which can be eliminated by application of either rule $\eta$ or $\beta$. If such a $\lambda$ exists, apply the corresponding rule and, trying to reach a regular formula, start from the beginning again. If such a $\lambda$ does not exist, then the formula is in normal form.

*Example*

$$\lambda x\lambda y(\lambda z(x(zz))y)\lambda u(uv) \xrightarrow{\beta} \lambda y(\lambda z(\lambda u(uv)(zz))y) \xrightarrow{\eta} \lambda z(\lambda u(uv)(zz)) \xrightarrow{\beta} \lambda z(zzv)$$

### 1. *The Notion of n-tuple and a Variant of the Algorithm More Suitable for efficient Automatic Computation*

Let us give, first of all, a CUCH formula for the notion of $n$-tuple, i.e.,

$$X \equiv \lambda x(xX_1 X_2 \cdots X_n) \qquad \text{or} \qquad Y \equiv \lambda x(xY_1 Y_2 \cdots Y_m)$$

where $X_i$ $Y_i$ are given formulas without $x$ and $n, m \geqslant 0$. Sometimes we shall also write for $X$ $\langle X_1, X_2, \ldots, X_n \rangle$, etc.

It is easy to prove that in this case the fundamental property of $n$-tuples holds:

$$X \leftrightarrow Y \qquad \text{iff} \quad n = m \text{ and } X_i \leftrightarrow Y_i$$

Moreover, we observe that the reduction algorithm proceeds always from left to right, while sometimes the number of steps or the length of the formulas could be less extensive if the reduction were carried out in a different way.

*Example.* Let us consider a composition $\alpha(\beta\gamma)$ and let us choose $\alpha \equiv \lambda x \lambda yy$, $\beta \equiv \lambda u \lambda v(u(u(uv)))$, $\gamma = \lambda zz$. Reaching the normal form we have

$$\lambda x \lambda yy(\lambda u \lambda v(u(u(uv)))\,\lambda zz) \xrightarrow{\beta} \lambda yy$$

that is, we obtain the normal form through one step only. If we first reduce $(\beta\gamma)$ we have

$$\lambda x \lambda yy(\lambda u \lambda v(u(u(uv)))\,\lambda zz) \xrightarrow{\beta} \lambda x \lambda yy(\lambda v(\lambda zz(\lambda zz(\lambda zzv))))$$

$$\xrightarrow{\beta} \lambda x \lambda yy(\lambda v(\lambda zz(\lambda zzv))) \xrightarrow{\beta} \lambda x \lambda yy(\lambda v(\lambda zzv))$$

$$\rightarrow \lambda x \lambda yy(\lambda vv) \xrightarrow{\beta} \lambda yy$$

In this way we obtain the normal form through 5 steps. On the other hand, if we choose

$$\alpha \equiv \lambda u \lambda v(u(u(uv))),\ \beta \equiv \lambda x \lambda y(x(x(xy))),\ \gamma \equiv \lambda zz$$

[i.e., the composition $\alpha(\alpha\gamma)$], using the usual method of reduction we have

$$\lambda u \lambda v(u(u(uv)))\,(\lambda x \lambda y(x(x(xy)))\,\lambda zz)$$

$$\xrightarrow{\beta} \lambda v(\lambda x \lambda y(x(x(xy)))\,\lambda zz(\lambda x \lambda y(x(x(xy)))\,\lambda zz(\lambda x \lambda y(x(x(xy)))\,\lambda zzv)))$$

$$\xrightarrow{\beta} \cdots \xrightarrow{\beta} \lambda vv$$

where $\cdots$ stay for 13 reduction steps. The total steps are then 16.

However, if we first reduce $(\alpha\gamma)$ we obtain the same result through 8 steps and the longest formula we encounter during the reduction process is

$$\lambda u \lambda v(u(u(uv)))(\lambda y(\lambda zz(\lambda zz(\lambda zzy))))$$

Finally we may say that in certain cases, if we know the order according to which the reduction method proceeds, it would be useful to have an algorithm which makes this choice possible.

A solution of this problem is given by the following variant of the algorithm. Proceed as in the algorithm of Section III,G,1, with the difference that, if the first $\lambda x$ to which the $\beta$-rule is applicable is the $\lambda x$ of an $n$-tuple $X$, its elimination must be postponed to the reduction in normal form of each of its components $X_1 X_2 \cdots X_n$.

Of course, if each $X$ is itself an $n$-tuple, the procedure must be iterated. By means of the variant just mentioned, it is possible to program the order according to which reductions must be carried out.[1]

*Example.* Let $X$, $Y$ be two formulas and $X$, $Y$ and $XY$ have normal form. Let us see what happens if we apply the modified algorithm to three formulas convertible to each other.

| | |
|---|---|
| $XY$ | If no $n$-tuple appears in it, the reduction process is that of the unmodified algorithm. |
| $\lambda u(uY)X$ | First of all, $Y$ is reduced to normal form; the remainder is treated as in the unmodified algorithm. |
| $\lambda u(uXY)I$ | First of all, $X$ and $Y$ are separately reduced to normal form; then as in the unmodified algorithm. |

## H. Heuristic Abstraction Principle (H.A.P.)

Sometimes we are interested in finding a formula $F$ which maps a class of formulas $\mathscr{U}$ into a class of formulas $\mathscr{V}$. We note that, if $\mathscr{U}$ is a proper subset of the set of all formulas $\Gamma$, $F$ will not be, in general, uniquely determined, because its action over the formulas of $\Gamma - \mathscr{U}$ is not defined.

If we succeed in expressing the unspecified $v \in \mathscr{V}$ by a formula $\mathfrak{F}[u]$ containing the unspecified $u \in \mathscr{U}$, we may write

$$Fu \Leftrightarrow \mathfrak{F}[u] \qquad \text{i.e., } Fu \Leftrightarrow \lambda x \mathfrak{F}[x]\, u$$

[1] Note that the modified algorithm is not a general one like the original one. So if it is applied carelessly, it may not reach its goal, i.e., the normal form.

An obvious choice for $F$ (of course not the only one), which, in any case, satisfies the relation just mentioned, is

$$F \equiv \lambda x \mathfrak{F}[x]$$

Any time that we make such a choice we shall say that we have applied the heuristic abstraction principle (H.A.P.).

### I. Historical Note

McCarthy [8b] first introduced the λ-notation into programming, to express substitution operations in his LISP-language. Because not every functional is representable in the LISP, he introduced a "label" operator to carry out recursive programming. Gilmore [7] described an abstract machine, whose operating mode contains the reduction algorithm with the $\beta$-rule only.

## IV. Use of the CUCH

The formulas admit several *interpretations*. For instance, they may be interpreted as operators, functions, numbers, functionals, and so on. Nevertheless, there do not exist interpretations such that to each formula there corresponds an entity, unless artificial entities are introduced.

### A. Essential Qualification for a Correct Interpretation

If a formula $F$ is interpreted in a certain way, every formula $G \Leftrightarrow F$ (convertible into $F$) must have the same interpretation.

### B. Various Interpretations of the Application Operation

Let us suppose that the formula $PQ$ is convertible into a formula $R$ which has an interpretation. Sometimes it is possible to find an operator corresponding to the application as its interpretation. This kind of correspondence, however, may *vary* with $P$ and $Q$. For instance, if $P$ has as interpretation a function $f$ of one variable and $Q$ an entity $\alpha$ in the domain of this function, $PQ$ has the interpretation of $f(\alpha)$. In that case, to the *application* corresponds the application of a function to one argument (whence the name application). On the other hand, if $P$ and $Q$ are interpreted as *statements* $p,q$ (in a determined way) then to $PQ$ may be given the interpretation $p \supset q$, in which case to the application corresponds the *implication*. If $P$, $Q$ are in some way interpreted as integers $m$, $n$, then $PQ$ may have the interpretation $n^m$, and in this case to the application corresponds the exponentiation.

## C. Operational Interpretation

Let $R$ be a formula and $\mathscr{P}_1, \mathscr{P}_2, \ldots, \mathscr{P}_n$ *classes* of formulas which have interpretations of different nature. Furthermore, let $RP_i \Leftrightarrow Q_i$, where $P_i \in \mathscr{P}_i$ have known interpretations. On the base of what has been said, this means that to the application of $R$ on $P_i$ corresponds a certain operation (depending on $i$) which allows us to pass from the entity interpretation of $P_i$ to the entity interpretation of $Q_i$. We may consider this operation as an interpretation of $R$ and we shall call it an *operational interpretation* of $R$. An operational interpretation of $R$ may coincide with the original one but also may differ from it. In this last case it depends on the position of the formula $R$ and on the interpretation of the formula or formulas which follow it.

*Example.* The formula $\lambda xx$ may be interpreted as the number 1. However, it is easy to see from $\lambda xxf \Leftrightarrow f$ that if $f$ is interpreted as a function, $\lambda xx$ has an operational interpretation as the identity operator. In the formula $\lambda xxPQ \Leftrightarrow PQ$ if $P$, $Q$ are interpreted as statements, $\lambda xx$ admits as operational interpretation implication [$\supset$].

The main possibilities of applications of the CUCH consist in the fact that in a given interpretation the same formula may admit *various* operational interpretations in its different occurrences. Briefly the same formula (by means of appropriate interpretations) may be used for very different purposes.

## D. Standard Number System

The most natural and usual way of representing nonnegative integers by means of $\lambda$-formulas consists in associating to every number $n$ the operator $\underline{n}$[1] such that, applied to any formula $f$ and $g$, it iterates $n$ times the application of $f$ to $g$.

[1] Sometimes we will denote this operator by **n**, if no misunderstanding will occur.

That is, we require that for every $f$ and $g$ holds

$$\underline{n}fg \Leftrightarrow \underbrace{(f(f(f\cdots(f}_{n \text{ times}}g)\cdots)))$$

what is obviously satisfied by

$$\mathbf{n} \equiv \lambda x \lambda y \underbrace{(x(x(x\cdots(x}_{n \text{ times}}y)\cdots)))$$

*Examples*

$$\mathbf{0} \equiv \lambda x \lambda y y \equiv \mathbf{0}, \mathbf{1} \equiv \lambda x \lambda y(xy),\ \mathbf{2} \equiv \lambda x \lambda y(x(xy))$$

Note that applying the $\eta$-rule, **1** reduces to **I**. Of course the way described here is not unique for representing numbers.

## E. Elementary Operations on Numbers and Useful Relations

Let **m**, **n** be any two standard numbers. It is easily seen that, if this is the case, we have

$$\mathbf{B}nm \Leftrightarrow \lambda z(\mathbf{n}(\mathbf{m}z)) \Leftrightarrow \lambda z \lambda y \underbrace{(\mathbf{m}z(\mathbf{m}z(\cdots(\mathbf{m}z}_{n \text{ times}}y)\cdots)))$$

$$\Leftrightarrow \lambda z \lambda y \underbrace{\underbrace{(z(z(\cdots z}_{m}(\underbrace{z(z(\cdots z}_{m}(\cdots\underbrace{(z(z(\cdots(z}_{m}}_{n \text{ times}}y)\cdots)\cdots)$$

That is, **B***nm* is the result of multiplication of $m$ by $n$. It is easy to show that **B**, thought of as an operator, is associative, i.e.,

$$\mathbf{B}(\mathbf{B}xy)z \Leftrightarrow \mathbf{B}x(\mathbf{B}yz) \qquad \text{for each } x, y, z$$

This suggests writing $x \circ y$ instead of **B***xy*, so that, since

$$(x \circ y) \circ z \Leftrightarrow x \circ (y \circ z)$$

the notation $x \circ y \circ z$ is now meaningful. This last will be preferred by us below.

To sum up, for standard numbers the symbol $\circ$ means the multiplication operator.

Let us consider now the operator[1]

$$\mathbf{B}' = \mathbf{CB} = \lambda x \lambda y \lambda z(y(xz))$$

and observe that

$$\mathbf{B}' xy = \mathbf{B} yx = y \circ x$$

Since the multiplication of numbers is commutative, $\mathbf{B}'$ could also be chosen as the multiplication operator.

Now let us introduce the usual notation

$$x^n \equiv \underbrace{x \circ x \circ \cdots \circ x}_{n \text{ times}}$$

where by definition $x^0 \equiv \mathbf{I}$, $x$ being any formula. We see that an alternative way for defining standard numbers could be

$$\mathbf{n} \equiv \lambda x \lambda y(x^n y)$$

i.e., owing to the $\eta$-rule,

$$\mathbf{n}x \equiv x^n$$

Since $\mathbf{0}x = \mathbf{I}$ for any $x$, the relation $x^0 \equiv \mathbf{I}$ is justified a posteriori. From the preceding relation we deduce that, if $x$ is a *standard number*, the application of a standard number to a second one consists in elevating the latter to an exponent equal to the first.

Now let

$$\Phi \equiv \lambda x \lambda y \lambda z \lambda t(x(yt)(zt))$$

and let us consider the operator

$$\Phi\mathbf{B} = \lambda y \lambda z \lambda t((yt) \circ (zt))$$

This one is, like $\mathbf{B}$, associative. If we apply this operator to numbers we have

$$\Phi\mathbf{B}\mathbf{n}\mathbf{m}p = (\mathbf{n}p) \circ (\mathbf{m}p) = p^n = p^m = p^{n+m} = (\mathbf{n} + \mathbf{m})p$$

from which it is natural to put

$$\Phi\mathbf{B} = +$$

The operator $+$ is defined in such a way that it corresponds to addition of standard numbers and is definite quite naturally from multiplication and exponentiation.

[1] Owing to the equivalence between the $\lambda$-calculus and the combinators-calculus, the symbol $=$ shall from now on be substituted even for the symbol $\Leftrightarrow$.

The following relations hold for any formulas if variables $x, y, z$ are used; they hold for standard numbers only if the variable $\mathbf{n}$ is used:

$$\mathbf{I} \circ x = x \circ \mathbf{I} = x \tag{24}$$

$$\mathbf{0} \circ x = \mathbf{0} \tag{25}$$

$$\mathbf{n} \circ \mathbf{0} = \mathbf{0},\ \mathbf{nI} = \mathbf{I},\ \mathbf{n0} = \begin{cases} \mathbf{0} & \text{if } n \neq 0 \\ \mathbf{I} & \text{if } n = 0 \end{cases} \tag{25'}$$

$$\mathbf{K} + x = \mathbf{K} \tag{26}$$

$$\mathbf{B}(xy) = (\mathbf{B} \circ x)y \tag{27}$$

$$\mathbf{B}(x \circ y) = (\mathbf{B}x) \circ (\mathbf{B}y) \tag{28}$$

$$(x + y) \circ z = (x \circ z) + (y \circ z),\ \mathbf{B} \circ (x + y) = (\mathbf{B} \circ x) + (\mathbf{B} \circ y) \tag{29}$$

$$\begin{aligned} (xy)^n &= (n \circ x)y = (\underbrace{x + x + \cdots + x}_{n \text{ times}})y \\ &= ((\underbrace{\mathbf{I} + \mathbf{I} + \cdots + \mathbf{I}}_{n \text{ times}}) \circ x)y \end{aligned} \tag{30}$$

$$\mathbf{n} + \mathbf{m} = \mathbf{m} + \mathbf{n} \tag{31}$$

$$(\mathbf{B}x) \circ (\mathbf{B}'y) = (\mathbf{B}'y) \circ (\mathbf{B}x) \tag{32}$$

As $x + y \neq y + x$ there are two different operators

$$S = \lambda x(\mathbf{I} + x) = \lambda x \lambda y \lambda z(y(xyz))$$

$$S' = \lambda x(x + \mathbf{I}) = \lambda x \lambda y \lambda z(xy(yz))$$

that, applied to a standard number, give the same result, i.e., its successor.

## F. Recursive Functions

Now we are able to give λ-formulas of partial-recursive functions and of functional rules generating the whole class of the partial-recursive functions.

### 1. *Function* $O^{(m)}$

By means of the application of the H.A.P. we obtain the following formula for the identically null function of $m$ variables:

$$O^{(m)} \equiv \mathbf{K}^m \mathbf{0} = \lambda x_1 \lambda x_2 \cdots \lambda x_m \lambda y \lambda z z \qquad m \geqslant 0$$

2. *Selective Functions* $U_i^{(m)}$ $(1 \leqslant i \leqslant m)$

A solution, through the H.A.P., is

$$U_i^{(m)} \equiv \mathbf{K}^{i-1}\mathbf{K}^{m-i} = \lambda x_1 \lambda x_2 \cdots \lambda x_m x_i$$

3. *Composition Operator* $\Phi_l^{(m)}$

We want to obtain a λ-formula of the composition operator $\Phi_l^{(m)}$ knowing that if a one variable partial-recursive function $h^{(m)}$ results from the composition of a recursive $l$ variables function (where $l > 0$) with $l$ functions $g_1^{(m)} \cdots g_l^{(m)}$ of $m$ variables each, then the corresponding λ-formulas

$$F, G_1, \ldots, G_l, H$$

must satisfy the relations

$$\begin{aligned} Hn_1 n_2 \cdots n_m &= \Phi_l^{(m)} FG_1 G_2 \cdots G_2 n_1 \cdots n_m \\ &= F(G_1 n_1 \cdots n_m)(G_2 n_1 \cdots n_m) \cdots (G_l n_1 \cdots n_m) \end{aligned}$$

where $n_1 \cdots n_m$ are any standard numbers. Applying the H.A.P. we obtain the following solution:

$$\Phi_l^{(m)} FG_1 \cdots G_l = \lambda x_1 \cdots \lambda x_m (F(G_1 x_1 \cdots x_m)(G_2 x_1 \cdots x_m) \cdots (G_l x_1 \cdots x_m))$$

from which, by a further application of the H.A.P.,

$$\Phi_l^{(m)} = \lambda f \lambda g_1 \cdots \lambda g_l \lambda x_1 \cdots \lambda x_m (f(g_1 x_1 \cdots x_m)(g_2 x_1 \cdots x_m) \cdots (g_l x_1 \cdots x_m))$$

*Examples*

$$\Phi_1^{(1)} = \mathbf{B},\ \Phi_2^{(1)} \mathbf{B} = +,\ \Phi_2^{(1)} + = \Phi_2^{(2)} \mathbf{B} = \oplus$$

where $\oplus$ may be thought of as the addition operator for one variable function

$$\oplus fg = \lambda x(+(fx)(gx))$$

4. *Operator* $\mathscr{P}_m$ *of Primitive Recursion*

It is known that this operator must satisfy

$$\mathscr{P}_m f^{(m)} g^{(m+2)} = h^{(m+1)} \tag{33}$$

according to the rule

$$\begin{aligned} h^{(m+1)} x_1 \cdots x_m \mathbf{0} &= f^{(m)} x_1 \cdots x_m \\ h^{(m+1)} x_1 \cdots x_m (Sy) &= g^{(m+2)} x_1 \cdots x_m (hx_1 \cdots x_m y) y \end{aligned} \tag{34}$$

To find a λ-formula for $\mathscr{P}_m$ means seeking a λ-formula for $h^{(m+1)}$ given the λ-formulas $f^{(m)}$, $g^{(m+2)}$. If we put

$$h^{(m+1)} x_1 \cdots x_m \equiv H \qquad f^{(m)} x_1 \cdots x_m \equiv F \qquad g^{(m+2)} x_1 \cdots x_m \equiv G$$

that is, $h^{(m+1)} \equiv \lambda x_1 \cdots \lambda x_m H$, etc., we are led to find $H$ such that

$$\begin{aligned} H\mathbf{0} &= F \\ H(S\mathbf{n}) &= G(H\mathbf{n})\,\mathbf{n} \end{aligned} \tag{35}$$

where $F$ and $G$ are given formulas. It is easy to show that a solution for (35) is

$$H \equiv \langle M, N, \mathbf{0} \rangle \tag{36}$$

where

$$M \equiv \lambda u \langle S(u\mathbf{K}), G(u\mathbf{0})(u\mathbf{K}) \rangle \equiv M[G] \tag{37}$$

and

$$N \equiv \langle \mathbf{0}, F \rangle \equiv N[F] \tag{38}$$

*Proof* (by mathematical induction on $n$)

$$H\mathbf{0} = \mathbf{0}MN\mathbf{0} = N\mathbf{0} = \mathbf{00}F = F$$

Now put $N \equiv N_0$. Applying $M$ to $N_i \equiv \langle \mathbf{i}, H\mathbf{i} \rangle$ we obtain

$$MN_i = \langle S\mathbf{i}, H(S\mathbf{i}) \rangle = N_{i+1}$$

Therefore,

$$N_n = nMN_0 = M^n N = M^n \langle \mathbf{0}, H\mathbf{0} \rangle = \langle \mathbf{n}, H\mathbf{n} \rangle$$

so that

$$H\mathbf{n} = \langle \mathbf{n}, H\mathbf{n} \rangle\, \mathbf{0} = M^n N\mathbf{0} = \mathbf{n}MN\mathbf{0}$$

Applying the H.A.P. we have

$$H = \lambda x(xMN\mathbf{0}) = \langle M, N, \mathbf{0} \rangle$$

To sum up, we can write (33) in the form

$$\mathscr{P}_m f^m g^{(m+2)} x_1 \cdots x_m y = h^{m+1} x_1 \cdots x_m y = \langle M[G], N[F], \mathbf{0} \rangle\, y$$

and by $m+2$ applications of the H.A.P. we reach the formula

$$\mathscr{P}_m = \lambda f \lambda g \lambda x_1 \cdots \lambda x_m \langle M[g x_1 \cdots x_m], N[f x_1 \cdots x_m], \mathbf{0} \rangle \tag{39}$$

*Examples.* It is well known that the "predecessor function" $P$ and the "characteristic function of to be greater as zero" $D$ can be defined by induction in the following way:

$$\begin{aligned} &P\mathbf{0} = \mathbf{0} & \quad &D\mathbf{0} = \mathbf{0} \\ &P(S\mathbf{n}) = \mathbf{n} & \quad &D(S\mathbf{n}) = \mathbf{I} \end{aligned}$$

Then we can choose for $F$ and $G$, respectively,

$$\begin{aligned} &F = \mathbf{0},\ G = \mathbf{0} & &\text{for the } P \text{ case} \\ &F = \mathbf{0},\ G = \mathbf{K0} = \mathbf{K}^2\mathbf{I} & &\text{for the } D \text{ case} \end{aligned}$$

and we obtain

$$M = \lambda u\langle S(u\mathbf{K}), u\mathbf{K}\rangle,\ N = \langle \mathbf{0}, \mathbf{0}\rangle \qquad \text{for the } P \text{ case}$$
$$M = \lambda u\langle S(u\mathbf{K}), \mathbf{I}\rangle,\quad N = \langle \mathbf{0}, \mathbf{0}\rangle \qquad \text{for the } D \text{ case}$$

It is possible to reach a more simple form for $D$ if we remark that

$$\begin{matrix} 0^0 = 1 \\ 0^{Sn} = 0 \end{matrix} \quad \text{or} \quad \begin{cases} \mathbf{00} = \mathbf{I} \\ (S\mathbf{n})\,\mathbf{0} = \mathbf{0} \text{ and, e.g., } \mathbf{I0} = \mathbf{0} \end{cases}$$

so that

$$\begin{matrix} D\mathbf{0} = \mathbf{000} = \mathbf{0} \\ D(S\mathbf{n}) = S\mathbf{n00} = \mathbf{I} \end{matrix} \qquad \text{and by the H.A.P. } D = \lambda x(x\mathbf{00} \equiv \langle \mathbf{0}, \mathbf{0}\rangle$$

5. *Note*

Before we leave the standard number system let us to point out two relations whose meaning is obvious:

$$\mathbf{n}S\mathbf{0} = S^n\mathbf{0} = \mathbf{n} \tag{40}$$

$$P(S\mathbf{n}) = \mathbf{n} \tag{41}$$

6. *Operator $\mathscr{R}_m$ of Recursion*

The following scheme is more suitable for programming purposes than the minimalization or $\mu$-scheme. Moreover, it can be easily specialized to either the $\mu$-scheme or the primitive recursion scheme:

$$\mathscr{R}_m f^{(m+1)} g^{(m+2)} r^{(m+1)} p = h^{(m+1)} \tag{42}$$

according to the rule

$$h^{(m+1)} x_1 \cdots x_m y = \begin{cases} f^{(m+1)} x_1 \cdots x_m y & \text{if } r^{(m+1)} x_1 \cdots x_m y = \mathbf{0} \\ g^{(m+2)} x_1 \cdots x_m (h^{m+1} x_1 \cdots x_m (py))(py) \\ \qquad \text{if } r^{(m+1)} x_1 \cdots x_m y \neq \mathbf{0} \end{cases} \tag{43}$$

We can get the $\mu$-scheme

$$\mu y\{r^{(m+1)} x_1 \cdots x_m y = \mathbf{0}\} = h x_1 \cdots x_m \mathbf{0}$$

if we choose

$$f^{(m+1)} \equiv U_{m+1}^{(m+1)},\ g^{(m+2)} \equiv U_{m+1}^{(m+2)},\ p = S$$

We recover the primitive recursive scheme if we put in (43) $r^{(m+1)} = U_{m+1}^{(m+1)}$, $p = P$. With a similar setting as in the preceding case, i.e.,

$$h^{(m+1)} x_1 \cdots x_m \equiv H,\ f^{(m+1)} x_1 \cdots x_m \equiv F,$$
$$g^{(m+2)} x_1 \cdots x_m \equiv G,\ r^{(m+1)} x_1 \cdots x_m \equiv R$$

we are led to the system

$$Hy = \begin{cases} Fy & \text{if } Ry = \mathbf{0} \\ G(H(py))(py) & \text{if } Ry \neq \mathbf{0} \end{cases} \tag{44}$$

Now we want to merge the two alternatives into a single formula. We remark that

$$\mathbf{Sn}(\mathbf{K}\alpha)\beta = \alpha, \ \mathbf{O}(\mathbf{K}\alpha)\beta = \beta \tag{45}$$

for every $\alpha$, $\beta$. So we can write

$$Hy = Ry(\mathbf{K}(G(H(py))(py)))(Fy) \tag{46}$$

A solution of the latter equation is (using the H.A.P.) a solution of

$$H = \lambda y(Ry(\mathbf{K}(G(H(py))(py)))(Fy)) = XH$$

where

$$X = \lambda x \lambda y(Ry(\mathbf{K}(G(x(py))(py)))(Fy)) \tag{47}$$

It is easy to see that the "feedback" equation

$$H = XH \tag{48}$$

$X$ being given, is satisfied by

$$H = \lambda u(X(uu))\lambda u(X(uu)) \tag{49}$$

In fact if we carry out a $\beta$-reduction in the right side of (49) we have

$$H = X(\lambda u(X(uu))\lambda u(X(uu))) = XH$$

Applying the H.A.P. to (49) we can write

$$H = \theta X \tag{50}$$

where[1]

$$\theta = \lambda x(\lambda u(x(uu))\lambda u(x(uu)))$$

which is, together with (47), a useful solution of (46). We leave to the reader, as an exercise, the construction of a formula for $\mathscr{R}_m$ like (39) for $\mathscr{P}_m$.

## G. Operations on $n$-tuples. $\lambda$-formulas Interpreting the Job of an Automaton

The standard number system is convenient for defining recursive functions in a relatively simple way. Nevertheless we must admit that integers are

[1] This $\theta$ is convertible into that defined in Section II,C. Note that $\theta$ does not have normal form but $\theta X\mathbf{n} = H\mathbf{n}$ will have one if there exists an integer $j$ such that $R'(p^j\mathbf{n}) = \mathbf{O}$.

represented in a manner more wasteful (looking at the length of the expressions) than that obtained by the unary alphabet {1} on the tape of Turing machines.

An improvement in efficiency is obtained using an alphabet with more than one symbol, for example, a binary or decimal alphabet, etc., either for abstract machines or for actual computers. The same thing is of course feasible by CUCH. So we are quite naturally led to introduce formulas for representing *words* or strings over a certain alphabet.

Let us note, at this point, that the already introduced notion of $n$-tuple $\langle X_1, X_2, \ldots, X_n \rangle$ generalizes that of word for the simple reason that no hypothesis has been made until now on the nature of the components $X_i$. We now want to outline a calculus about $n$-tuples which can be useful for further development of the formulas within the CUCH. Let us consider a triplet $(\mathscr{V}, \triangle, \square)$, where $\mathscr{V}$ is a class of $\lambda$-formulas, $\square$ is a formula $\notin \mathscr{V}$ and $\triangle$ is a discriminating formula between $\square$ and any element $X_i$ of $\mathscr{V}$; i.e., we claim that

$$\triangle\square = \mathbf{0} \qquad \triangle X_i = \mathbf{K}$$

*Example.* If we choose for $\mathscr{V}$ the standard numbers class, remembering that $1^n = 1$, we may write $\mathbf{nI} = \mathbf{I}$ [see (25′)].

The relations

$$\mathbf{nIK} = \mathbf{K} \qquad \mathbf{K}^2\mathbf{OIK} = \mathbf{0}$$

suggest the choice

$$\triangle = \lambda x(x\mathbf{IK}) = \langle \mathbf{I}, \mathbf{K} \rangle \qquad \square = \mathbf{K}^2\mathbf{0} = \lambda x \lambda y \lambda z \lambda tt$$

Now we are interested in operations about $n$-tuples whose components $X_i, Y_j \in \mathscr{V}$. That is, let us consider the formulas

$$X \equiv \lambda x(xX_1 \cdots X_n) \qquad Y \equiv \lambda x(xY_1 \cdots Y_m) \tag{51}$$

First of all, we observe that the empty $n$-tuple is $\lambda xx \equiv \mathbf{I}$. Now we give the $\lambda$-formulas concerning elementary operations on $n$-tuples and we leave this verification to the reader as an exercise. To find the formulas, we used the H.A.P. systematically.

*Add a component to the left* ($\bar{S}$):

$$\bar{S}XY_1 = \langle Y_1, X_1, \ldots, X_n \rangle = \lambda z(X(zY_1)) \tag{52}$$

from which

$$\bar{S} = \lambda x \lambda y \lambda z(x(zy)) \tag{53}$$

*Erase the first component* ($\bar{P}$):

$$\bar{P}X = \langle X_2, \ldots, X_n \rangle = \lambda z(X(\mathbf{K}z)) = \mathbf{B}X\mathbf{K} = X \circ \mathbf{K}$$
$$\bar{P} = \mathbf{CBK} = \mathbf{B}'\mathbf{K} = \lambda x \lambda y(x \lambda z y)$$

*Add a component to the right* ($\bar{S}'$):

$$\bar{S}'XY_1 = \langle X_1, \ldots, X_m, Y_1 \rangle = \lambda z(XzY_1) = \mathbf{C}XY_1$$

from which $\bar{S}' = \mathbf{C}$.

*Concatenate two n-tuples* ($\mathbf{B}'$):

$$Z = \langle X_1, \ldots, X_m, Y_1, \ldots, Y_m \rangle$$

be the $(m+n)$-tuple resulting from the concatenation of $X$ to $Y$. It is easily seen that

$$Z = Y \circ X = \mathbf{B}'XY$$

*Extract the first component* ($U_1$):

We want to find $U_1$ such that

$$U_1 X = \begin{cases} \square & \text{if } X = \lambda xx \\ X_1 & \text{if } X \neq \lambda xx \end{cases}$$

A solution is

$$U_1 = \lambda u(u \lambda z(\theta M_1 zz) \square) = \langle \lambda z(\theta M_1 zz), \square \rangle$$

where

$$M_1 \equiv \lambda t \lambda x \lambda y(\triangle x \lambda v(tvy) y) \quad \text{or} \quad M_1 \equiv \lambda t \lambda x \lambda y(\triangle y(tx)x)$$

*Extract the last component* ($U_\infty$):

We want

$$U_\infty X = \begin{cases} \square & \text{if } X = \lambda xx \\ X_n & \text{if } X = \lambda x(xX_1 \cdots X_n) \text{ for each } n > 0 \end{cases}$$

A solution is

$$U_\infty = \lambda u(u \lambda z(\theta M_\infty zz) \square) = \langle \lambda z(\theta M_\infty zz), \square \rangle$$

where

$$M_\infty \equiv \lambda t \lambda x \lambda y(\triangle y(ty) x)$$

*Homomorphism relative to the concatenation of n-tuples* ($\bar{H}f$)

We want to construct $\bar{H}$ such that, given the operator $f$, we have

$$\bar{H}fX = \langle fX_1, \ldots, fX_n \rangle \qquad \text{for each } n > 0$$
$$\bar{H}f\mathbf{I} = \mathbf{I}$$

A solution is

$$\bar{H} = \lambda f \lambda u(u(\theta M_f \mathbf{I})\,\square)$$

where

$$M_f \equiv \lambda t \lambda u \lambda x(\triangle x(t \lambda s(us(fx)))\,u)$$

*Sequential mapping on n-tuples* ($\bar{M}$)

Given any two formulas $f$ and $Y_0$, and an $n$-tuple $X$, we want to construct a formula $\bar{M}$ such that

$$\bar{M} f Y_0 X = \begin{cases} \langle Y_0 \rangle & \text{if } X = \lambda xx \\ \langle Y_0, f Y_0 X_1, \ldots, f(f \cdots (f Y_0 X_1) \cdots X_{n-1}) X_n \rangle & \text{if } n > 0 \end{cases}$$

$\bar{M}$ may obviously be interpreted as a generalized automaton (eventually with infinite states or symbols over an infinite alphabet) because $f$ may be interpreted as the state-transition function (output function), $Y_0$ as the initial state, and the result as the $n$-tuple of the internal states (output $n$-tuple) of the automaton.

If we put

$$\bar{Y}_0 \equiv \langle Y_0, \langle Y_0 \rangle \rangle$$
$$G[x,f] \equiv \lambda v \langle f(v\mathbf{K})\,x, \lambda u(v\mathbf{O}u(f(v\mathbf{K})\,x)) \rangle$$

it is easy to prove that a solution is the following formula:

$$\bar{M} = \lambda f \langle \theta \lambda t \lambda u \lambda x(\triangle x(t(G[x,f]\,u))\,(u\mathbf{O}))\ \bar{Y}_0, \square \rangle$$

## H. Real-Number Standard System—CUCH Formulas for Continuous Functions[1]

If $r$ is a real positive number having the following decimal representation:

$$r \leftrightarrow R_{-n} R_{j-n} \cdots R_1 R_0 .\ R_1 R_2 \cdots R_i \cdots$$

We shall call a *real standard formula* any formula $\tilde{r}$ such that

$$\tilde{r}\mathbf{i} = \underline{ri}$$

where

$$\underline{ri} = \underline{\sum_{j=-n}^{i} R_j 10^{j+n}} \quad \text{or} \quad \underline{\sum_{j=-n}^{i} R_j 10^{j+n} - 1}$$

*Example.* $\pi = 3.14\ldots$ may be represented

$$\tilde{\pi}\mathbf{0} = \mathbf{2},\ \tilde{\pi}\mathbf{1} = \underline{31},\ \tilde{\pi}\mathbf{2} = \underline{313}, \text{ etc.}$$

[1] This section is due to the collaboration of G. Jacopini, researcher at the C.N.R.

Of course, given $r$, $\tilde{r}$ is not uniquely determined and it does not always exist (it is sufficient to observe that formulas constitute only an enumerable infinity). Anyway, we are interested only in formulas that can be constructed.

The real standard number $\tilde{1}$, applied to **i** will give, for what we said, the result $\underline{10}^i$, and then it can be written $\tilde{1} = \langle\underline{10}\rangle$ (in fact, $\langle\underline{10}\rangle\mathbf{i} = \mathbf{i}\underline{10} = \underline{10}^i$).

In the same way if $N$ is an integer, the real standard number is such that

$$\tilde{N} = \mathbf{iBN}(\mathbf{i}\underline{10}) = \mathbf{BN}(\tilde{1}\mathbf{i}) = \mathbf{B}(\mathbf{BN})\,\tilde{1}\mathbf{i}$$

from which, by means of the H.A.P., we have

$$\tilde{N} = \mathbf{B}(\mathbf{BN})\,\tilde{1}$$

It may be interesting to represent functions of real numbers as combinators such that when applied to real standard numbers they yield other real standard numbers.

Since $+$ and $\oplus$ are combinators corresponding, respectively, to the addition of standard numbers and to the addition of functions of one variable,

$$\tilde{t} = \oplus\tilde{r}\tilde{s}$$

may be thought of as the addition combinator $\widetilde{r+s}$. Well, this is not true; in fact it is enough to think that if $\tilde{r}$ and $\tilde{s}$ applied to any **i** yield the first $i$ digits with 1 as the negative error (as the definition of a real standard number allows) $\tilde{t}\mathbf{i}$ may have 2 as the negative error (which is not possible). So we must consider also the $(i+1)$th digit of the numbers $r$ and $s$. To this end let us introduce the combinator $Q$ such that if **x** and **y** are two standard numbers, $Q\mathbf{xy}$ represents the integer part of $x/y$ (the combinator $Q$ certainly exists because its correspondent function is a primitive recursive one). Then we may write, from

$$\widetilde{r+s} \equiv \Sigma\tilde{r}\tilde{s}$$

that

$$\Sigma\tilde{r}\tilde{s}\mathbf{i} = Q(\oplus\tilde{r}\tilde{s}(S))\,\underline{10}$$

and so we can define

$$\Sigma \equiv \lambda x\lambda y\lambda z(Q(\oplus xy(Sz))\,\underline{10})$$

In the same way we may obtain, for example, the combinator $\Pi$ and $X$, the first of which represents the multiplication operation between real numbers and the second one the division operation between real and positive integer numbers.

Using the last operation we could λ-define the *rational real standard numbers*. We leave these exercises to the reader.

## I. Investigations of CUCH as a Description Language

Some years ago F. B. Fitch [6] used combinatory logic for describing sequential circuits. Fitch's work is interesting from many aspects: Circuits are treated from a purely logical point of view; so the notion of "state" of a machine is not mentioned, and combinatory logic is used for describing circuits.

At I.N.A.C. in Rome [2] a more general description of sequential circuits has been obtained by means of CUCH. Following the same method, it has been possible also to describe analogical circuits.

λ-formulas concerning circuits have been constructed in such a way as to receive contemporarily two different interpretations, the first one giving the complete description of block schemes of circuits and the second one the behavior of them. So CUCH formulas give exactly all information about the circuits they represent.

For describing analogical circuits it has been necessary to introduce many constants and their reduction rules (laws of the mathematical analysis). It is interesting to note that, owing to the recent work on real numbers (see Section IV,H), it seems possible to λ-define most of these constants; if all of them were λ-defined, every CUCH constant could vanish.

At I.N.A.C. CUCH has also been applied in another direction. It has been precisely pointed out [14] how it is possible to interpret the λ-**K**-calculus as a programming language. This aim has been reached giving a λ-formulation of K. E. Iverson's programming language, because that in a certain way pursues aims which are proper of the λ-calculus.

At I.C.C. [13] the computer Elea 6001 has been instructed to carry out λ-reductions; i.e., it has written the program of the CUCH general-reduction algorithm.

## References

1. C. Böhm, Macchine a indirizzi, dotate di un numero minimo di istruzioni, *Atti accad. nazl. Lincei. Rend. Classe sci. fis. mat. e nat.* [serie VIII] **32**, 923–930 (1962).
2. C. Böhm and R. Giovannucci, *Circuiti sequenziali ed analogici e loro descrizione mediante il CUCH*, I.N.A.C.–C.N.R., Rome (unpublished).
3. A. Church, The calculi of lambda-conversion, *Ann. Math. Studies* **6**, Princeton University Press, Princeton, N.J., 2nd ed., 1951.

4. A. Church, Combinatory logic as a semigroup (abstract), *Bull. Am. Math. Soc.* **43**, 333 (1937).
5. H. B. Curry and R. Feys, *Combinatory Logic*, North-Holland, Amsterdam, 1958.
6. F. B. Fitch, Representation of sequential circuits in combinatory logic, *Phil. Sci.* **25**, 263–279 (1958).
7. P. C. Gilmore, An abstract computer with a lisp-like machine language without a label operator, in *Computer Programming and Formal Systems*, North-Holland, Amsterdam, 1963, pp. 71–86.
8a. H. Hermes, *Aufzählbarkeit, Entscheidbarkeit, Berechenbarkeit*, Springer, Berlin, 1961.
8b. J. McCarthy, A basis for a mathematical theory of computation, in *Computer Programming and Formal Systems*, North-Holland, Amsterdam, 1963, pp. 33–70.
9. A. A. Markov, *Teoriya algoritmov, Trudy Mat. Inst. im. V. A. Steklova* **No. 42** (1954).
10. P. C. Rosenbloom, *The Elements of Mathematical Logic*, Dover, New York, 1950.
11. M. Schönfinkel, Über die Bausteine der mathematische Logik, *Math. Ann.* **92**, 305–316 (1924).
12. J. C. Shepherdson and H. E. Sturgis, Computability of recursive functions, *J. Assoc. Comp. Mach.* **10**, 217–255 (1963).
13. M. Venturini-Zilli, CUCH—algorithm program (unpublished), I.C.C., Rome.
14. M. Venturini-Zilli, λ-K-formulae for vector operators, *I. C. C. Bulletin, Rome* (in press).
15. H. Wang, A variant to Turing's theory of computing machines, *J. Assoc. Comp. Mach.* **4**, 63–92 (1957).

# Quelques Remarques sur la Détermination de l'Algorithme Optimal pour la Recherche du Plus Court Chemin dans un Graphe sans Circuits[1]

MARIO BORILLO

*EURATOM*
*Ispra, Italy*

De nombreux algorithmes ont été proposés pour la détermination des chemins optimaux dans les graphes, mais il ne semble pas jusqu'à présent que le problème de comparer ces algorithmes du point de vue de la quantité de calculs qu'ils impliquent ait été étudié systématiquement.

Nous nous proposons de montrer ici que, pour une famille de graphes donnés, un algorithme peut être considéré comme optimal quant au nombre de comparaisons à effectuer entre éléments du module libre engendré par les arcs du graphe pour arriver à la détermination du chemin optimal.

## I. Algorithme de Recherche du Plus Court Chemin

**Définition 1.** $G = (X, U)$ sera un graphe ou multigraphe orienté, fini, sans boucle, sans circuits, possédant deux sommets $x_0$ et $z$ tels que $\Gamma^{-1} x_0 = \phi \Gamma_z = \phi$ et tel que tout arc se trouve sur au moins un chemin élémentaire allant de $x_0$ à $z$ — ou: chemin $[x_0, z]$ (pour les notations, cf. [1]).

Soit $\bar{U}$ l'espace vectoriel engendré par $U$ sur les réels, $\bar{E}$ le sous-espace vectoriel engendré par l'ensemble $\mathscr{E}$ des chemins élémentaires $[x_0, z]$, et soit $\Omega'$ l'ensemble des homomorphismes $\omega, \omega: \bar{U} \to R$.

On considère pour simplifier le sous-ensemble $\Omega \subset \Omega'$ des $\omega$ tels que pour toute paire $e, e'$ de chemins élémentaires:

$$e \neq e' \Rightarrow \omega e \neq \omega e'$$

[1] L'auteur remercie le Professeur M. P. Schützenberger, qui a été à l'origine de ce travail, pour ses conseils et ses critiques.

**Définition 2.** On appelle chemin élémentaire optimal, pour chaque $\omega \in \Omega$, un élément $e_\omega \in \mathscr{E}$, unique, tel que

$$\forall^{e'}_{\mathscr{E}} = \omega e_\omega \leqslant \omega e'$$

Remarquons qu'à chaque $e \in \mathscr{E}$ correspondra le sous-ensemble $\Omega_e \in \Omega$ des homomorphismes $\omega \in \Omega$ tels que

$$\forall^{\omega}_{\Omega_e}: e_\omega = e$$

Soit $I \subset N$ un ensemble d'indices appliqués bijectivement sur $X \backslash \{z\}$ de telle sorte que pour tout $i \in I$ le sommet $x_i$ n'ait aucun de ses ancêtres d'indice $i'' \geqslant i$ ce qui est toujours possible puisque le graphe est sans circuits.

Considérons pour chaque sommet $x_i \neq x_0$ le dernier arc du chemin optimal $[x_0, x_i]_\omega$. Les arcs considérés forment un graphe partiel $(X, V)$ qui est une arborescence de centre $x_0$. Chaque arc de $U - V$ détermine avec cette arborescence un cycle et l'on sait que le nombre de ces cycles de fermeture est égal à **Card** $U$ − **Card** $X + 1$. Remarquons que chaque cycle de fermeture est une différence de deux chemins élémentaires $[x_0, z]$; en effet, si l'on ferme un cycle avec l'arc $(x_i, x_j)$:

1. $x_j \notin [x_0, x_i]_\omega$, car le graphe est sans circuits.
2. il existe au moins un chemin $[x_j, z]_0$, puisque tout sommet se trouve sur au moins un chemin $[x_0, z]$.
3. $[x_j, z]_0$ ne rencontre ni $[x_0, x_i]_\omega$ ni $[x_0, x_j]_\omega$ car le graphe est sans circuits.

Le cycle de fermeture $\mu_j$ est donc égal à la différence entre le chemin $[x_0, x_i]_\omega + (x_i, x_j) + [x_j, z]_0$ et le chemin $[x_0, x_j]_\omega + [x_j, z]_0 \cdot \bar{C}$, le sous-espace vectoriel de $\bar{U}$ engendré par l'ensemble $C$ des différences de chemins élémentaires est donc l'espace vectoriel des cycles de $G$. **sgn** $\omega\mu_j$ est l'inégalité indiquant le signe de $\omega\mu_j$.

**Propriété 1.** *Pour tout graphe G on peut associer le chemin élémentaire optimal* $[x_0, z]_\omega$ *à la paire* $(\{\mathbf{sgn}\, \omega\mu_j\}, \omega)$ *avec*

$$\mathbf{Card}\{\mathbf{sgn}\, \omega\mu_j\} = \mathbf{Card}\, U - \mathbf{Card}\, X + 1$$

De ce qui prècède on déduit un algorithme permettant de déterminer $[x_0, z]_\omega$. Supposons déja déterminé pour tout $i' < i$, le chemin élémentaire optimal $[x_0, x_{i'}]_\omega$. Soit $\{x_{i_1'}, x_{i_2'}, \ldots, x_{i_p'}\}$, avec $i_1' < i_2' < \cdots < i_p'$ l'ensemble $\Gamma^{-1} x_i$. Posons

$$\mu_{j-1} = [x_0, x_i]_{j-1} - [x_0, x_{i_j'}]_\omega - a(i_j', i)$$

On définit inductivement une séquence de chemins $[x_0, x_i]_1, [x_0, x_i]_2, \ldots,$ $[x_0, x_i]_p$ et de "comparaisons" par les définitions suivantes:

$$[x_0, x_i]_1 = [x_0, x_{i_1'}]_\omega + a(i_1', i)$$

(a) $$[x_0, x_i]_j = [x_0, x_i]_{j-1} \qquad \text{si } \omega\mu_{j-1} < 0$$

(b) $$[x_0, x_i]_j = [x_0, x_{i_j'}]_\omega + a(i_j', i) \qquad \text{si } \omega\mu_{j-1} \geqslant 0$$

Il est clair que $[x_0, x_i]_p \equiv [x_0, x_i]_\omega$ où $[x_0, x_i]_\omega$ est le chemin élémentaire $[x_0, x_i]$ optimal. Ce résultat sera obtenu, pour le sommet $x_i$, en demandant le signe de $p-1$ différences de chemins élémentaires. Comme tout chemin élémentaire joignant $x_0$ à $x_i$ ne passera que par des sommets $x_{i'}$ tels que $i' < i$, $[x_0, x_i]_\omega$ ne sera pas modifié dans une étape ultérieure de l'algorithme par la détermination de $[x_0, x_{i''}]_\omega$, quel que soit $i'' > i$. En procédant identiquement pour tout sommet jusqu'en $z$ on pourra toujours déterminer le chemin élémentaire optimal $[x_0, z]_\omega$ par $\mathbf{Card}\, U - \mathbf{Card}\, X + 1$ inégalités.

## II. Optimalité de L'Algorithme Naturel

**Définition 3.** Un sous-ensemble $\{\mathbf{sgn}\, \omega\mu_j\}_0$ d'inégalités (de "comparaisons") sera dit minimal pour un graphe $G$ si on peut faire correspondre le chemin élémentaire optimal $[x_0, z]_\omega$ à toute paire $(\{\mathbf{sgn}\, \omega\mu_j\}_0, \omega)$, $\forall^{\omega}_{\Omega}$, et si pour tout $\mathbf{sgn}\, \omega\mu_j = \mathbf{sgn}\, \omega\mu_m$ on peut trouver un homomorphisme $\omega = \omega_m$ tel qu'on ne puisse associer $[x_0, z]_\omega$ à la paire $(\{\mathbf{sgn}\, \omega\mu_j\}_0 \setminus \mathbf{sgn}\, \omega\mu_m, \omega_m)$.

**Propriété 2.** *Pour tout graphe $G$ le sous-ensemble minimal d'inégalités sera tel que* $\mathbf{Card}\{\mathbf{sgn}\, \omega\mu_j\}_m = \mathbf{Card}\, U - \mathbf{Card}\, X + 1$.

Soit, par exemple,

$$\omega\mu_m = \omega([x_0, x_i]_{j-1} - [x_0, x_{i'_j}]_\omega - a(i_j', i)) \tag{1}$$

La séquence des $p-2$ "comparaisons" restantes relatives au sommet $x_i$ conduira à déterminer un chemin $[x_0, x_i]$, supposé optimal, qui sera, par exemple,

$$[x_0, x_i]_{p-2} = [x_0, x_{i_k'}]_\omega + a(i_k', i)$$

D'après la bijection de $I$ sur $X \setminus \{z\}$, $a(i_j', i)$ ne figure dans aucun des termes des $(p-2)$ différences dont on a demandé le signe. L'homomorphisme $\omega_m$ étant tel qu'on puisse attribuer à tout arc, $a(i_j', i)$ en particulier, n'importe quelle valeur réelle arbitraire, le signe de la différence (1) sera indépendant du signe des $(p-2)$ différences ainsi que du signe des différences relatives aux sommets $x_{i'}$, $i' < i$. Nous aurons donc nécessairement: $a(i_k', i) \neq a(i_j', i)$.

De cette relation on déduit que lorsqu'on aura demandé les signes des différences relatives aux sommets $x_{i''}, i'' > i$, jusqu'en $z$, on déterminera un chemin élémentaire $[x_0, z]$ supposé optimal qui ne pourra pas passer par $a(i'_j, i)$.

Or il existe au moins un $\omega = \omega_m$ tel qu'il soit défini, par exemple, par

$$\begin{array}{lll} 0 \leqslant \omega a(i_l, i_m) \leqslant L & \text{pour tout} & a(i_l, i_m) \in U,\ a(i_l, i_m) \neq a(i'_j, i) \\ \omega a(i'_j, i) = -10^L & \text{pour } L \text{ tel que} & 10^L > \displaystyle\sum_{a(i_m, i_l) \in U \setminus \{a(i_j', i)\}} \omega a(i_m, i_l) \end{array}$$

et cet $\omega_m$ est tel qu'à la paire $(\{\mathbf{sgn}\,\omega\mu_j\}, \omega_m)$ on peut par la Propriété 1 faire correspondre le chemin élémentaire $[x_0, z]_{\omega_m}$ optimal qui passera évidemment par $a(i'_j, i)$.

Or, nous avons vu que pour tout $\omega \in \Omega$ la paire $(\{\mathbf{sgn}\,\omega\mu_j\} \setminus \mathbf{sgn}\,\omega\mu_m, \omega)$ détermine un chemin élémentaire $[x_0, z]$ supposé optimal qui ne pourra en aucun cas passer par $a(i'_j, i)$. $\{\mathbf{sgn}\,\omega\mu_j\}$ est donc un sous-ensemble minimal d'inégalités.

*Remarque. Interprétation de la Propriété* 2. Pour un graphe $G$ et un homomorphisme $\omega \in \Omega$ toute stratégie $\sigma$ de recherche du chemin élémentaire optimal $[x_0, z]$ sera définie comme étant une fonction

$$\sigma\colon \omega \times \mathfrak{P}(\bar{U}) \to \bar{U}$$

définie récursivement par

$$\sigma\{\mathbf{sgn}\,\omega\phi\} \to u_1$$
$$\sigma\{\mathbf{sgn}\,\omega\phi, \mathbf{sgn}\,\omega u_1, \ldots, \mathbf{sgn}\,\omega u_{i-1}\} \to u_i$$

où $\mathfrak{P}(\bar{U})$ représente l'ensemble des parties de $\bar{U}$ et $\phi, u_1, \ldots, u_i \in \bar{U}$.

On appelle coût de l'algorithme une fonction $\mathfrak{C}(\sigma, \omega)$ prenant ses valeurs dans $N$. Si $u_1, \ldots, u_n$, sont les éléments de $\bar{U}$ qui déterminent le chemin élémentaire optimal $[x_0, z]_\omega$

$$\mathfrak{C}(\sigma, \omega) = n$$

Des Propriétés 1 et 2 on déduit immédiatement que pour les graphes $G$ la stratégie $\sigma_m$ définie par $\{u_1, \ldots, u_n\} = \{\mu_j\}$ sera optimale ce qui s'écrit

$$\min_{\sigma} \max_{\omega} \mathfrak{C}(\sigma, \omega) = \mathbf{Card}\, U - \mathbf{Card}\, X + 1$$

## Bibliographie


1. C. Berge, *Théorie des graphes et ses applications*. Dunod, Paris, 1958.
2. C. Berge et A. Ghouila-Houri, *Programmes, jeux et réseaux de transport*. Dunod, Paris, 1962.
3. B. Roy, *Cheminement et connexité dans les graphes: application aux problèmes d'ordonnancement*. Thèse, Paris, 1961.

# Algebraic Theory of Feedback in Discrete Systems, Part I[1]

J. RICHARD BÜCHI

*Department of Mathematics, Ohio State University*
*Columbus, Ohio*

## I. Introduction

Our world, both natural and technological, abounds in systems which may be thought of, at least in a first approximation, as operating in accordance with the following specifications:

1. *Finite number of internal states.* At each instance the system is in one, out of a finite number $n$, of well distinguishable internal configurations.

2. *Finite number of input and output states.* The system is connected to the environment by an input channel, through which at each instance one out of a finite number $k$ of well distinguishable stimuli can be imposed on the system. In turn, the system can influence the environment through an output channel, capable of taking on but a finite number $n$ of states.

Because of 1 and 2 the input, internal, and output states can change only at discrete time instances $t = 0, 1, 2, \ldots$.

3. *Determinism.* At time $t = 0$ the system is in a specific state $A$, called the *initial state.* The internal state at time $t + 1$ is uniquely determined by the pair consisting of the internal state at time $t$ and the input state at time $t$. The output state at time $t$ is uniquely determined by the internal state at time $t$.

Mechanical devices, or parts of machines working on mechanical principles, provide obvious examples of such discrete deterministic systems. (Clocks may be mentioned as input-free examples; a combination lock is clearly meant to operate according to specifications 1, 2, and 3.) It is rather tempting to consider certain biological systems (nerve nets, interaction among organs) from this point of view. Last but not least, we mention electronic devices, such as digital computers and their components.

[1] These notes were prepared under a grant from the National Science Foundation.

We are presenting here an outline of a mathematical theory of such discrete deterministic systems and their behavior. *Finite automaton* is the mathematical concept which renders precise the intuitive idea of *discrete deterministic system*. In his pioneering work of 1952, Kleene [1] gave a rigorous definition of "behavior," and he proved two theorems about the behavior of finite automata, which provide a clear understanding of what discrete deterministic systems can, and what they cannot, do. Much work has since been done in this field, so that it is now possible to present concisely the rudiments of a mathematical theory, which is appealing both to the practitioner and the mathematician:

(a) The rigorous development of basic concepts and theorems on automata provides a kind of understanding of discrete deterministic systems which cannot be obtained by empirical methods and experience alone.

(b) There are many intriguing solved and unsolved problems which well deserve attention, especially the attention of the mathematician with an interest in discrete questions. There is a strong intuitive background, and there are obvious connections to algebra (finite semigroups), graph theory, and logic.

Most of the material presented here is not new. However, we have chosen a strongly algebraic presentation. If the definition of "finite automata" is appropriately chosen, it turns out that all the basic concepts and results concerning structure and behavior of finite automata are in fact just special cases of the fundamental concepts (homomorphism, congruence relation, free algebra) and facts of abstract algebra. Automata theory is simply the theory of universal algebras (in the sense of Birkhoff [2]) with unary operations, and with emphasis on finite algebras. In turn, all the material presented here can be generalized to universal algebras with $n$-ary operations, and in part leads to novel conceptions in this field. From another point of view, the theory of finite automata may be viewed as a chapter in the arithmetic of words. It is a study of congruences of finite index on words, and these are a very natural generalization of the elementary congruences on natural numbers.

Finite automata and their theory are clearly of interest to the designer of digital systems; in fact, such a theory might well be called the "theory of switching through feedback." As a contribution to the study of words (i.e., sequences of symbols) the theory is of interest to formal linguistics (finite-state grammars are but another version of finite automata). But also for more theoretical purposes, finite automata have proved to be useful. The solution of a decision problem of logic, posed by Tarski and solved by

Büchi [3], and some preliminary results of Büchi [4], are based on the understanding of regular sets of words. We do not discuss these matters here, but refer to Church [5], where the history of results on design algorithms for finite automata is presented.

## II. The Transition Algebra of a Logical Net

The purpose of this section is to motivate the claim that the study of finite algebras with unary operations is the study of feedback in discrete

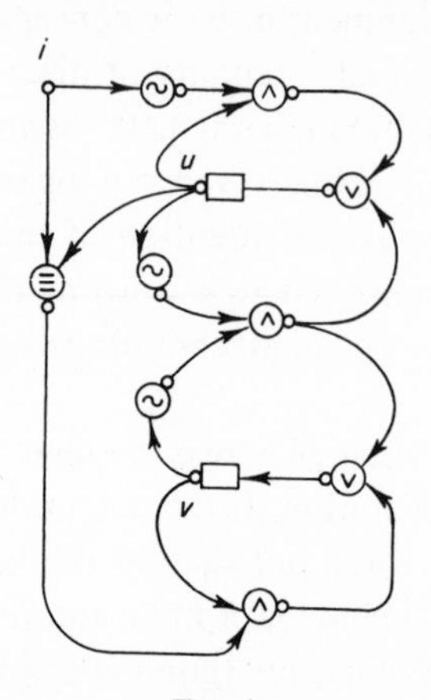


FIG. 1.

systems. We shall therefore discuss the concepts of logical nets and restricted recursion, by way of examples. For extensive studies of these matters we refer to Burks and Wright [6], Kleene [1], and Church [7].

**Definition 1.** A $k$-algebra is a system $\mathfrak{A} = \langle \mathbf{A}, A, f_1, \ldots, f_k \rangle$ consisting of a set $\mathbf{A}$, an element $A$ of $\mathbf{A}$, and unary operations $f_1, \ldots, f_k$ which map $\mathbf{A}$ into $\mathbf{A}$.

The value of $f_i$ at $U \in \mathbf{A}$ will be denoted by $U^{f_i}$.

Figure 1 represents an example of a (*well formed*) *logical net* with one input junction, labeled $i$; various *switch junctions*, marked by small circles; and two *delay junctions*, labeled $u$ and $v$. The *logical elements* $\sim$, $\wedge$, $\vee$, and $\equiv$ behave in the usual manner. The *delay elements* behave thus: At time 0 the junction of a delay is $F$ (inactive); at time $t' = t + 1$ the junction is $F$, if the input wire at time $t$ is $F$ [otherwise the junction is $T$ (active)]. It is now clear how the net transforms an input predicate $i = i0, i1, i2, \ldots$ into delay-output predicates $u$ and $v$. In fact, this transformation $i \rightarrow u, v$ is also defined by the *restricted recursion*

$$\begin{aligned} u0 &\equiv F \\ v0 &\equiv F \\ ut' &\equiv [\widetilde{it} \wedge ut] \vee [\widetilde{ut} \wedge \widetilde{vt}] \\ vt' &\equiv [[it \equiv ut] \wedge vt] \vee [\widetilde{ut} \wedge \widetilde{vt}] \end{aligned} \tag{1}$$

This recursion clearly provides the same information as the net. According to taste, one may prefer to deal either with logical nets or restricted recursions. In the sequel we shall discuss the recursions, simply because printing of nets is more expensive. Let us now consider the general form of a restricted recursion:

$$\begin{aligned} u0 &= A \\ ut' &= B[it, ut] \end{aligned} \tag{2}$$

Here $i$ and $u$ stand for vectors $i_1, \ldots, i_n$ and $u_1, \ldots, u_m$ of predicates, i.e., for sequences $i0, i1, i2, \ldots$ and $u0, u1, u2, \ldots$ of $n$-vectors ($m$-vectors) of truth values $T$ and $F$. $A$ stands for a given $m$-vector of truth values $A_1, \ldots, A_m$. $B[it, ut]$ is a given $m$-vector of Boolean expressions $B_1[it, ut], \ldots, B_m[it, ut]$, and "$=$" in (2) stands for componentwise equivalence. The recursion (2) is uniquely described by the pair $\langle A, B[X, Y] \rangle$.

Let $k = 2^n$, and let $C_1, \ldots, C_k$ be an enumeration of all $n$-vectors of truth values; call these the *input states* of the recursion (2). Let $\mathbf{A}$ be the set of all $m$-vectors of truth values, called the *internal states* of (2). For $i = 1, \ldots, k$, let $f_i$ be the unary operation on $\mathbf{A}$, defined by the vector of expressions $B[C_i, Y]$ (i.e., $Y^{f_i} = B[C_i, Y]$ for all $Y \in \mathbf{A}$). The $k$-algebra $\mathfrak{A} = \langle \mathbf{A}, A, f_1, \ldots, f_k \rangle$ may be called the *transition algebra* of the recursion (2) and of the corresponding logical net.

From the transition algebra $\mathfrak{A}$ of a recursion (2), one can clearly reconstruct the recursion, at least up to equivalent expressions $B'[X, Y]$. More exactly, if the transition operators $f_1, \ldots, f_k$ are given in some fashion, one can find a vector $B'[X, Y]$ of Boolean expressions, such that $Y^{f_i} = B'[C_i, Y]$ for all $i = 1, \ldots, k$ and all $Y \in \mathbf{A}$. While these expressions $B'$ may be different from $B$, they will define the same Boolean functions, i.e., $B'[X, Y] \equiv B[X, Y]$ must be valid, and the recursion $\langle A, B'[X, Y] \rangle$ defines the same input-to-output transformation $i \rightarrow u$ as (2). Suppose we do not possess the algebra $\mathfrak{A}$ itself but only an isomorphic $k$-algebra $\mathfrak{A}'$. In this case there is, in addition to the matter just discussed, an arbitrary choice of a one-to-one correspondence between the set of elements of $\mathfrak{A}'$ and $\mathbf{A}$, i.e., of a coding of the elements of $\mathfrak{A}'$ as vectors of truth values. We may express this situation as follows: *The theory of (isomorphism types of) finite k-algebras is the theory of logical nets, modulo matters of coding and switching.*

Because the study of logical nets (or restricted recursions) is the study of switching through feedback (in finite discrete systems) we may also say:

*The theory of finite k-algebras is the theory of feedback in discrete systems.*

We hope that this discussion will be clearer after the reader has worked out the following exercises.

*Exercise 1.*

(a) Find the transition algebra of the net in Fig. 1. Let $C_1 = T$, $C_2 = F$, and make up a table for the transition functions $f_1$ and $f_2$. Find expressions $B_1'[X, U, V]$, different from those occurring in (1), which yield a recursion, defining the same transformation $i \to u, v$ as (1).

(b) Find a logical net whose transition algebra $\mathfrak{A}$ is isomorphic to the algebra on the set $\mathbf{A} = \{1, \ldots, 8\}$, whose distinguished element is $A = 1$, and whose operators $f_1, f_2, f_3, f_4$ are given by Table 1.

TABLE 1

| | 1 | 2 | 3 | 4 | 5 | 6 | 7 | 8 |
|---|---|---|---|---|---|---|---|---|
| $f_1$ | 2 | 2 | 2 | 5 | 5 | 5 | 5 | 5 |
| $f_2$ | 2 | 2 | 4 | 7 | 7 | 8 | 7 | 8 |
| $f_3$ | 1 | 2 | 3 | 4 | 6 | 6 | 8 | 8 |
| $f_4$ | 1 | 3 | 3 | 8 | 8 | 8 | 8 | 8 |

(c) Find a logical net with two input functions $i, j$, which realizes the algebra $\mathfrak{A}$ given by $\mathbf{A} = \{1, 2, 3, 4, 5\}$, $A = 1$, and $f_1, f_2, f_3$ as shown in Table 2. Note that three delay junctions are required, so that the net will have to possess eight internal states and four input states. Choose the "don't-care" states and transitions wisely, to obtain a simple net.

TABLE 2

| | 1 | 2 | 3 | 4 | 5 |
|---|---|---|---|---|---|
| $f_1$ | 2 | 2 | 3 | 3 | 3 |
| $f_2$ | 1 | 2 | 3 | 4 | 4 |
| $f_3$ | 5 | 4 | 3 | 2 | 1 |

### III. The Response Function of a $k$-Algebra

Let $N_k$ denote the set consisting of all *words* (i.e., finite sequences) over the alphabet $1,\ldots,k$. Thus, examples of members of $N_3$ are 122, 221, 33213, and also the *empty word* 0. The *length* of a word $x$ will be denoted by $\ln(x)$. Thus, $\ln(122) = 3$ and $\ln(0) = 0$. The result of juxtaposing the word $x$ to the left of the word $y$ will be denoted by $x^\frown y$. $^\frown$ thus becomes a binary operation on $N_k$, called *concatenation*. If no confusion arises we shall sometimes abbreviate "$x^\frown y$" by "$xy$." The members of $N_k$ may be called $k$–ary *input signals*.

Let $\mathfrak{A} = \langle \mathbf{A}, A, f_1,\ldots,f_k \rangle$ be a $k$-algebra as defined in Sec. II. Compare this mathematical concept with the idea of a discrete deterministic system, as described in Sec. I. To preserve the intuitive background we shall call $A$ the *initial state* of $\mathfrak{A}$; the numerals $1,\ldots,k$ are called the *input states* of $\mathfrak{A}$; the elements $U \in \mathbf{A}$ are called the (*internal*) *states* of $\mathfrak{A}$; and for $i = 1,\ldots,k$ the map $f_i$ is called the *transition operator* of the input state $i$. Note that we shall later have to add additional structure to $\mathfrak{A}$, to provide for an output channel.

Words $x$ in $N_k$ are called *input signals* (or input histories) of $\mathfrak{A}$. The intended interpretation is as follows: The transition algebra $\mathfrak{A}$ at first is in its initial state $A$, and whenever it is in state $U$ and the input state $j$ is applied it will go into state $V = U^{f_j}$. Thus, $\mathfrak{A}$ reacts to the input signal 2113 by successively passing through the states $A$, $A^{f_2}$, $A^{f_2 f_1}$, $A^{f_2 f_1 f_1}$, $A^{f_2 f_1 f_1 f_3}$. The final state $rp(2113) = A^{f_2 f_1 f_1 f_3}$ may be called the *response* of $\mathfrak{A}$ to the input signal 2113. More precisely this may be put as follows.

**Definition 2.** Let $\mathfrak{A} = \langle \mathbf{A}, A, f_1,\ldots,f_k \rangle$ be a $k$-algebra. Then its binary *response function* $V = U/x$ is the function with arguments $U \in \mathbf{A}$, $x \in N_k$ defined by the recursion

$$U/0 = U \qquad\qquad U \in \mathbf{S}$$
$$U/xj = (U/x)^{f_j} \qquad j = 1,\ldots,k,\ x \in N_k$$

The *response function* $rp(x)$ of $\mathfrak{A}$ is defined by $rp(x) = A/x$. For a fixed $a \in N_k$ the *a-transition operator* $f_a$ on $\mathbf{A}$ is defined by $U^{f_a} = U/a$.

Somewhat less precisely, $U/i_1 i_2 \cdots i_l = U^{f_{i_1} f_{i_2} \cdots f_{i_l}}$, and $U^{f_{221}} = U^{f_2 f_2 f_1}$. Thus, $f_{221}$ is but the result of *composing* the operators $f_2, f_2, f_1$. Note also that $f_0$ is the identity operator of $\mathbf{A}$. Thus the transition operators $f_a$, $a \in N_k$ form a *monoid* (semigroup with identity) $G(\mathfrak{A})$ of mappings from $\mathbf{A}$ into $\mathbf{A}$. $G(\mathfrak{A})$ is generated by the direct transition operators $f_1,\ldots,f_k$. Because a monoid $G(\mathfrak{A})$ may be attached to the transition part of an automaton, it is sometimes claimed that monoids should be used to provide an algebraic approach to finite automata. This, however, appears somewhat strained; unary algebras serve the purpose much more appropriately, and, in addition, they are in a sense simpler algebraic objects than monoids.

*Note:* The operators $f_a$ and $f_b$ may be equal, even for $a \neq b$. In fact if $\mathfrak{A}$ is finite then $G(\mathfrak{A})$ must be finite also.

Often without reference we shall use the following elementary properties of $U/x$ and $rp(x)$. The proofs are left to the reader. The binary response function of a $k$-algebra $\mathfrak{A}$ may also be calculated by the following recursions "from the left":

$$\text{(a)} \qquad \begin{array}{ll} U/0 = U & U \in \mathbf{S} \\ U/jx = U^{f_j}/x, & j = 1,\ldots,k, \; x \in N_k \end{array}$$

From this it follows more generally that

$$\text{(b)} \qquad \begin{array}{rl} (\forall U)_{\mathbf{A}}(\forall x, y)_{N_k} & U/(x \frown y) = (U/x)/y \\ (\forall x, y)_{N_k} & rp(x \frown y) = rp(x)/y \end{array}$$

This in turn yields

$$\text{(c)} \qquad \begin{array}{rl} (\forall U)_{\mathbf{A}}(\forall x, y, v)_{N_k} & U/x = U/y \supset U/(x \frown v) = U/(y \frown v) \\ (\forall x, y, v)_{N_k} & rp(x) = rp(y) \supset rp(x \frown v) = rp(y \frown v). \end{array}$$

Clearly the direct transition operators $f_1,\ldots,f_k$ of a $k$-algebra $\mathfrak{A} = \langle \mathbf{A}, A, f_1,\ldots,f_k \rangle$ may be recovered from the *binary transition operator* $\mathrm{tr}(U, X) = U/X$, defined for $U \in \mathbf{A}$, $X \in \mathbf{I} = \{1,\ldots,k\}$, and taking values in $\mathbf{A}$. Namely, $U^{f_j} = \mathrm{tr}(U, j)$. Therefore, in place of our unary transition operators $f_1,\ldots,f_k$ one could take the binary transition operator tr as primitive. In place of transition algebras one would then have to investigate systems of the form $\langle \mathbf{I}, \mathbf{A}, A, \mathrm{tr} \rangle$ whereby $A \in \mathbf{A}$ and tr maps $\mathbf{A} \times \mathbf{I}$ into $\mathbf{A}$. This actually is more commonly done in the literature on automata theory, and various other variants of the concept of a $k$-algebra are also in use. However, our $k$-algebras are just as natural intuitively and have the advantage of being algebraic systems of a more conventional sort. Consequently, it will be possible to apply standard ideas concerning such fundamental algebraic concepts as homomorphisms, congruence relations on free algebras, and direct products (see the following sections).

Note that *time* enters implicitly into our discussion through the definition of the response function $rp$. This time is discrete: At time 0 the algebra is in state $A$, at time 1 it is in a new state $A^{f_j}$ corresponding to an input state $j$ which has been injected at some instance between 0 and 1, etc. Whether or not a physical realization of $\mathfrak{A}$ is such that the time intervals $0-1, 1-2, \ldots$ must be of equal length does not concern us, and our theory also abstracts from the question whether the input state is to be injected at time $t$, or sometimes between $t$ and $t'$. It might be good here to consider the following two universal principles:

1. The more abstract the theory, the wider the range of applications.
2. The more abstract the theory, the less it will say in any one application.

The positive side of (2) can be brought out thus: If properly carried out an abstraction emphasizes the essential aspects of a more concrete situation.

Concluding this section we shall now introduce a graphical representation of a finite $k$-algebra $\mathfrak{A}$. In essence it is equivalent to the operation table. However, the graph is much more suggestive, and often provides a very

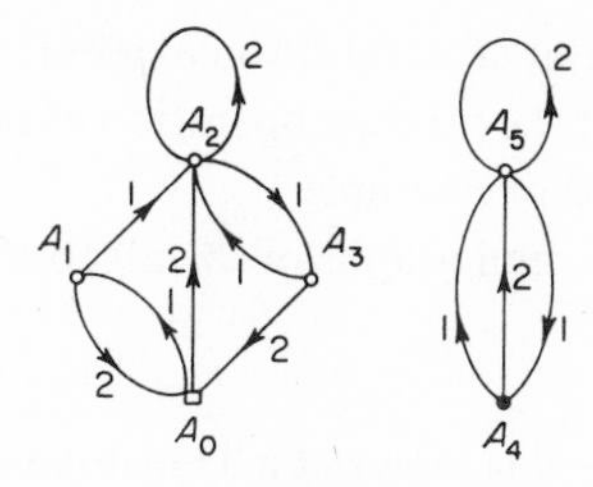


FIG. 2.

handy method of dealing with $k$-algebras. Instead of stating the general definition of the *transition graph* of $\mathfrak{A}$, we shall show it for an example of a 2-algebra.

*Example 1.* Let $\mathfrak{A}$ be the finite 2-algebra whose states are $\mathbf{A} = \{A_0, \ldots, A_5\}$, whose initial state is $A = A_0$, and whose transition operators $f_1, f_2$ are given by Table 3.

TABLE 3

| | $A_0$ | $A_1$ | $A_2$ | $A_3$ | $A_4$ | $A_5$ |
|---|---|---|---|---|---|---|
| $f_1$ | $A_1$ | $A_2$ | $A_3$ | $A_2$ | $A_5$ | $A_4$ |
| $f_2$ | $A_2$ | $A_0$ | $A_2$ | $A_0$ | $A_5$ | $A_5$ |

The transition graph of $\mathfrak{A}$ is the directed graph with labeled edges and marked root, shown in Fig. 2. Clearly from it one can recover the algebra $\mathfrak{A}$. Note that we could drop the labeling of vertices by states; the graph would still describe the algebra $\mathfrak{A}$ up to an isomorphism. In this example the transition graph splits into two disconnected components.

*Exercise 2.*

(a) Let $\mathfrak{A}$ be as in Example 1. Calculate $rp(122)$ and $rp(221)$. Calculate $A_2/122$, first by using the right recursions of Definition 2, and second by using the left recursion of (a). Make up a table and graph for the transition operator $f_{12}$. Find two input signals $a$ and $b$ such that $rp(a) = rp(b)$ but $f_a \neq f_b$. Find two different input signals $a$ and $b$ such that $f_a = f_b$.

(b) Let $\mathbf{A} = \{A_0, A_1, A_2, A_3\}$, $\mathbf{I} = \{1, 2, 3\}$, and let the binary transition operator tr: $\mathbf{A} \times \mathbf{I} \rightarrow \mathbf{A}$ be defined by $\text{tr}(A_i, j) = A_{i+j}$, whereby $i + j$ stands for adding $i$ and $j$ modulo 4. If $\mathfrak{A}$ is the 3-algebra corresponding to the system $\langle \mathbf{I}, \mathbf{A}, A_1, \text{tr} \rangle$, draw the transition graph of $\mathfrak{A}$.

(c) Suppose $G$ is a directed graph, on the set of vertices $\mathbf{A}$, each of whose edges is labeled by either 1 or 2. State necessary and sufficient conditions for $G$ to be the transition graph of a transition algebra.

(d) Make up a table for the product operation of the monoid of transition operators of the algebra $\mathfrak{A}$ of Example 1.

(e) Construct the transition graphs of the algebras of Exercise 1, (b) and (c).

## IV. Accessible States of a Transition Algebra

Note that not every state $U$ of a $k$-algebra need occur as a response to an input signal. Clearly such states are inessential, in the sense that they do not enter into the calculation of $rp(x)$.

**Definition 3.** A state $U$ of a $k$-algebra $\mathfrak{A}$ is called accessible if it occurs as a response to some input signal. The set of accessible states of $\mathfrak{A}$ will be denoted by $as(\mathfrak{A})$. Thus, $as(\mathfrak{A}) = rp(N_k)$. A $k$-algebra is called *reduced* if all its states are accessible, i.e., if $as(\mathfrak{A}) = \mathbf{A}$. The reduced *transition algebra* $rd(\mathfrak{A})$ of $\mathfrak{A}$ is the algebra $\langle as(\mathfrak{A}), A, g_1, \ldots, g_k \rangle$, whereby the operators $g_1, \ldots, g_k$ are obtained by restricting $f_1, \ldots, f_k$ to the subset $as(\mathfrak{A})$ of $\mathbf{A}$.

We shall also say that $U$ is *accessible from* $V$, if $U/x = V$ for some $x$ in $N_k$. In more algebraic terminology, $\mathfrak{A} = \langle \mathbf{A}, A, f_1, \ldots, f_k \rangle$ is reduced just in case $A$ is a *generator* of $\mathfrak{A}$; i.e., a reduced $k$-algebra is but an "algebra with only monadic operators and one generator."

Note that $rd(\mathfrak{A})$ is reduced. Furthermore, $\mathfrak{A}$ and $rd(\mathfrak{A})$ have identical response functions. Because we are using algebras to generate response functions, this means that in essence we need only be concerned with reduced

$k$-algebras. We shall now discuss a simple method for reducing a finite $k$-algebra.

It is hoped that Fig. 3 sufficiently explains what is meant by the *right tree* over $N_k$ for $k = 3$. Its vertices correspond one-to-one to the elements of $N_k$. The vertices in the $m$th *level* correspond to the $x \in N_k$ of length $\ln(x) = m$. The *response tree* of a $k$-algebra $\mathfrak{A}$ is obtained by attaching the state $rp(x)$ as a label to the vertex $x$ of the right tree over $N_k$. Thus the response tree is but a graphical description of the response function $rp$. Note that only accessible states occur as labels.

The *transition tree* of $\mathfrak{A}$ is obtained by labeling the vertices of the right tree just as in the response tree, except that in case $U$ occurs a second time as a label, say at $x$, we delete all vertices $y \geqslant x$ which stand over $x$ in the right

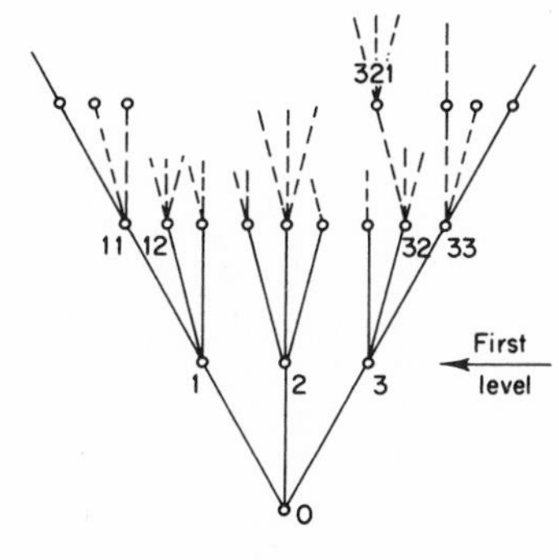


FIG. 3.

tree. Furthermore, the labeling is done by starting at 0 and running through successive levels from left to right.

*Example 2.* Let $\mathfrak{A}$ be the 3-algebra on the states $\mathbf{A} = \{A, B, C, D, E, F\}$, with initial state $A$ and transit operators given by Table 4. Fig. 4 shows the transition tree.

TABLE 4

| | $A$ | $B$ | $C$ | $D$ | $E$ | $F$ |
|---|---|---|---|---|---|---|
| $f_1$ | $B$ | $C$ | $A$ | $D$ | $F$ | $A$ |
| $f_2$ | $C$ | $B$ | $C$ | $B$ | $B$ | $E$ |
| $f_3$ | $A$ | $D$ | $D$ | $C$ | $C$ | $F$ |

It is clear that just the accessible states of $\mathfrak{A}$ occur in the transition tree. Furthermore, the transition tree fully describes the $rd(\mathfrak{A})$; it is but a modified version of the transition graph of $rd(\mathfrak{A})$. In particular, the initial state of $rd(\mathfrak{A})$ can be read from the transition tree; it is the root. To further clarify the idea we add the following comments: (a) The labeling of edges is omitted in the transition tree; it is intended that the branches, in left-to-right order, correspond to the input states $1, 2, \ldots, k$. Thus our trees include an orientation of branches, coming off a vertex. (b) The tree of a $k$-algebra is is $k$-branching (c) Each accessible state of $\mathfrak{A}$ occurs exactly once as interior vertex; it may or may not recur at the frontier.

Transition trees turn out to be a useful device for describing and handling finite reduced $k$-algebras. In particular, constructing the transition tree of $\mathfrak{A}$ is the most efficient method to obtain the accessible states, and at the same time one obtains $rd(\mathfrak{A})$.

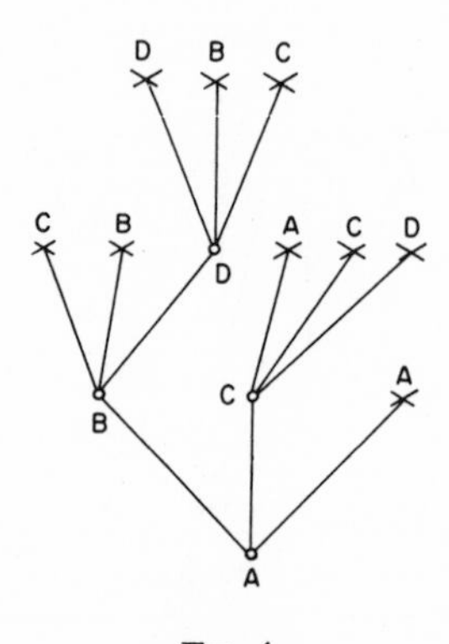


FIG. 4.

**Lemma 1.** If $\mathfrak{A}$ is a finite $k$-algebra with $n$ states, then every accessible state $U$ of $\mathfrak{A}$ can be obtained as a response $U = rp(x)$ to an input signal $x$ of length $< n$; i.e., there are at most $n$ levels in the transition tree of $\mathfrak{A}$.

*Proof.* Let $U$ be an accessible state of $\mathfrak{A}$. Then $U = rp(y)$ for some $y \in N_k$. To prove the lemma it is clearly sufficient to show that if $U = rp(y)$ and $\ln(y) \geqslant n$, then there is a $z$ such that $U = rp(z)$ and $\ln(y) > \ln(z)$.

Suppose therefore that $U = rp(y)$, $y = X_1 X_2 \cdots X_l$, $l \geqslant n$, and $X_1, \ldots, X_l$ are input states. Let $U_0, U_1, \ldots, U_l$ be the states $\mathfrak{A}$ passes through if the input states $X_1, X_2, \ldots, X_l$ are applied in succession, i.e., $U_0 = A$, $U_1 = U_0/X_1$, $U_2 = U_1/X_2, \ldots, U_l = U_{l-1}/X_l = rp(y) = U$. Because there are but $n$ states in $\mathfrak{A}$ and $l \geqslant n$, there must be a repetition $U_p = U_q$ for some $0 \leqslant p < q \leqslant l$. Thus we have $U_0 = A$, $U_1 = U_0/X_1, \ldots, U_p = U_{p-1}/X_p$, $U_{q+1} = U_p/X_{q+1}, \ldots$, $U_l = U_{l-1}/X_l = U$. Thus $A = U_0, U_1, \ldots, U_p, U_{q+1}, \ldots, U_l = U$ is the succession of states $\mathfrak{A}$ passes through if the input signal $z = X_1 X_2 \cdots X_p X_{q+1} X_{q+2} \cdots X_l$ is applied. Therefore, $U = rp(z)$. But $\ln(z) < \ln(y)$, because $p < q$, and we have found a $z$ such that $rp(z) = U$ and $\ln(z) < \ln(y)$. Q.E.D.

This simple proof is typical for many similar but more sophisticated arguments used in the theory of finite automata.

*Exercise 3*

(a) Let $\mathfrak{A}$ be as in Example 1. Find $as(\mathfrak{A})$ by constructing the transition tree. Note that in this particular case there is a better bound on the number of levels than the one predicted by Lemma 1.

(b) Let $\mathfrak{A}$ be as in Example 2. Construct the transition graph of $rd(\mathfrak{A})$ from the transition tree.

(c) Find a function $h: N_2 \to \{A_0, A_1, A_2\} = \mathbf{A}$ which is not the response function of an algebra on the states **A**. If $g$ is a function from $N_k$ into a finite set **S**, find a necessary and sufficient condition for existence of an algebra on the set **S** whose response function is $g$.

(d) Construct the transition tree of the algebra of Exercise 1, b and c, and of Exercise 2b.

(e) Give a survey over all reduced 1-algebras, up to isomorphism. How many of these are infinite? Find two nonisomorphic infinite 2-algebras.

(f) Show that if a $k$-algebra has $n$ states, then to every word $y$ there is a word $z$ such that $\ln(z) \leqslant n^2$ and the transition operators $f_y$ and $f_z$ are equal.

## V. The Basic Concepts of Algebra

In this section we shall discuss the universal algebraic concepts of *subalgebra, homomorphism, congruence relation, direct product,* and *free algebra,* in the special case of $k$-algebras. We shall see that each one of these general notions is of significance for the understanding of discrete deterministic systems. Had not the algebraists invented them, these ideas would sooner or later have independently grown out of the study of states transitions. In fact, something of the sort has actually happened during the past decade.

We have already used the notion of subalgebra of a $k$-algebra $\mathfrak{A}$. The reduced $rd(\mathfrak{A})$ of $\mathfrak{A}$ is simply the smallest among all subalgebras of $\mathfrak{A}$. $\mathfrak{A}$ is reduced in case it admits no proper subalgebra. In the sequel we shall often deal with reduced algebras only, the reason for this having been stated in Sec. IV.

A $k$-algebra $\mathfrak{A} = \langle \mathbf{A}, A, f_1, \ldots, f_k \rangle$ is called (*totally*) *free* if it satisfies the "generalized Peano axioms":

$$U^{f_j} \neq A \qquad \text{for } U \in \mathbf{A}, i = 1, \ldots, k \tag{3}$$

$$U^{f_i} \neq V^{f_j} \qquad \text{for } U, V \in \mathbf{A}, i < j = 1, \ldots, k \tag{4}$$

$$U^{f_i} = V^{f_i} \supset U = V \qquad \text{for } U, V \in \mathbf{A}, i = 1, \ldots, k \tag{5}$$

For any $\mathbf{X} \subseteq \mathbf{A}$, if $A \in \mathbf{X}$ and $(\forall U).\ U \in \mathbf{X} \supset U^{f_i}, \ldots, U^{f_k} \in \mathbf{X}$, then $\mathbf{X} = \mathbf{A}$ (6)

Note that (4) and (5) may be expressed thus: $A^{f_{i_1} \cdots f_{i_n}} = A^{f_{j_1} \cdots f_{j_m}}$ holds only in case $n = m$ and $i_1 = j_1, \ldots, i_n = j_n$, and condition (6) simply states that $\mathfrak{A}$ is reduced. On the set $N_k$ of words one defines the *right-successor functions* $\sigma_1, \ldots, \sigma_k$; thus

$$x^{\sigma_i} = xi \qquad \text{for } x \in N_k, i = 1, \ldots, k \tag{7}$$

It is easy to see that the $k$-algebra $\mathfrak{F}_k = \langle N_k, 0, \sigma_1, \ldots, \sigma_k \rangle$ is free, and that every free $k$-algebra $\mathfrak{A}$ must be isomorphic to $\mathfrak{F}_k$. The transition tree of $\mathfrak{F}_k$ is the right tree of words, discussed in Sec. IV. In fact, to say that a reduced $k$-algebra $\mathfrak{A}$ is free simply means that no feedback occurs in its transition tree (or graph).

A *homomorphism* of the $k$-algebra $\mathfrak{A} = \langle \mathbf{A}, A, f_1, \ldots, f_k \rangle$ onto the $k$-algebra $\mathfrak{B} = \langle \mathbf{B}, B, g_1, \ldots, g_k \rangle$ is a mapping $h$ from $\mathbf{A}$ onto $\mathbf{B}$ such that $hA = B$ and

$$h(U^{f_i}) = (hU)^{g_i} \qquad \text{for } U \in A, i = 1, \ldots, k \tag{8}$$

An *isomorphism* is a one-to-one homomorphism; the inverse $h^{-1}$ of an isomorphism of $\mathfrak{A}$ onto $\mathfrak{B}$ is an isomorphism of $\mathfrak{B}$ onto $\mathfrak{A}$. We use the symbol $\mathfrak{A} \Leftarrow \mathfrak{B}$ to denote that $\mathfrak{A}$ is the *homomorphic image* of $\mathfrak{B}$, and $\mathfrak{A} \simeq \mathfrak{B}$ means that $\mathfrak{A}$ and $\mathfrak{B}$ are *isomorphic*.

We have already dealt with homomorphisms. The response function $rp$ of a reduced $k$-algebra $\mathfrak{A}$ is, by its very definition, a homomorphism of the free algebra $\mathfrak{F}_k$ onto $\mathfrak{A}$. Thus $\mathfrak{F}_k \Rightarrow \mathfrak{A}$ holds for any reduced algebra. In fact $rp$ is the only homomorphism of $\mathfrak{F}_k$ onto $\mathfrak{A}$; more generally one easily shows:

> If $\mathfrak{A}$ is reduced and $\mathfrak{A} \Rightarrow \mathfrak{B}$, then $\mathfrak{B}$ is reduced and the homomorphism from $\mathfrak{A}$ onto $\mathfrak{B}$ is uniquely determined. (9)

Isomorphic algebras $\mathfrak{A} \simeq \mathfrak{B}$ have identical response functions. Conversely, if $\mathfrak{A}$ and $\mathfrak{B}$ are reduced and $rp_{\mathfrak{A}} = rp_{\mathfrak{B}}$, then $\mathfrak{A} \simeq \mathfrak{B}$. The transition graphs and trees of isomorphic algebras are identical up to renaming of the vertices. The significance of the notion of isomorphism is that it provides a rigorous definition of "$\mathfrak{A}$ *is structurally identical to* $\mathfrak{B}$." The *isomorphism type* $\mathfrak{A}$, i.e., the class of all $k$-algebras $\mathfrak{B}$ which are isomorphic to $\mathfrak{A}$, may well be called the structure of $\mathfrak{A}$. We are usually interested in a $k$-algebra $\mathfrak{A}$ only up to isomorphism. However, we shall often follow the common practice of talking about $\mathfrak{A}$, when in fact we mean $\mathfrak{A}^{\simeq}$. The intuitive meaning of $\mathfrak{A} \Rightarrow \mathfrak{B}$ is "$\mathfrak{A}$ is *structurally stronger* than $\mathfrak{B}$."

Let $\mathfrak{A} = \langle \mathbf{A}, A, f_1, \ldots, f_k \rangle$ be a $k$-algebra, and let $h : \mathbf{A} \to \mathbf{B}$ be a mapping of $\mathbf{A}$ onto some set $\mathbf{B}$. We will say that $h$ is *compatible with* $f_1, \ldots, f_k$ (or with $\mathfrak{A}$) if

$$hU = hV \supset h(U^{f_i}) = h(V^{f_i}) \qquad \text{for } U, V \in \mathbf{A}, i = 1, \ldots, k \tag{10}$$

Clearly a homomorphism $h$ of $\mathfrak{A}$ onto $\mathfrak{B}$ is compatible with $\mathfrak{A}$, i.e., (10) is a simple consequence of (8). Conversely, if $h$ is a mapping from $\mathbf{A}$ onto $\mathbf{B}$ which is compatible with $\mathfrak{A}$, then on $\mathbf{B}$ one can introduce a $k$-algebra $\mathfrak{B} = \langle \mathbf{B}, B, g_1, \ldots, g_k \rangle$ such that $h$ is a homomorphism of $\mathfrak{A}$ onto $\mathfrak{B}$. Namely, let $B = hA$, and note that, because (10) is assumed to hold, formula (8) properly defines mappings $g_i$ from $\mathbf{B}$ onto $\mathbf{B}$. Thus,

> A mapping $h : \mathbf{A} \to \mathbf{B}$ is compatible with $\mathfrak{A} = \langle \mathbf{A}, A, f_1, \ldots, f_k \rangle$, if and only if on $\mathbf{B}$ there is an algebra $\mathfrak{B} = \langle \mathbf{B}, B, g_1, \ldots, g_k \rangle$ such that $h$ is homomorphism of $\mathfrak{A}$ onto $\mathfrak{B}$. $\mathfrak{B}$, of course, is uniquely determined by $h$. (11)

In other words, finding homomorphic images of $\mathfrak{A}$ is the same as finding mappings which are compatible with $\mathfrak{A}$. This analysis can be carried one step further, and leads to the concept of congruence relation. We first note that many homomorphic images of $\mathfrak{A}$ will be equal up to an isomorphism; in particular,

> If $h_1 : \mathfrak{A} \Rightarrow \mathfrak{B}_1$, $h_2 : \mathfrak{A} \Rightarrow \mathfrak{B}_2$ are homomorphisms such that the equivalence relations $h_1 U = h_1 V$ and $h_2 U = h_2 V$ on $\mathbf{A}$ are identical then $\mathfrak{B}_1 \simeq \mathfrak{B}_2$. (12)

We therefore call an equivalence relation $\frown$ on $\mathbf{A}$ a *congruence* (*relation*) on $\mathfrak{A}$ if

$$U \frown V \supset U^{f_i} \frown V^{f_i} \qquad \text{for } U, V \in \mathbf{A}, i = 1, \ldots, k \tag{13}$$

Inspection of (10) and (13) shows the following: To say that $\frown$ is a congruence of $\mathfrak{A}$ is the same as saying that the *canonical map* $U \to \overset{\frown}{U}$ of $\mathbf{A}$ onto $\overset{\frown}{\mathbf{A}} = \{\overset{\frown}{U}, U \in A\}$ is compatible with $\mathfrak{A}$. Thus, by (11), to a congruence $\frown$ on $\mathfrak{A}$ there corresponds an algebra $\mathfrak{A}/\frown$ on $\overset{\frown}{\mathbf{A}}$, namely, the homomorphic image of $\mathfrak{A}$ under the canonical map $U \to \overset{\smile}{U}$. This algebra $\mathfrak{A}/\smile = \langle \overset{\smile}{\mathbf{A}}, \overset{\smile}{A}, \overset{\smile}{f_1}, \ldots, \overset{\smile}{f_k} \rangle$ is called the quotient of $\mathfrak{A}$ by $\smile$; its initial state is the congruence class $\overset{\smile}{A}$ of the initial state $A$ of $\mathfrak{A}$, and its operators $\overset{\smile}{f_i}$ are given by

$$\overset{\smile}{U}^{\overset{\smile}{f_i}} = (U^{f_i})^{\smile} \qquad \text{for } U \in \mathbf{A},\ i = 1, \ldots, k \tag{14}$$

Note that, owing to (13), formula (14) unambiguously defines operators $\overset{\smile}{f_i}$ on $\overset{\smile}{\mathbf{A}}$. Reconsidering (12) we see the significance of congruences and their quotients:

> The homomorphisms $h$ of a $k$-algebra $\mathfrak{A}$ come in classes $K(\smile)$ which correspond one-to-one to the congruences $\smile$ on $\mathfrak{A}$. Namely, $h$ belongs to $K(\smile)$ just in case $hU = hV$ means $U \smile V$. All images $h(\mathfrak{A})$ of congruences $h \in K(\smile)$ are isomorphic among each other and isomorphic to the quotient $\mathfrak{A}/\smile$. (15)

In other words, the canonical map $U \to \overset{\smile}{U}$ of a congruence $\smile$ on $\mathfrak{A}$ may be viewed as a normalized version of any one of the homomorphisms $h$ in $K(\smile)$. Every homomorphic image of $\mathfrak{A}$ is isomorphic to some quotient of $\mathfrak{A}$. In the case of reduced algebras, which are of special interest to us, the relationship between homomorphisms and congruences is particularly simple. Using (9), one shows that for reduced algebras the converse to (12) also holds, i.e.,

> Let $\mathfrak{A}$ be a reduced $k$-algebra. Two homomorphic images $h_1(\mathfrak{A})$ and $h_2(\mathfrak{A})$ are isomorphic if and only if $h_1$ and $h_2$ belong to the same class $K(\smile)$; i.e., if $\mathfrak{A}/\smile_1 \simeq \mathfrak{A}/\smile_2$, then $\smile_1 = \smile_2$. (16)

For later reference we restate this as

**Lemma 2.** The isomorphism types of homomorphic images of a reduced $k$-algebra $\mathfrak{A}$ correspond one-to-one to the congruence relations on $\mathfrak{A}$. If $\smile$ is a congruence on $\mathfrak{A}$, then $\mathfrak{A}/\smile$ represents the corresponding isomorphism type. If $h : \mathfrak{A} \Rightarrow \mathfrak{B}$ is a homomorphism, then $hU = hV$ is the congruence corresponding to $\mathfrak{B}$.

In papers concerned with digital systems one often encounters a process called *merging of states*. In fact, this always means passing from a $k$-algebra (or similar algebraic system) $\mathfrak{A}$ to some quotient $\mathfrak{A}/\smile$. The point is: The basic facts about congruences (which we are here discussing, and which are well known to the algebraist) yield a clear and satisfactory understanding of the idea of merging of states. See in particular the discussion of Moore's minimality theory in Sec. VI.

A congruence relation on the free $k$-algebra $\mathfrak{F}_k = \langle N_k, 0, \sigma_1, \ldots, \sigma_k \rangle$ we shall also call a *right congruence* on the set $N_k$ of words. Thus a right congruence on $N_k$ is an equivalence relation on $N_k$ satisfying

$$(x \backsim y) \supset (xu \backsim yu) \qquad \text{for } x, y, u \in N_k \tag{17}$$

As we have already remarked, every reduced $k$-algebra $\mathfrak{A}$ is a homomorphic image of $\mathfrak{F}_k$, and the (unique) homomorphism is the response function $rp$ of $\mathfrak{A}$. The corresponding congruence relation on $\mathfrak{F}_k$ we denote by $\perp(\mathfrak{A})$, and we call it the *equi-response* relation of $\mathfrak{A}$. Thus,

$$x \perp y(\mathfrak{A}) \equiv rp_{\mathfrak{A}}\, x = rp_{\mathfrak{A}}\, y \qquad \text{for } x, y \in N_k \tag{18}$$

Note that $\perp(\mathfrak{A})$ has a very natural intuitive meaning; $x \perp y(\mathfrak{A})$ simply means that the input signals $x$ and $y$ produce the same internal state, when fed through the input channel of $\mathfrak{A}$. Note also,

> If $\mathfrak{A}$ is a reduced $k$-algebra, then the index[1] $id(\mathfrak{A})$ of the equi-response relation $\perp$ of $\mathfrak{A}$ is equal to the number of states of $\mathfrak{A}$. (19)

Using this terminology we can state the following corollary to Lemma 2:

**Lemma 2′.** The isomorphism types of reduced $k$-algebras correspond one-to-one to the right-congruence relations on $N_k$. This correspondence and its inverse are given by

$$\backsim \text{ right congruence} \rightarrow \mathfrak{F}_k/\backsim \text{ reduced } k\text{-algebra}$$
$$\mathfrak{A} \text{ reduced } k\text{-algebra} \rightarrow \perp(\mathfrak{A}) \text{ right congruence}$$

Furthermore, if $\mathfrak{A} \leftrightarrow \backsim$, then $id(\backsim) =$ number of states of $\mathfrak{A}$. Thus, the study of (finite) reduced $k$-algebras is equivalent to a study of right congruences (of finite index) on the set $N_k$ of words.

The *direct product* $\mathfrak{A} \times \mathfrak{B}$ of two $k$-algebras, $\mathfrak{A} = \langle \mathbf{A}, A, f_1, \ldots, f_k \rangle$ and $\mathfrak{B} = \langle \mathbf{B}, B, g_1, \ldots, g_k \rangle$, is the $k$-algebra $\langle \mathbf{A} \times \mathbf{B}, (A, B), h_1, \ldots, h_k \rangle$, whose states are the pairs $(U, V), U \in \mathbf{A}, V \in \mathbf{B}$, whose initial state is $(A, B)$ and whose transition functions are defined by

$$(U, V)^{h_i} = (U^{f_i}, V^{g_i}) \qquad \text{for } U \in \mathbf{A}, V \in \mathbf{B}, i = 1, \ldots, k$$

[1] By the *index* $id(\backsim)$ of an equivalence relation $\backsim$ we mean the number of its equivalence classes. Clearly, $id(\backsim)$ is the number of states of the quotient $\mathfrak{A}/\backsim$ of $\mathfrak{A}$ by a congruence $\backsim$ on $\mathfrak{A}$.

The *projections* $p$ and $q$, defined below, clearly are homomorphisms of $\mathfrak{A} \times \mathfrak{B}$ onto $\mathfrak{A}$ and $\mathfrak{B}$, respectively.

$$\left.\begin{aligned} p(U,V) &= U \\ q(U,V) &= V \end{aligned}\right\} \qquad \text{for } U \in \mathbf{A}, V \in \mathbf{B}$$

Note that $\mathfrak{A} \times \mathfrak{B}$ does not need to be reduced, even in case $\mathfrak{A}$ and $\mathfrak{B}$ are reduced. We define $\mathfrak{A} \otimes \mathfrak{B}$ to be the reduction of $\mathfrak{A} \times \mathfrak{B}$ and we call this the *reduced product*. A very natural construction will yield the transition tree of $\mathfrak{A} \otimes \mathfrak{B}$ (without going through $\mathfrak{A} \times \mathfrak{B}$) from the trees of $\mathfrak{A}$ and $\mathfrak{B}$. We show this construction in an example; see Fig. 5.

Clearly $\mathfrak{A} \otimes \mathfrak{B}$ has at most $n \cdot m$ states if $\mathfrak{A}$ has $n$ and $\mathfrak{B}$ has $m$ states. One easily verifies that the projections $p$ and $q$, restricted to $\mathfrak{A} \otimes \mathfrak{B}$, are homomorphisms of $\mathfrak{A} \otimes \mathfrak{B}$ onto $\mathfrak{A}$ and $\mathfrak{B}$, respectively, if $\mathfrak{A}$ and $\mathfrak{B}$ are

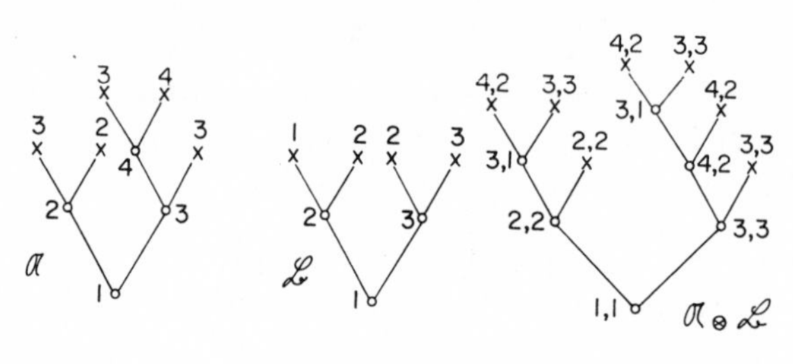

FIG. 5.

reduced. We now show that, for reduced algebras, $\mathfrak{A} \otimes \mathfrak{B}$ is the smallest $k$-algebra having $\mathfrak{A}$ and $\mathfrak{B}$ as homomorphic images.

**Lemma 3.** Let $\mathfrak{A}$ and $\mathfrak{B}$ be reduced $k$-algebras. Then $\mathfrak{A} \otimes \mathfrak{B} \Rightarrow \mathfrak{A}, \mathfrak{A} \otimes \mathfrak{B} \Rightarrow \mathfrak{B}$ Furthermore, if $\mathfrak{C}$ is a reduced $k$-algebra such that $\mathfrak{C} \Rightarrow \mathfrak{A}$, $\mathfrak{C} \Rightarrow \mathfrak{B}$, then $\mathfrak{C} \Rightarrow \mathfrak{A} \otimes \mathfrak{B}$; i.e., among all reduced $k$-algebras $\mathfrak{A} \otimes \mathfrak{B}$ is the smallest having $\mathfrak{A}$ and $\mathfrak{B}$ as homomorphic images.

*Proof.* Let $\mathfrak{C}$ be reduced $k$-algebras. Let $h_1 : \mathfrak{C} \Rightarrow \mathfrak{A}$ and $h_2 : \mathfrak{C} \Rightarrow \mathfrak{B}$. Define the mapping $h : \mathbf{C} \to (\mathbf{A} \times \mathbf{B})$ by

$$hQ = (h_1 Q, h_2 Q) \qquad \text{for } Q \in \mathbf{C}$$

Because $\mathfrak{C}$ is reduced, $h$ clearly is a homomorphism of $\mathfrak{C}$ into $\mathfrak{A} \otimes \mathfrak{B}$. That all states of $\mathfrak{A} \otimes \mathfrak{B}$ are actually values of $h$ follows because $h_1$ is onto $\mathfrak{A}$ and $h_2$ is onto $\mathfrak{B}$. Thus, $h$ is a homomorphism of $\mathfrak{C}$ onto $\mathfrak{A} \otimes \mathfrak{B}$, and therefore $\mathfrak{C} \Rightarrow \mathfrak{A} \otimes \mathfrak{B}$. Q.E.D.

If $\mathbf{A}_s, s \in S$ is a family of sets, let $\underset{s \in S}{\times} \mathbf{A}_s$ denote the set of all functions $U$, defined on $S$, and such that $U_s \in \mathbf{A}_s$ for all $s \in S$. For every $s \in S$ let $\mathfrak{A}_s = \langle \mathbf{A}_s, A_s, f_{1s}, \ldots, f_{ks} \rangle$ be a $k$-algebra. The *direct product* $\underset{s \in S}{\times} \mathfrak{A}_s$ is the algebra whose states are $\underset{s \in S}{\times} \mathbf{A}_s$, whose initial state is the function $A$ which takes $s$ into $A_s$, and whose transition operators $f_i$ are defined by $(U^{f_i})_s = U_s^{f_{is}}$. Reducing the direct product yields the reduced *product*, denoted by $\underset{s \in S}{\otimes} \mathfrak{A}_s$. Lemma 3 easily generalizes to arbitrary reduced products.

*The case* $k = 1$. It is quite instructive to reconsider the discussion of this section in the special case $k = 1$, which is properly termed the *input-free case*. The free algebra $\mathfrak{F}_1$ is $\langle N, 0, ' \rangle$, whereby $N = N_1$ is the set of natural numbers (including 0) and $x' = x + 1$ is the ordinary successor function on $N$. This turns out to be, up to isomorphism, the only infinite reduced 1-algebra. Every finite reduced 1-algebra is, up to isomorphism, uniquely characterized by two numbers $s \geqslant 0$ (called the *phase*) and $p \geqslant 1$ (called the *period*). Figure 6 shows the transition graph of the 1-algebra $\mathfrak{A}_{s,p}$ of phase

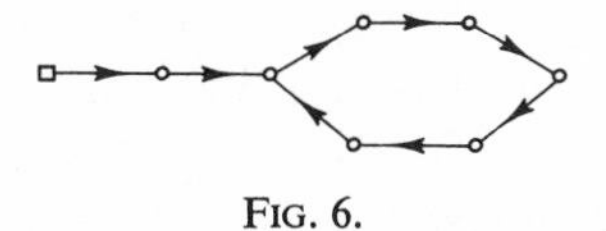

FIG. 6.

$s = 2$ and period $p = 6$. The congruence relation $\approx (s,p)$ on $\mathfrak{F}_1$, corresponding to the algebra $\mathfrak{A}_{s,p}$, is given by

$$x \approx y(s,p) \;.\!\equiv\!.\; [x < s \wedge x = y] \wedge [s \leqslant x \wedge s \leqslant y \wedge x \equiv y (\operatorname{mod} p)] \qquad (20)$$

We may extend these notations to $p = 0$; for any $s$ $\mathfrak{F}_1 = \mathfrak{A}_{s,0}$ and $\approx (s,0)$ is the equality relation on $N$. Thus, the study of 1-algebras simply means the study of the usual congruences of elementary number theory.

*k-ary notation for natural numbers.* Also, the words on $k$ symbols $1, \ldots, k$ may be interpreted as natural numbers. Note that the free algebra $\mathfrak{F}_k = \langle N_k, 0, \sigma_1, \ldots, \sigma_k \rangle$ is isomorphic to the algebra $\mathfrak{F}'_k = \langle N, 0, k \cdot x + 1, \ldots, k \cdot x + k \rangle$; the isomorphism $h: N \to N_k$ yields a $k$-ary notation for natural numbers. (This is not the standard $k$-ary notation! It has the advantage of using every word in a one-to-one fashion as the notation for a natural number). Results on finite $k$-algebras and finite automata may therefore be viewed as contributions to elementary number theory with emphasis on $k$-ary, rather than 1-ary notation. The first task in this field is to provide a survey over all congruences of finite index of the functions $k \cdot x + 1, \ldots, k \cdot x + k$ on $N$ (i.e., of all congruences of finite index on $\mathfrak{F}_k$). As a distant goal one may hope to eventually reach an understanding of these congruences which compares to the understanding we possess of the ordinary congruences (20) on the natural numbers. The results on finite automata which are available today should be considered as a humble contribution to such an understanding. That the step from $k = 1$ to $k = 2$ is not a trivial one is most clearly shown by the lattice-theoretic difficulties we shall discuss in Sec. VI. That things become much more interesting for $k \geqslant 2$ is also clear from the following.

*Congruences on $\mathfrak{F}_k$ of infinite index.* While there is but one infinite reduced 1-algebra, it is clear that there are many nonisomorphic infinite reduced 2-algebras. In fact, there are congruences of $2x + 1$, $2x + 2$ which are of infinite index and are intricate in a much deeper sense. The result of Post and Markov, which states that the word problem for semigroups is unsolvable, may be restated thus: For $k \geqslant 2$, there is a congruence relation $\backsim$ on $\mathfrak{F}_k$ which is a non-recursive relation.

*Commutative k-algebras.* A $k$-algebra $\mathfrak{A}$ is called *commutative* if its transition operators $f_1,\ldots,f_k$ commute with each other, i.e., $U^{f_i f_j} = U^{f_j f_i}$. From the viewpoint of sequential systems, finite commutative $k$-algebras may be called *modular counters.* Note that 1-algebras are trivially commutative. The *free commutative* $k$-algebra $\mathfrak{C}_k$, of which all other reduced commutative $k$-algebras are homomorphic images, is a sort of product $\mathfrak{C}_k = \mathfrak{F}_1 \times \cdots \times \mathfrak{F}_1$ of $k$ copies of $\mathfrak{F}_1$. Thus the states of $\mathfrak{C}_k$ are the $k$-tuples $x_1,\ldots,x_k$ of natural numbers; the initial state is $0,\ldots,0$; and the transition operators are $\langle x_1,\ldots,x_i,\ldots,x_k\rangle^{\lambda_i} = \langle x_1,\ldots,x_i + 1,\ldots,x_k\rangle$. We leave it to the reader to give a satisfactory survey over all finite reduced commutative $k$-algebras, i.e., to classify the congruences of finite index of $\mathfrak{C}_k$. This can actually be done, using well-known facts of elementary number theory or the basic facts about finite commutative monoids.

*Exercise 4.*

(a) Let $\mathfrak{A}$ be as in Example 1. Does $122 \perp 2211(\mathfrak{A})$ hold? Is there an input signal $x \neq 0$ such that $x \perp 0(\mathfrak{A})$? Find a set of representatives for the congruence classes of $\perp$.

TABLE 5

| | 1 | 2 | 3 | 4 | 5 | 6 |
|---|---|---|---|---|---|---|
| $g_1$ | 2 | 3 | 4 | 2 | 4 | 1 |
| $g_2$ | 3 | 5 | 4 | 3 | 3 | 3 |
| $g_3$ | 4 | 6 | 6 | 1 | 6 | 3 |

(b) Construct the transition tree of a 3-algebra $\mathfrak{C}$ which has $\mathfrak{A}$ and $\mathfrak{B}$ as homomorphic images. $\mathfrak{A}$ is the algebra of Fig. 4; $\mathfrak{B}$ is given by Table 5.

(c) Let $T$ be the transition tree of the finite $k$-algebra $\mathfrak{A}$. What does it mean for $T$ that $\backsim$ is a congruence of $\mathfrak{A}$? From $T$, how does one construct the transition tree of the quotient $\mathfrak{A}/\backsim$? Find all congruences of the algebra given by Table 6. Find the transition trees of the corresponding quotients.

TABLE 6

| | 1 | 2 | 3 | 4 | 5 |
|---|---|---|---|---|---|
| $f_1$ | 2 | 4 | 5 | 4 | 5 |
| $f_2$ | 3 | 4 | 5 | 4 | 5 |

(d) Find all homomorphic images of the algebra $\mathfrak{A}$ given by Table 7. Represent $\mathfrak{A}$ as a reduced product of a two-state algebra and a four-state algebra.

TABLE 7

| | 1 | 2 | 3 | 4 | 5 | 6 |
|---|---|---|---|---|---|---|
| $f_1$ | 2 | 4 | 6 | 6 | 4 | 6 |
| $f_2$ | 3 | 5 | 2 | 5 | 5 | 5 |

(e) Describe the relations $\approx(0,1)$, $\approx(s,1)$, $\approx(s,0)$, $\approx(0,p)$. Find the index of $\approx(s,p)$. Show that $\approx(s,p)$ is a congruence relation of the operations $x+y$ and $x{\cdot}y$.

(f) Show that $\approx(3,12)$ is the equi-response relation of $\mathfrak{A}_{3,6} \otimes \mathfrak{A}_{1,4}$. Which is the equi-response relation of $\mathfrak{A}_{s,p} \otimes \mathfrak{A}_{r,q}$? Find $u,v$ such that $\approx(u,v)$ is the intersection of $\approx(s,p)$ and $\approx(r,p)$. State a theorem concerning these matters.

(g) Prove that every congruence relation $\backsim$ of $\langle N,0,'\rangle$ is one of the relations $\approx(s,p)$. Do not use Lemma 2 but only the defining property $(x \backsim y) \supset (x' \backsim y')$.

(*h*) Find an infinite reduced commutative 2-algebra which is not isomorphic to the free commutative algebra $\mathfrak{C}_2$; i.e., find a congruence of infinite index on $\mathfrak{C}_2$ which is not the equality relation.

(i) Find all reduced 2-counters with six states, and the corresponding congruences on $\mathfrak{C}_2$.

(j) Show that the 3-algebra $\mathfrak{F}_3' = \langle N, 0, 3x+1, 3x+2, 3x+3 \rangle$ is totally free. Draw its transition tree, and compare the corresponding ternary notation for natural numbers with the standard ternary notation. Set up an algorithm for adding two natural numbers in this modified ternary notation.

(k) Which of the following equivalence relations on $N_2$ are right congruences and left congruences; find the indices. For notation see below.

1. $\ln_1 x \approx \ln_1 y(1,2) \wedge \ln_2 x \approx \ln_2 y(2,4)$
2. $(12 \leqslant x) \equiv (12 \leqslant y)$
3. $\ln_1 x \approx \ln_1 y(1,2) \wedge (\ln_2 x \geqslant 1) \equiv (\ln_2 y \geqslant 1)$
4. $(\ln_1 x + 2\ln_2 x) \approx (\ln_1 y + 2\ln_2 y)(1,3)$

(l) Show that the binary relations on $N_2$ defined by the following expressions are right congruences on $N_2$, of finite index. In each case construct a 2-algebra which has the relation as its equi-response relation. For notation see below.

1. $(12 \leqslant x) \equiv (12 \leqslant y) \wedge (x=0) \equiv (y=0) \wedge (x=1) \equiv (y=1)$
2. $(x \geqslant 12) \equiv (y \geqslant 12) \wedge (x \geqslant 1) \equiv (y \geqslant 1)$
3. $\ln_1 x \approx \ln_1 y(1,4)$
4. $\ln_{12} x \approx \ln_{12} y(1,2)$

(m) Find the right congruences $\backsim$ on $N_2$ of smallest index such that $\backsim$ is contained in the relation.

$$1\colon (112 \leqslant x) \equiv (112 \leqslant y) \qquad 2\colon (x \geqslant 112) \equiv (y \geqslant 112)$$

Construct the transition trees of the quotients.

*Notation.* If $x, y$ are words in $N_k$, define

| | |
|---|---|
| $x \leqslant y\colon (\exists u)\, xu = y$ | "$x$ is left segment of $y$" |
| $y \geqslant x\colon (\exists u)\, ux = y$ | "$x$ is right segment of $y$" |
| $x \preceq y\colon (\exists uv)\, uxv = y$ | "$x$ occurs in $y$" |
| $x < y\colon (x \leqslant y) \wedge (x \neq y)$ | "$x$ is proper left segment of $y$" |
| $y > x\colon (y \geqslant x) \wedge (x \neq y)$ | "$x$ is proper right segment of $y$" |
| $\ln_x y$: number of occurrences of $x$ in $y$ | |

## VI. The Structure Lattice of $k$-Algebras

It seems clear that mathematical results concerning the following general problems will be of interest for the understanding of deterministic digital systems.

*Problem A*. To give a survey over all isomorphism types of finite reduced $k$-algebras.

*Problem B*. To decompose finite reduced $k$-algebras, i.e., to find operations of composition of $k$-algebras, such that every finite reduced $k$-algebra $\mathfrak{A}$ can be represented as a composite of $k$-algebras $\mathfrak{P}$, which are of simple structure.

As the algebraist would say, we would like to see significant contributions to the *structure theory* of finite reduced $k$-algebras. Of course these problems are not precisely stated. In fact, an essential part of the task at hand is to invent significant principles of ordering (A) and operations of composition (B) of (isomorphism types of) $k$-algebras. In this section we shall present the basic results which are available in case we choose $\mathfrak{A} \Rightarrow \mathfrak{B}$ (the homomorphism or quotient relation) as ordering, and $\mathfrak{A} \otimes \mathfrak{B}$ (the reduced product) as composition. It turns out that $\mathfrak{A} \Rightarrow \mathfrak{B}$ is a lattice order on reduced $k$-algebras, and $\mathfrak{A} \otimes \mathfrak{B}$ is the "join" operation in this lattice. Furthermore, every reduced $k$-algebra $\mathfrak{A}$ is decomposable into $\otimes$-indecomposable components.

### *1. Lattices*

A partially ordered set $\langle L, \leqslant \rangle$ is called a *lattice order* if the *meet* (greatest lower bound) $x \wedge y$, and the *join* (smallest upper bound) $x \vee y$ exist for any

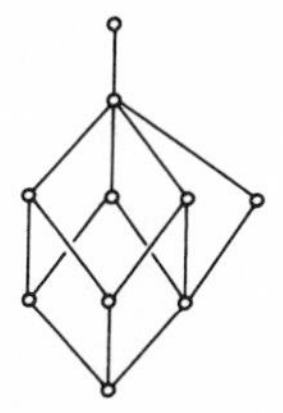

FIG. 7.

members $x, y$ of $L$. It is called a *complete lattice order* if the meet $\wedge_\gamma x_\gamma$ and the join $\wedge_\gamma x_\gamma$ exist for arbitrary families $\{x_\gamma\}$ of members of $L$. Note that

$$\bigvee_{\gamma} x_\gamma = \bigwedge_{(\forall \gamma) x\gamma \leqslant y} y \tag{21}$$

Thus, if all $\wedge$'s exist, so do all $\vee$'s, and $\langle L, \leqslant \rangle$ is a complete lattice. The join (meet) of the empty family of members of $L$, if it exists, is the smallest (largest) member of $L$. Thus a complete lattice order must possess a smallest element 0 and a largest element $e$. A finite lattice order is always complete, and can be represented by a diagram, as exemplified in Figs. 7 and 10. It is left to the reader to learn to understand such diagrams, i.e., to find out in which manner they represent a partial order $x \leqslant y$ on the vertices, and how one goes about finding $x \wedge y$ and $x \vee y$. A *lattice* $\langle L, \wedge, \vee \rangle$ is an algebra with two binary operations $\wedge$, $\vee$, which are meet and join of some partial order $\leqslant$ on $L$. Note that $x \leqslant y$ means $x = x \wedge y$ $(y = x \vee y)$.

A *complete lattice* $\langle L, \bigwedge, \bigvee \rangle$ is an algebra with infinitary operations, which are the operations of meet and join of a partial order on $L$.

A one-to-one mapping $h$ of $L_1$ onto $L_2$ is called an *anti-isomorphism* of the partial order $\langle L_1, \leqslant_1 \rangle$ onto $\langle L_2, \leqslant_2 \rangle$ if $(x \leqslant_1 y) \equiv (hy \leqslant_2 hx)$ holds for all $x, y \in L_1$. Clearly an anti-isomorphism $h$ takes meets into joins and vice versa, i.e.,

$$h(x \wedge y) = (hx \vee hy)$$
$$h(x \vee y) = (hx \wedge hy)$$

and similarly for $\bigwedge$ and $\bigvee$. We shall now discuss lattices of equivalence relations.

## 2. *Algebraic Closure Lattices*

Let $S$ be a set; let $\mathbf{L}$ be a set of subsets of $S$ such that $S \in \mathbf{L}$ and $\mathbf{L}$ is closed under intersection, i.e.,

$$\bigcap_{\gamma} X_\gamma \in \mathbf{L} \qquad \text{for any family } \{X_\gamma\} \text{ of members of } \mathbf{L} \tag{22}$$

Such a pair $\langle S, \mathbf{L} \rangle$ is called a *closure space*. The operation $U^c$, defined by

$$U^c = \bigcap_{U \subseteq X \in \mathbf{L}} X \qquad \text{for } U \subseteq S \tag{23}$$

is a closure operator on $S$, i.e., $U \subseteq U^c$, $(U \subseteq V) \supset (U^c \subseteq V^c)$, $U^{cc} = U^c$. $\mathbf{L}$ just consists of the closed sets $X = X^c$.

By remark (21) it is clear that $\langle \mathbf{L}, \subseteq \rangle$ is a complete lattice order. Its meet operation is the operation $\bigcap$ of set intersection; its join operation $\bigvee$ is defined by

$$\bigvee_{\gamma} X_\gamma = (\bigcup_{\gamma} X_\gamma)^c \qquad \text{for any family } \{X_\gamma\} \text{ of members of } \mathbf{L} \tag{24}$$

By a *closure lattice* we understand a complete lattice $\langle \mathbf{L}, \bigcap, \bigvee \rangle$ whose elements are subsets of a set $S$, whose largest element is $S$, and whose meet operation is set intersection; i.e., a closure lattice is the lattice of all closed sets of a closure space $\langle S, \mathbf{L} \rangle$. A closure lattice (and the corresponding space) is called *algebraic* if it satisfies either one of the following equivalent conditions:

$$\bigvee_{\gamma} X_\gamma = \bigcup_{\gamma_1, \ldots, \gamma_i} (X_{\gamma_1} \vee \cdots \vee X_{\gamma_i}) \qquad \text{for any family } \{X_\gamma\} \text{ in } \mathbf{L} \tag{25a}$$

$$\bigvee_{\gamma} X_\gamma = \bigcup_{\gamma} X_\gamma \qquad \text{for any directed family in } \mathbf{L} \tag{25b}$$

A family of sets $X_\gamma$ is called *directed* if to any two members $X_{\gamma_1}$ and $X_{\gamma_2}$ there is a third member $X_\gamma$, such that $(X_{\gamma_1} \cup X_{\gamma_2}) \subseteq X_\gamma$. It is left to the reader to show that (25a) and (25b) are equivalent, and in fact are equivalent to the assertion that $U^c$ is the union of closures $\{u_1, \ldots, u_i\}^c$ of all finite subsets of $U$.

Algebraic closure lattices naturally arise in algebra and logic. For example, one easily sees that the subalgebras of any algebra form an algebraic closure lattice. More important yet is the fact that all congruences on an algebra $\mathfrak{A}$ form an algebraic closure lattice $Cg(\mathfrak{A})$; below we shall show this for $k$-algebras. We shall now discuss a basic result of Birkhoff's and provide some hints to the proof.

**Definition 4.** Let $X$ be an element of the closure lattice $\langle \mathbf{L}, \bigcap, \bigvee \rangle$ over the set $S$. $X$ is called $\bigcap$*-irreducible* if $X \neq S$, and $X = \bigcap_\gamma X_\gamma$ implies that $X = X_\gamma$, for some member of the family $\{X_\gamma\}$ in $\mathbf{L}$. $X$ is called maximal relative $a \in S$ if $a \notin X$ and there is no $U \in \mathbf{L}$ such that $a \notin U$, $X \subset U$. $X$ is called maximal if $S$ is the only element of $\mathbf{L}$ which properly contains $X$.

Note that every maximal $X$ is relatively maximal. Furthermore, it is not hard to establish that

In every closure lattice $\langle \mathbf{L}, \bigcap, \bigvee \rangle$, the relatively maximal elements of $\mathbf{L}$ are exactly the $\bigcap$-irreducibles of $\mathbf{L}$. (26)

Birkhoff's theorem says that in an algebraic closure lattice every $X \in \mathbf{L}$ is an intersection of $\bigcap$-irreducibles; i.e.,

**Lemma 4.** In an algebraic closure lattice $\langle \mathbf{L}, \bigcap, \bigvee \rangle$ the $\bigcap$-irreducible (i.e., the relatively maximal elements) form a $\bigcap$-basis.

*Proof.* Let $Y \in \mathbf{L}$; let $\boldsymbol{M} = \{X;\ Y \subseteq X;\ X \text{ relatively maximal}\}$; let $Z$ be the intersection of all $X \in \boldsymbol{M}$. By (26) it is sufficient to show that $Y = Z$. But $Y \subseteq Z$ is obvious; thus it remains to show that $(a \notin Y) \supset (a \notin Z)$ for any $a \in S$. This is proved as follows (using the axiom of choice):

Suppose $a \notin Y$. Let $\mathbf{P} = \{X;\ Y \subseteq X \wedge a \notin X \in \mathbf{L}\}$. Clearly $Y \in \mathbf{P}$, so that $\mathbf{P}$ is not empty. Furthermore, from the assumption (25b) that the space is algebraic, it follows that $\mathbf{P}$ is closed under directed union. Therefore, by Zorn's lemma, $\mathbf{P}$ contains a maximal member $X_0$; i.e., (a) $Y \subseteq X_0$, (b) $a \notin X_0 \in \mathbf{L}$, and (c) $Y \subseteq X$, $a \notin X \in \mathbf{L}$ implies $X_0 \not\subset X$. Because of (b) and (c) $X_0$ is maximal relative $a$. Therefore by ($a$), $X_0 \in \boldsymbol{M}$. Thus we have $a \notin X_0 \in \boldsymbol{M}$, so that $a \notin Z$. Q.E.D.

*3. Lattices of Equivalence Relations*

It is easy to see that the intersection $\bigcap_\gamma E_\gamma$ of a family of equivalence relations $\{E_\gamma\}$ on a set **A** is again an equivalence relation on **A**. The set of all equivalence relations on **A** therefore forms a closure lattice $Eq(\mathbf{A})$. The smallest member of $Eq(\mathbf{A})$ is the equality relation $=(\mathbf{A})$ on the set **A**; the largest member is the universal relation $\mathbf{A} \times \mathbf{A}$. The join operation on equivalences will be denoted by $\bigsqcup$, while $X^e$ is used to denote the equivalence closure of the relation $X \subseteq \mathbf{A} \times \mathbf{A}$. Thus, by (23) and (24),

$$X^e = \text{intersection of all equivalence relations } E \text{ on } \mathbf{A},\ X \subseteq E$$
$$\bigsqcup_\gamma E_\gamma = (\bigcup_\gamma E_\gamma)^e \qquad \text{for any family of equivalences on } \mathbf{A} \tag{27}$$

$X^e$ is usually called the *equivalence relation generated* by the relation $X \subseteq \mathbf{A} \times \mathbf{A}$.

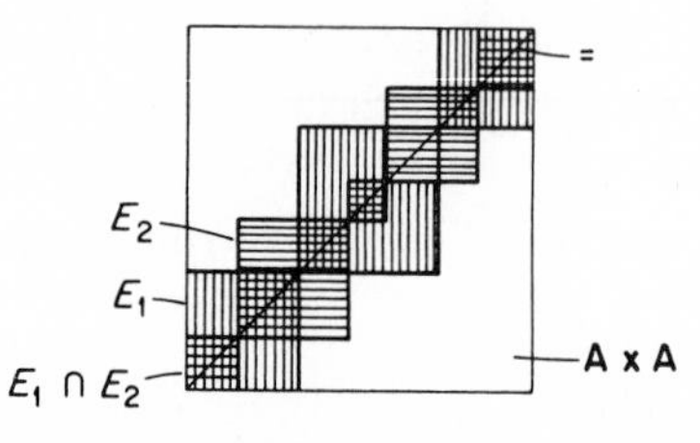


FIG. 8.

As shown in Fig. 8, there is a nice graphic way of thinking of equivalence relations and their intersection. (*Caution:* The picture depends on the order which is arbitrarily introduced among the members of **A**!) Also, it is well known that instead of talking about equivalences $E$ on **A**, one may talk about the corresponding partition of **A**. The reader should establish the meaning of $\subseteq, \cap$, and $\bigsqcup$ in terms of partition. The following are obvious remarks on the index of equivalence relations.

$$E_1 \subseteq E_2 . \supset . \operatorname{ind}(E_2) \leqslant \operatorname{ind}(E_1)$$
$$\operatorname{ind}(E_1 \cap E_2) \leqslant \operatorname{ind}(E_1) \cdot \operatorname{ind}(E_2) \tag{28}$$

We leave it to the reader to show that the closure operator $X^e$ on the set $\mathbf{A} \times \mathbf{A}$ is algebraic, i.e., $X^e = \bigcup U^e$, whereby $U$ ranges over all finite subrelations of $X$. Actually, we need this only in case $X$ is a symmetric relation; for these the assertion easily follows from

$$xR^e y . \equiv . (\exists x_0 \cdots x_m)[x_0 = x \wedge x_0 R x_1 \wedge \cdots \wedge x_{m-1} R x_m \wedge x_m = y] \qquad \text{if } R \text{ is symmetric} \tag{29}$$

To prove (29) one has to prove three facts about the relation $xSy$ defined by the expression on the right. Namely, (a) $S$ is an equivalence relation, (b) $R \subseteq S$, and (c) if $E$ is an equivalence and $R \subseteq E$, then $S \subseteq E$. These are easy to establish (and it seems clear how the expression for $S$ has to be modified in case $R$ is not symmetric). Using (29) and (27), and the fact that $\bigcup_\gamma E_\gamma$ is symmetric if the $E_\gamma$'s are equivalences, we obtain a more constructive method for finding the join of a family of equivalences:

$$x(\bigsqcup_\gamma E_\gamma)y \ .\equiv.\ (\exists_{\gamma_1}^{x_0} \cdots \exists_{\gamma_m}^{x_m})[x = x_0 \wedge x_0 E_{\gamma_1} x_1 \wedge \cdots \wedge x_{m-1} E_{\gamma_m} x_m \wedge x_m = y] \tag{30}$$

From (30) one easily proves that $Eq(\mathbf{A})$ is an algebraic closure space, i.e.,

$$\bigsqcup_\gamma E_\gamma = \bigcup_{\gamma_1,\ldots,\gamma_m} (E_{\gamma_1} \sqcup \cdots \sqcup E_{\gamma_m}) \qquad \text{for any family of equivalences} \tag{31}$$

We will now establish a second important consequence of (30). Let $\mathfrak{A} = \langle \mathbf{A}, A, f_1, \ldots, f_k \rangle$ be a $k$-algebra, and let $\{E_\gamma\}$ be a family of equivalence relations on $\mathbf{A}$ which are congruences of $\mathfrak{A}$, i.e., $(XE_\gamma Y) \supset (X^{f_i} E_\gamma Y^{f_i})$. From (30) it clearly follows that $\bigsqcup_\gamma E_\gamma$ is again a congruence relation of $\mathfrak{A}$.

**Theorem 1.** The congruence relations on a $k$-algebra $\mathfrak{A}$ form a closure lattice $Cg(\mathfrak{A})$. The join operation of this lattice is $\sqcup$, i.e., $Cg(\mathfrak{A})$ is a sublattice of $Eq(\mathbf{A})$. Furthermore, formula (31) holds in $Cg(\mathfrak{A})$, so that it is an algebraic closure lattice. In particular, the right congruences on the set of words $N_k$ form a closure lattice $Cg_k$. It is algebraic, and its join operation is $\sqcup$.

*Proof.* That the intersection $\bigcap_\gamma E_\gamma$ of congruences is again a congruence is easily seen. Therefore $Cg(\mathfrak{A})$ is a closure lattice. That $\bigsqcup_\gamma E_\gamma$ is a congruence, if the $E_\gamma$'s are, was shown above. Thus $\sqcup$ is the join operation of $Cg(\mathfrak{A})$, and by (31) the lattice is algebraic. Q.E.D.

As a consequence of Lemma 4 and Theorem 1 we obtain

**Corollary 1.** Every congruence $E$ of a $k$-algebra $\mathfrak{A}$ is an intersection $E = \bigcap_\gamma P_\gamma$ of $\bigcap$-irreducible congruences $P_\gamma$ of $\mathfrak{A}$. In particular, every right congruence $E$ on $N_k$ is the intersection of $\bigcap$-irreducible right congruences.

It remains to discuss the congruence-closure-operator $R^c$ = intersection of all congruence relations $X$ on $\mathfrak{A}$, $R \subseteq X$. $R^c$ is also called the *congruence generated* by the relation $R \subseteq \mathbf{A} \times \mathbf{A}$. We leave it to the reader to show that $R^c$ can be calculated as follows. If $R_i, E_i$ are defined inductively by

$$R_0 = R \qquad E_i = R_i^e \tag{32}$$

$$XR_{i+1}\, Y \ .\equiv.\ XE_i\, Y \vee X^{f_1} E_i\, Y^{f_1} \vee \cdots \vee X^{f_k} E_i\, Y^{f_k}$$

then

$$R^c = \bigcup_{i=0}^{\infty} E_i$$

Note that if $\mathfrak{A}$ is finite and has $n$ states, then for some $j \leqslant 2^{(n^2)}$, $E_{j+1} = E_j$. If this holds for $j$, then $R = E_j$.

*Example 3.* Let $\mathfrak{A}$ be the $k$-algebra, on the set of states $\mathbf{A} = \{1,2,3,4,5\}$, Exercise 4(c). Using the method described above one easily finds the congruences induced by the relations $R \subseteq \mathbf{A} \times \mathbf{A}$, starting with one-member relations. This process yields 10 congruences of $\mathfrak{A}$. Inspection will show that the lattice $Cg(\mathfrak{A})$ is that of Fig. 7. We leave it to the reader to mark the five $\bigcap$-irreducible elements (just one of them is maximal), and to verify Corollary 1. Note that the decomposition into $\bigcap$-irreducibles is not unique!

## 4. *The Structure Lattice of k-Algebras*

In the sequel we shall follow the common practice of talking about the $k$-algebra $\mathfrak{A}$, when in fact we mean its isomorphism-type $\mathfrak{A}^{\simeq}$. In other words, we "identify" isomorphic $k$-algebras. Note that this ambiguity is even less dangerous than usual, because we are dealing with reduced algebras (the isomorphism between reduced algebras is unique if it exists, and a reduced algebra cannot be isomorphic to a proper subalgebra).

As announced at the beginning of this section, we wish to study the relation $\mathfrak{B} \Rightarrow \mathfrak{A}$ (i.e., $\mathfrak{A}$ is a homomorphic image of $\mathfrak{B}$) between all homomorphic images of a reduced $k$-algebra $\mathfrak{C}$. It is easy to see that this is a partial order. Furthermore, Lemma 3 (which easily extends to general reduced products) says that $\mathfrak{A} \otimes \mathfrak{B}$ is the join operation in this partial order. Thus all homomorphic images of a reduced $k$-algebra $\mathfrak{A}$ form a complete lattice $SL(\mathfrak{A})$ relative $\Rightarrow$, and the reduced product $\otimes$ is the join operation in this lattice. We call $SL(\mathfrak{A})$ the *structure lattice* of $\mathfrak{A}$. We already know from Lemma 2 that $E \to \mathfrak{A}/E$ establishes a one-to-one map of the congruences of $\mathfrak{A}$ onto the homomorphic images of $\mathfrak{A}$. This map is in fact an anti-isomorphism of $Cg(\mathfrak{A})$ onto $SL(\mathfrak{A})$.

**Theorem 2.** The structure lattice $SL(\mathfrak{A})$ of a reduced $k$-algebra $\mathfrak{A}$ is anti-isomorphic to the lattice $Cg(\mathfrak{A})$ of all congruences on $\mathfrak{A}$. The anti-isomorphism from $Cg(\mathfrak{A})$ onto $SL(\mathfrak{A})$ is given by $E \to \mathfrak{A}/E$, i.e.

$$\begin{aligned} &E_1 \subseteq E_2 \,.\!\equiv\!.\, (\mathfrak{A}/E_2) \Leftarrow (\mathfrak{A}/E_1) \qquad \text{for congruences } E_1, E_2 \text{ on } \mathfrak{A} \\ &\mathfrak{A}/(\bigcap_{\gamma} E_\gamma) = \bigotimes_{\gamma} (\mathfrak{A}/E_\gamma) \qquad \text{for a family } \{E_\gamma\} \text{ of congruences on } \mathfrak{A} \end{aligned} \tag{33}$$

In particular, the structure lattice $SL_k$ of the free $k$-algebra $\mathfrak{F}_k$ is anti-isomorphic to the lattice $Cg_k$ of all right congruences on $N_k$. The anti-isomorphism is given by $\mathfrak{C} \to \perp(\mathfrak{C})$; its inverse is $E \to \mathfrak{F}_k/E$; i.e.,

$$\mathfrak{C}_1 \Leftarrow \mathfrak{C}_2 \,.\!\equiv\!.\, \perp(\mathfrak{C}_2) \subseteq \perp(\mathfrak{C}_1) \qquad \text{for reduced } k\text{-algebras}$$
$$E_1 \subseteq E_2 \,.\!\equiv\!.\, (\mathfrak{F}_k/E_2) \Leftarrow (\mathfrak{F}_k/E_1) \qquad \text{for right congruences on } N_k \qquad (34)$$

*Proof.* Suppose $E_1 \subseteq E_2$ are congruences on the reduced $k$-algebra $\mathfrak{A}$. Let $X^{E_i}$ denote the congruence class, modulo $E_i$, of the state $X$ of $\mathfrak{A}$. Then clearly $X^{E_1} \to X^{E_2}$ is a homomorphism of $\mathfrak{A}/E_1$ onto $\mathfrak{A}/E_2$. Thus $E_1 \subseteq E_2$ implies $(\mathfrak{A}/E_2) \Leftarrow (\mathfrak{A}/E_1)$. Suppose next that $(\mathfrak{A}/E_2) \Leftarrow (\mathfrak{A}/E_1)$. Let $h$ be the homomorphism. Then $gX = h(X^{E_1})$ is a homomorphism from $\mathfrak{A}$ onto $\mathfrak{A}/E_2$. Because $\mathfrak{A}$ is reduced, there is but one homomorphism of $\mathfrak{A}$ onto $\mathfrak{A}/E_2$, namely, $X \to X^{E_2}$. Consequently, $gX = X^{E_2}$, i.e., $h(X^{E_1}) = X^{E_2}$. Therefore we have $(X^{E_1} = Y^{E_1}) \supset (X^{E_2} = Y^{E_2})$, i.e., $(XE_1\,Y) \supset (XE_2\,Y)$, i.e., $E_1 \subseteq E_2$. Thus, $(\mathfrak{A}/E_2) \Leftarrow (\mathfrak{A}/E_1)$ implies $E_1 \subseteq E_2$. This establishes the first formula (33); i.e., $Cg(\mathfrak{A})$ is anti-isomorphic to $SL(\mathfrak{A})$.

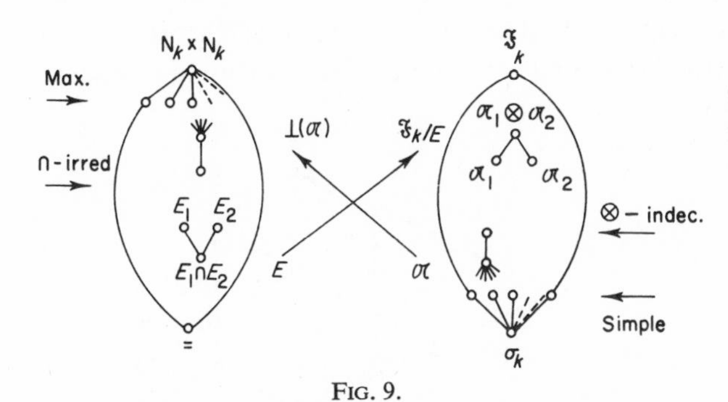


FIG. 9.

The second part of (33) follows, because an anti-isomorphism takes meets into joins, and we have already seen (Lemma 2) that $\otimes$ is the join in the lattice $SL(\mathfrak{A})$. The rest of Theorem 2 is just a restatement of the first part, in the special case $\mathfrak{A} = \mathfrak{F}_k$. Q.E.D.

A reduced $k$-algebra $\mathfrak{A}$ is called $\otimes$-*indecomposable* (reduced directly indecomposable) if $\mathfrak{A} = \otimes_\gamma \mathfrak{C}_\gamma$ implies $\mathfrak{A} \simeq \mathfrak{C}_\gamma$ for some member of the family $\{\mathfrak{C}_\gamma\}$.

**Corollary 2.** Every reduced $k$-algebra $\mathfrak{A}$ is isomorphic to a reduced product $\otimes_\gamma \mathfrak{P}_\gamma$ of $\otimes$-indecomposable reduced $k$-algebras $\mathfrak{P}_\gamma$.

This clearly follows from Theorem 1, Corollary 1, and the remark that a right congruence $E$ is $\bigcap$-irreducible if and only if its quotient $\mathfrak{F}/_kE$ is $\otimes$-indecomposable. We remark further that the maximal right congruences

$E$ on $N_k$ correspond to the *simple* reduced $k$-algebras. A reduced $k$-algebra $\mathfrak{A}$ is called simple if the one-state algebra $\mathfrak{O}_k$ and $\mathfrak{A}$ are the only homomorphic images of $\mathfrak{A}$. In other words, $\mathfrak{A}$ is simple if it admits no congruence, except the equality and universal relations. Figure 9 represents the anti-isomorphism between the lattices $Cg_k$ and $SL_k$.

*Example 4*. Figure 10 shows the structure lattice $SL(\mathfrak{B})$ of the 2-algebra $\mathfrak{B}$ given by Table 8; the $\otimes$-indecomposable elements are marked. We leave it to the reader to develop his own streamlined method of finding all homo-

TABLE 8

| | 0 | 1 | 2 | 3 | 4 | 5 | 6 | 7 | 8 | 9 |
|---|---|---|---|---|---|---|---|---|---|---|
| $f_1$ | 1 | 3 | 5 | 7 | 4 | 8 | 8 | 3 | 6 | 9 |
| $f_2$ | 2 | 4 | 6 | 4 | 3 | 9 | 6 | 7 | 9 | 8 |

morphic images of $\mathfrak{B}$. It seems quite clear that Theorem 2 is of much help; it is easier to manipulate congruences than homomorphisms. We have

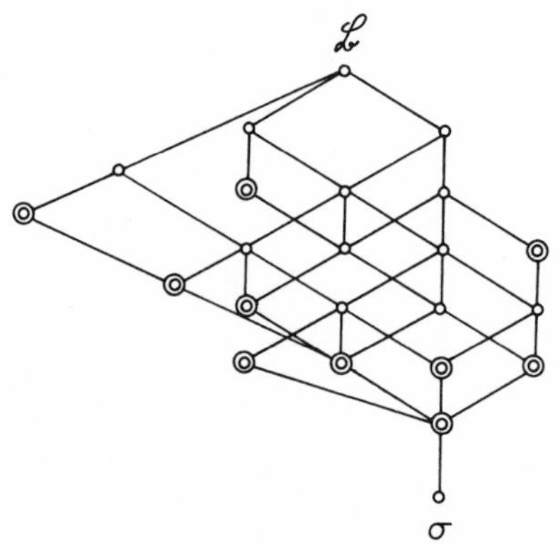


FIG. 10.

chosen this example because it shows how bad structure lattices of reduced $k$-algebras can get. Note the following features:

a. The representation of $\mathfrak{B}$ as a reduced product of indecomposable algebras is far from unique. There are very different irredundant decompositions of $\mathfrak{B}$.

b. Some of the indecomposable members of $SL(\mathfrak{B})$ are not small, in any obvious sense. Compare their strange distribution in $SL(\mathfrak{B})$ with the orderly one in $SL_1$.

c. There are maximal chains from $\mathfrak{O}$ to $\mathfrak{B}$, which are of different length. The lattice is not modular nor even semimodular.

Of course, the idea of studying the structure of an algebra via congruences is not new. What we have done here is to show that, by choosing the proper mathematical formulation, these classical algebraic methods become available in the study of finite automata. To the algebraist our presentation of Corollary 2 may be of interest. This is just another version of Birkhoff's result: Every universal algebra is a subdirect product of subdirectly indecomposable algebras.

We do not want to give the impression that the basic lattice-theoretic results, discussed in this section, settle the structure theory of finite reduced $k$-algebras. On the contrary, there are good reasons to suspect that this structure theory is just as difficult and interesting a field as the structure theory of finite monoids and groups. Much solid mathematical work is needed to make the lattice-theoretic approach more significant (see Problems 1, 2, 3 below). Furthermore, there are very natural non-lattice-theoretic operations on $k$-algebras, which might be the key to a satisfactory structure theory (see Problem 3 below). We mention only the idea of cascading, where an output of the $k$-algebra $\mathfrak{A}$ is used to drive (part of) the input of a $k$-algebra $\mathfrak{B}$. Finally, we would like to stress that Corollary 2 is trivial for finite algebras. Thus, as far as the lattice $SL_k^0$ of all finite reduced $k$-algebras is concerned, we are left with only the most elementary results.

In spite of the present lack of deeper results concerning the structure of finite reduced $k$-algebras, investigating the lattice $SL(\mathfrak{A})$ of a particular finite $\mathfrak{A}$ might still yield practical information on $\mathfrak{A}$. Furthermore, in the case of finite commutative $k$-algebras, the lattice-theoretic approach can actually be worked out to yield a satisfactory structure theory, and it is quite reasonable to expect that this systematic survey should be of interest to people who design counters. Finally, we remark that congruences and the forming of quotients are the basis for a clear understanding of minimality algorithms for finite automata. Minimality and Kleene's theory of behavior will be presented as Part II of these lectures.

## PROBLEMS

1. Classify the simple and $\otimes$-indecomposable finite reduced $k$-algebras; i.e., give a survey over all maximal and $\bigcap$-irreducible right congruences on $N_k$.

2. Investigate the nonuniqueness of $\otimes$-decompositions for finite reduced $k$-algebras.

3. Characterize those lattices which are isomorphic to $SL(\mathfrak{A})$, for some finite reduced $k$-algebra $\mathfrak{A}$.

4. Even in the case $k = 1$, the relationship between simple (primes) and $\otimes$-indecomposables (prime powers) can be better understood if nonlattice operations (product, powers) are considered. Is there a reasonable operation on $k$-algebras, which would clear up these matters for $k \geqslant 2$?

*Exercise 5*

(a) Draw the lattice $Eq$ of all equivalence relations on the set $\{1,2,3,4\}$.

(b) Find the relation $(s,p) \Leftarrow (r,q)$ and the operation $(s,p) \otimes (r,q)$ on pairs of natural numbers, which correspond to the relation $\mathfrak{A}_{s,p} \Leftarrow \mathfrak{A}_{r,q}$ and the operation $\mathfrak{A}_{s,p} \otimes \mathfrak{A}_{r,q}$ on finite reduced 1-algebras. Draw the structure lattice $SL(\mathfrak{A}_{2,12})$. Which $\mathfrak{A}_{s,p}$ are simple, which are $\otimes$-indecomposable? Show that the structure lattice $SL_1$ (all reduced 1-algebras) is isomorphic to the lattice of divisibility on natural numbers, i.e., isomorphic to the infinite direct power of the lattice $\langle N, \leqslant \rangle$. (Consequently, $SL_1$ is distributive!) Which is the irredundant $\otimes$-representation of $\mathfrak{A}_{s,p}$?

(c) Let the 2-algebra $\mathfrak{A}$ be given by Table 9. Find the congruence $E$ generated by (the relation whose only element is) the pair $BC$. Find the transition tree of $\mathfrak{A}/E$. This process is called *merging of the states* $B, C$ of $\mathfrak{A}$.

TABLE 9

| | $A$ | $B$ | $C$ | $D$ | $E$ | $F$ | $G$ | $H$ |
|---|---|---|---|---|---|---|---|---|
| $f_1$ | $B$ | $D$ | $F$ | $H$ | $C$ | $H$ | $H$ | $F$ |
| $f_2$ | $C$ | $E$ | $G$ | $D$ | $B$ | $D$ | $C$ | $G$ |

(d) Construct a 2-algebra $\mathfrak{A}$ whose equi-response relation is

$$E = E_1 \cap E_2 \cap E_4.$$

$E_1, E_2, E_4$ are given by the corresponding expressions in Exercise 4b. *Hint:* Use the reduced-product operation.

(e) Work out Examples 2 and 4. Note that $\mathfrak{A}$ occurs in $SL(\mathfrak{B})$.

REFERENCES

1. S. C. Kleene, Representation of events in nerve nets and finite automata, *Automata Studies*, Princeton University Press, Princeton, N.J., 1956, pp. 3–41.
2. G. Birkhoff, *Lattice Theory*, Am. Math. Soc., New York, 1948.

3. J. R. Büchi, On a decision method in restricted second order arithmetic, in *Proc. Intern. Congr. Logic Phil. Sci.*, Stanford University Press, Stanford, Calif., 1962, pp. 1–11.
4. J. R. Büchi, Weak second order arithmetic and finite automata, *Z. Math. Logik und Grundlagenforschung der Math.* **6**, 66–92 (1960).
5. A. Church, Logic, Arithmetic, and Automata. *Proc. Intern. Congr. Math.*, Stockholm, 1962, pp. 23–35.
6. A. W. Burks and J. B. Wright, Theory of logical nets, *Proc. IRE* **41**, 1357–65 (1953).
7. A. Church, Application of recursive arithmetic to the problem of circuit synthesis, in *Proc. Logic Conf.*, Cornell University, Ithaca, New York, 1957.

# Une Méthode de Généralisation d'Algorithmes de la Théorie des Graphes en Algèbre Linéaire

P. CAMION[1]

*EURATOM–CETIS, Ispra (Varese)*
*Italy*

## I. Introduction

On connait les propriétés remarquables, [1], [2], des modules des flots et des tensions sur un graphe orienté. L'objet de notre recherche a été de trouver la généralisation de ces propriétés dans certains sous-modules des modules sur un anneau d'intégrité totalement ordonné, dans l'esprit de [3] et en se guidant sur les résultats de [4]. Des résultats plus généraux obtenus, on déduit immédiatement des propriétés des cycles et des cocycles d'un graphe. De plus la généralisation du lemme de Minty des arcs colorés permet de trouver en programmation linéaire des algorithmes correspondant à ceux qui utilisent ce lemme en théorie des graphes [5].

*Graphe.* Un graphe est défini par un ensemble fini de sommets $X$ et un ensemble $Y$ de couples ordonnés de sommets appelés arcs. Les deux sommets de l'arc sont ses extrémités.

## II. Cycle Elémentaire

Sous ensemble $\mu$ d'arcs de $Y$ tel que si un sommet est l'extrémité d'un arc de $\mu$, il est l'extrémité d'exactement deux arcs de $\mu$.

## III. Cocycle Elémentaire

Tout $A \subset X$ définit un cocycle $\omega(A)$ qui est l'ensemble des arcs ayant une extrémité dans $A$ et l'autre dans $X - A$. Un cocycle qui n'est pas la réunion de cocycles non vides est élémentaire.

$$\mu = \mu^+ \cup \mu^-$$

[1] *Present address:* Faculté des Sciences, Université de Toulouse, France.

où $\mu^+$ est l'ensemble des arcs orientés dans le sens d'un parcours et $\mu^-$ l'ensemble $\mu - \mu^+$.

$$\omega = \omega^+ \cup \omega^-$$

où $\omega^+$ est l'ensemble des arcs orientés de $A$ vers $X - A$ et $\omega^-$ l'ensemble $\omega - \omega^+$.

Soit $S$ un anneau d'intégrité; pour nous, $S$ sera soit l'anneau $Z$ des entiers rationnels, soit le corps $Q$ des nombres rationnels, soit le corps $R$ des nombres réels ou les anneaux de polynômes à coefficients dans $Z$, $Q$, ou $R$. Chaque élément $x$ d'un module sur $S$ ayant une base finie $Y$ de $m$ éléments peut être défini par ses coordonnées dans $Y$, donc $x = (x_j)_{j \in Y}$. Réciproquement, l'ensemble des $m$-tuples $(x_j)_{j \in Y}$, $x_j \in S$, avec la base $Y$ définissent le module $S^m$. Les modules que nous étudierons sont des sous-modules de $S^m$, $Y$ étant fixée. Il seront définis par les propriétés de leurs composantes dans $Y$.

Pour les modules que nous définirons sur un graphe, la base $Y$ sera confondue avec l'ensemble des arcs du graphe. Module $\Phi$ des *flots* d'un graphe.

$$x = (x_j)_{j \in Y},\ x_j \in S$$

est un flot si, et seulement si, pour tout cocycle élémentaire $\omega$:

$$\sum_{j \in \omega^+} x_j = \sum_{j \in \omega^-} x_j$$

Module $\Theta$ des *tensions* d'un graphe.

$$x = (x_j)_{j \in Y},\ x_j \in S$$

est une tension si, et seulement si, pour tout cycle élémentaire $\mu$:

$$\sum_{j \in \mu^+} x_j = \sum_{j \in \mu^-} x_j$$

On trouvera de nombreuses propriétés de ces modules dans [1, 2].

*Support* $s(x)$ d'un flot (tension) $x$ pour la base $Y$:

$$s(x) = \{i \mid i \in Y \text{ and } x_i \neq 0\}$$

$x$ est un flot (tension) de *support minimal* si pour tout flot (tension) $y$,

$$s(y) \subset s(x) \to y = x \text{ ou } y = 0$$

## IV. Vecteur-Cycle, Vecteur-Cocycle

Au cycle $\mu$ on associe le vecteur dont les composantes sont 1 dans $\mu^+$, $-1$ dans $\mu^-$ et 0 partout ailleurs. On définit de façon analogue un vecteur cocycle. Rappelons quelques propriétés.

**Propriété 1.** *Un flot (tension) de support minimal est multiple d'un vecteur-cycle (vecteur-cocycle).*

*Matrice d'incidence $A$* d'un graphe $(X, Y)$. Chaque sommet de $(X, Y)$ définit un cocycle élémentaire, donc un vecteur-cocycle. Les vecteurs-lignes de $A$ sont les vecteur-cocycles définis par les sommets de $(X, Y)$. Supposons de plus que $S$ possède l'élément unité 1.

**Propriété 2.** *Le module des tensions $\Theta(A, Y)$ est le module engendré par les vecteurs-lignes de $A$, le module des flots $\Phi(A, Y)$ est le module orthogonal de $\Theta(A, Y)$.*

*Matrice principale de $A$.* Si $A$ est une matrice $n \times m$ sur $S$, $A_J$ définie par un sous-ensemble $J$ de $n$ colonnes de $A$ est principale si $\text{Dét}(A_J) \neq 0$.

*Matrice localement unimodulaire sur $S$.* Matrice sur $S$ dont toutes les sous-matrices principales ont des déterminants inversibles sur $S$.

**Propriété 3.** *La matrice formée d'un sous-ensemble de vecteurs lignes linéairement indépendants de la matrice d'incidence d'un graphe, est localement unimodulaire sur $Z$.*

Un *u-module* $\Theta(A, Y)$ est le module engendré par les vecteurs lignes d'une matrice localement unimodulaire sur $S$.

**Théorème** (*W. Tutte*). *$\Theta(A, Y)$ est un u-module si et seulement si tout vecteur de support minimal est multiple d'un vecteur à coordonnées inversibles ou nulles.*

W. Tutte a démontré ce théorème pour $S = Z$, nous l'avons démontré pour $S$, anneau d'intégrité.

Donc, parmi les vecteurs d'un *u*-module, ayant même support minimal, il en existe au moins un dont les composantes sont inversibles ou nulles. Nous appellerons *vecteur élémentaire* un tel vecteur. Nous démontrons:

**Propriété 4.** *Les vecteurs-lignes des transformées principales de $A$ sont les vecteurs élémentaires de $\Theta(A, Y)$.*

**Propriété 5.** *Le module orthogonal $\Phi(A, Y)$ d'un u-module $\Theta(A, Y)$ est u-module.*

Soit $S$ un anneau d'intégrité totalement ordonné. Soient $\Gamma_{i(i \in Y)}$ une famille d'intervalles de $S$ tels que chaque intervalle borné inférieurement (supérieurement) a un infemum (supremum).

Soit $M = \{x | Ax = b\}$ où $A$ est une matrice $n \times m$ localement unimodulaire sur $S$ et $b$ un élément de $S^n$. Soit

$$\Gamma = \Gamma_1 \times \Gamma_2 \cdots \times \Gamma_m$$

**Théorème.** *$M \cap \Gamma \neq \phi$ si et seulement si pour tout vecteur élémentaire $x = tA$, $tb \in \Sigma_{i \in Y} x_i \Gamma_i$.*

Un théorème proche de celui-ci, dans le cas où $Z = S$ et $A \geqslant 0$ a été démontré par A. J. Hoffman [4].

Le théorème ci-dessus permet de vérifier dans les $u$-modules de nombreuses propriétés connues pour les modules de flots et de tensions d'un graphe.

Enonçons dans une forme un peu moins générale que dans [5] une généralisation du lemme de Minty. Partionnons arbitrairement l'ensemble $Y$ des axes en trois parties, celle des axes noirs, des axes rouges et des axes verts. Soit $j$ un axe noir.

**Lemme.** Il existe dans l'$u$-module $\Theta(A, Y)$ un vecteur élémentaire ayant sa composante $j$ non nulle et des composantes non nulles uniquement rouges et noires, les composantes nonnulles noires étant positives, si et seulement s'il n'existe pas dans l'$u$-module orthogonal $\Phi(A, Y)$ un vecteur élémentaire ayant sa composante $j$ nonnulle et des composantes nonnulles uniquement vertes et noires, ses composantes non nulles noires étant positives.

Nous observons que dans tous les cas que nous connaissons où un algorithme sur un graphe peut être basé sur le lemme de Minty (C. Berge a montré qu'ils étaient nombreux), l'algorithme peut être étendu aux $u$-modules. En particulier l'algorithme de Ford et Fulberson fournit un algorithme de programmation linéaire (par exemple $S = R$) où l'on peut partir d'un point intérieur au polyèdre et aboutir à la solution en un nombre fini d'étapes. On peut aussi généraliser le théorème et l'algorithme de T. C. Hu [6].

Donnons pour terminer à titre d'exemple une propriété des $u$-modules d'où l'on peut déduire deux propriétés connues de la théorie des graphes.

**Propriété 6.** *Si un u-module contient un vecteur à composantes toutes* $\geqslant 1$, *il est engendré par ses vecteurs élémentaires non négatifs.*

On en déduit: "Un graphe fortement connexe possède une base de circuits" et "Un graphe sans circuits possède une base de cocircuits."

La conclusion de ceci en ce qui concerne la théorie des graphes est que l'on devrait y modifier certaines définitions de manière à ne plus privilégier les cocycles associés aux sous-ensembles de sommets réduits à un seul élément.

Un *(co)circuit hamiltonien* [7] serait alors: (co)circuit élémentaire avec un arc dans chaque cocycle (cycle). Un *graphe complet* [7] serait un graphe pour lequel deux cocycles quelconques ont un arc en commun.

Certains resultats de [5] avaient été obtenus dans [8] en généralisant les modules de flots et tensions à des $u$-modules, sous-modules des $Z$ modules $G^m$, $G$ étant un groupe abélien.

Après une discussion avec M. Schützenberger nous avons repris ce travail qui a abouti à [5].

## Références

1. C. Berge, Les problèmes de flot et de tension, *Cahiers Centre Etudes* K.O. **3**[2] (1961).
2. C. Berge et A. Ghouila-Houri, *Programmes linéaires, jeux et problèmes de transport*, Dunod, Paris, 1962.
3. W. T. Tutté, A ring in graph theory, *Proc. Cambridge Phil. Soc.* **43** (1947); A class of abelian groups, *Can. J. Math.* **8**, 13–28 (1953).
4. A. J. Hoffman, Some recent applications of the theory of linear inequalities to extremal combinatorial analysis, *Proc. Symp. Appl. Math.* **10**.
5. P. Camion, Inégalités linéaires sur un anneau d'intégrité totalement ordonné, *J. Can. Math.* (à paraître).
6. T. C. Hu, Multicommodity network flows, *J.* O.R.S.A. **11**[3] (1963).
7. C. Berge, *Theorie des graphes et ses applications*, Dunod, Paris, 1958.
8. P. Camion, Matrices totalements unimodulaires et problèmes combinatoires. Thèse, Université de Bruxelles, Fevriér 1963, et Rapport Euratom.

# $m$-Valued Logics and $m$-Ary Selection Functions

ALFONSO CARACCIOLO DI FORINO

*Centro Studi Calcolatrici Elettroniche del C.N.R.*
*Pisa, Italy*

## I. Introduction

In this lecture we are going to present some basic results concerning the relationship between $m$-valued logics and the concept of $m$-ary selection function (as defined in [1]), which is essentially equivalent, as already noted there, to McCarthy's concept of "conditional expression" [2].

## II. $m$-Valued Logics

An $m$-valued logic is, by definition, a calculus of "proposition" which may take one out of $m$ truth values $t_1, \ldots, t_m$.

Historically, the concept of many-valued logics has arisen from the concept of modal logics, which are logical systems which classify proposition under a richer variety than the classical binary truth-value dichotomy: *true, false*. The first modern treatment of modal logics is due to Lewis [3], who introduced a kind of five-valued modal logic: *true*, *false*, *possible*, *impossible*, *necessary*.

A different, more abstract approach was taken a few years later by Post [4] with his "general theory of elementary propositions," and, wholly independent of him, by Lukasiewicz with his system of three-valued logics [5], later extended by himself and Tarski [6] to the $m$-valued case.

The Lukasiewicz-Tarski approach consists in extending to $m$-valued logics the theory of implication based on a generalization of the two-valued logical connectives *Cpq* (material implication) and *Nq* (negation) by defining them by means of the following truth tables, Tables 1 and 2, which obviously reduce, for $m = 2$, to the classical two-valued truth tables, Table 3.

TABLE 1

| $Cpq$ | $t_1 t_2 - t_m$ |
|---|---|
| $t_1$ | $t_1 t_2 - t_m$ |
| $t_2$ | $t_1 t_1 - t_{m-1}$ |
| ... | ......... |
| $t_m$ | $t_1 t_1 - t_1$ |

$Ctptq = t_{\max(1,\,1+p-q)} \qquad (p, q = 1, m)$

TABLE 2

| | $Np$ |
|---|---|
| $t_1$ | $t_n$ |
| $t_2$ | $t_{m-1}$ |
| ... | ..... |
| $t_n$ | $t_1$ |

$Nt_p = t_{n-p} \qquad (p = 1, m)$

TABLE 3

| $Cpq$ | $t_1$ | $t_2$ |
|---|---|---|
| $t_1$ | $t_1$ | $t_2$ |
| $t_2$ | $t_1$ | $t_1$ |

| | $Np$ |
|---|---|
| $t_1$ | $t_2$ |
| $t_2$ | $t_1$ |

The Lukasiewicz-Tarski system has later [7] been shown to be "incomplete" in the sense that it is impossible to define an arbitrary $m$-valued logical connective characterized by an arbitrary truth table as a combination of the two basic connectives $C$, $N$.

A complete system has been obtained by Post (the very notion of completeness is due to him), who based his system [4] on the extension of the connectives $A$ (or) and $S$ (negation) given in Tables 4 and 5, where $\oplus$ denotes the sum modulo $m$.

As for two-valued logics, it is possible to define $m$-valued complete logical systems based on a single $m$-valued connective. Any such logic will be called a Sheffer logic and any single connective which gives rise to a complete logical system is called a Sheffer connective. It can be shown that for $m = 3$ there is a very large number of such Sheffer connectives [8], and this number increases very rapidly with increasing $m$.

TABLE 4

| $Apq$ | $t_1 t_2 - t_m$ |
|---|---|
| $t_1$ | $t_1 t_1 - t_1$ |
| $t_2$ | $t_1 t_2 - t_2$ |
| ... | ......... |
| $t_m$ | $t_1 t_2 - t_m$ |

$Atptq = t_{\max(p,q)} \qquad (p, q = 1, m)$

TABLE 5

| | $Sp$ |
|---|---|
| $t_1$ | $t_2$ |
| $t_2$ | $t_3$ |
| ... | ... |
| $t_{m-1}$ | $t_m$ |
| $t_m$ | $t_1$ |

$St_p = St_{p \oplus 1} \qquad (p = 1, m)$

As an example of a Sheffer connective (definable in the Post system but not in the Lukasiewicz-Tarski system) we can cite the two-place "not-or" connective:

$$Fpq = SApq$$

## III. Logical Systems

In order to define as abstractly as possible an $m$-valued logical system we shall proceed, following Halmos [9], by defining a logical system as a set of expressions together with an appropriate equivalence relation.

To proceed in the most general way, we shall define an $m$-valued logic as a system $\left(A(B, C, \varphi), \underset{Q/L}{\approx}\right)$, where:

(a) $A(B, C, \varphi)$ is a "closed set of algebraic expressions" consisting of the set $\hat{B}$ of expressions recursively defined as follows:

$$\sigma \in B \Rightarrow \sigma \in \hat{B} \tag{1}$$

$$K \in C;\ \sigma_1, \ldots, \sigma_{\varphi(K)} \in \hat{B} \Rightarrow K\sigma_1 - \sigma_{\varphi(K)} \in \hat{B} \tag{2}$$

where $B$ is any set of basic symbols, $C$ is a finite set of "connectives," and $\varphi\colon C \to \{1,2,\ldots\}$ is a mapping defining for each $K \in C$ the number of its "arguments."

(b) $\underset{Q/L}{\approx}$ is an equivalence relation on $\hat{B}$ depending on a family $L$ of "finite functions"

$$L = \{f_K\colon \mathcal{N}^{\varphi(K)} \to \mathcal{N}\}_{K \in C} \qquad \mathcal{N} = \{1, 2, \ldots, m\} \tag{3}$$

and defined by the condition

$$\forall \alpha', \alpha'' \in \hat{B}\colon \alpha' \underset{Q/L}{\approx} \alpha'' \qquad \text{iff} \quad \eta(\alpha') = \hat{\eta}(\alpha'') \tag{4}$$

where $\hat{\eta}$ is the mapping

$$\hat{\eta}\colon \hat{B} \to \mathcal{N} \tag{5}$$

obtained by extending to $\hat{B}$ an arbitrary basic mapping (valuation)

$$\eta\colon B \to \mathcal{N} \tag{6}$$

in such a way that

$$\forall \sigma \in B\colon \hat{\eta}(\sigma) = \eta(\sigma) \tag{7}$$

$$\forall K \in C;\ \forall \sigma_1, \ldots, \sigma_{\varphi(K)} \in \hat{B}\colon \hat{\eta}(K\sigma_1 - \sigma_{\varphi(K)}) = f_K(\hat{\eta}(\sigma_1), \ldots, \hat{\eta}(\sigma_{\varphi(K)})) \tag{8}$$

For instance, the Lukasiewicz-Tarski system will be defined as the system

$$\left(A_{LT}(B, C_{LT}, \varphi_{LT}), \underset{Q/L_{LT}}{\approx}\right)$$

where $B$ is any set of elementary symbols, $C_{LT} = \{C, N\}$, $\varphi_{LT}(C) = 2$, $\varphi_{LT}(N) = 1$, and $L_{LT} = \{f_C, f_N\}$ is defined as

$$f_C(p, q) = \max_{(1, 1+p-q)} \qquad p, q \in \mathcal{N}$$
$$f_N(p) = (m - p) \qquad p \in \mathcal{N}$$

In the same way the Post system is defined as the system

$$\left(A_{PS}(B, C_{PS}, N_{PS}), \underset{Q/L_{PS}}{\approx}\right)$$

where $B$ is any set of elementary symbols, $C = \{A, S\}$, $\varphi_{PS}(S) = 1$, $\varphi_{PS}(A) = 2$, and $L_{PS} = \{f_A, f_S\}$ is defined as

$$f_A(pq) = \max_{(p,q)} \qquad p, q \in \mathcal{N}$$
$$f_S(p) = p \oplus 1 \qquad p \in \mathcal{N}$$

## IV. *m*-ary Selection Functions

By an *m*-ary selection function we shall understand any mapping

$$h: B \cdot E^m \to E \tag{9}$$

where $B$ and $E$ are any two nonempty sets satisfying the following set of basic properties:

$$h(\sigma, a, \ldots, a) = a \tag{10}$$

$$h(\sigma, h(\sigma, a_{11}, \ldots, a_{1m}), \ldots, (\sigma, a_{m1}, \ldots, a_{mm})) = h(\sigma, a_{11}, \ldots, a_{mm}) \tag{11}$$

$$\begin{aligned} &h(\sigma, h(\rho, a_{11}, \ldots, a_{1m}), \ldots, h(\rho, a_{m1}, \ldots, a_{mm}) \\ &\quad = h(\rho, h(\sigma, a_{11}, \ldots, a_{m1}), \ldots, h(\sigma, a_{1m}, \ldots, a_{mm})) \end{aligned} \tag{12}$$

The name "selection function" given to such functions derives from the fact that if we assume

$$h(\sigma, a_1, \ldots, a_m) = a_{\gamma(\sigma)} \tag{13}$$

where

$$\gamma: B \to \mathcal{N} \qquad (\mathcal{N} = \{1, 2, \ldots, m\}) \tag{14}$$

is a numerical valuation for the elements of $B$, we obtain a function $h: B \cdot E^m \to E$, which satisfies exactly the defining set of properties (10) to (12).

For reasons already explained in [1], we shall proceed as abstractly as possible, by defining the concept of formal selective systems and studying their relationship with *m*-valued logical systems as previously defined.

## V. Simple Formal Selective Systems

We shall call a simple formal selective system (over $B, E$) a system $\left(H(B,E,m), \underset{H}{\approx}\right)$, where

(a) $$H(B, E, m) = \hat{H}_B$$

is the set of expressions recursively defined by

$$\alpha \in E \Rightarrow \alpha \in \hat{H}_B \tag{15}$$

$$\sigma \in B, \alpha_1 - \alpha_m \in \hat{H}_B \Rightarrow H\sigma\alpha_1 - \alpha_m \in \hat{H}_B \tag{16}$$

where $B, E$ are any two sets of symbols.

(b) $\underset{H}{\approx}$ is the smallest equivalence relation on $\hat{H}_B$ such that

$$H\sigma\alpha - \alpha \underset{H}{\approx} \alpha \tag{17}$$

$$H\sigma H\sigma\alpha_{11} - \alpha_{1m} - H\sigma\alpha_{m1} - \alpha_{mm} \underset{H}{\approx} H\sigma\alpha_{11} - \alpha_{mm} \tag{18}$$

$$H\sigma H\rho\alpha_{11} - \alpha_{1m} - H\rho\alpha_{m1} - \alpha_{mm} \underset{H}{\approx} H\rho H\sigma\alpha_{11} - \alpha_{m1} - H\sigma\alpha_{1m} - \alpha_{mm} \tag{19}$$

Since we shall frequently have to consider $H$-expressions such as $H\sigma\alpha_1 - \alpha_m$, where $\alpha_i = H\rho\alpha_{i1} - \alpha_{im}$ and so on, we shall introduce the following notational convention:

$$H\sigma_1 - \sigma_p A_{i_1-i_p} = H\sigma_1 H\sigma_2 - \sigma_p A_{1i_2-i_p} - H\sigma_2 - \sigma_p A_{mi_2-i_p} \tag{20}$$

where

$$A_{i_1-i_p} = \|a_{i_1-i_p}\| \, i_1, \ldots, i_p \in \{1, m\} \tag{21}$$

is a $p$-dimensional square matrix of order $m$ of $H$-expressions.

Moreover, we shall call a "canonical form" any expression of the form (20) such that $A_{i_1-i_p}$ is a matrix of elementary $E$-symbols. Canonical forms, as shown in [1], play an important role in the theory of selective expressions, since it can be shown that two expressions are equivalent if and only if they can be reduced to the same canonical form. This gives rise, as already noted by McCarthy [2], to a mechanical procedure for testing whether two selective expressions are equivalent.

## VI. Formal Algebraic Selective Systems

To study the relationship between $m$-valued logics and formal selective systems, let us now introduce the concept of formal algebraic selective systems.

We shall call a formal algebraic selective system a system

$$\left(H(A(B, C, \varphi), E, m), \underset{H/L}{\approx}\right)$$

where

(a) $$H(A(B, C, \varphi), E, m) = \hat{H}_{\hat{B}}$$

is the set of all $H$-expressions which can be formed as in (15) and (16) by assuming for $B$ the set $\hat{B} = A(B, C, \varphi)$ defined as in (1) to (2).

(b) $\underset{H/L}{\approx}$ is the smallest equivalence relation defined on $H(A(B, C, \varphi), E,m)$ satisfying the basic set of properties (17) to (19) plus a family $L$ of additional properties:

$$L = \{HK\sigma_1 - \sigma_{\varphi(K)}\, a_1 - a_m \underset{H/L}{\approx} H\sigma_1 - \sigma_{\varphi(K)}\, A^K_{i_1 - i\varphi(K)}\}\, K \in C \tag{22}$$

where

$$a^K_{i_1 - i\varphi(K)} \in \{a_1, \ldots, a_m\} \tag{23}$$

The preceding formulas can be considered as defining an "interpretation" for the connectives $K \in C$ in terms of simple selective expression.

Let us note that such an interpretation is characterized by the family

$$\{A^K_{i_1 - i\varphi(K)}\}\, K \in C \tag{24}$$

of matrices appearing in (22) and satisfying (23). Now any such matrix can be characterized by a finite function $f_K\colon \mathcal{N}^{(K)} \to \mathcal{N}$ such that

$$a^K_{i_1 - i\varphi(K)} = a_{f_K(i_1 - i\varphi(K))} \tag{25}$$

As it is shown in [1] the $\underset{L/H}{\approx}$ equivalence relation defined on $H(A(B, C, \varphi), E,m)$ induces an equivalence relation $\underset{L/H}{\approx}$ on $A(B, C, \varphi)$ such that

$$\forall \alpha', \alpha'' \in A(B, C, \varphi)$$

$$\alpha' \underset{L/H}{\approx} \alpha'' \Leftrightarrow H\alpha'\, a_1 - a_m \underset{L/H}{\approx} H\alpha''\, a_1 - a_m \tag{26}$$

for every $a_1 - a_m \in E$.

Thus associated with each family of selective interpretations (22) for the connectives $K \in C$, we can define, by means of (26), an induced equivalence relation on $A(B, C, \varphi)$.

## VII. Formal Selective Systems

The main result of the theory of formal selective systems, which shows the deep relationship between such formal systems and $m$-valued logics, can be stated as follows.

Given any closed set of algebraic expression $A(B, C, \varphi)$ and a family $= L\{f_K\colon \mathcal{N}^{\varphi(K)} \to \mathcal{N}\}$ of finite functions, we can define an $m$-valued logic

$\left(A(B, C, \varphi), \underset{Q/L}{\approx}\right)$ and an $m$-ary algebraic selective system $\left(H\ (A(B, C, \varphi), E, m) \underset{H/L}{\approx}\right)$ such that the latter induces an equivalence relation $L/H$ on $A(B, C, \varphi)$ such that

$$\forall \alpha', \alpha'' \mathrel{\hat{\in}} B: \alpha' \underset{L/H}{\approx} \alpha'' \Leftrightarrow \alpha' \underset{Q/L}{\approx} \alpha''$$

A formal proof of this assertion will appear in the continuation of paper [1].

This theorem shows:

(a) that we can define any $m$-valued logics by making use of the induced $\underset{L/H}{\approx}$ equivalence relation on $A(B, C, \varphi)$ derived from any $\underset{H/L}{\approx}$ equivalence relation defined on $H(A(B, C, \varphi) E, m)$ by means of $3 + |C|$ basic relations or "postulates" where $|C|$ is the number of connectives occurring in $C$,

(b) that any $m$-valued logic admits a selective interpretation which can be simply obtained from the truth-table definition of its connectives.

These latter remarks, in their turn, show that the concepts of selection function and selective system appear as a basic concept for logic underlying any logical system.

As already noted in [1], there are still many open problems in the theory of selective systems whose investigation should lead to a deeper insight into the relationships among algebras, selective systems, and logics.

## References


1. A. Caracciolo di Forino, *N*-selection function and formal selective systems, I, *Calcolo* **1**, 1 (1964).
2. J. McCarthy, A basis for a mathematical theory of computation, in *Computer Programming and Formal Systems*, North-Holland, Amsterdam, 1963.
3. C. I. Lewis, *A Survey of Symbolic Logic*, Univ. Calif. Press. Berkeley, Calif., 1918.
4. E. L. Post, Introduction to a general theory of elementary propositions, *Am. J. Math.* **43**, 163–185 (1921).
5. T. Lukasiewicz, *Logiche trowartasciowes* (*On three-valued logic*), *Przeglad fil.* **23**, 1921, 189–205 (1921).
6. T. Lukasiewicz and A. Tarski, Untersunchungen über den Aussagenkalkül, *C.p. Soc. Sci. Lett. Varsovie* [classe III] **23**, 1–21 (1930). English trans. in A. Tarski, *Logics, Mathematics, Metamathematics*, Oxford University Press, New York, 1956.
7. J. Slupecki, Der volle dreivertige Aussogenkalkül, *C.p. Soc. Sci. Lett. Varsovie* [classe III] **29**, 9–11 (1936).
8. N. N. Martin, The Sheffer function of 3-valued logic, *J. Symbolic Logic* **27**, 409–423 (1962).
9. P. R. Halmos, *Algebraic Logic*, Chelsea, New York, 1962.

# Generalized Markov Algorithms and Automata

ALFONSO CARACCIOLO DI FORINO

*Centro Studi Calcolatrici Elettroniche del C.N.R.*
*Pisa, Italy*

## I. Introduction

Markov normal algorithms (MNA) were introduced by Markov [1, 2] to define computational procedures by means of string transformation procedures as a basis for studies in computability theory. MNA are in fact equivalent [3] to Turing machines, and all theorems concerning Turing machines can be restated with little or no modification in terms of MNA.

Owing to the more complex nature of their basic operations, MNA are somewhat easier to handle than Turing machines, although both of them are quite unsuitable for a practical definition of computational procedures. However, making use of some concepts derived from the theory of formal languages [4], it is possible to generalize MNA in such a way as to get not only a theoretical device, but a real practical tool for defining both numerical and nonnumerical computations in a rather natural way.

Two such generalizations, as well as some hints for further generalizations, have been described in a joint work with Wolkenstein [5] and have been assumed as an actual base for setting up programming languages for symbol manipulation. As already noted in [5], these programming systems show many similarities to other programming systems (for instance, Comit, LISP, and Syntax directed compilers), but they differ from them for a more direct derivation from the theory of MNA.

In this lecture we shall first recall the concept of MNA and compare it with that of Turing machines. We shall then introduce the concept of generalized Markov algorithms (GMA), limiting our present exposition to the simplest type, called $S$-generalized Markov algorithms [5], and we shall apply it to the definition of partial-recursive functions. Finally, we shall give some hints of other possible applications, as, for instance, the description of a digital computer.

## II. Markov Normal Algorithms

We shall define an MNA as a triple $(\mathscr{A},\mathscr{R},\mathscr{N})$, where $\mathscr{A}$ is a finite set of symbols, called the alphabet, and $\mathscr{R}=(R_i)_{i=1,n}$ is a sequence of expressions of the form $T_i'\,\beta_i T_i''$ where $T_i', T_i''$ are words belonging to the set $\mathscr{A}^*$ of all finite strings of length $1 \geqslant 0$ on $\mathscr{A}$ and $\beta \in \{\rightarrow, \dot{\rightarrow}\}$. We shall call these expressions "transformation rules." $\mathscr{N}$ is a fixed "transformation procedure" for transforming an "argument string" $P \in \mathscr{A}^*$, defined as follows:

- $L0$: set $i=1$
- $L1$: *if* $R_i$ is "applicable" to $P$ (i.e., if $T_i'$ occurs in $P$), *then go to* $L2$, *else go to* $L3$
- $L2$: "apply" $R_i$ to $P$ (i.e., substitute the "first" occurrence of $T_i'$ in $P$ with $T_i''$); *go to* $L21$
- $L21$: *if* $\beta_i = \dot{\rightarrow}$, *then go to* $LS$, *else go to* $L0$
- $L3$: $i=i+1$; *if* $i \leqslant n$, *then go to* $L1$, *else go to* $LS$
- $LS$: stop

We shall call the above procedures the "normal Markov sequencing scheme."

As can be seen by the definition of $\mathscr{N}$, a MNA defines a sequence of transformations of the argument string, which comes to an end if and only if either there exists no transformation rule applicable to $P$, or immediately after a transformation rule $R_i$ such that $\beta_i = \dot{\rightarrow}$ has been applied.

We can, therefore, think of an MNA as defining a partial mapping of $\mathscr{A}^*$ into $\mathscr{A}^*$ which is defined on the (possibly empty) subset $\mathscr{D} \subseteq \mathscr{A}^*$ of those initial argument strings for which the transformation procedure comes to an end and which assigns to each such initial string the correspondent final string.

## III. Markov Normal Algorithms, Turing Machines, and Finite Automata

Let us now apply the concept of MNA to the definition of Turing machines as well as to various types of finite automata.

We shall assume as a definition of Turing machines that given by Davis [6]. A Turing machine is a system $(\mathscr{A}, Q, \mathscr{T})$ where

$\mathscr{A}=\{\mathfrak{b}, a_1, \ldots\}$ is a finite "alphabet" containing at least two symbols, one of which, "$\mathfrak{b}$," is the blank symbol

$Q$ is a finite set of "internal states"
$\mathscr{T}$ is a finite set of quadruples of the form

$$\chi_i \alpha_i \chi'_i \beta_i$$

where $\alpha_i \in \mathscr{A}$; $\chi_i, \chi'_i \in Q$; $\beta_i \in \mathscr{A} \cup \{+, -\}$ such that no two quadruples begin with the same pair of symbols.

Given now an "instantaneous configuration" $P = \alpha'_1 \cdots \alpha'_{n'} \chi \alpha''_1 \cdots \alpha''_{n''}$, where $(\alpha_i)_{i=1,n'}$, $(\alpha_i)_{i=1,n''} \in \mathscr{A}$, $\chi \in Q$, and $n'$, $n'' \geqslant 0$, a Turing machine defines a sequence of transformations of $P$ which can be characterized by the following Markov normal algorithm $M_T$:

$$\text{(a)} \quad \chi_i \alpha_i \to \chi'_i \alpha'_i$$

for every quadruple such that $\beta_i = \alpha_i \in \mathscr{A}$;

$$\text{(b)} \quad \begin{array}{l} \alpha_j \chi_i \alpha_i \to \chi'_i \alpha_j \alpha_i \\ \chi_i \alpha_i \to \chi'_i \mathfrak{b} \alpha_i \end{array}$$

for every quadruple such that $\beta_i = +$;

$$\text{(c)} \quad \begin{array}{l} \chi_i \alpha_i \to \alpha_i \chi'_i \\ \chi_i \to \mathfrak{b} \chi'_i \end{array}$$

for every quadruple such that $\beta_i = -$.

This algorithm ends if and only if an instantaneous configuration is reached such that there exists no quadruple in $\mathscr{T}$ (i.e., no transformation rule in $M_T$) which begins with the corresponding pair $\chi\alpha$.

This definition of Turing machines, directly in terms of MNA, shows by itself the first half of the theorem which states the equivalence between Turing machines and MNA.

To show the second half of the equivalence theorem one should prove that for any Markov normal algorithm $M$ one can define a Turing machine $T_M$ and an initial tape configuration such that $T_M$ will perform a sequence of cycles of tape-configuration transformations, each cycle corresponding to the application of a simple Markov transformation rule. In other words, one has to "program" in terms of Turing machines the procedure which defines the normal Markov sequencing scheme. This is not at all difficult in principle, but the resulting Turing machine is rather complicated, because of the relatively complex nature of the procedure $\mathscr{N}$ with respect to the elementary moves of Turing machines.

A different way to obtain the same result is in building a kind of universal Turing machine which accepts a tape of the form $DP$, where $D$ is an appropriate description of an arbitrary MNA and $P$ is a representation of the initial argument string. The corresponding Markov algorithm is then obviously a universal Markov algorithm, which plays in the theory of Markov normal algorithms exactly the same role which universal Turing machines play in the theory of Turing machines.

Markov normal algorithms can be directly applied to define various types of finite automata. For example, a finite automaton $G(\mathscr{I},Q,\mathscr{P},\delta,\lambda)$, where

$\mathscr{I}$ is the input alphabet
$Q$ is the set of states
$\mathscr{P}$ is the output alphabet
$\delta:\mathscr{I}\cdot Q \to Q$ is the next state function
$\lambda:\mathscr{I}\cdot Q \to \mathscr{P}$ is the output function

can be simply defined as an MNA,

$$\chi_i\,\alpha_i \to \lambda(\chi_i,\alpha_i)\,\delta(\chi_i,\alpha_i)$$

for each

$$\chi \in Q, \quad \alpha \in \mathscr{I}.$$

Similarly, a finite-recognition device $A(\mathscr{I},Q,\delta,q_0,\mathscr{F})$, where $\mathscr{I},Q,\delta$ are defined as before, $q_0$ is a selected initial state $\in Q$, and $\mathscr{F} \subseteq Q$ is the set of "designated final states," can be simply defined by the following Markov normal algorithms $M_A$:

$$\begin{array}{ll} \chi\alpha \to \delta(\chi,\alpha) & \chi \in Q,\ \alpha \in \mathscr{I} \\ \chi \overset{\cdot}{\to} + & \chi \in \mathscr{F} \\ \chi \overset{\cdot}{\to} - & \chi \in Q\backslash\mathscr{F} \\ \to q_0 & \end{array}$$

This is a total MNA, which defines a mapping of $\mathscr{I}:\mathscr{A}^* \to \{+,-\}$, in such a way that

$$\{x|M_A(x) = +\} = T(A)$$

where $T(A)$ denotes the set of tapes "accepted" by the automaton $A$.

## IV. Generalized Markov Algorithms

We shall now introduce the concept of generalized Markov algorithms, as they have been defined in [5].

We shall limit ourselves here to what we have called in [5] $S$-generalized Markov algorithms (where $S$ stands for "simple"), since they are sufficient both to present the basic ideas and to develop our present discussions and applications.

The basic idea is to substitute for the elementary transformation rules

$$R_i \equiv T_i' \beta_i T_i'' \tag{1}$$

where $T_i', T_i'' \in \mathscr{A}^*$, a higher type of transformation rule, which we have called "structural transformation rules." To define them let us first introduce the following concepts and notations.

By a *compound formal language* we shall understand a finite family $\mathscr{F} = \{\mathscr{A}_X\}_{X \in \mathscr{C}}$ of decidable languages over a common alphabet $\mathscr{A}$ (i.e., of recursive subset of $\mathscr{A}^*$).

Given a compound formal language $(\mathscr{A}, \mathscr{C}, \mathscr{F})$ and a set $\Sigma$ of "subscripts," we shall say that a word $P \in \mathscr{A}^*$ is *of structure T*,

$$T = t_1 t_2 \cdots t_k \tag{2}$$

where $t_i \in \mathscr{A} \cup \mathscr{C}_\Sigma (i = 1, k)$ if there exists a decomposition of $P$ in $k$ words,

$$P = P_1 P_2 \cdots P_k \tag{3}$$

such that

(a) $P_i = t_i$ if $t_i \in \mathscr{A}$

(b) $P_i \in \mathscr{A}_{\hat{t}_i}$ if $P_{\hat{t}_i} \in \mathscr{C}$, where $\hat{t}_i$ represents the $\mathscr{C}$-symbol obtained by deriving $t_i$ of its subscript

(c) $P_i = P_j$ for all $t_i = t_j$

For example, given

$$\begin{aligned} \mathscr{A} &= \{a, b, c, p, q, r\} \\ \mathscr{C} &= \{X, Y\} \\ \mathscr{A}_X &= \{p, pq, pqr, rp\} \\ \mathscr{A}_Y &= \{q, pr\} \\ \Sigma &= \{B, C, 1\} \end{aligned}$$

the word

$$P = a\ pr\ qrp\ b\ pr\ q\ p = P_1 P_2 P_3 P_4 P_5 P_6 P_7 \tag{4}$$

is a word of structure

$$T = a Y_B X_1 b Y_B Y_C X_C = t_1 t_2 t_3 t_4 t_5 t_6 t_7 \tag{5}$$

since

$$\begin{aligned} t_1 &= a & P_1 &= a \\ t_2 &= Y_B & P_2 &= pr \\ t_3 &= X_1 & P_3 &= qrp \\ t_4 &= b & P_4 &= b \\ t_5 &= Y_B = t_2 & P_5 &= pr = P_2 \\ t_6 &= Y_C & P_6 &= q \\ t_7 &= X_C & P_7 &= p \end{aligned}$$

It can happen that a word $P$ can be said to be of structure $T$ under more than one decomposition. For example, the word

$$P = pqpp = P_1 P_2 \tag{6}$$

is a word of structure

$$T = X_B X_C = t_1 t_2 \tag{7}$$

both because it can be decomposed as

$$P_1 = pqr \quad P_2 = p \tag{8a}$$

and as

$$P_1 = pq \quad P_2 = rp \tag{8b}$$

In such a case we shall say that

$$P = P_1 P_2 \cdots P_k$$

is a *canonical* decomposition of $P$ under $T = t_1 t_2 \cdots t_k$ if, calling

$$Q_i = P_i P_{i+1} \cdots P_k \qquad i = 1, k \tag{9}$$

it happens that for each $i = 1, k-1$, $P_i$ is the "shortest initial" string of $Q_i$ such that $Q_{i+1}$ is a word of structure $t_{i+1} \cdots t_k$. In the last example the canonical decomposition is the one defined by (8b).

We shall now call a *structural transformation rule* an expression of the form

$$T' \, \beta \, T'' \tag{10}$$

where

$$\beta \in \{\rightarrow, \dot{\rightarrow}\} \tag{11}$$

$$T' = t_1' \cdots t_p' \in (\mathscr{A} \cup \mathscr{C}_\Sigma)^* \tag{12}$$

$$T'' = t_1'' \cdots t_q'' \in (\mathscr{A} \cup T_C')^* \tag{13}$$

where $T_C'$ is the set of symbols belonging to $\mathscr{C}_\Sigma$ and occurring in $T'$. For instance,

$$a Y_B X_1 \rightarrow b X_1 X_1 \tag{14}$$

$$Y_B X_1 b Y_B \rightarrow c X_1 Y_B \tag{15}$$

A structural transformation rule (10) is said to be "applicable" to a word $P$ if there exists a decomposition $P = P' P_{T'} P''$, where $P_{T'}$ is a word of structure $T'$.

In such a case, "to apply it" to $P$ means to substitute for $P$ the word

$$Q = Q' \, Q_{T''} \, Q''$$

where

$$\begin{aligned}
&\text{(a)}\quad Q' = P', \qquad Q'' = P''\\
&\text{(b)}\quad Q_{T''} = Q_{t_1''} \cdots Q_{t_q''}\\
&\text{(c)}\quad Q_i = t_i'' \qquad \text{for} \qquad t_i'' \in \mathscr{A}\\
&\text{(d)}\quad Q_i = P_j \qquad \text{for} \qquad t_i'' = t_j' \in \mathscr{C}_\Sigma
\end{aligned}$$

and where $P_{T'}$ is the leftmost occurrence of a word of structure $T'$ in $P$, and $P_i (i = 1, p)$ is defined by the canonical decomposition of $P_{T'}$.

For example, both (14) and (15) are applicable to the word $P$ defined in (4) and would transform it into

$$Q_1 = bqepqrpbprqp$$
$$Q_2 = acqrpprqp$$

We shall now define a generalized Markov algorithm as a triple $(\mathscr{L}, \mathscr{R}, \mathscr{N})$ where $\mathscr{L}$ is a compound formal language, $\mathscr{R}$ is a sequence $\mathscr{R} = (T_i' \beta_i T_i'')_{i=1,N}$ of structural transformation rules, and $\mathscr{N}$ is the normal Markov sequencing scheme defined in Sec. III, modified only for the meaning of the words "applicable" and "to apply," which are now to be understood as defined in the present section.

In the following sections we shall give some examples of GMA's all of which are based on compound formal languages defined by means of context free productions [6], which can be used (by assuming each auxiliary symbol as an initial symbol) as a rather powerful tool for defining families of decidable languages.

## V. Partial-Recursive-Function Definition by Means of Generalized Markov Algorithms

We shall now apply the concept of GMA to the definition of partial-recursive functions. More exactly we shall show how to define a GMA which if applied to an argument string of the form

$$F(n_1, \ldots, n_p) \tag{16}$$

where $F$ is a "name" of a particular partial-recursive function and $n_1, \ldots, n_p$ is an appropriate representation of a $p$-ple of natural numbers, yields a sequence of successive transformations of (16) which ends by the representation of the value of $F$ for the given set of arguments if, and only if, $n_1, \ldots, n_p$ belongs to the domain of $F$.

To do this we have to recall the concept of partial-recursive function, for which we shall adopt the following definition [6]:

A function

$$F:\mathscr{D}\to\mathscr{N} \tag{17}$$

where $\mathscr{N}$ is the set of natural numbers and $\mathscr{D}\subseteq\mathscr{N}$, is "partial-recursive" if it can be obtained by a finite number of applications of the operations of composition ($\gamma$), primitive recursion ($\rho$), and minimalizations ($\mu$) to the following basic functions:

$$S(n)=n+1 \qquad n\in\mathscr{N} \tag{18}$$

$$N(n)=0 \qquad n\in\mathscr{N} \tag{19}$$

$$U_i^p(n_1,\ldots,n_p)=n_i \qquad n_i\in\mathscr{N}(1\leqslant i\leqslant p) \tag{20}$$

to which, we shall add, for convenience, the predecessor function

$$P(n)=n-1 \qquad (n\geqslant 1) \tag{21}$$

Equivalently, we can say that a function $F$ is partial-recursive if there exists a finite sequence of partial-recursive functions $F_1, F_2,\ldots, F_m$, the last of which is $F$ and such that, for each $k\leqslant m$, $F_m$ can be defined by means of an operation of composition:

$$\begin{aligned}&F_k^{(p)}(n_1,\ldots,n_p)\\&\quad=\gamma(G_{k_0}^{(q)};\,G_{k_1}^{(p)},\ldots,G_{k_q}^{(p)};\,n_1,\ldots,n_p)\end{aligned} \tag{22}$$

or of primitive recursion:

$$\begin{aligned}&F_k^{(p)}(n_1,\ldots,n_p)\\&\quad=\rho(G_{k_0}^{(p-1)};\,G_{k_1}^{(p+1)};\,n_1,\ldots,n_p)\end{aligned} \tag{23}$$

or of minimalization:

$$\begin{aligned}&F_k^{(p)}(n_1,\ldots,n_p)\\&\quad=\mu(G_{k_0}^{(p+1)};\,n_1,\ldots,n_p)\end{aligned} \tag{24}$$

where $G_i\in\{F_1,\ldots,F_{k-1}\}$ and where

$$\begin{aligned}&\gamma(G_0;\,G_1,\ldots,G_q;\,n_1,\ldots,n_p)\\&\quad=G_0(G_1(n_1,\ldots,n_p),\ldots,G_q(n_1,\ldots,n_p))\end{aligned} \tag{25}$$

$$\begin{aligned}&\rho(G_0;\,G_1;\,n_1,\ldots,n_p)\\&\quad=\begin{cases}G_0(n_2,\ldots,n_p) & \text{if } n_1=0\\ G_1(n_1,\ldots,n_p,\rho(G_0;\,G_1;\,P(n_1),n_2,\ldots,n_p)) & \text{if } n_1\neq 0\end{cases}\end{aligned} \tag{26}$$

$$\begin{aligned}&\mu(G_0;\,n_1,\ldots,n_p)\\&\quad=\min_y[G_0(y;\,n_1,\ldots,n_p)=0]\end{aligned} \tag{27}$$

To show that we can define any such partial-recursive function by means of GMA, what we have to do is simply to show that we can define a sequence of structural transformation rules which define: (A), the set of basic functions (18) to (21); (B) a sequence of derived functions (22) to (24); (C), computational rules for developing the derived functions according to (25) to (27).

First of all, we shall agree to represent a positive number $p$ with a sequence of "1" of length $p$, and the number zero with a "0." We shall then introduce a compound formal language, by means of the following set of context-free productions:

$$\begin{aligned} \mathbf{p} &::= 1|\mathbf{p}1 \\ \mathbf{n} &::= 0|\mathbf{p} \\ \mathbf{nl} &::= \mathbf{n}|\mathbf{nl}, \mathbf{n} \\ \mathbf{f} &::= \mathbf{a}|\mathbf{fa} \\ \mathbf{a} &::= A|B|C|\ldots|Z \\ \mathbf{fl} &::= \mathbf{f}|\mathbf{fl}, \mathbf{f} \end{aligned} \tag{28}$$

We can now define the basic functions (18) to (21) by means of the following set of structural transformation rules:

(A1.1) $S(0) \to 1$
(A1.2) $S(\mathbf{p}) \to \mathbf{p}1$
(A2.1) $P(\mathbf{p}1) \to \mathbf{p}$
(A2.2) $P(1) \to 0$
(A3) $N(\mathbf{n}) \to 0$
(A4.1) $U(1, \mathbf{n}) \to \mathbf{n}$
(A4.2) $U(1, \mathbf{n}, \mathbf{nl}) \to \mathbf{n}$
(A4.3) $U(\mathbf{p}, \mathbf{n}, \mathbf{nl}) \to U(P(\mathbf{p}), \mathbf{nl})$

We can then define computational rules for developing $\gamma$-, $\rho$-, and $\mu$-expressions according to (25) to (27) as:

(C$\gamma$1) $\gamma(\mathbf{f}; \mathbf{fl}; \mathbf{nl}) \to \mathbf{f}(\Delta\mathbf{fl}; \mathbf{nl})$
(C$\gamma$2) $\Delta\mathbf{f}, \mathbf{fl}; \mathbf{nl}) \to \mathbf{f}(\mathbf{nl}), \Delta\mathbf{fl}; \mathbf{nl})$
(C$\gamma$3) $\Delta\mathbf{f}; \mathbf{nl}) \to \mathbf{f}(\mathbf{nl}))$
(C$\rho$1) $\rho(\mathbf{f}_0; \mathbf{f}_1; 0, \mathbf{nl}) \to \mathbf{f}_0(\mathbf{nl})$
(C$\rho$2) $\rho(\mathbf{f}_0; \mathbf{f}_1; \mathbf{p}, \mathbf{nl}) \to \mathbf{f}_1(\mathbf{p}, \mathbf{nl}, \rho(\mathbf{f}_0; \mathbf{f}_1; P(\mathbf{p}), \mathbf{nl}))$
(C$\mu$1) $\mu\mathbf{f}_0(\xi, \mathbf{nl}) \to \mathbf{f}_0(0, \mathbf{nl})\,?0\mu\mathbf{f}_0(\xi, \mathbf{nl})$
(C$\mu$2) $\mathbf{p}\,?\mathbf{n}\mu\mathbf{f}_0(\xi, \mathbf{nl}) \to \mathbf{f}_0(S(\mathbf{n}), \mathbf{nl})\,?S(\mathbf{n})\,\mu\mathbf{f}_0(\xi, \mathbf{nl})$
(C$\mu$3) $0\,?\mathbf{n}\mu\mathbf{f}_0(\xi, \mathbf{nl}) \to \mathbf{n}$

Finally we have to add a set $B$ of structural transformation rules in correspondence with each function definition (22)–(24). Each structural transformation rule can be simply obtained by assigning a distinct "function name" belonging to the set **f**, to each function $F_k$ and then rewriting formulas (22), (23), (24), making use of these function names and substituting the symbol "=" which appears in (22) to (24) with the symbol "→," which characterizes structural transformation rules.

The set of structural transformation rules (A), (B), (C) characterizes a GMA which, if applied to a string of the form

$$\mathbf{f}(\mathbf{n}_1, \ldots, \mathbf{n}_p)$$

where **f** is one of function names introduced by a $C$-structural transformation rule, and $\mathbf{n}_1, \ldots, \mathbf{n}_p$ is a $p$-ple of natural numbers represented as elements belonging to the set **n** as defined in (28), yields either the value of the function if that particular set of arguments belongs to the domain $\mathscr{D}$ of the function of $f$ or else an unending sequence of successive transformations.

To show that such a GMA does in fact compute any partial-recursive function which is defined in it, we shall observe that if we take as the initial argument string

$$\mathbf{f}(\mathbf{n}_1, \ldots, \mathbf{n}_p) \tag{29}$$

and there is a $B$-transformation rule whose left-hand side has exactly the form (29), then the argument string will be substituted by the corresponding right-hand side. This means that we get one of the forms appearing on the left-hand side of (C$\gamma$1) or (C$\rho$1) or (C$\mu$1).

Now, although in this particular case the order in which the structural transformation rules are given does not affect the final result (provided there exists a final result) we shall suppose that the rules (C) appear first in GMA and are followed by the rules (A) and (B) in that order.

Under this assumption it can be easily seen that in case a $\gamma$-form has been generated, the next transformation rule which becomes applicable is exactly (C$\gamma$1) followed by a repetition of (C$\gamma$2) until (C$\gamma$3) becomes applicable. The net result of all these transformation is the substitution of a form

$$\mathbf{f}(\mathbf{nl})$$

with a form

$$\mathbf{f}_0(\mathbf{f}_1(\mathbf{nl}), \ldots, \mathbf{f}_p(\mathbf{nl}))$$

Similarly if a $\rho$-form has been generated, then we shall apply $p$ times the transformation rule (C$\rho$2) followed by an application of (A2) until (C$\rho$1) becomes applicable. The net result of all these transformations is the substitution of a form

$$\mathbf{f(nl)}$$

with a nested structure of the type

$$\mathbf{f_2(p, nl, f_2(``p-1", nl, f_2(\cdots f_2(1, nl, f_1(nl))\cdots))}$$

In both cases the process will go on by applying the proper transformation rules to the first "pure" functional form **f(nl)** which is encountered when scanning the resulting argument string from left to right, until we get some of the basic functions which are directly reduced to their value by means of the substitution rules (A1.1) to (A4.3).

The only remaining case to be discussed is the case when a $\mu$-form is generated. In this case the next applicable transformation rule is (C$\mu$1), which must be followed by the complete process of reducing **f(0, nl)** to a number.

If this number turns out to be positive, then the next applicable transformation is (C$\mu$2), which starts the same process again by substituting the tested number **n** which appears after the symbol "?" with its successor $S(\mathbf{n})$.

The process ends if and only if the number thus computed turns out to be "0", in which case (C$\mu$3) becomes applicable, yielding the generated number $n$ as the result of the minimalization process.

Primitive recursion can also be defined by using a different system of rules which is more "efficient" and more similar to the way primitive-recursive functions are programmed in actual programming practice, i.e., as an iteration or loop. This system consists in introducing for each function $F(\mathbf{n}_1, \ldots, \mathbf{n}_p)$ to be generated by a primitive recursion process of the type

$$\begin{aligned} F(0, \mathbf{n}_2, \ldots, \mathbf{n}_p) &= F_0(\mathbf{n}_2, \ldots, \mathbf{n}_p) \\ F(\mathbf{n}_1, \mathbf{n}_2, \ldots, \mathbf{n}_p) &= F_1(\mathbf{n}_1, \mathbf{n}_2, \ldots, \mathbf{n}_p, F(P(\mathbf{n}_1), \mathbf{n}_2, \ldots, \mathbf{n}_p)) \end{aligned}$$

a $B$-transformation rule of the form

$$\mathbf{f}_F(\mathbf{n}_1, \mathbf{n}_2, \ldots, \mathbf{n}_p) \to \rho'(\mathbf{f}_1; 0, \mathbf{n}_1, \mathbf{n}_2, \ldots, \mathbf{n}_p; \mathbf{f}_0(\mathbf{n}_2, \ldots, \mathbf{n}_p)) \qquad (23')$$

and in introducing, instead of (C$\rho$1), (C$\rho$2), (C$\rho$3), the following set of general transformation rules:

(C$\rho'$1) $\rho'(\mathbf{f}_1; \mathbf{n}_1, \mathbf{n}_1, \mathbf{nl}; \mathbf{n}_x) \to \mathbf{n}_x$

(C$\rho'$2) $\rho'(\mathbf{f}_1; \mathbf{n}_0, \mathbf{n}_1, \mathbf{nl}; \mathbf{n}_x)$

$$\to (\mathbf{f}_1; S(\mathbf{n}_0), \mathbf{n}_1, \mathbf{nl}; \mathbf{f}_1(S(\mathbf{n}_0), \mathbf{nl}; \mathbf{n}_x))$$

It is easy to see that whenever the transformation (23′) is applied it will be followed by the computation of $\mathbf{f}_0(\mathbf{n}_1,\ldots,\mathbf{n}_p)$. Afterward, ($C\rho'2$) becomes successively applicable for $\mathbf{n}_1$ times, performing the successive steps of the recursive process until the process terminates by becoming applicable to ($C\rho'1$).

There are still other ways to define GMA for computing partial-recursive functions, as, for example, by directly writing the structural transformation rules for the composition of functions in the form

$$\mathbf{f}(\mathbf{n}_1,\ldots,\mathbf{n}_p) \\ \rightarrow \mathbf{f}_0(\mathbf{f}_1(\mathbf{n}_{\alpha_{11}},\ldots,\mathbf{n}_{\alpha_{1p_1}}),\ldots,\mathbf{f}_q(\mathbf{n}_{\alpha_{q_1}},\ldots,\mathbf{n}_{\alpha_{qp_q}}))$$

where $\mathbf{f}_0, \mathbf{f}_1, \ldots, \mathbf{f}_q$ are function names for previously defined functions and the indexes $\alpha_{ij}$ are $\Sigma$-symbols belonging to the set $\{1,\ldots,p\}$. Such a structural transformation rule would introduce a direct definition of the function $\mathbf{f}(\mathbf{n}_1,\ldots,\mathbf{n}_p)$ and makes it possible to dispense with the set of structural transformation rules ($C\gamma1$), ($C\gamma2$), $C\gamma3$).

Similarly, it is possible to eliminate the transformation rules ($C\rho1$), ($C\rho2$) and define directly functions to be obtained by a primitive-recursion operation by introducing for each such function a pair of transformation rules of the form

$$\mathbf{f}_F(0,\mathbf{n}_2,\ldots,\mathbf{n}_p) \rightarrow \mathbf{f}_0(\mathbf{n}_2,\ldots,\mathbf{n}_p)$$
$$\mathbf{f}_F(\mathbf{n}_1,\mathbf{n}_2,\ldots,\mathbf{n}_p) \rightarrow \mathbf{f}_1(\mathbf{n}_1,\mathbf{n}_2,\ldots,\mathbf{n}_p,\mathbf{f}_F(P(\mathbf{n}_1),\mathbf{n}_2,\ldots,\mathbf{n}_p))$$

This shows that generalized Markov algorithms are not only a complete system for defining every partial-recursive function, which is obvious since they include Markov normal algorithms, but also that they can be used to define such functions in a "natural" way, transforming just the ordinary function definition, by means of equations, into an operational one.

## VI. Further Examples of Applications of Generalized Markov Algorithms

As was noted in [5], and as has been shown in the preceding section, generalized Markov algorithms provide a basis for defining in a rather natural way a sort of "pictorial" description of algorithms and computational processes, based upon structural transformation rules, to be applied to structured strings of symbols.

As a further example of the applicability of GMA's we shall roughly sketch how they can be applied to define "multistring" computations.

Suppose we have a set of labelled strings $\langle A:S_1\rangle$, $\langle B:S_2\rangle$, $\langle C:S_3\rangle$ and we want to substitute the first occurrence of a certain string of class $Z$ occurring in $C$ with the expression which results by taking the second occurrence of an expression of class $X$ ocurring in $A$ followed by the first occurrence of an expression of class $Y$ occurring in $B$. In order to do this we have simply to write a structural transformation rule of the following kind:

$$\langle A:P_{A_1}X_{A_1}P_{A_2}X_{A_2}P_{A_3}\rangle\langle B:P_{B_1}Y_BP_{B_2}\rangle\langle C:P_{C_1}Y_CP_{C_2}\rangle$$
$$\rightarrow\langle A:P_{A_1}X_{A_1}P_{A_2}X_{A_2}P_{A_3}\rangle\langle B:P_{B_1}Y_BP_{B_2}\rangle\langle C:P_{C_1}X_{A_2}Y_BP_{C_2}\rangle$$

where $X$, $Y$, $Z$ are the designated class names and $P$ is a name for the class of all strings not containing the symbols "$\langle$" and "$\rangle$", which are here used as a kind of metasymbol.

Much along the same lines it is possible to use GMA's for defining conventional digital computers as well as various types of abstract and unconventional computers.

For example, a conventional binary computer with 4096 memory location locations of 18 bits each, an instruction counter **IC** of 12 bits, an instruction register **IR** of 18 bits, an accumulator **AC** of 18 bits, can be represented by an argument string $\mathscr{P}$ of the form

$$\mathscr{P}\equiv\langle\mathbf{IC}:\alpha\rangle\langle\mathbf{IR}:\gamma_I\rangle\langle\mathbf{AC}:\gamma_A\rangle\langle 000000000000:\gamma_0\rangle$$
$$\cdot\langle 000000000001:\gamma_1\rangle\cdots\langle 111111111111:\gamma_{4095}\rangle$$

where $b=0|1$

$\theta=bbbbbb$

$\alpha=\theta\theta$

$\gamma=\theta\theta\theta$

to which we shall add, for later use, the following class definitions:

$$\beta=\text{"empty"}\ |b|\beta b$$
$$\diamondsuit=\text{"empty"}\ |\langle\alpha:\gamma\rangle|\diamondsuit\langle\alpha:\gamma\rangle$$

as well as a certain number of classes with a single $\gamma$-bits member, one for each "instruction code," as for instance

**stop** = 000000
**jump** = 000001
. . . . . . . . . . . . .
**copy** = 100000
**store** = 100001
**add** = 100010
. . . . . . . . . . . . .

We can then define the functioning of such a computer by means of a GMA consisting of four successive sets of transformation rules:

1. A first set of transformation rules for performing actual logical or arithmetical operation as, for instance:

(a) rules for computing $(\beta + 1) \bmod 2^l$, where $l =$ length of $\beta$:

$$
\begin{gathered}
(\beta + 1) \rightarrow (\beta') \\
(\beta_1 0' \beta_2) \rightarrow (\beta_1 1 \beta_2) \\
(\beta_1 1' \beta_2) \rightarrow (\beta_1' 0 \beta_2) \\
('\beta) \rightarrow \beta
\end{gathered}
$$

(b) rules for computing $(\beta_1 + \beta_2) \bmod 2^l$, where $l =$ common length of $\beta_1$ and $\beta_2$:

$$
\begin{array}{l}
(\beta_1 + \beta_2) \rightarrow (\beta_1 + \beta_2 =) \\
(\beta_1 0 + \beta_2 0 = \beta_3) \rightarrow (\beta_1 + \beta_2 = 0\beta_3) \\
(\beta_1 0 + \beta_2 0 = \phi\beta_3) \rightarrow (\beta_1 + \beta_2 = 1\beta_3) \\
\dots\dots\dots\dots\dots\dots\dots\dots\dots\dots \\
(\beta_1 1 + \beta_2 1 = \beta_3) \rightarrow (\beta_1 + \beta_2 + \phi 0 \beta_3) \\
(\beta_1 1 + \beta_2 1 = \phi\beta_3) \rightarrow (\beta_1 + \beta_2 = \phi 1 \beta_3) \\
(+ = \phi\beta_1) \rightarrow \beta_1
\end{array}
$$

2. A second set of transformation rules defining, for each instruction in the instruction code, the "execution phase." Such a set will be exemplified here by the following set of rules:

$$*\langle \mathbf{IR{:}\,stop}\ \alpha\rangle \overset{\cdot}{\rightarrow} \langle \mathbf{IR{:}\,stop}\ \alpha\rangle$$

$$
\begin{array}{l}
\langle \mathbf{IC}{:}\,\alpha_1\rangle * \langle \mathbf{IR{:}\,jump}\ \alpha_2\rangle \\
\quad \rightarrow *\langle \mathbf{IC}{:}\,\alpha_2\rangle\langle \mathbf{IR{:}\,jump}\ \alpha_2\rangle
\end{array}
$$

$$
\begin{array}{l}
\langle \mathbf{IC}{:}\,\alpha_1\rangle * \langle \mathbf{IR{:}\,copy}\ \alpha_2\rangle\langle \mathbf{AC}{:}\,\gamma_a\rangle \Diamond \langle \alpha_2{:}\,\gamma_1\rangle \\
\quad \rightarrow *\langle \mathbf{IC}{:}\,(\alpha_1 + 1)\rangle\langle \mathbf{IR{:}\,copy}\ \alpha_2\rangle\langle \mathbf{AC}{:}\,\gamma_1\rangle \Diamond \langle \alpha_2{:}\,\gamma_1\rangle
\end{array}
$$

$$
\begin{array}{l}
\langle \mathbf{IC}{:}\,\alpha_1\rangle * \langle \mathbf{IR{:}\,store}\ \alpha_2\rangle\langle \mathbf{AC}{:}\,\gamma_a\rangle \Diamond \langle \alpha_2{:}\,\gamma_1\rangle \\
\quad \rightarrow * \langle \mathbf{IC}{:}\,(\alpha_1 + 1)\rangle\langle \mathbf{IR{:}\,store}\ \alpha_2\rangle\langle \mathbf{AC}{:}\,\gamma_a\rangle \Diamond \langle \alpha_2{:}\,\gamma_a\rangle
\end{array}
$$

$$
\begin{array}{l}
\langle \mathbf{IC}{:}\,\alpha_1\rangle * \langle \mathbf{IR{:}\,add}\ \alpha_2\rangle\langle \mathbf{AC}{:}\,\gamma_a\rangle \Diamond \langle \alpha_2{:}\,\gamma_1\rangle \\
\quad \rightarrow * \langle \mathbf{IC}{:}\,(\alpha + 1)\rangle\langle \mathbf{IR{:}\,add}\ \alpha_2\rangle\langle \mathbf{AC}{:}\,(\gamma_a = \gamma_1)\rangle \Diamond \langle \alpha_2{:}\,\gamma_1\rangle
\end{array}
$$

. . . . . . . . . . . . . . . . . . . . . . . . . . . . . . . . . . . . . . . . . . . . . .

3. A third set of rules for defining the "calling phase" of an instruction and consisting simply of the following rule:

$$
\begin{array}{l}
* \langle \mathbf{IC}{:}\,\alpha_1\rangle\langle \mathbf{IR}{:}\,\gamma_1\rangle\langle \mathbf{AC}{:}\,\gamma_a\rangle \Diamond \langle \alpha_1{:}\,\gamma_2\rangle \\
\qquad\qquad \rightarrow \langle \mathbf{IC}{:}\,\alpha_1\rangle * \langle \mathbf{IR}{:}\,\gamma_2\rangle\langle \mathbf{AC}{:}\,\gamma_a\rangle \Diamond \langle \alpha_1{:}\,\gamma_2\rangle
\end{array}
$$

4. A final rule which simply defines the starting condition, i.e., pressing the "start button" on the console, which makes the computer start its operation:

$$\rightarrow *$$

As a last example we shall roughly sketch how we can define a "multitape Turing machine."

The functioning of such an automaton can be readily described by the following transformation rule:

$$\begin{aligned}&\langle \boldsymbol{\alpha}\mathbf{I}\rangle\langle \mathbf{x}\rangle\langle \mathbf{T}_{1A} * \mathbf{t}_1\ \mathbf{T}_{1B}\rangle \cdots \langle \mathbf{T}_{nA} * \mathbf{t}_n\ \mathbf{T}_{nB}\rangle \\ &\quad\rightarrow \langle I\rangle\langle \delta(\boldsymbol{\alpha}, \mathbf{x}, \mathbf{t}_1, \ldots, \mathbf{t}_n)\rangle\langle \mathbf{T}_{1A}\ \mu_1(\boldsymbol{\alpha}, \mathbf{x}, \mathbf{t}_1, \ldots, \mathbf{t}_n)\ \lambda_k(\boldsymbol{\alpha}, \mathbf{x}, \mathbf{t}_1, \ldots, \mathbf{t}_n)\ \mathbf{T}_{1B}\rangle \\ &\quad\ldots \langle \mathbf{T}_{nA}\ \mu_n(\boldsymbol{\alpha};\ \mathbf{x}, \mathbf{t}_1, \ldots, \mathbf{t}_n)\ \lambda_n(\boldsymbol{\alpha}, \mathbf{x}, \mathbf{t}_1, \ldots, \mathbf{t}_n)\ \mathbf{T}_{nB}\end{aligned} \tag{30}$$

preceded by the transformation rules for moving a tape configuration $\langle \mathbf{T}_{iA}\mu\mathbf{T}_{iB}\rangle$ one character right or left according to the class symbol $\mu$ standing for $+$ (right) or $-$ (left):

$$\begin{aligned}-\mathbf{t}_k &\rightarrow \mathbf{t}_k* \\ \mathbf{t}_k+ &\rightarrow *\mathbf{t}_k \\ \langle * &\rightarrow \langle \not{b}* \\ *\rangle &\rightarrow *\not{b}\rangle\end{aligned}$$

where

| | |
|---|---|
| $\mathbf{I} = \boldsymbol{\alpha}\|\mathbf{I}\boldsymbol{\alpha}$ | defines the set of input strings |
| $\boldsymbol{\alpha} = a_1\|a_2\| - \|\mathbf{a}_n$ | defines the input alphabet |
| $\mathbf{x} = q_0\|q_1\| - \|q_{nx}$ | defines the set of internal states |
| $\mathbf{T}_k = \mathbf{t}_k\|\mathbf{T}_k\,\mathbf{t}_k$ | defines the set of non null strings of characters on the alphabet *tk* |
| $\mathbf{t}_k = \not{b}\ \|\ \overset{k}{b_1}\ \|\ \overset{k}{b_2}\ \|-\|\ \overset{k}{b}_{nk}$ | defines the alphabet $\mathbf{t}_k$ which includes for each $k = 1, n$ the common blank symbol "$\not{b}$" |

and

| | |
|---|---|
| '*' | is a primitive symbol respresenting the positioning of a tape with respect to the automaton identifying the character in reading position as the first symbol on the right of * |
| '⟨' and '⟩' | are a sort of metasymbol identifying the various components |

and where

| | |
|---|---|
| $\delta(\boldsymbol{\alpha}, \mathbf{x}, \mathbf{t}_1, \ldots, \mathbf{t}_n)$ | denotes the value of the "next state function" which belongs to the set $\mathbf{x}$ |

$\lambda_k(\boldsymbol{\alpha}, \mathbf{x}, \mathbf{t}_1, \ldots, \mathbf{t}_n)$ denotes the value of the "printing function" for each tape $k = 1, n$, which belongs to $\mathbf{t}_k$

$\mu_k(\boldsymbol{\alpha}, \mathbf{x}, \mathbf{t}_1, \ldots, \mathbf{t}_n)$ denotes the value of the "moving function" for each tape $k = 1, n$, which belongs to the set $(+, *, -\}$, where "$+$" stands for moving the tape to the right, "$-$" stands for moving the tape to the left, and * implies no tape movement

In a very similar fashion one can define single and multiple push down automata as well as the kind of automata considered by Rabin in [7].

## References

1. A. A. Markov, Theory of algorithms (in Russian), *Akad. Nauk SSSR* (1954) (English trans. published by the Israel Program for Scientific Translation, Jerusalem, Vol. XLII 1962).
2. A. A. Markov, The theory of algorithms (in Russian), *Tr. Math. Inst. Akad. Nauk SSSR* **38**, 176–189 (1951) (English trans., *Am. Math. Soc.*, 1958, pp. 1–14).
3. G. Asser, Turing-Maschinen und Markovsche Algorithmen, *Z. Mat.*[2]**5**, 346–365 (1959).
4. N. Chomsky and G. A. Miller, Introduction to the formal analysis of natural languages, in *Handbook of Mathematical Psychology*, Vol. 2, Wiley, New York, 1963.
5. A. Caracciolo di Forino and N. Wolkenstein, On a Class of Programming Languages for Symbol Manipulation Based on Extended Markov Algorithms, *Rept. Centro Studi Calcolatrici Elettroniche*, C.N.R., Pisa, Italy, 1963.
6. M. Davis, *Computability and Unsolvability*, McGraw-Hill, New York, 1958.
7. M. O. Rabin, Real Time Automata (lectures given during this same course on automata theory, Ravello, June 1964).

# Synthesis of Reliable Automata from Unreliable Components[1]

JACK D. COWAN

*Department of Electrical Engineering*
*Imperial College of Science and Technology*
*London, England*

## I. Introduction

Modern computing systems contain many devices or *modules* and many *connections*. We call such modules, and their connections, *elements*. Networks of these elements, known as *modular nets*, are required to execute, at high speeds, long sequences of precise computations at high levels of reliability. In analog computers (wherein physical quantities are generally represented by such quantities as voltage, current, impedance, and so forth) precision is limited by intrinsic fluctuations or *noise* present in the nets comprising the computer. In digital computers (wherein physical quantities are represented by numbers) arbitrarily high precision may be obtained by increasing the number of digits used in the representation of the given objects of computation. However, such an increase in precision is obtained at the cost of decreased *reliability*. That is, the longer the digital expansion, the greater the expected number of errors in the computation, owing to possible malfunctions or failures of the many elements comprising modular nets.

For example, the overloading of electrical networks may cause short-circuiting and breakdown of modules such as valves or transistors. The contacts of a relay switching network may stick from time to time, resulting in occasional errors in the output of the network; similarly, noise in modules comprising gating circuits, for example, may result in occasional output errors. A power failure may result in complete loss of function of modular nets. In addition, the modules used in the system may be old or may have suffered radiation damage, and so forth. Finally the connections may be

[1] Under U.S. Dept. Navy, Contract Nonr-62558/3820.

faulty; dry joints, mistakes in wiring, short- or open-circuiting, etc., all may contribute to the over-all unreliability of the system. We call these various sources of error *faults*.

In general, *faults* may be split into two classes: *malfunctions*, whose effect is to produce *transient errors*, and *failures*, whose effect is to produce *stationary errors* in computing systems. Associated with this classification are different definitions of what is meant by reliability. In the case of transient errors, we use as a reliability measure the probability of system malfunction when given the probability of modular and connection mal-

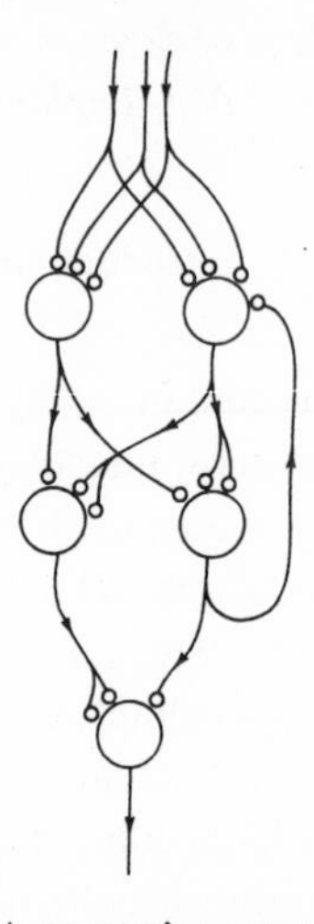

FIG. 1. A computing automaton $A$.

function. In the case of stationary errors, we use as our measure the expected lifetime to failure of the system when given the lifetime to failure of modules. The problem of reliable system design is that of finding ways of designing systems which operate at requisite levels of reliability, given fixed levels of elemental reliability.

We may express this formally as follows: Consider the computing system or *automaton* $A$ shown in Fig. 1. Let $N$ be the number of modules comprising $A$, let $t_i$ be the number of times that the output of the $i$th module ($i = 1, \ldots, N$) influences a single output of $A$, and let $\Sigma_{i=1}^{N} t_i = Q < \infty$. That is, there can be loops within $A$, but their effect is of finite duration. Let $p$ be the probability of any single modular malfunction and let $P$ be the probability that $A$ malfunctions. It is easily seen that

$$(1 - p)^Q \leqslant 1 - P \tag{1}$$

This equation implies, for fixed values of $p$, a positive lower bound on $P$, i.e., arbitrarily high reliability cannot be directly attained from $A$ alone. Similar considerations apply to the cases of connection errors and of failures.

Evidently an automaton $A'$ must be designed which will compute the same function as $A$, and which will contain mechanisms for limiting errors due to faults. In general, there exist several possible strategies. $A'$ may incorporate a *fault detection and location* mechanism coupled to an element removal and replacement mechanism, or else the latter mechanism may be automatic. Alternatively $A'$ may be designed so that faults have little or no effect on the system; i.e., a *fault-masking* mechanism may be incorporated. Yet another strategy is to make $A'$ *adaptive*. Faulty elements are given progressively less "weight" in the system than correctly functioning elements. In what follows we shall give a brief outline of some of these strategies, and the resultant automata.

## II. Fault Masking of Transient Errors

We consider first the case of malfunctions resulting in transient errors. We distinguish between *contact networks* ($c$-nets) and *gating networks* ($g$-nets). The basic difference between these types of network is that in the former, the output of each element, given faultless operation, uniquely specifies the input, whereas in the latter such is not the case. Thus relay switching circuits are $c$-nets, whereas networks of modules such as NOR-gates are $g$-nets. In masking the effects of transient errors in such nets, a basic principle employed is that of *replication by redundancy*. That is, more elements are used in the design of $A'$ than in $A$, and the extra elements are used to provide repetitions of the basic operations executed in $A$.

For example, consider an idealized relay whose malfunctions comprise the failure of its contacts to open or close when signalled to do so by the current flowing in the coil. If the relay is energized, the contact is closed with probability $a$, open with probability $1 - a$. If the relay is not energized, the contact is closed with probability $c$, open with probability $1 - c$. If $a > c$, we have what is called a *make-contact*; if $a < c$, we have a *break-contact*. In general, to preserve closure of a contact network (i.e., to guarantee that at least one essential contact is closed) we need only construct a parallel contact network; conversely, to preserve an open circuit we need only construct a series network. Replacement of the single relay with associated make-contact of Fig. 2 by the parallel relay network with associated series parallel contact network of Fig. 3 will produce a large improvement in reliability.

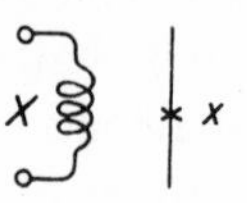


FIG. 2. Single relay $X$ with make-contact $x$.

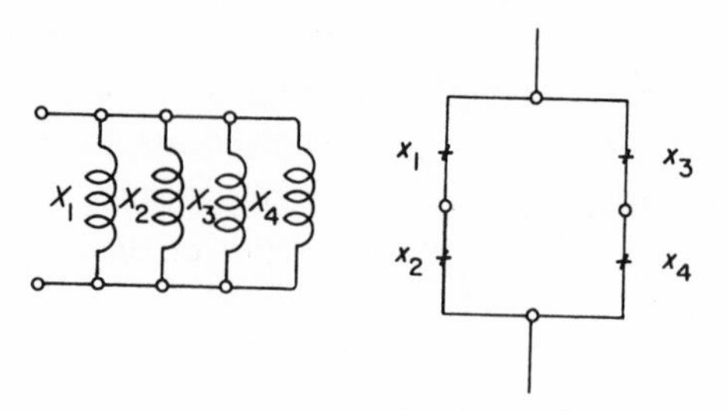


FIG. 3. Series-parallel relay network.

If each of the contacts $x_1, \ldots, x_4$ has the probability $p$ of being closed, then the probability of the network being closed is

$$h(p) = 1 - (1 - p^2)^2 = 2p^2 - p^4 \tag{2}$$

A plot of this function is shown in Fig. 4.

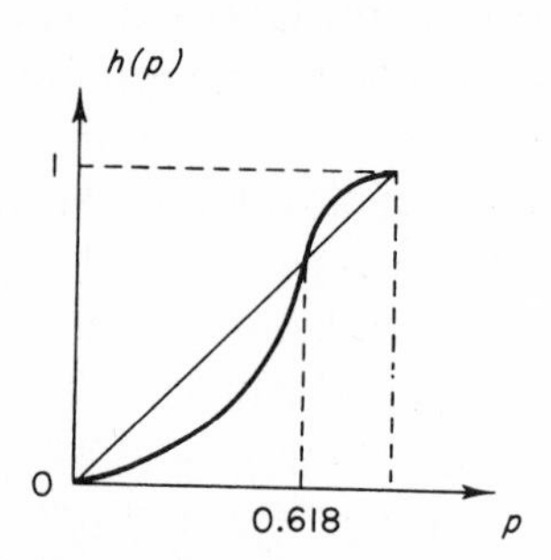


FIG. 4. Plot of $h(p)$, the probability of closure of the four-contact network, against $p$, the closure probability of a single relay.

Clearly, if $a < 0.618 < c$ we shall now have a better relay in respect to closure than the single relay system. For example, if $1 - a = c = 0.01$, the multiterminal circuit makes errors when the coils are energized, with probability $3.96 \times 10^{-4}$, and when the coils are not energized with probability $2 \times 10^{-4}$.

In general, many multicontact relay networks have this property, characterized by a polynomial of the form

$$h(p) = \sum_{n=0}^{m} A_n p^n (1-p)^{m-n} \tag{3}$$

where $m$ is the number of contacts in the network and $A_n$ is the number of ways in which a subset of $n$ contacts can be selected so that if those contacts are closed and the remainder are open, the total network is closed. Such networks are sometimes called *hammock nets*, after Moore and Shannon (1956).

In $g$-nets, fault-masking of transient errors, via replication by redundancy, is used both at the network level and at the elemental level, in a somewhat similar manner to that of $c$-nets. The simplest example [attributed to von Neumann (1956)] is the *triplication* of an entire $g$-net (see Fig. 5) followed

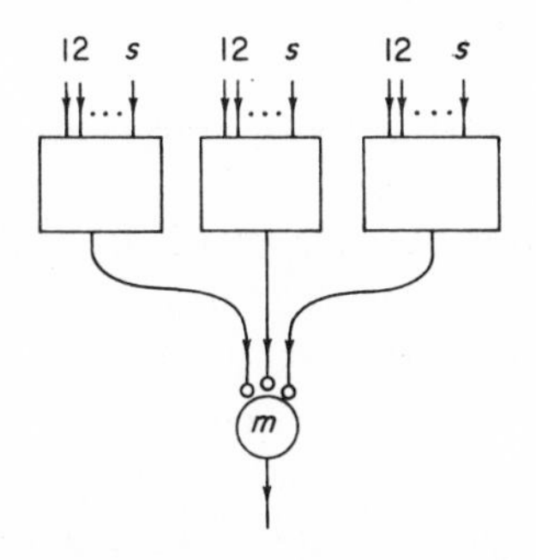


FIG. 5. A triplicated gating network plus majority organ *m*.

by a so-called majority vote-taker or *majority organ*. This module computes a function such that if at least two of the $g$-nets give similar outputs, then so does the majority organ. It follows that only if at least two g-nets are simultaneously malfunctioning does an error propagate through the majority organ. More succinctly, we say that the majority organ is single-error insensitive. Assuming independence of malfunctions in $g$-nets and in the majority organ, we may calculate the probability of network malfunction. Let $p$ be the probability of malfunction of each $g$-net, and $\delta$ that of the majority organ. Then the probability of at least two of the $g$-nets being in error is

$$\begin{aligned} \theta &= 3p^2(1-p) + p^3 \\ &= 3p^2 - 2p^3 \end{aligned} \tag{4}$$

and the probability of system malfunction (assuming, of course, no interconnection errors) is

$$\begin{aligned} P(\delta, p) &= (1-\delta)\,\theta + \delta(1-\theta) \\ &= \delta + (1-2\delta)(3p^2 - 2p^3) \end{aligned} \tag{5}$$

The graph of this function of $p$ is shown in Fig. 6.

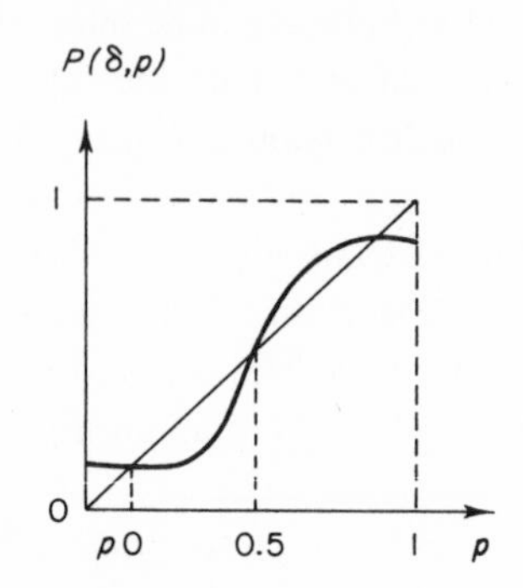


FIG. 6. Plot of $P(\delta,p)$, the probability of error of the triplicated network of Fig. 5

It can be shown that by suitable modification of the redundant network (i.e., by using two layers of majority organs, one layer triplicated), and by iteration of such networks, that the steady-state value $P(\delta,p) \sim P_0$ will be attained, provided $\delta < 0.0073$. For example, an error level of $P = 2 \times 10^{-2}$ can be maintained in such a system provided $\delta \leqslant 0.0041$ and $p < 0.5$. Unfortunately, such a design requires the use of a very large number of redundant modules. Thus, if $\mu$ is the longest chain of logical operations to be executed in such a network, then approximately $3^{\mu}$ modules are required in the redundant network. Consequently, the procedure is impracticable for all but a small range of values of $\mu$.

Similarly, it may be shown that malfunctions in $g$-nets may be controlled by elemental replication rather than by replication of entire $g$-nets. It is known that networks executing arbitrary logical functions may be composed from so-called *universal logical elements*, and that *mutatus mutandis*, the majority organ, is universal in this sense. Thus any Boolean function may be computed by $g$-nets comprising only majority organs. The elemental replication technique [introduced by von Neumann (1956)], known as *multiplexing*, entails the replacement of all single connections in the given $g$-nets by groups of connections or *bundles*, and all modules of the $g$-nets by aggregates of similar modules (see Fig. 7).

It can be shown, with suitable randomization of these input and output bundles to and from aggregates, and in the absence of malfunctions, that these redundant $g$-nets approximate the function computed by a single module, i.e., the function computed by the majority organ, sometimes called

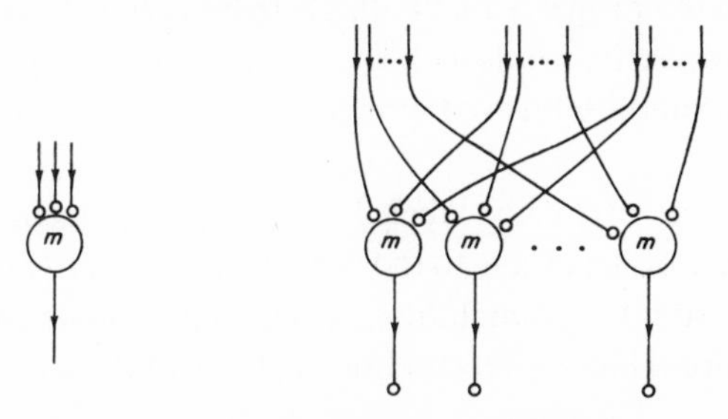


FIG. 7. The technique of multiplexing.

the *quorum function* [Moore and Shannon, (1956)]. In the presence of malfunctions, however, an error-controlling network is required to maintain the approximation. It was shown by von Neumann that the network of Fig. 8 will control transient errors.

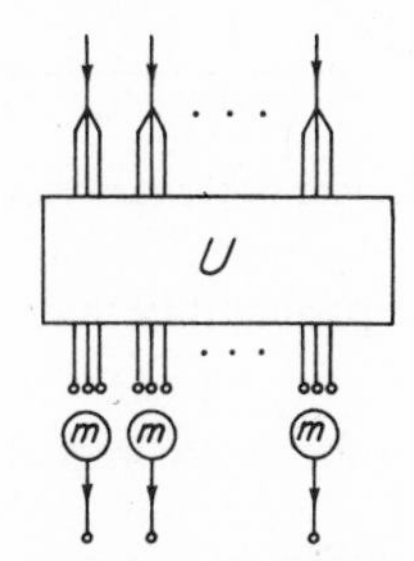


FIG. 8. An error-controlling network.

The redundancy created by the multiplexing is used in a certain *encoding and decoding* of the signal patterns within the network. The details of this code are as follows:

Each bundle comprises $n$ connections, each the carrier of a binary impulse (signal or no-signal). There are thus $2^n$ distinct signal patterns in the bundle ranging from $(111\cdots1)$ to $(000\cdots0)$. If no malfunctions were to occur, these extreme levels of excitation would be the only ones existent in the bundle. Let the number of ones in any pattern be $x$, and set a fiduciary level $\Delta$ so that $n \geqslant x \geqslant (1-\Delta)n$ represents signal (1), $\Delta n \geqslant x \geqslant 0$ represents no-signal (0), and any intermediate level of excitation $(1-\Delta)n > x > \Delta n$ represents the occurrence of a malfunction. The problem of obtaining reliable computation is now reduced to the problem of maintaining levels of excitation throughout the multiplexed network sufficiently close to $x = n$ or else 0. Von Neumann was able to show that the $g$-net of Fig. 8 had only two stable states of activity corresponding to the above extrema. Therefore, this network has the property that with probability fairly close to one, any input bundle with excitation level fairly close to one of the extrema gives rise to an output bundle with excitation level even closer to the extremum in question.

The basic function of the box labeled $U$ in Fig. 8 is to maintain the statistical independence of the inputs to the next layer of majority organs, and in fact it executes a suitable permutation of these inputs sufficient to maintain such independence. Under such conditions, if any of the $n$ inputs are active

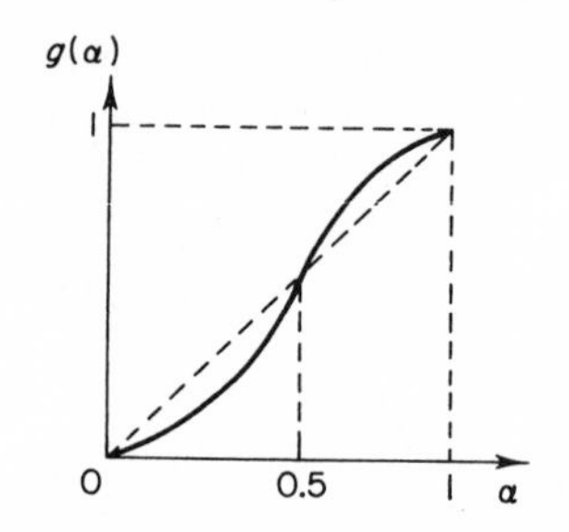


FIG. 9. Behavior of the restoring organ.

(transmitting signals), then the probability that any majority organ is active is

$$\alpha^* = 3\alpha^2 - 2\alpha^3 = g(\alpha) \tag{6}$$

For sufficiently large $n$, it is therefore highly probable that approximately $\alpha n$ outputs will be active. Figure 9 shows the graph of the function $g(\alpha)$. It will be seen that only the levels $g(\alpha) = 0$ or else 1 are stable, and they represent the asymptotic behavior of the network for any initial activity level $\alpha \neq 0.5$. This is clearly an error-controlling process, in that with respect to the chosen code, any initial state corresponding to malfunctions of some majority organs will be restored, by suitable iterations of the process to a final state corresponding to the signal states 1 or 0. This process is clearly analogous to the use of certain circuits in actual automata for *amplification* rather than for gating or detection.

Equation (6) is obtained on the assumption that the error-controlling network is not itself subject to internal malfunctions. It can be shown that if malfunctions are assumed to occur with some nonzero probability $p$ in all elements of the redundant $g$-net, there exists an optimum fiduciary level $\Delta$, so that for sufficiently large redundancy $n$, the probability of network malfunction $P(n,p)$ can be made lower than any given fidelity level $\delta$. In particular, for $p < 0.0107$ and $\Delta = 0.07$, and for $n$ sufficiently large,

$$P(n,p) \sim (1/\sqrt{2\pi}k)\exp(-k^2/2) \tag{7}$$

where $k = 0.062\sqrt{n}$. Table 1 gives some figures for this result for $p = 0.005$.

TABLE 1

$P(n,p)$ AS A FUNCTION OF $n$

| $n$ | $P(n,p)$ |
|---|---|
| 1000 | $2.7 \times 10^{-2}$ |
| 2000 | $2.6 \times 10^{-3}$ |
| 3000 | $2.5 \times 10^{-4}$ |
| 5000 | $4.0 \times 10^{-6}$ |
| 10,000 | $1.6 \times 10^{-10}$ |

It will be seen that a redundancy greater than 1000 is required before $P$ drops below $p$. Such a design is therefore extremely inefficient. These results concerning system and component replication can be viewed as no more than existence proofs of the theorem that reliable automata may be constructed from networks of unreliable elements.

We note, however, that the basic elements comprising such networks are all majority organs, and as such are "simple" in the sense that they compute functions of only three variables. (Certain other universal elements can be used, e.g., the Sheffer-stroke organ—neither $x$ nor $y$, and this is even simpler.) If more "complex" elements are used, which compute functions of an indefinitely large number of variables, a rather different existence theorem can be proved, wherein the levels of redundancy required for the synthesis of reliable automata can be minimized [Winograd and Cowan (1963)]. The basis for this theorem is to be found in the theory of *error-correcting codes.* Such codes are presently used in the design of reliable long-range communication and telemetry systems, and in the design of reliable computer storage systems. These codes are essentially rules of transformation to and from one set of symbols to another. Thus if $x_1 x_2 \cdots x_k$ is an initial message to be transmitted through a noisy channel, what is in fact transmitted is a sequence of signals $x'_1 x'_2 \cdots x'_n$, where $x'_\beta = e'_\beta(x_1, x_2, \ldots, x_k)$,

($\beta = 1, 2, \ldots, n$). The function $e_\beta$ is called an *encoding function*. In general this means that any $x'_\beta$ is a function of many $x_\alpha (\alpha = 1, \ldots, k)$, and *a fortiori* any $x_\alpha$ is represented in many of the $x'_\beta$. It is this multiple representation which permits the message to be recovered from a signal sequence distorted by transmission through some noisy channel. That is, at the receiver a *decoding function* operates according to the transformation $x_\alpha = d_\alpha(x''_1, \ldots, x''_n)$, where $x''_\beta$ is a (possibly) distorted version of $x'_\beta$. Thus the message $x_1 x_2 \cdots x_k$ is reconstructed.

It will be seen that there are essentially two parameters associated with such a code: the ratio $n/k$, which is a measure of the *redundancy* in the code, and the *complexity* inherent in the coding functions, which we relate to the number of variables over which the functions $e_\beta$ and $d_\alpha$ range. The associated probability of decoding error $P_c$, averaged over a certain collection of codes

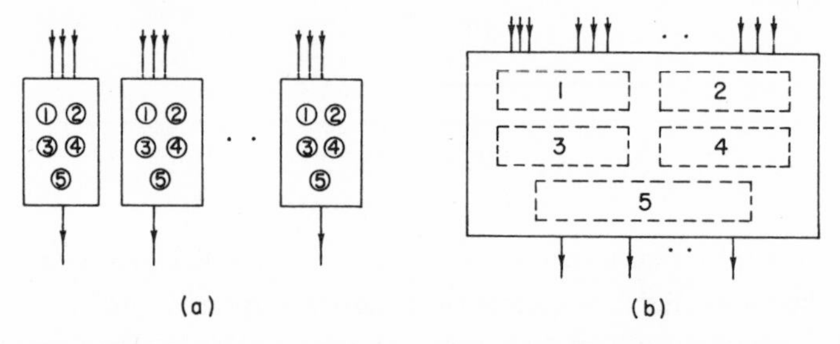


FIG. 10. (a) $k$ copies of $A$. (b) $A'$, a redundant version of the $k$ copies.

which map long sequences of messages into long sequences of signals (and conversely), has been related to the redundancy $n/k$ and to the *noise* in the channel in a famous theorem [Shannon and Weaver (1949)]. It was proved that noisy communication channels could be described by a certain number (the *channel capacity*) which specified a certain minimum redundancy requir-ed for any level of reliable communication through the channel. Thus if $C$ is the channel capacity and $R$ is the so-called *rate* of transmission of informa-tion through the channel (the reciprocal of redundancy) then on the average, for the specified collection of codes,

$$P_c \sim \exp_2(-n(C - R)) \tag{8}$$

Evidently, arbitrarily small error rates ($P_c \to 0$) can be obtained in principle, provided $R \leqslant C$, i.e., provided $K \leqslant nC$, by using sufficiently long message and signal sequences and by preserving the ratio $k/n$. However, this implies that the complexity of the requisite coding equipment increases fairly rapidly with $n$.

Consider now the modular net shown in Fig. 10. As we have noted, (1) implies, for fixed values of $p$, a positive lower bound on $P$. To circumvent this, and to obtain arbitrarily small values of $P$ with fixed $p$, we design a redundant automaton $A'$ in which error-correcting codes are imbedded. We first consider $k$ *copies of the design for* $A$, rather than one copy. However the copies may operate on different sets of inputs or on different programs. We replace each set of $k$ corresponding modules and associated connections by an aggregate of $n$ modules with associated connections, via the following transformation. Let each set of $k$ modules compute the functions $f_{i\alpha}(\mathbf{x}_i)$ $(i=1,\ldots,N;\ \alpha=1,\ldots,k)$, where $\mathbf{x}_i=(x_1,x_2,\ldots,x_s)$ represents the set of input connections to the $i$th module of $A$. Then the functions computed by the $n$ modules of $A'$ are given by

$$f'_{i\beta}=e_\beta\begin{pmatrix} f_{i1}(d'_1(\mathbf{x}''_{in}),d'_1(\mathbf{x}''_{2n}),\ldots,d'_1(\mathbf{x}''_{sn})) \\ f_{i2}(d'_2(\mathbf{x}''_{in}),d'_2(\mathbf{x}''_{2n}),\ldots,d'_2(\mathbf{x}''_{sn})) \\ \cdots \\ f_{ik}(d'_k(\mathbf{x}''_{in}),d'_k(\mathbf{x}''_{2n}),\ldots,d'_k(\mathbf{x}''_{sn})) \end{pmatrix} \tag{9}$$

where the decoding function $d'_\alpha$ is such that it equals $d_\alpha$ if $\mathbf{x}''$ is not an external input, and equals the identity function otherwise. Thus the $k$ modules which compute the functions $f_{i1},f_{i2},\ldots,f_{ik}$ are replaced by $n$ modules which compute the functions $f'_{i1},f'_{i2},\ldots,f'_{in}$, respectively.

It will be seen that each of these functions operates on at most $ns$ input variables, whereas each of the $f_{i\alpha}$ operates on $s$ input variables. Thus each of the modules computing $f'_{i\beta}$ is at most $n$ times more complicated than the modules computing $f_{i\alpha}$. What is gained by this increased complexity is that each module of $A'$ *decodes all its inputs and so corrects errors in modules feeding directly into it, executes its requisite function, and then encodes this computation for transmission to the next aggregate of modules.* Since an $(n,k)$ error-correcting code is obviously imbedded in $A'$, so that the structure of $A'$ is isomorphic to that of $A$, we may combine (1) and (8) to obtain a formula relating $P$, the probability that $A'$ malfunctions, to $P_c$, the average error probability for sufficiently large $n$ and $k$, of $(n,k)$ codes; i.e.,

$$P\leqslant 1-(1-\exp_2(n(C-R)))^Q \tag{10}$$

Equation (10) implies that $P$ may be made arbitrarily small, for fixed $Q$ and $p$, by increasing $n$ in such a way that the ratio $n/k$ is maintained, provided that the modules used have a capacity greater than $k/n$.

In a somewhat similar fashion it can be shown, provided errors of interconnection are not too frequent, that modular redundancy can control such errors.

That is, if each connection of the automaton $A'$ is improper with probability $p$, and proper with probability $1-p$, then if $p \log 1/(1-p) \leqslant (C-R)$, with probability arbitrarily close to 1, $A'$ may still be made to function with arbitrarily high reliability. Thus the quantity $C-R$ defines an ensemble of interconnection patterns over which $A'$ may function reliably. If $C-R$ is very small, the corresponding ensemble has few members, and the interconnections must be made with high precision; on the other hand, if $C-R$ is large, the corresponding ensemble is large, so that interconnections may be made imprecisely, the resultant errors being controlled by the error-correcting codes present in the automaton.

It is clear that this solution to the problem of synthesizing reliable automata from unreliable elements differs radically from von Neumann's solution. In his construction, redundancy was introduced locally, each module being replaced by $n$ copies. This corresponds to the use of an $(n, 1)$ error-correcting code, with associated coding equipment constructed from the simplest of modules. In the Winograd-Cowan theorem, redundancy is introduced nonlocally over an aggregate of $k$ modules via an $(n, k)$ error-correcting code, with the associated (complex) coding equipment imbedded in the $n$ modules comprising the redundant aggregate. In a sense, this construction represents the other extrme to von Neumann's solution, wherein complexity is minimized at the cost of redundancy, to attain arbitrarily small error rates. In this case redundancy is minimized at the cost of complexity. However, it is a crucial requirement of the theorem that modular malfunctions do not become more probable with increased modular complexity. This is not a requirement that can be met by present technological methods of module fabrication, and so neither of the designs represents a practical method for obtaining very high levels of reliable computation. For fixed levels of reliable computation, however, some application seems feasible. See, for example, Tryon (1962), wherein a $(4, 1)$ code is used for single-error correction.

It is clear that suitable combinations of the two techniques of transient error control, multiplexing and coding, may lead to practical solutions to the problem. Given modules of fixed complexity, a certain amount of nonlocal coding may be possible and would result in a lowered error rate for certain aggregate of modules. If still lower error rates are required, there will be a level at which further application of the coding technique will require the use of more complex machines than are available. Such modules would have to be constructed from the (less complex) given ones, in which case (since the number required of these less complex modules increases rapidly with *ns*) there will exist a level where the outputs of the complex modules are statistically independent of the inputs ($C = 0$). This suggests a scheme in which coding is applied at the lowest (elemental) level of organization until either complexity or channel capacity is used up, whence multiplexing is applied *to the coded aggregates.*

It seems reasonable to expect that this method will result in efficient designs for controlling transient errors. That is, for given requirements of reliability, and for given modules, the method will result in some kind of minimum redundancy design. Pierce (1964a, b) has in fact produced results consistent with these ideas.

## III. Control of Stationary Errors

In case the errors occurring in $A$ are stationary, resulting from permanent failures of its elements, the techniques discussed in Section II do not provide completely satisfying answers to the reliability problem, which now becomes the problem of designing an automaton $A'$ whose expected lifetime to failure is arbitrarily longer than the expected lifetime to failure of any of its elements. (In certain cases the problem is that of designing integrated circuit configurations so as to increase the *yield* of usable circuits resulting from a given manufacturing process.)

An important technique recently discovered uses *adaptive* majority organs [Pierce (1962)]. A basic defect in the multiplexing technique in respect of stationary errors is that since some inputs to majority organs are permanently in error, a consistently reliable minority may be "outvoted" by a consistently unreliable majority. Such a limitation may be overcome by the generalized majority organ of Fig. 11. This module computes the quorum function

$$x' = \operatorname{signum}\left[a_0 + \sum_{i=1}^{s} a_i x_i\right] \tag{11}$$

all inputs $x_i$ taking the values $\pm 1$. If input errors are statistically independent, the vote weights $a_i$ can be chosen so that the output $x'$ is the digit most likely to be correct, under the assumption that what is required of the module is a reliable computation of the quorum function on the $x_i$. If the error probability of the $i$th input is $p_i$, then the weights $a_i$ giving such an output are

$$a_0 = \ln(a\ priori \text{ probability of } +1/a\ priori \text{ probability of } -1)$$
$$a_i = \ln(1 - p_i/p_i) \qquad i = 1, \ldots, s \tag{12}$$

If an input is completely random, $p_i = 0.5$; then $a_i = 0$. Thereafter $a_i$ increases monotonically as $p_i$ approaches zero or one. These requisite

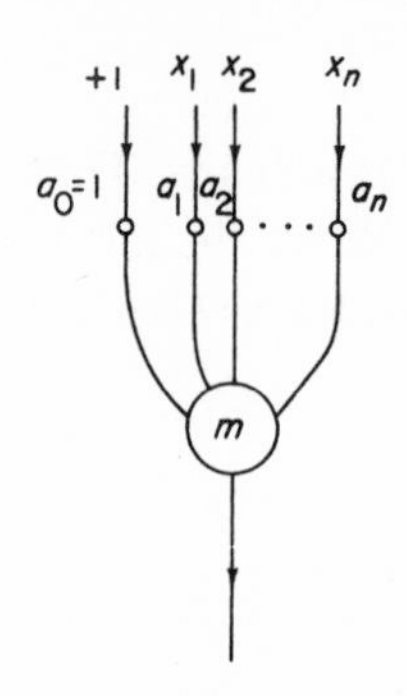


FIG. 11. Generalized majority organ.

settings may be obtained by comparing the inputs $x_i$ with the output $x'$ of the module, and counting the number of coincidences between the values. Thus in a cycle of $M$ operations, if $P_i$ is the number of coincidences and $Q$ the number of disagreements, the settings

$$a_i = \ln(P_i/Q_i) \tag{13}$$

will give (12). It can be shown, provided suitable limits are placed on the possible values of $a_i$, that automatic setting of these weights controlled by feedback from the output is feasible, and that it can be used practically, to optimize the weights.

If errors have the further property that they are catastrophic, i.e., they tend to influence neighboring elements, a modified technique can be used in which a threshold of unreliability $\theta$ is set, so that if $(P_i/Q_i)$ ever exceeds $\theta$, $a_i$ is set to zero. A practical implementation of this is to couple $\theta$ to a fuse-blowing mechanism.

Several other techniques exist for dealing with stationary errors, which generally comprise a combination of fault detection and location (which is a special case of fault masking), with either a component replacement mechanism, or with a switching mechanism, with switches redundant aggregates of unused components (or newly serviced components) into the system, upon receipt of a signal from the fault-location circuits (Löfgren (1962), Griesmer *et al.* (1962)]. Interesting questions concerning the relation between these techniques and the theory of self-reproducing automata [von Neumann (1965)] remain to be investigated.

## References

Griesmer, J. H., R. E. Miller, and J. P. Roth (1962), in *Redundancy Techniques in Computing Systems* (R. H. Wilcox and W. C. Mann, eds.), Spartan Books, Washington, D.C.

Löfgren, L. (1958), *Inform. and Control* **1**, 127–147.

Löfgren, L. (1962), in *Biological Prototypes and Synthetic Systems* (E. Bernard and M. Kare, eds.), Plenum Press, New York.

Moore, E. F., and C. E. Shannon (1956), Reliable circuits using less reliable relays, *J. Franklin Inst.* **262**, 191–208, 281–297.

Pierce, W. H. (1962), in *Redundancy Techniques in Computing Systems* (R. H. Wilcox and W. C. Mann, eds.), Spartan Books, Washington, D.C.

Pierce, W. H. (1964a), *J. Franklin Inst.* **277**, 55–85.

Pierce, W. H. (1964b), *Inform. and Control* **7**, 340–359.

Shannon, C. E., and W. Weaver (1949), *Mathematical Theory of Communication*, Univ. Illinois Press, Urbana.

Tryon, J. G. (1962), in *Redundancy Techniques in Computing Systems* (R. H. Wilcox and W. C. Mann, eds.), Spartan Books, Washington, D.C.

von Neumann, J. (1956), in *Automata Studies* (C. E. Shannon and J. McCarthy, eds.), Princeton University Press, Princeton, N.J.

von Neumann, J. (1965), in *The Theory of Automata: Construction, Reproduction, and Homogeneity* (A. W. Burks, ed.) (to be published by Univ. Illinois Press, Urbana).

Winograd, S., and J. D. Cowan (1963), *Reliable Computation in the Presence of Noise*, M.I.T. Press, Cambridge, Mass.

# Diophantine Equations and Recursively Enumerable Sets

MARTIN DAVIS

*Belfer Graduate School of Science*
*Yeshiva University, New York, New York*

The tenth problem in Hilbert's famous list (see [7]) is to give an algorithm for determining whether or not a polynomial diophantine equation

$$P(x_1, \ldots, x_m) = 0$$

has a solution in integers. We shall discuss the evidently (using the fact that positive integers are just those which can be represented as one more than the sum of four squares) equivalent form of this problem, which seeks positive integer solutions. In fact, Hilbert's tenth problem remains open. If however, we permit

$$P = \sum_{i=1}^{N} t_i$$

where each

$$t_i = C a_1^{b_1} a_2^{b_2} \cdots a_n^{b_n}$$

where in turn $C$ is a positive or negative integer and each $a_i$, $b_i$ is a positive integer or a variable, and then pose the analog of Hilbert's tenth problem for such "exponential diophantine equations," then it may be asserted (see [5]) that this latter problem is recursively unsolvable.

A set $S$ which can be defined as follows:

$$S = \{(x_1, \ldots, x_n) | (Ey_1, \ldots, y_m) [P(x_1, \ldots, x_n, y_1, \ldots, y_m) = 0]\}$$

where $P$ is a polynomial, is called a *diophantine set*. If $P = 0$ is permitted to be an exponential diophantine equation, then $S$ is called an *exponential diophantine* set. So let

$\mathscr{D}$ = set of all diophantine sets
$\mathscr{E}$ = set of all exponential diophantine sets
$\mathscr{R}$ = set of all recursively enumerable (re) sets

Then we have trivially,

$$\mathscr{D} \subset \mathscr{E} \subset \mathscr{R}$$

The interesting problems are to replace these inclusions with equations. Suppose, e.g., that we could show that $\mathscr{D} = \mathscr{R}$. Then $K$ [an re set which is not recursive] would be diophantine. So we could write

$$K = \{x | (Ey_1, \ldots, y_m) [P(x, y_1, \ldots, y_m) = 0]\}$$

where $P$ is a polynomial. Since $K$ is not recursive, there could be no algorithm for testing for given $x_0$, whether or not the diophantine equation

$$P(x_0, y_1, \ldots, y_m) = 0$$

has a solution; so, Hilbert's tenth problem would be unsolvable. The question of whether $\mathscr{D} = \mathscr{R}$ is still open. However, we have the theorem whose proof will be outlined later (see also [5]):

**Theorem.** $\mathscr{E} = \mathscr{R}$.

Hence (by the same argument used above), there is no algorithm for testing exponential diophantine equations for solutions! (For an application to automata theory of the fact that $\mathscr{E} = \mathscr{R}$, see [6].)

So, $\mathscr{D} = \mathscr{R}$ if and only if $\mathscr{D} = \mathscr{E}$. Let us define $x * n$ by

$$x * 1 = x$$
$$x * (n+1) = x^{(x * n)}$$

and let J.R. stand for the proposition

*There is a diophantine set $S$ of ordered pairs such that for some $n$,*

$$(x, y) \in S \rightarrow y \leqslant (x * n)$$

*but for each $k$, there is $(x, y) \in S$ with $y > x^k$.*

Then, Julia Robinson (see [9]) has shown that

J.R. *if and only if* $\mathscr{D} = \mathscr{E}$

Since $\mathscr{E} = \mathscr{R}$, we have

J.R. *if and only if* $\mathscr{D} = \mathscr{R}$

So further investigation seeks to prove J.R. We now give several hypotheses (due to Hilary Putnam and myself) which imply J.R.

Consider the equation $x^3 - my^3 = 1$

It is known (see [8]), that (with one exception which we may ignore) this equation has a solution $(x, y)$ just in case $x - y\sqrt[3]{m}$

is the generator of the group of units of the ring of integers in $R(\sqrt[3]{m})$

By known estimates of the size of this fundamental unit (see [1]), we may deduce that $x^3 - my^3 = 1$ implies $x < m^{m^m} = m * 3$.
Hence, the following proposition implies J.R. and hence that $\mathscr{D} = \mathscr{R}$, and Hilbert's tenth problem is unsolvable:

**Hypothesis.** For each $k$, there are $x, y, m$ such that

$$x^3 - my^3 = 1 \qquad \text{and} \qquad x > m^k$$

Similar considerations regarding the equation $Ax^3 - By^3 = 1$ lead to the following proposition implying J.R.:

**Hypothesis.** For every $k$ there are $A, B, x, y$ with

$$Ax^3 - By^3 = 1 \qquad \text{and} \qquad x \text{ or } y > (A + B)^k$$

This hypothesis is in turn implied by the following proposition:

**Hypothesis.** There are arbitrarily long geometric progressions of integers beginning with 1, whose sum is a perfect cube.

For,

$$1 + r + \cdots + r^{n-1} = z^3$$

becomes

$$r^n - (r - 1)\, z^3 = 1$$

Since this is to hold for arbitrarily large values of $n$, it must hold in particular for arbitrarily large values belonging to one of the three residue classes: $3k$, $3k + 1$, $3k + 2$. But these cases lead, respectively, to

$$(r^k)^3 - (r - 1)\, z^3 = 1$$
$$r(r^k)^3 - (r - 1)\, z^3 = 1$$
$$r^2(r^k)^3 - (r - 1)\, z^3 = 1$$

Julia Robinson has noted (see [5]) that the results given here lead to the following theorem about the rate of growth of solutions of a diophantine equation:

**Theorem.** Suppose that for every diophantine equation

$$P(x, y, t_1, \ldots, t_m) = 0$$

such that for each $x$ the equation is solvable for at most finitely many $y$'s, there is an $n$ such that

$$P(x, y, t_1, \ldots, t_m) = 0 \quad \& \quad x > 1 \rightarrow y \leqslant (x * n)$$

Then for each such $P$ there is an $N$ such that

$$P(x,y,t_1,\ldots,t_m)=0 \quad \& \quad x>1 \rightarrow y<x^N$$

*Proof.* Under our assumption, we must have $\mathscr{D} \neq \mathscr{R}$. For if $\mathscr{D} = \mathscr{R}$, then $\{(x,y) | y=(x*x)\}$ would be diophantine:

$$y=(x*x) \leftrightarrow (Et_1,\ldots,t_m)[P(x,y,t_1,\ldots,t_m)=0]$$

Hence

$$y=(x*x) \quad \& \quad x>1 \rightarrow y \leqslant (x*n)$$

for some $n$. But, $(n+1)*(n+1)>(n+1)*n$.

Since $\mathscr{D} \neq \mathscr{R}$, J.R. is false. But each $P(x,y,t_1,\ldots,t_m)=0$ of the sort being discussed is a candidate for making J.R. true. Hence, the conclusion.

**Proof that $\mathscr{D} = \mathscr{E}$.** We begin by recalling the result (see [2,3]) that a set $S$ is re if and only if it satisfies a condition of the form

$$S=\{x|(Ey)(k)_{\leqslant y}(Ex_1,\ldots,x_m)_{\leqslant y}[P(k,x,y,x_1,\ldots,x_m)=0]\}$$

We call this a normal form for $S$.

Given a polynomial

$$P(k,x,y,x_1,\ldots,x_m)=\sum_{i=1}^{N} t_i$$

where the $t_i$ are terms, let

$$Q(x,y)=\sum_{i=1}^{N} |t_i(y,x,y,\ldots,y)|+y$$

Then

$$Q(x,y) \geqslant y \tag{1}$$

For

$$k,x_1,\ldots,x_m \leqslant y \tag{2}$$

we have

$$|P(k,x,y,x_1,\ldots,x_m)| \leqslant Q(x,y)$$

Then, we have

**Lemma 1.**

$$(k)_{\leqslant y}(Ex_1,\ldots,x_m)_{\leqslant y}[P(k,x,y,x_1,\ldots,x_m)=0] \leftrightarrow (Ec,t,a_1,\ldots,a_m)$$
$$[P(c,x,y,a_1,\ldots,a_m)\equiv 0 \bmod 1+ct \quad \& \quad t=Q(x,y)!$$
$$\& \quad 1+ct=\prod_{k=1}^{y}(1+kt) \quad \& \quad 1+ct | \prod_{j=1}^{y}(a_i-j),\ i=1,2,\ldots,m]$$

*Proof.* Suppose the left side to be true and for each $k \leqslant y$, let $x_1^{(k)},\ldots,x_m^{(k)} \leqslant y$ satisfy

$$P(k,x,y,x_1^{(k)},\ldots,x_m^{(k)})=0$$

Set $t = Q(x,y)!$ and note that $\Pi_{k=1}^{y}(1+kt) \equiv 1 \bmod t$, so that there is a unique $c$ such that

$$1 + ct = \prod_{k=1}^{y} (1 + kt)$$

Since $Q(x,y) \geqslant y$ and $t = Q(x,y)!$ the numbers $1 + kt$, $k \leqslant y$ are relatively prime in pairs. So by the Chinese remainder theorem, for each $i = 1,2,\ldots,m$, there is a number $a_i$ such that *Remainder* $(a_i, 1 + kt) = x_i^{(k)}$.
Now,

$$\begin{aligned} c &\equiv c - c(1 + kt) \\ &\equiv - kct \\ &\equiv k \ (\text{mod } 1 + kt) \end{aligned}$$

since $1 + ct \equiv 0(\text{mod } 1 + kt)$. So,

$$\begin{aligned} 0 &\equiv P(k, x, y, x_1^{(k)}, \ldots, x_m^{(k)}) \\ &\equiv P(c, x, y, a_1, \ldots, a_m)(\text{mod } 1 + kt) \end{aligned}$$

Hence

$$P(c, x, y, a_1, \ldots, a_m) = 0(1 + ct)$$

[since the $(1 + kt)$'s are relatively prime in pairs]. Finally,

$$1 + kt | a_i - x_i^{(k)}$$

and

$$a_i - x_i^{(k)} | \prod_{j=1}^{y} (a_i - j)$$

Hence

$$1 + ct | \prod_{j=1}^{y} (a_i - j)$$

Conversely, suppose the right side is true. Let $p_k$ be a prime factor of $1 + kt$, and let

$$x_i^{(k)} = \textit{Remainder}\ (a_i, p_k)$$

As before,

$$c \equiv k \bmod p_k$$

Hence

$$P(k, x, y, x_1^{(k)}, \ldots, x_m^{(k)}) \equiv 0 \bmod p_k$$

Since

$$p_k | \prod_{j=1}^{y} (a_i - j)$$

*Remainder* $(a_i, p_k) \leqslant y$; i.e., $x_i^{(k)} \leqslant y$. Finally,

$$|P(k, x, y, x_1^{(k)}, \ldots, x_m^{(k)})| \leqslant Q(x, y)$$

But, since

$$p_k | 1 + kt$$

and $t = Q(x, y)!$, it follows that

$$Q(x, y) < p_k$$

Hence

$$P(k, x, y, x_1^{(k)}, \ldots, x_m^{(k)}) = 0$$

This proves the lemma.

Now, we note that by Lagrange's form of Taylor's theorem:

$$\begin{aligned} a^{(2k+1)}(1 + a^{-2})^\alpha &= \sum_{j=0}^{k} \binom{\alpha}{j} a^{2k-2j+1} + R_k(a) \\ &= S_k(a) + R_k(a) \end{aligned}$$

where

$$\begin{aligned} R_k(a) &= \binom{\alpha}{k+1} a^{-1}(1 + \theta a^{-2})^{\alpha-k-1} \\ &= a^{-1}\,\alpha^{k+1}\,2^{\alpha-k-1}\,\theta' \end{aligned}$$

and $0 < \theta, \theta' < 1$. This yields at once

**Lemma 2.** If $a > \alpha^{k+1}2^{\alpha-k}$ and $\alpha > k$, and if $S_{k-1}(a)$ and $S_k(a)$ are integers, then

$$\binom{\alpha}{k} = a^{-1}[a^{2k+1}(1 + a^{-2})^\alpha] - a[a^{2k-1}(1 + a^{-2})^\alpha]$$

(Here $[\mu]$ is the greatest integer $\leqslant \mu$).

**Lemma 3.**

$$y = \binom{m}{k}$$

is exponential-diophantine.

*Proof.* Immediate from Lemma 2.

**Lemma 4.**

$$x! = \left[ r^x \bigg/ \binom{r}{x} \right] \qquad \text{if } r > 2^x x^{x+1}$$

*Proof*

$$\begin{aligned} r^x \bigg/ \binom{r}{x} &= x! \frac{1}{(1 - (1/r)) \cdots (1 - (x-1)/r)} \\ &< x! + \frac{2^x x^{x+1}}{r} \end{aligned}$$

using elementary inequalities. This proves the lemma.

**Lemma 5.** $y = x!$ is exponential-diophantine.

*Proof.* Clear from Lemma 4.

**Lemma 6.**

$$y = \binom{p/q}{k} \qquad p/q > k$$

is exponential-diophantine.

*Proof.* In Lemma 2 we take $a = 2^p p^{k+1} q^k k!$. Then $q^k k! | a$; so $S_{k-1}(a)$ and $S_k(a)$ are integers. The result follows at once.

**Lemma 7.**

$$y = \prod_{k=1}^{y} (a + bk)$$

is exponential-diophantine.

*Proof.*

$$\prod_{k=1}^{y} (a + bk) = \binom{(a/b) + y}{y} b^y y!$$

The theorem now follows at once by writing the given set in its normal form and using Lemmas 1, 5, and 7.

## References


1. H. Cohn, Some algebraic number theory estimates based on the Dedekind etafunction. *Am. J. Math.* **78**, 791–796 (1956).
2. M. Davis, Arithmetical problems and recursively enumerable predicates. *J. Symbolic Logic* **18**, 33–41 (1953).
3. M. Davis, *Computability and Unsolvability*. McGraw-Hill, New York, 1958.
4. M. Davis and H. Putnam. Reduction of Hilbert's tenth problem. *J. Symbolic Logic* **23**, 183–187 (1958).
5. M. Davis, H. Putnam, and J. Robinson, The decision problem for exponential diophantine equations. *Ann. Math.* **74**, 425–436 (1961).
6. C. C. Elgot and J. Rutledge, RS-Machines with almost blank tapes, *J. Assoc. Comp. Mach.* **11**, 313–337 (1964).
7. D. Hilbert, "Mathematische Probleme," Vortrag, gehalten auf dem internationalen Mathematiker-Kongress zu Paris 1900, *Nach. Akad. Wiss. Goettingen. Math. Physik. Kl.* **1900**, 253–297. Reprinted in *Arch. Math. Phys.*, **1**, 44–63, 213–237 (1901). English trans. *Bull. Am. Math. Soc.* **8**, 437–479 (1901–1902).
8. T. Nagell, Solution complète de quelques équations cubiques à deux indéterminées, *J. Mathématique* (9e serie) **4**, 209–270 (1925).
9. J. Robinson, Existential definability in arithmetic, *Trans. Am. Math. Soc.* **72**, 437–449 (1952).

# Recursive Functions—An Introduction

MARTIN DAVIS

*Belfer Graduate School of Science*
*Yeshiva University, New York, New York*

## I. What Is Recursive Function Theory?

Although recursive function theory has, perhaps, little to do with automata theory, Turing machines are being discussed here, and surely recursive function theory is the raison d'être for Turing machines.

Recursive function theory is, in a suitable sense, the theory of computation, or better, of computability. To see what is involved, consider the usual elementary-school algorithm for adding a pair of integers given in decimal notation. For numbers of what size does this algorithm work? The immediate reply, "for numbers of any size," is certainly not literally correct; e.g., we cannot use the algorithm for adding numbers too large to be written on a blackboard the size of the Pacific Ocean. Nevertheless, everyone feels that he understands what is meant by saying that the algorithm works for all numbers. It is with *computation procedures in this somewhat metaphorical sense* that recursive function theory is concerned.

Since an actual digital computer is a finite object subject to limitations of space and time (of which practical programmers are only too aware), one might at first sight assume that digital computers have little to do with the notion of computation being proposed here. But when one considers the availability of auxiliary storage (tapes, cards, etc.), it is seen that the precise limits of a given machine are not well defined. To summarize, we may say that in contexts where it is proper to think of a computing machine augmented with as much storage as needed, and computing as long as necessary to solve a given problem, we are using the word "computation" in the sense intended in recursive function theory.

A function $f$ defined and with values on the nonnegative integers $0, 1, 2, 3, \ldots$ (e.g., $f(x) = x^2$) is called *recursive* or *computable* if there is a computing procedure (in the sense indicated) for computing the values of $f$.

This is not, of course, a rigorous definition, because the meaning of the term "computing procedure" has been indicated only in an informal manner. What makes the theory of recursive (or computable) functions possible is that the class of recursive functions (as defined alone) turns out to be *quite insensitive* to the details of the definition given of computing procedure—definitions which vary widely among themselves all lead to the same class!

## II. Turing's Analysis of Computation

Here, we shall follow Turing's analysis of computation as carried out by a human computer, which led him, by the process of simplification by omission of the inessential, to what we now called Turing machines.

A human computer is observed writing symbols on a sheet of paper in a two-dimensional array, e.g.,

$$\begin{array}{r} 32 \\ 62 \\ \hline 64 \\ 192\phantom{0} \\ \hline 1984 \end{array}$$

Our first simplification is to note that with no loss in computing power, a one-dimensional "strip" of paper would do as well, e.g.,

$$32, 62; 64, 1920; 1984.$$

The computer is at any moment of time aware only of the symbols appearing in a small part of the paper. This is really the essential idea in the notion of a Turing machine—that is behavior is influenced by "local" information only. Our next simplification is to regard as our atomic symbols the data actually "scanned" at a given instant. Finally, we assume that the Turing machine has a finite number of internal *states* or *configurations* and that the next action of a given Turing machine is entirely determined by its present internal configuration, together with the symbol currently scanned. This next action is taken to be either a replacement of the symbol scanned by another, or motion of one square to the left or to the right, followed, in either case, by transition to a new internal configuration.

The fact that a given Turing machine in state $q$ scanning symbol $S$ replaces $S$ by $S'$ and goes into state $q'$ can be expressed by the "quadruple" $qSS'q'$.

Similarly, motions to the left or right are associated with quadruples $qS \leftarrow q'$, $qS \rightarrow q'$. Mathematically, we can simply define a Turing machine to be a finite set of quadruples in which no two quadruples begin with the same pair $qS$. (This last stipulation is just to avoid contradictory instructions.)

We may think of Turing machines in two ways:

1. As above, the $q$'s are configurations (of toothpicks and rubber bands—if these are what the machine is made of) of the machine.
2. The $q$'s are instructions carried out by an abstract machine which can only overprint or move one square.

The latter point of view was the one taken by Post in his work (independent of Turing's) and recently revived by Hao Wang.

In a rigorous development of the subject, each assertion of the recursiveness of a function should be justified by showing that there is a Turing machine which computes the function. Here we shall content ourselves with indicating heuristically that an algorithm exists for computing the function, relying on the cogency of Turing's analysis to convince ourselves that a corresponding Turing machine exists.

## III. Gödel Numbers and a Universal Function

When a Turing machine arrives at a state $q$, scanning a symbol $S$, where the machine contains no quadruple beginning $qS$, the machine will stop, and the computation will be over. However, there may well be arguments for which the machine never stops, but simply continues computing forever. In this case, the machine "computes" a function whose domain of definition is a subset of the set of natural numbers. Such a function is called *partial recursive* or *partially computable*. An example is $f(x) = 10 - x$, undefined for $x > 10$. Also, we shall speak of recursive or partial recursive functions of more than one argument. It is simply necessary to put all the arguments on the tape initially, separated by punctuation marks.

Let us use integers (written decimally) as subscripts on $q$ and $S$ to yield notations for the various internal states and symbols of a Turing machine. Rewriting the subscripts "on the line" the description of a Turing machine becomes a sequence of the symbols $0, 1, 2, 3, 4, 5, 6, 7, 8, 9, q, S, \leftarrow, \rightarrow$. Taking $q, S, \leftarrow, \rightarrow$ as new digits denoting the numbers 10, 11, 12, and 13, respectively, our description of a Turing machine becomes a number written to the base 14. This number is called the Gödel number of the Turing machine.

We now define the important function $\mathscr{A}_z(x)$ as follows: $\mathscr{A}_z(x)$ is the partial recursive function computed by the Turing machine with Gödel number $z$, if there is such; otherwise $\mathscr{A}_z(x) = 0$.

We have:

1. For each partial recursive function $f(x)$ there is a $z$ such that

$$f(x) = \mathscr{A}_z(x)$$

i.e., the sequence

$$\mathscr{A}_0(x), \mathscr{A}_1(x), \mathscr{A}_2(x), \ldots$$

is an enumeration of all partial recursive functions (of one argument).

*Proof.* Let $z$ be the Gödel number of a Turing machine which computes $f(x)$.

2. $\mathscr{A}_z(x)$ is a partial recursive function of two arguments.

For, given $z$ and $x$, to compute $\mathscr{A}_z(x)$, write $z$ to the base 14 and check whether $z$ is a Gödel number of a Turing machine. If not, continue computing forever. If it is, apply the quadruples of that machine to $x$ on its tape. This is an algorithm; hence $\mathscr{A}_z(x)$ is partially computable.

Let $U$ be a Turing machine which computes $\mathscr{A}_z(x)$. Then $U$ is called *universal*, because by placing a suitable $z_0$ on its tape it can be made to compute any partial recursive function.

## IV. Recursive and Recursively Enumerable Sets

Let

$$\omega_i = \{x | \mathscr{A}_i(x) \text{ is defined}\}$$

Then $\omega_0, \omega_1, \omega_2, \ldots$ is an enumeration of all sets which can serve as a domain of definition of partial recursive functions. Such sets are called *recursively enumerable* (re). A set $R$ is *recursive* if its characteristic function

$$C_R(x) = \begin{cases} 1 & \text{if } x \in R \\ 0 & \text{if } x \notin R \end{cases}$$

is recursive. Clearly to say that $R$ is recursive is to say that there is an algorithm by means of which we can test a given number to determine whether or not it belongs to $R$.

**Theorem.** $R$ is recursive if and only if $R$ and $\bar{R}$ (i.e., the set of integers not in $R$) are both re.

*Proof.* If $R$ is recursive, then the functions

$$f_1(x) = \begin{cases} 1 & \text{if } x \in R \\ \text{undefined} & \text{otherwise} \end{cases}$$

$$f_2(x) = \begin{cases} 0 & \text{if } x \in \bar{R} \\ \text{undefined} & \text{otherwise} \end{cases}$$

are both partial recursive, as is readily seen by considering the Turing machine which computes $C_R(x)$. Hence, $R$ and $\bar{R}$ are re.

Conversely, let $R$ and $\bar{R}$ be re so that they are the domains of definition of partial recursive functions computed by Turing machines $T_1$ and $T_2$, respectively. Then, the following is an algorithm for testing whether or not a given integer $x$ belongs to $R$:

Place $x$ on the tapes of $T_1$ and $T_2$, and let both begin computing. Wait until one of them halts. If it is $T_1$, then $x \in R$; if $T_2$, then $x \notin R$.

The question is suggested by this theorem: Is there a re but nonrecursive set? Set $K = \{i \mid i \in \omega_i\}$, so that $K$ is the set of Gödel numbers of Turing machines which halt when their own Gödel number is initially placed on their tape. Then, we have

**Theorem.** $K$ is re, but $\bar{K}$ is not. So, *$K$ is not recursive.*

*Proof.* Since $K$ is the domain of definition of the partial recursive function $\mathscr{A}_i(i)$, $K$ is re.

Suppose $\bar{K}$ is re so that

$$\bar{K} = \omega_q$$

Then

$$i \in \bar{K} \Leftrightarrow i \in \omega_q$$

But

$$i \in \bar{K} \Leftrightarrow i \notin \omega_i$$

Hence, for every $i$,

$$i \in \omega_q \Leftrightarrow i \notin \omega_i$$

Setting $i = q$,

$$q \in \omega_q \Leftrightarrow q \notin \omega_q$$

This is a contradiction.

The argument used in this last proof will be recognized at once as an application of Cantor's diagonal method.

## V. Gödel's Incompleteness Theorem

Mathematicians are in the habit of proving theorems and communicating their results to others. For the purpose of this communication, a *language* either natural or artificial must be used. Thus, to each assertion and to each proof must correspond a finite sequence of symbols (i.e., a linguistic expression). To serve its purpose, one must be able to check mechanically that an alleged proof really is a proof. In practice this last is an unrealized ideal (as everyone who has struggled with "obviouslies" and "clearlies" will readily admit). However, the formal systems of logic constructed by logicians do meet this demand. The content of Gödel's theorem is that if this demand is met, then not all true statements of arithmetic can be proved.

We shall take the following fixed set of mathematical assertions:

$$0 \in \bar{K}$$
$$1 \in \bar{K}$$
$$2 \in \bar{K}$$
$$3 \in \bar{K}$$
$$\cdots$$
$$\cdots$$
$$\cdots$$

Let us suppose that for each $n$ we can obtain (by means of an algorithm) a certain expression $S_n$ which we think of as stating that $n \in \bar{K}$ in a language we construct. Let us further assume that methods of proof have been provided and that we have an algorithm such that given $n$ and an alleged proof of $S_n$, we can determine using the algorithm whether or not the alleged proof of $S_n$ really is one. Finally, let us assume that no false statement can be proved using the rules of proof, that is, that

$$\text{If } \vdash S_i, \text{ then } i \in \bar{K}$$

Here $\vdash S_i$ means that $S_i$ can be proved according to the rules of proof under discussion.

Then we have:

**Gödel's Theorem (Kleene-Post Form).** There is a number $q$ such that $q \in \bar{K}$ but $\not\vdash S_q$.

That is the assertion that $q \in \bar{K}$, is true but unprovable by the given rules of proof.

*Proof.* Let $M = \{i \mid \vdash S_i\}$. First we note that by what we have assumed above,

$$M \subset \bar{K} \tag{1}$$

Second, $M$ is re. For, let

$$f(i) = \begin{cases} 0 & \text{if } \vdash S_i \\ \text{undefined} & \text{otherwise} \end{cases}$$

Clearly $M$ is the domain of definition of $f$. So we need to show that $f$ is partial-recursive. To see that it is, let us first associate integers with each proof, according to the present rules of proof, in a manner similar to what was done above for Turing machines. Now, given an $i$ for which we wish to compute $f(i)$, we generate the integers $0, 1, 2, 3, \ldots$ in order and check each one to see whether or not it is the number of a proof of $S_i$. If it is, we are done, and $f(i) = 0$; otherwise we go on to the next integer.

Since $M$ is re and $\bar{K}$ is not, we have

$$M \neq \bar{K}. \tag{2}$$

Combining (1) and (2) we conclude that some number $q$ belongs to $\bar{K}$ but not to $M$. This completes the proof.

One should note:

1. The "undecidability" of "$q \in \bar{K}$" is a relative matter—in the very act of showing it to be undecidable from certain rules of proof, we show that it is true!
2. Using "stronger" rules of proof can only change the value of $q$.

### VI. The Halting Problem for Turing Machines

Let $R$ be a Turing machine which computes a partial-recursive function whose domain of definition is $K$. Then, we claim that the *halting problem for $R$* is unsolvable in the following sense:

*There is no algorithm by means of which we may test for given input whether or not $R$ will eventually halt when starting with that input.*

For if such an algorithm were available, we could use it to check whether or not a given integer $x$ belongs to $K$: if and only if $R$ halts eventually when it begins with $x$ written on its tape. Since $K$ is not recursive, no such algorithm can exist.

### VII. The Word Problem for Semi-Groups

Let us begin with some alphabet, say $a, b, c, d, e$, and certain equations between words on this alphabet, e.g.

$$bad = cad$$
$$ecc = becd$$
$$aca = bd$$

Then certain derived equations will result, e.g.,

$$\begin{aligned} abade &= acade \\ &= bdde \end{aligned}$$

Generally, given a finite set of equations,

$$\begin{aligned} g_1 &= \bar{g}_1 \\ g_2 &= \bar{g}_2 \\ &\cdots \\ &\cdots \\ g_K &= \bar{g}_K \end{aligned}$$

the resulting *word problem* is to give an algorithm for determining whether two given words are equal according to the given equations. We shall show how to construct a set of equations for which no such algorithm can exist, i.e., an unsolvable word problem.

We begin with a Turing machine $R$ whose halting problem is unsolvable. Let the internal states of $R$ be $q_1, q_2, \ldots, q_M$ and let the symbols it "prints" be $S_0, S_1, \ldots, S_N$, where we take $S_0$ to be the blank so that "erasing" is taken to mean printing $S_0$. We take the tape of $R$ at any given moment to be *finite*. However motion off the end of the tape is always to be prevented by the addition of a blank square. The entire subsequent history of $R$'s computation is determined by specifying at a given moment the corresponding *Post word*:

$$hS_{i_1}S_{i_2}\cdots S_{i_k}q_jS_{i_{k+1}}\cdots S_{i_q}h$$

where

$$S_{i_1}S_{i_2}\cdots S_{i_q}$$

is the word on the tape at this moment of time, $q_j$ is the internal state of $R$, and $S_{i_{k+1}}$ is the symbol scanned. The course of a computation is reflected in a succession of Post words according to the rules (called *semi-Thue* productions):

$$Pq_iS_jQ \rightarrow Pq_lS_kQ \tag{3}$$

whenever $q_iS_jS_kq_l$ is a quadruple of $R$.

$$\left.\begin{aligned} Pq_iS_jS_kQ &\rightarrow PS_jq_lS_kQ \\ Pq_iS_jhQ &\rightarrow PS_jq_lS_0hQ \end{aligned}\right\} \tag{4}$$

whenever $q_iS_j \rightarrow q_l$ is a quadruple of $R$.

$$PS_k q_i S_j Q \to Pq_l S_k S_j Q$$
$$Phq_i S_j Q \to Phq_l S_0 S_j Q \tag{5}$$

whenever $q_i S_j \leftarrow q_l$ is a quadruple of $R$.

We introduce two new symbols $q$ and $q'$ and the additional semi-Thue productions:

$$Pq_i S_j Q \to PqS_j Q \tag{6}$$

if no quadruple beginning $q_i S_j$ belongs to $R$, and the productions:

$$Pq\, S_j Q \to PqQ \tag{7}$$

$$PqhQ \to Pq' hQ \tag{8}$$

$$PS_j q' Q \to Pq' Q \tag{9}$$

The effect of (6) to (9) is to transform the Post word corresponding to the end of a computation (i.e., a time when the machine stops for lack of further instructions) into the word $hq'h$. Hence we have:

$R$ will eventually halt when it begins in a situation described by a given Post word, if and only if the productions (3) to (9) can transform that Post word into $hq'h$.

Now we consider the following equations obtained from (3) to (9):

$$q_i S_j = q_l S_k \tag{3'}$$

$$q_i S_j S_k = S_j q_l S_k \tag{4'a}$$

$$q_i S_j h = S_j q_l S_0 h \tag{4'b}$$

$$S_k q_i S_j = q_l S_k S_j \tag{5'a}$$

$$hq_i S_j = hq_l S_0 S_j \tag{5'b}$$

$$q_i S_j = qS_j \tag{6'}$$

$$qS_j = q \tag{7'}$$

$$qh = q' h \tag{8'}$$

$$S_j q' = q' \tag{9'}$$

where the same restrictions are to be observed as in the statements of the corresponding semi-Thue productions.

Then we have:

**Lemma.** The equation $P = hq'h$, where $P$ is a Post word, is induced by equations (3′) to (9′) if and only if Turing machine $R$ eventually halts when beginning in a situation described by Post word $P$.

*Proof.* Suppose that $R$ will eventually halt when beginning in a situation described by Post word $P$. Then, using (3′) to (5′) we have

$$P = T$$

where $T$ is a post word corresponding to the end of the computation. Next, using (6′) to (9′) we have

$$T = hq'h$$

Next, suppose

$$P = hq'h$$

Then we have a sequence

$$P_1, P_2, \ldots, P_q$$

where $P_1$ is $P$ and $P_q$ is $hq'h$ and $P_{i+1}$ is obtained directly from $P_i$ using *one* of the equations (3′) to (9′).

We wish to show that we can obtain such a sequence in which we use (3′) to (9′), but *reading from left to right*, i.e., using just the semi-Thue productions (3) to (9). To see this, let

$$P_{k+1}, P_{k+2}, \ldots, P_q$$

be obtained using (3) to (9) (as indeed $P_q$ must be obtained from $P_{q-1}$), but let $P_{k+1}$ be obtained from $P_k$ using one of the equations (3′) to (9′) from right to left. But then $P_k$ can be obtained from $P_{k+1}$ using one of equations (3) to (9), i.e., both $P_k$ and $P_{k+2}$ are obtained from $P_{k+1}$ using (3) to (9). But then $P_k$ and $P_{k+2}$ are identical, since no Post word can have more than one successor under (3) to (9). (This is the "monogenic" character of Turing machines.) Hence, we may eliminate $P_k$ and $P_{k+1}$ from the sequence. Continuing this process, we obtain the desired result.

From the lemma it follows at once that equations (3′) to (9′) give rise to an unsolvable word problem. For any algorithm for testing the correction of equations could be used to check whether or not

$$P = hq'h$$

for a Post word $P$ and hence to solve the (unsolvable) halting problem for $R$.

## VIII. Some Concluding Remarks

In conclusion we should like to indicate various directions which work in the theory of recursive functions has taken.

1. There has been work on the unsolvability of various specific mathematical problems. Here the unsolvability of the word problem for groups has been the outstanding result.
2. The classification of recursively enumerable sets.
3. How unsolvable is a problem? For example, consider the set

$$U = \{z \mid \mathscr{A}_z(x) \text{ is everywhere defined}\}$$

It can be shown that $U$ is not only recursive, but that it is more unsolvable than $K$ in the sense that given an "oracle" which will correctly answer our questions about membership in $U$, we can give an algorithm for testing for membership in $K$, but not conversely.

For further details and a bibliography, the reader is referred to the author's *Computability and Unsolvability*, McGraw-Hill, New York, 1958.

# The Reduced Form of a Linear Automaton[1]

ARTHUR GILL

*Department of Electrical Engineering*
*University of California*
*Berkeley, California*

## I. Characterization of Linear Automata

Linear automata are of interest for two reasons: First, these systems constitute a subclass of the class of general automata, where powerful results in the theories of finite groups, rings, and fields, and of linear vector spaces can be exploited to advantage. As such, linear automata serve as a bridge between the theory of finite-state machines and the theory of linear systems. Second, linear automata have found wide application in computer control circuitry, implementation of error-correction codes, random-number generation, and other digital tasks; this provides ample justification for their study from the practical point of view.

One way of defining linear automata is by starting with the characterization of a general automaton:

$$s(t+1) = (s(t), u(t)) \tag{1}$$

$$y(t) = (s(t), u(t)) \tag{2}$$

where $u(t)$, $y(t)$, and $s(t)$ denote the input, output, and state, respectively, at time $t$. An automaton is *linear* if $u(t)$, $y(t)$, and $s(t)$ are vectors [say $\mathbf{u}(t)$ of dimension $l$, $\mathbf{y}(t)$ of dimension $m$, and $\mathbf{s}(t)$ of dimension $n$] over $GF(p)$, and if (1) and (2) assume the form

$$\mathbf{s}(t+1) = \mathbf{A}\mathbf{s}(t) + \mathbf{B}\mathbf{u}(t) \qquad \text{or} \qquad \mathbf{s}' = \mathbf{A}\mathbf{s} + \mathbf{B}\mathbf{u} \tag{3}$$

$$\mathbf{y}(t) = \mathbf{C}\mathbf{s}(t) + \mathbf{D}\mathbf{u}(t) \qquad \text{or} \qquad \mathbf{y} = \mathbf{C}\mathbf{s} + \mathbf{D}\mathbf{u} \tag{4}$$

[1] This study was supported by the Information Systems Branch of the Office of Naval Research under Contract Nonr-222(53), and by the Air Force Office of Scientific Research Grant AFOSR-639-64.

where

$$\mathbf{A} = [a_{ij}]_{nxn} \qquad \mathbf{B} = [b_{ij}]_{nxl}$$
$$\mathbf{C} = [c_{ij}]_{mxn} \qquad \mathbf{D} = [d_{ij}]_{mxl} \tag{5}$$

**A**, **B**, **C**, and **D** are called the *characterizing matrices* of the automaton. **A** is called the *characteristic matrix* and $n$ the *order* of the automaton.

It should be remarked at this point that instead of $GF(p)$, the preceding definition could be made with any finite field $GF(p^k)$. As it turns out, however, any linear automaton over $GF(p^k)$ can be simulated by a linear automaton over $GF(p)$, so that the definition as stated above is more general than may be inferred at first sight [1].

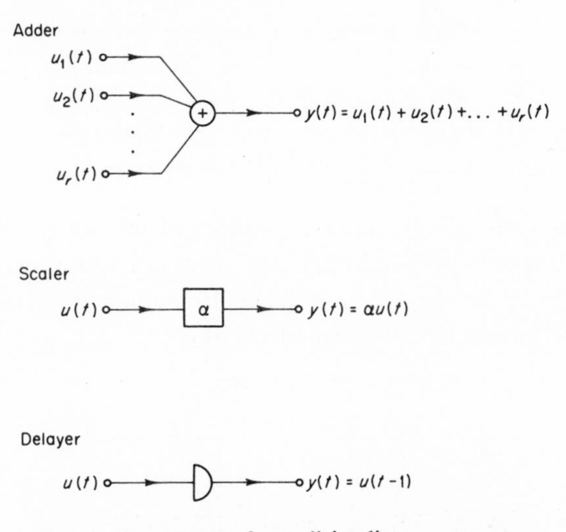


FIG. 1. Components for realizing linear automata.

Linear automata can be realized with elements called *adders*, *scalers*, and *delayers*, whose input-output characteristics are summarized in Fig. 1. In this figure, $u(t)$ or $u_i(t)$ are inputs, $y(t)$ the output, and $\alpha$ an arbitrary element from $GF(p)$; the inputs are elements from $GF(p)$, and all additions and multiplications are performed modulo $p$. Given **A**, **B**, **C**, and **D** as denoted by Eq. (5), a circuit such as the one shown in Fig. 2 can be constructed to simulate the operation of the corresponding automaton.

Conversely, given any interconnection of adders, scalers, and delayers (provided every closed loop contains at least one delayer, to avoid indeterminacy), one can describe its operation via a set of equations of the form (3) and (4). The characterizing matrices can be found as follows:

"Extract" from the circuit all delayers and all terminals assigned as external input and output terminals; label them as shown in Fig. 3. Trace the paths

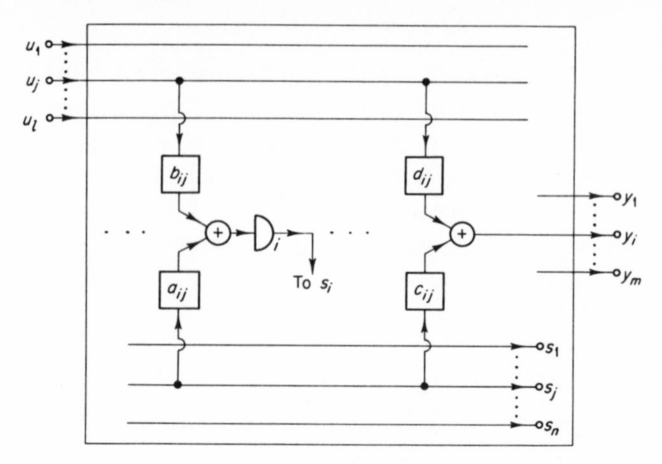


FIG. 2. Realization of linear automata.

leading from $s_j$ to $s'_i$; compute the product of the scaler constants encountered along each path and add the products (all operations are modulo $p$); this sum is $a_{ij}$. Similarly, $b_{ij}$ is obtained from the paths $u_j$ to $s'_i$, $c_{ij}$ from the paths $s_j$ to $y_i$, and $d_{ij}$ from the paths $u_j$ to $y_i$.

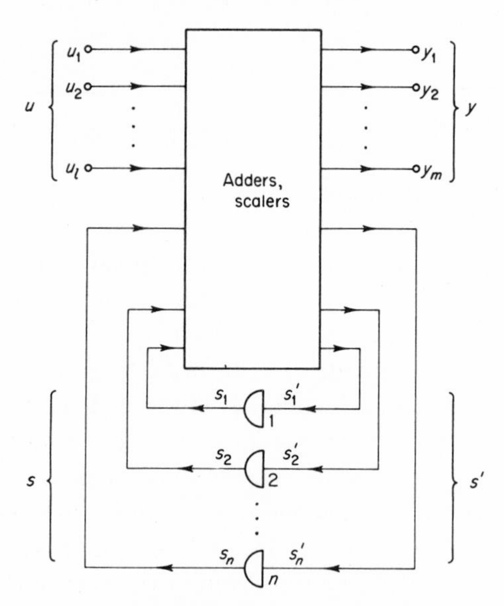


FIG. 3. Evaluation of characterizing matrices.

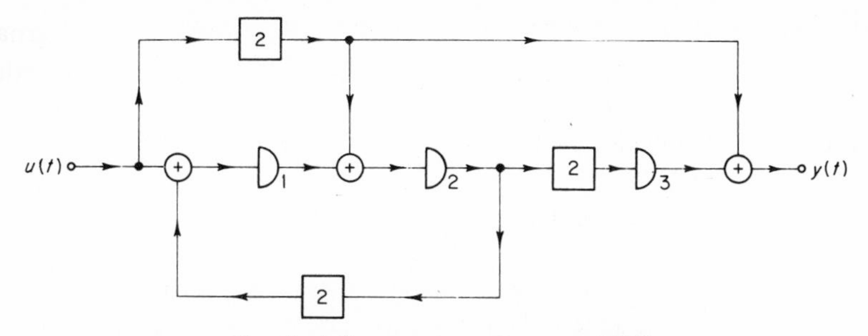


Fig. 4. A linear automation over $GF(3)$.

*Example 1.* Figure 4 shows a 3-delayer automaton over $GF(3)$, where

$$\mathbf{A} = \begin{pmatrix} 0 & 2 & 0 \\ 1 & 0 & 0 \\ 0 & 2 & 0 \end{pmatrix} \qquad \mathbf{B} = \begin{pmatrix} 1 \\ 2 \\ 0 \end{pmatrix} \tag{6}$$

$$\mathbf{C} = (0 \quad 0 \quad 1) \qquad \mathbf{D} = (2)$$

**Assertion 1** [2].

$$\mathbf{s}(t) = \mathbf{A}^t \mathbf{s}(0) + \sum_{\nu=0}^{t-1} \mathbf{A}^{t-\nu-1} \mathbf{B}\mathbf{u}(\nu) \tag{7}$$

*Proof* (by induction on $t$). Setting $t = 0$ in (3), we have

$$\mathbf{s}(1) = \mathbf{A}\mathbf{s}(0) + \mathbf{B}\mathbf{u}(0) \tag{8}$$

which proves (7) for $t = 1$. Hypothesizing (7) for $t$, we have by (3),

$$\begin{aligned} \mathbf{s}(t+1) &= \mathbf{A}[\mathbf{A}^t \mathbf{s}(0) + \sum_{\nu=0}^{t-1} \mathbf{A}^{t-\nu-1} \mathbf{B}\mathbf{u}(\nu)] + \mathbf{B}\mathbf{u}(t) \\ &= \mathbf{A}^{t+1} \mathbf{s}(0) + \sum_{\nu=0}^{t} \mathbf{A}^{t-\nu} \mathbf{B}\mathbf{u}(\nu) \end{aligned} \tag{9}$$

which proves (7) for $t + 1$.

Substituting (9) in (4),

$$\mathbf{y}(t) = \mathbf{C}[\mathbf{A}^t \mathbf{s}(0) + \sum_{\nu=0}^{t-1} \mathbf{A}^{t-\nu-1} \mathbf{B}\mathbf{u}(\nu)] + \mathbf{D}\mathbf{u}(t) \tag{10}$$

or

$$\mathbf{y}(t) = \mathbf{C}\mathbf{A}^t \mathbf{s}(0) + \sum_{\nu=0}^{t} \mathbf{H}(t-\nu)\mathbf{u}(\nu) \tag{11}$$

where

$$\mathbf{H}(t) = \begin{cases} \mathbf{D} & (t = 0) \\ \mathbf{C}\mathbf{A}^{t-1}\mathbf{B} & (t > 0) \end{cases} \tag{12}$$

Thus, $\mathbf{y}(t)$ is the sum of two components: the *free response*

$$\mathbf{y}(t)\big|_{\text{free}} = \mathbf{C}\mathbf{A}^t\mathbf{s}(0) \tag{13}$$

obtained by setting $\mathbf{u}(t) = 0$ for all $t \geqslant 0$, and the *forced response*

$$\mathbf{y}(t)\big|_{\text{forced}} = \sum_{\nu=0}^{t} \mathbf{H}(t-\nu)\,\mathbf{u}(\nu) \tag{14}$$

Given any initial state and input sequence, these components can be found separately and then added. This is a fortunate circumstance, as there are excellent techniques for finding the components individually (involving natural periods for the free response and transfer function for the forced response) but no single method for finding them simultaneously.

## II. Determination of Equivalence Classes

For the ensuing discussion we need the following definition: Let $\mathbf{s}_1$ and $\mathbf{s}_2$ be states in a linear automaton $\mathscr{A}$. Then $\mathbf{s}_1$ and $\mathbf{s}_2$ are *k-equivalent* if $\mathscr{A}$ at $\mathbf{s}_1$ and $\mathscr{A}$ at $\mathbf{s}_2$ yield the same output sequence when excited by any input sequence of length $k$ or less. It is a well-known result [3] that if $\mathscr{A}$ has $p^n$ states and $\mathbf{s}_1$ and $\mathbf{s}_2$ are $(p^n - 1)$-equivalent, then they are equivalent. This leads us to the following:

**Assertion 2.** Let $\mathscr{A}$ be an $n$th-order linear automaton with the characteristic matrix $\mathbf{A}$. Then the states $\mathbf{s}_1$ and $\mathbf{s}_2$ of $\mathscr{A}$ are equivalent if and only if

$$\mathbf{C}\mathbf{A}^t\mathbf{s}_1 = \mathbf{C}\mathbf{A}^t\mathbf{s}_2 \qquad \text{for all } t \geqslant 0 \tag{15}$$

*Proof.* By definition and (11), $\mathbf{s}_1$ and $\mathbf{s}_2$ are equivalent if and only if

$$\mathbf{C}\mathbf{A}^t\mathbf{s}_1 + \sum_{\nu=0}^{t} \mathbf{H}(t-\nu)\,\mathbf{u}(\nu) = \mathbf{C}\mathbf{A}^t\mathbf{s}_2 + \sum_{\nu=0}^{t} \mathbf{H}(t-\nu)\,\mathbf{u}(\nu) \tag{16}$$

for all $\mathbf{u}(t)$ and all $t \geqslant 0$.

The set of all states which are equivalent to the null state $\mathbf{0}$ will be denoted by $E_0$:

$$E_0 = \{\mathbf{s} \mid \mathbf{C}\mathbf{A}^t\mathbf{s} = \mathbf{0} \text{ for all } t \geqslant 0\} \tag{17}$$

If $\mathbf{s}_1$ and $\mathbf{s}_2$ are in $E_0$, then $\alpha_1\mathbf{s}_1 + \alpha_2\mathbf{s}_2$ is in $E_0$ for any $\alpha_1$ and $\alpha_2$ in $GP(p)$. Hence, if $S_n$ denotes the state space of the automaton, $E_0$ is a subspace of $S_n$. Consequently, $E_0$ is a subgroup of the additive Abelian group $S_n$. This subgroup induces a coset partition consisting of the classes $E_0, E_1, \ldots, E_{r-1}$ on $S_n$, which can be found by inspection once $E_0$ is determined.

**Assertion 3** [4]. The coset partition induced by $E_0$ on $S_n$ is the equivalence partition of $S_n$.

*Proof.* $\mathbf{s}_1$ and $\mathbf{s}_2$ are in the same coset $E_i$ if and only if $\mathbf{s}_1 - \mathbf{s}_2$ is in $E_0$, hence if and only if $\mathbf{CA}^t(\mathbf{s}_1 - \mathbf{s}_2) = \mathbf{0}$ for all $t \geqslant 0$, hence if and only if $\mathbf{CA}^t\mathbf{s}_1 = \mathbf{CA}^t\mathbf{s}_2$ for all $t \geqslant 0$, and hence—by Assertion 2—if and only if $\mathbf{s}_1$ and $\mathbf{s}_2$ are equivalent.

Let $N_i$ denote the null space of $\mathbf{CA}^i$:

$$N_i = \{\mathbf{s} | \mathbf{CA}^i = \mathbf{0}\} \tag{18}$$

The set of all states which are $k$-equivalent to $\mathbf{0}$ is given by $N_0 \cap N_1 \cap \cdots \cap N_{k-1}$. Hence

$$E_0 = N_0 \cap N_1 \cap \cdots \cap N_{p^n-2} \tag{19}$$

(See the Appendix for an alternative method for finding $E_0$).

*Example 2.* Consider the 4th-order linear automaton, over $GF(2)$, whose characterizing matrices are

$$\mathbf{A} = \begin{pmatrix} 0 & 1 & 1 & 1 \\ 1 & 0 & 1 & 1 \\ 0 & 0 & 0 & 1 \\ 0 & 0 & 1 & 0 \end{pmatrix} \qquad \mathbf{B} = \begin{pmatrix} 1 \\ 0 \\ 0 \\ 0 \end{pmatrix} \tag{20}$$
$$\mathbf{C} = (0 \quad 0 \quad 0 \quad 1) \qquad \mathbf{D} = (0)$$

Thus

$$\mathbf{CA} = (0 \quad 0 \quad 1 \quad 0) \tag{21}$$

$$\mathbf{CA}^2 = (0 \quad 0 \quad 0 \quad 1) = \mathbf{C} \tag{22}$$

By inspection,

$$\begin{aligned} N_0 &= \{0000, 0010, 0100, 0110, 1000, 1010, 1100, 1110\} \\ N_1 &= \{0000, 0001, 0100, 0101, 1000, 1001, 1100, 1101\} \end{aligned} \tag{23}$$

$$\begin{aligned} E_0 = N_0 \cap N_1 &= \{0000, 0100, 1000, 1100\} \\ E_1 &= \{0001, 0101, 1001, 1101\} \\ E_2 &= \{0010, 0110, 1010, 1110\} \\ E_3 &= \{0011, 0111, 1011, 1111\} \end{aligned} \tag{24}$$

The reduced form of the automaton in this case consists of four states.

## III. The Generating Matrix for $E_0$

From the theory of linear vector spaces we know that a basis for any subspace of $S_n$—and in particular a basis of $E_0$—can be chosen to form a matrix in a column-reduced echelon form. This matrix, denoted by $\mathbf{G}_{E_0}$, is exemplified by the following one:

$$\mathbf{G}_{E_0} = \begin{pmatrix} 1 & 0 & 0 \\ \alpha_{21} & 0 & 0 \\ 0 & 1 & 0 \\ \alpha_{24} & \alpha_{42} & 0 \\ \alpha_{51} & 0 & 0 \\ 0 & 0 & 1 \end{pmatrix} \tag{25}$$

(In this form every leading term in each column is 1, every row containing such a leading term has all its other entries 0, and the leading term of any column is below the leading term in any preceding column.) To simplify the ensuing discussion, we shall assume that $\mathbf{G}_{E_0}$ is of the form

$$\mathbf{G}_{E_0} = \begin{pmatrix} \mathbf{I}_k \\ \mathbf{Q} \end{pmatrix} \tag{26}$$

where $\mathbf{I}_k$ is a $k \times k$ identity matrix and $\mathbf{Q}$ an $(n-k) \times k$ matrix. The form (26) can always be obtained from (25) by permuting rows of the original form. This, however, amounts to renaming the states and hence to considering an automaton isomorphic to the original one, which has no bearing on the minimization process.

**Assertion 4.** $E_0$ is the set of all states of the form

$$s_0 = \begin{pmatrix} \boldsymbol{\sigma} \\ \mathbf{Q}\boldsymbol{\sigma} \end{pmatrix} \tag{27}$$

where $\boldsymbol{\sigma}$ is any $k$-dimensional vector.

*Proof.* $E_0$ is the set of all linear combinations of columns of $\mathbf{G}_{E_0}$; hence, if $\mathbf{Q}_j$ is the $j$th column of $\mathbf{Q}$,

$$\mathbf{s}_0 = \begin{pmatrix} \alpha_1 \\ \alpha_2 \\ \vdots \\ \alpha_k \\ \cdots\cdots\cdots\cdots\cdots\cdots \\ \alpha_1 \mathbf{Q}_1 + \alpha_2 \mathbf{Q}_2 + \cdots + \alpha_k \mathbf{Q}_k \end{pmatrix} \tag{28}$$

which becomes (27) if we let

$$\boldsymbol{\sigma} = \begin{pmatrix} \alpha_1 \\ \alpha_2 \\ \vdots \\ \alpha_k \end{pmatrix} \tag{29}$$

**Assertion 5.** If $\boldsymbol{\sigma}$ is any $k$-dimensional vector and $\boldsymbol{\sigma}_1$ any $n-k$ dimensional vector, then

$$\begin{pmatrix} \boldsymbol{\sigma} \\ \boldsymbol{\sigma}_1 \end{pmatrix} \text{ is equivalent to } \begin{pmatrix} \mathbf{0} \\ \boldsymbol{\sigma}_1 - \mathbf{Q}\boldsymbol{\sigma} \end{pmatrix} \tag{30}$$

*Proof*

$$\begin{pmatrix} \boldsymbol{\sigma} \\ \boldsymbol{\sigma}_1 \end{pmatrix} - \begin{pmatrix} \mathbf{0} \\ \boldsymbol{\sigma}_1 - \mathbf{Q}\boldsymbol{\sigma} \end{pmatrix} = \begin{pmatrix} \boldsymbol{\sigma} \\ \mathbf{Q}\boldsymbol{\sigma} \end{pmatrix} \tag{31}$$

which, by Assertion 4, is a state in $E_0$. The two states, therefore, are in the same coset induced by $E_0$ and hence—by Assertion 3—are equivalent.

**Assertion 6.** Let $\mathbf{A}$ have the partitioned form

$$\mathbf{A} = \overset{\rightarrow k \leftarrow}{\begin{pmatrix} \mathbf{A}_1 & \mathbf{A}_2 \\ \mathbf{A}_3 & \mathbf{A}_4 \end{pmatrix}} \begin{matrix} \downarrow \\ k \\ \uparrow \end{matrix} \tag{32}$$

Then

$$(\mathbf{Q}\mathbf{A}_2 - \mathbf{A}_4)\mathbf{Q} = \mathbf{A}_3 - \mathbf{Q}\mathbf{A}_1 \tag{33}$$

*Proof*

$$\mathbf{A}\mathbf{s}_0 = \begin{pmatrix} \mathbf{A}_1 & \mathbf{A}_2 \\ \mathbf{A}_3 & \mathbf{A}_4 \end{pmatrix} \begin{pmatrix} \boldsymbol{\sigma} \\ \mathbf{Q}\boldsymbol{\sigma} \end{pmatrix} = \begin{pmatrix} (\mathbf{A}_1 + \mathbf{A}_2\mathbf{Q})\boldsymbol{\sigma} \\ (\mathbf{A}_3 + \mathbf{A}_4\mathbf{Q})\boldsymbol{\sigma} \end{pmatrix} \tag{34}$$

Since $\mathbf{A}\mathbf{s}_0$, like $\mathbf{s}_0$, must be in $E_0$, it must be of the form $\begin{pmatrix} \boldsymbol{\sigma} \\ \mathbf{Q}\boldsymbol{\sigma} \end{pmatrix}$. Hence,

$$(\mathbf{A}_3 + \mathbf{A}_4\mathbf{Q})\boldsymbol{\sigma} = \mathbf{Q}(A_1 + \mathbf{A}_2\mathbf{Q})\boldsymbol{\sigma} \tag{35}$$

which yields (33).

## IV. The Minimization Procedure

Let $\mathscr{A}$ be a linear automaton with the characterizing matrices

$$\mathbf{A} = \underset{\rightarrow k \leftarrow}{\overset{\rightarrow k \leftarrow}{\begin{pmatrix} \mathbf{A}_1 & \mathbf{A}_2 \\ \mathbf{A}_3 & \mathbf{A}_4 \end{pmatrix}}} \begin{matrix} \downarrow \\ k \\ \uparrow \end{matrix} \qquad \mathbf{B} = \begin{pmatrix} \mathbf{B}_1 \\ \mathbf{B}_2 \end{pmatrix} \begin{matrix} \downarrow \\ k \\ \uparrow \end{matrix} \tag{36}$$

$$\mathbf{C} = (\mathbf{C}_1 \quad \mathbf{C}_2) \qquad \mathbf{D}$$

Consider a new automaton $\check{\mathscr{A}}$ with the characterizing matrices

$$\begin{aligned} \check{\mathbf{A}} &= \mathbf{A}_4 - \mathbf{Q}\mathbf{A}_2 & \check{\mathbf{B}} &= \mathbf{B}_2 - \mathbf{Q}\mathbf{B}_1 \\ \check{\mathbf{C}} &= \mathbf{C}_2 & \check{\mathbf{D}} &= \mathbf{D} \end{aligned} \tag{37}$$

**Assertion 7.** $\check{\mathscr{A}}$ is equivalent to $\mathscr{A}$.

*Proof.* We shall show that every state $\mathbf{s} = \begin{pmatrix} \boldsymbol{\sigma} \\ \boldsymbol{\sigma}_1 \end{pmatrix}$ in $\mathscr{A}$ is equivalent to the state $\check{\mathbf{s}} = \boldsymbol{\sigma}_1 - \mathbf{Q}\boldsymbol{\sigma}$ in $\check{\mathscr{A}}$. This implies that every state $\boldsymbol{\sigma}_1$ of $\check{\mathscr{A}}$ is equivalent to $\begin{pmatrix} \boldsymbol{\sigma} \\ \boldsymbol{\sigma}_1 \end{pmatrix}$ of $\mathscr{A}$. Thus for every state in $\mathscr{A}$ there is a state equivalent to it in $\check{\mathscr{A}}$, and conversely, and hence $\mathscr{A}$ and $\check{\mathscr{A}}$ are equivalent. Now, for any given $\mathbf{u}$, the output $\mathbf{y}$ of $\mathscr{A}$ is, by (30), given by

$$\begin{aligned} \mathbf{y} = \mathbf{Cs} + \mathbf{Du} &= (\mathbf{C}_1\,\mathbf{C}_2)\begin{pmatrix} \boldsymbol{\sigma} \\ \boldsymbol{\sigma}_1 \end{pmatrix} + \mathbf{Du} \\ &= (\mathbf{C}_1\,\mathbf{C}_2)\begin{pmatrix} \mathbf{0} \\ \boldsymbol{\sigma}_1 - \mathbf{Q}\boldsymbol{\sigma} \end{pmatrix} + \mathbf{Du} \\ &= \mathbf{C}_2(\boldsymbol{\sigma}_1 - \mathbf{Q}\boldsymbol{\sigma}) + \mathbf{Du} \end{aligned} \tag{38}$$

The corresponding output $\check{\mathbf{y}}$ of $\check{\mathscr{A}}$ is given by

$$\check{\mathbf{y}} = \check{\mathbf{C}}\check{\mathbf{s}} + \check{\mathbf{D}}\mathbf{u} = \mathbf{C}_2(\boldsymbol{\sigma}_1 - \mathbf{Q}\boldsymbol{\sigma}) + \mathbf{Du} = \mathbf{y} \tag{39}$$

Hence $\mathbf{s}$ and $\check{\mathbf{s}}$ are 1-equivalent. The next state of $\mathscr{A}$ is given by

$$\begin{aligned} \mathbf{s}' = \mathbf{As} + \mathbf{Bu} &= \begin{pmatrix} \mathbf{A}_1 & \mathbf{A}_2 \\ \mathbf{A}_3 & \mathbf{A}_4 \end{pmatrix}\begin{pmatrix} \boldsymbol{\sigma} \\ \boldsymbol{\sigma}_1 \end{pmatrix} + \begin{pmatrix} \mathbf{B}_1 \\ \mathbf{B}_2 \end{pmatrix}\mathbf{u} \\ &= \begin{pmatrix} \mathbf{A}_1\,\boldsymbol{\sigma} + \mathbf{A}_2\,\boldsymbol{\sigma}_1 + \mathbf{B}_1\,\mathbf{u} \\ \mathbf{A}_3\,\boldsymbol{\sigma} + \mathbf{A}_4\,\boldsymbol{\sigma}_1 + \mathbf{B}_2\,\mathbf{u} \end{pmatrix} = \begin{pmatrix} \boldsymbol{\sigma}' \\ \boldsymbol{\sigma}_1' \end{pmatrix} \end{aligned} \tag{40}$$

The next state of $\check{\mathscr{A}}$ is given by

$$\begin{aligned} \check{\mathbf{s}}' = \check{\mathbf{A}}\check{\mathbf{s}} + \check{\mathbf{B}}\mathbf{u} &= (\mathbf{A}_4 - \mathbf{QA}_2)(\boldsymbol{\sigma}_1 - \mathbf{Q}\boldsymbol{\sigma}) + (\mathbf{B}_2 - \mathbf{QB}_1)\,\mathbf{u} \\ &= \mathbf{A}_4\,\boldsymbol{\sigma}_1 + \mathbf{B}_2\,\mathbf{u} - \mathbf{Q}(\mathbf{A}_2\,\boldsymbol{\sigma}_1 + \mathbf{B}_1\,\mathbf{u}) + (\mathbf{QA}_2 - \mathbf{A}_4)\,\mathbf{Q}\boldsymbol{\sigma} \end{aligned} \tag{41}$$

Using (35), the last term can be replaced with $(\mathbf{A}_3 - \mathbf{QA}_1)\,\boldsymbol{\sigma}$. Hence,

$$\begin{aligned} \check{\mathbf{s}}' &= (\mathbf{A}_3\,\boldsymbol{\sigma} + \mathbf{A}_4\,\boldsymbol{\sigma}_1 + \mathbf{B}_2\,\mathbf{u}) - \mathbf{Q}(\mathbf{A}_1\,\boldsymbol{\sigma} + \mathbf{A}_2\,\boldsymbol{\sigma}_1 + \mathbf{B}_1\,\mathbf{u}) \\ &= \boldsymbol{\sigma}_1' - \mathbf{Q}\boldsymbol{\sigma}' \end{aligned} \tag{42}$$

Repeating (40) with $\boldsymbol{\sigma}'$ replacing $\boldsymbol{\sigma}$, and $\boldsymbol{\sigma}_1'$ replacing $\boldsymbol{\sigma}_1$, it can be shown that $\mathbf{s}$ and $\check{\mathbf{s}}$ are 2-equivalent. Repeating $p^n - 1$ times proves that $\mathbf{s}$ and $\check{\mathbf{s}}$ are equivalent.

**Assertion 8.** $\check{\mathscr{A}}$ is a reduced automaton.

*Proof.* Suppose $\boldsymbol{\sigma}_1$ and $\boldsymbol{\sigma}_2$ in $\check{\mathscr{A}}$ are equivalent. This implies that $\begin{pmatrix} \mathbf{0} \\ \boldsymbol{\sigma}_1 \end{pmatrix}$ and $\begin{pmatrix} \mathbf{0} \\ \boldsymbol{\sigma}_2 \end{pmatrix}$ in $\mathscr{A}$ are equivalent, and hence that $\begin{pmatrix} \mathbf{0} \\ \boldsymbol{\sigma}_1 \end{pmatrix} - \begin{pmatrix} \mathbf{0} \\ \boldsymbol{\sigma}_2 \end{pmatrix} = \begin{pmatrix} \mathbf{0} \\ \boldsymbol{\sigma}_1 - \boldsymbol{\sigma}_2 \end{pmatrix}$ is in $E_0$

and hence of the form $\begin{pmatrix}\boldsymbol{\sigma} \\ \mathbf{Q}\boldsymbol{\sigma}\end{pmatrix}$. Thus we must have $\boldsymbol{\sigma}_1 - \boldsymbol{\sigma}_2 = \mathbf{Q}\mathbf{0} = \mathbf{0}$ and $\boldsymbol{\sigma}_1 = \boldsymbol{\sigma}_2$.

**Corollary.** If an automaton is linear, then its minimal form is also linear.

*Example 3*. Consider the 5th-order linear automaton over $GF(2)$, whose characterizing matrices are (see Fig. 5)

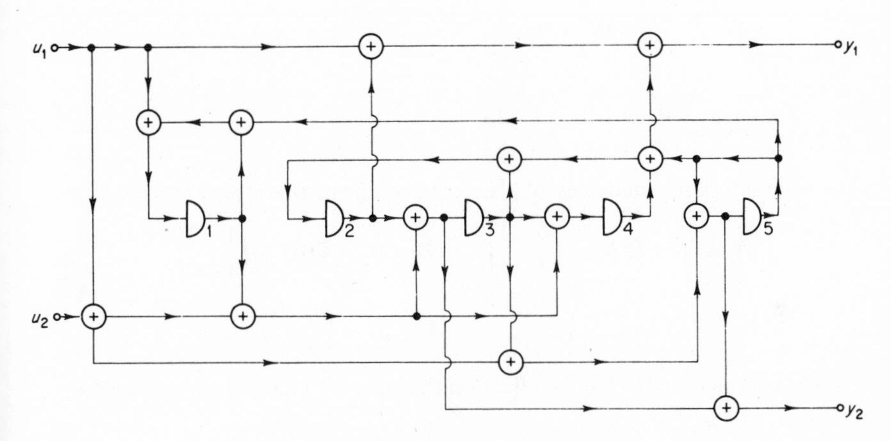


FIG. 5. A linear automaton over $GF(2)$.

$$\mathbf{A} = \begin{pmatrix} 1 & 0 & 0 & 0 & 1 \\ 0 & 0 & 1 & 1 & 1 \\ 1 & 1 & 0 & 0 & 0 \\ 1 & 0 & 1 & 0 & 0 \\ 0 & 0 & 1 & 0 & 1 \end{pmatrix} \qquad \mathbf{B} = \begin{pmatrix} 1 & 0 \\ 0 & 0 \\ 1 & 1 \\ 1 & 1 \\ 1 & 1 \end{pmatrix} \tag{43}$$

$$\mathbf{C} = \begin{pmatrix} 0 & 1 & 0 & 1 & 1 \\ 1 & 1 & 1 & 0 & 1 \end{pmatrix} \qquad \mathbf{D} = \begin{pmatrix} 1 & 0 \\ 0 & 0 \end{pmatrix}$$

In this case,

$$\mathbf{G}_{E_0} = \begin{pmatrix} 1 & 0 & 0 \\ 0 & 1 & 0 \\ 0 & 0 & 1 \\ \cdots & \cdots & \cdots \\ 1 & 0 & 1 \\ 1 & 1 & 1 \end{pmatrix} \begin{matrix} \uparrow \\ k \\ \downarrow \\ \\ \left.\begin{matrix} \\ \\ \end{matrix}\right\} \mathbf{Q} \end{matrix} \tag{44}$$

The partitioning of **A**, **B**, and **C** takes the form

$$\mathbf{A} = \left(\begin{array}{ccc:cc} 1 & 0 & 0 & 0 & 1 \\ 0 & 0 & 1 & 1 & 1 \\ 1 & 1 & 0 & 0 & 0 \\ \hdashline 1 & 0 & 1 & 0 & 0 \\ 0 & 0 & 1 & 0 & 1 \end{array}\right) \qquad \mathbf{B} = \left(\begin{array}{cc} 1 & 0 \\ 0 & 0 \\ 1 & 1 \\ \hdashline 1 & 1 \\ 1 & 1 \end{array}\right) \tag{45}$$

where $\mathbf{A}_1$ is the upper left block, $\mathbf{A}_2$ the upper right, $\mathbf{A}_3$ the lower left, $\mathbf{A}_4$ the lower right; $\mathbf{B}_1$ the upper three rows and $\mathbf{B}_2$ the lower two rows.

$$\mathbf{C} = \left(\begin{array}{ccc:cc} 0 & 1 & 0 & 1 & 1 \\ 1 & 1 & 1 & 0 & 1 \end{array}\right)$$

with $\mathbf{C}_1$ the left block and $\mathbf{C}_2$ the right block.

The characterizing matrices of the reduced form, therefore, are given by

$$\check{\mathbf{A}} = \mathbf{A}_4 - \mathbf{Q}\mathbf{A}_2 = \begin{pmatrix} 0 & 1 \\ 1 & 1 \end{pmatrix} \qquad \check{\mathbf{B}} = \mathbf{B}_2 - \mathbf{Q}\mathbf{B}_1 = \begin{pmatrix} 1 & 0 \\ 1 & 0 \end{pmatrix}$$
$$\check{\mathbf{C}} = \mathbf{C}_2 = \begin{pmatrix} 1 & 1 \\ 0 & 1 \end{pmatrix} \qquad \check{\mathbf{D}} = \mathbf{D} = \begin{pmatrix} 1 & 0 \\ 0 & 0 \end{pmatrix} \tag{46}$$

(Note that the input $u_2$ has no effect on the circuit.) The reduced automaton is shown in Fig. 6.

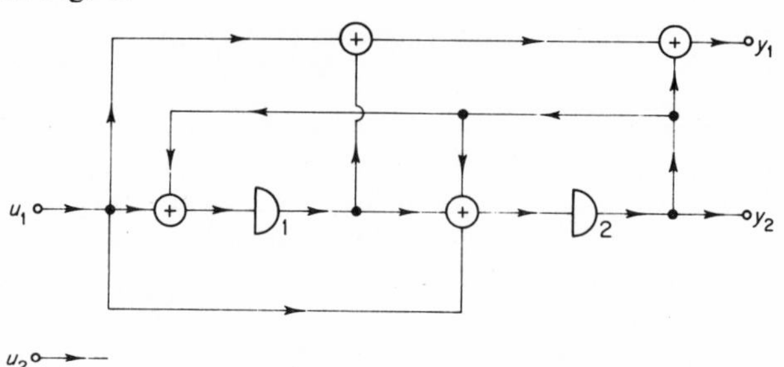


FIG. 6. The reduced form of automaton of Fig. 5.

It should be noted that nowhere in the proposed minimization procedure has the fact been exploited that the underlying field is finite. In fact, if $E_0$ is determined as shown in the Appendix, the procedure remains valid for infinite underlying fields, as well as finite fields of any order.

### Appendix: Determination of $E_0$

An improved method for determining $E_0$ was proposed to the author by M. A. Arbib. It is based on the following:

**Assertion 9.** $E_0$ is the null space of

$$\mathbf{M} = \begin{pmatrix} \mathbf{C} \\ \mathbf{CA} \\ \vdots \\ \mathbf{CA}^{n-1} \end{pmatrix} \tag{47}$$

i.e.,

$$E_0 = \{\mathbf{s} | \mathbf{Ms} = \mathbf{0}\} \tag{48}$$

*Proof.* If $\mathbf{Ms} = \mathbf{0}$, then

$$\mathbf{Cs} = \mathbf{0}, \mathbf{CAs} = \mathbf{0}, \ldots, \mathbf{CA}^{n-1}\mathbf{s} = \mathbf{0} \tag{49}$$

Since the minimum polynomial of $\mathbf{A}$ is of degree at most $n$, any $\mathbf{CA}^t$ can be expressed as a linear combination of rows of $\mathbf{M}$, and hence $\mathbf{CA}^t\mathbf{s} = \mathbf{0}$ for all $t$. Thus, if $\mathbf{Ms} = \mathbf{0}$, $\mathbf{s}$ is in $E_0$. Conversely, if $\mathbf{s}$ is in $E_0$, it must at least satisfy $\mathbf{Ms} = \mathbf{0}$.

## References

1. T. L. Booth, Representation of signal flow through linear and nonlinear sequential networks, Ph.D. Thesis, Univ. Conn., Storrs, 1962.
2. B. Friedland, Linear modular sequential circuits, *IRE Trans.* **CT-6**, 61–68 (1959).
3. A. Gill, *Introduction to the Theory of Finite-State Machines*, McGraw-Hill, New York, 1962, Chap. 3.
4. G. Hotz, On the mathematical theory of linear sequential networks, *in* "Switching Theory in Space Technology" (H. Aiken and W. F. Main, eds.), pp. 11–19. Stanford Univ. Press, Stanford, California, 1963.

# State Graphs of Autonomous Linear Automata[1]

ARTHUR GILL

*Department of Electrical Engineering*
*University of California*
*Berkeley, California*

## I. Autonomous Linear Automata

An autonomous linear automaton $\mathscr{A}$ of order $n$ is characterized by

a. A finite field $GF(p) = \{0, 1, \ldots, p-1\}$ (where all operations are modulo $p$).

b. An $n$-dimensional state space $S_n$ with vectors $\mathbf{s}$ over $GF(p)$.

c. A rule of operation given by

$$\mathbf{s}(t+1) = \mathbf{A}\mathbf{s}(t) \qquad \text{or} \qquad \mathbf{s}' = \mathbf{A}\mathbf{s} \tag{1}$$

where $\mathbf{A}$ is an $n \times n$ matrix over $GF(p)$, called the *characteristic matrix* of $\mathscr{A}$.

The *state graph* of $\mathbf{A}$ or $\mathscr{A}$ has a vertex for every one of the $p^n$ states and an arrow leading from $\mathbf{s}$ to $\mathbf{s}'$ whenever $\mathbf{s}' = \mathbf{A}\mathbf{s}$. Two graphs $G$ and $\bar{G}$ are *isomorphic* if a one-to-one correspondence can be established between $G$ and $\bar{G}$ in the following manner: State $\mathbf{s}$ of $G$ corresponds to state $\bar{\mathbf{s}}$ of $\bar{G}$ if and only if the successor of $\mathbf{s}$ corresponds to the successor of $\bar{\mathbf{s}}$.

**Assertion 1.** If $\mathbf{A}$ and $\bar{\mathbf{A}}$ are similar, their state graphs are isomorphic.

*Proof.* Let $\bar{\mathbf{A}} = \mathbf{P}\mathbf{A}\mathbf{P}^{-1}$. Establish the correspondence $\bar{\mathbf{s}} \to \mathbf{P}\mathbf{s}$. Since $\mathbf{P}$ is nonsingular, this correspondence is one-to-one. Moreover,

$$\bar{\mathbf{s}}' = \bar{\mathbf{A}}\bar{\mathbf{s}} = (\mathbf{P}\mathbf{A}\mathbf{P}^{-1})(\mathbf{P}\mathbf{s}) = \mathbf{P}(\mathbf{A}\mathbf{s}) = \mathbf{P}\mathbf{s}'.$$

In particular, the graph of $\mathbf{A}$ is isomorphic to the graph of $\mathbf{A}^*$, the rational canonical form of $\mathbf{A}$. If $d_1(x), d_2(x), \ldots, d_W(x)$ are the elementary divisors of

[1] This study was supported by the Information Systems Branch of the Office of Naval Research under Contract Nonr-222(53), and by the Air Force Office of Scientific Research Grant AFOSR-639-64.

**A** [each being a power of an irreducible monic polynomial over $GF(p)$], and if $\mathbf{M}_{d_i(x)}$ denotes the companion matrix of $d_i(x)$, then

$$\mathbf{A}^* = \begin{pmatrix} \mathbf{M}_{d_1(x)} & \mathbf{0} & \cdots & \mathbf{0} \\ \mathbf{0} & \mathbf{M}_{d_2(x)} & \cdots & \mathbf{0} \\ \vdots & & & \\ \mathbf{0} & \mathbf{0} & & \mathbf{M}_{d_w(x)} \end{pmatrix} \tag{2}$$

The submatrices $\mathbf{M}_{d_i(x)}$ are called the *elementary blocks* of $\mathbf{A}^*$; if

$$d_i(x) = \alpha_0 + \alpha_1 x + \cdots + \alpha_{k-1} x^{k-1} + x^k, \tag{3}$$

then

$$\mathbf{M}_{d_i(x)} = \begin{pmatrix} 0 & 0 & \cdots & 0 & -\alpha_0 \\ 1 & 0 & & 0 & -\alpha_1 \\ \vdots & & & & \\ 0 & 0 & & 1 & -\alpha_{k-1} \end{pmatrix} \tag{4}$$

$\mathbf{M}_{d_i(x)}$ is nonsingular if and only if $\alpha_0 \neq 0$.

If one is interested in analyzing the state graph of **A** only up to isomorphism, $\mathbf{A}^*$ is just as adequate as **A** and offers considerable advantages. (In synthesis, the rational canonical form implies that, up to isomorphism, the state graph of **A** can be realized by means of feedback shift registers [1].)

## II. Nonsingular Automata

When **A** is nonsingular, $\mathscr{A}$ is called a *nonsingular* automaton. In this case $\mathbf{s} = \mathbf{A}^{-1}\mathbf{s}'$ and each state has a unique predecessor (as well as a unique successor). The state graph, therefore, consists of cycles only (at least one cycle—that consisting of the null state—is of length 1). For the remainder of this section, **A** will be assumed to be nonsingular.

The period of a state **s** is the least integer such that $\mathbf{A}^T\mathbf{s} = \mathbf{s}$ (i.e., the length of the cycle which contains **s**).

**Assertion 2.** Let

$$\mathbf{A} = \begin{pmatrix} \mathbf{A}_1 & \mathbf{0} \\ \mathbf{0} & \mathbf{A}_2 \end{pmatrix} \tag{5}$$

and let $\begin{pmatrix} \mathbf{s}_1 \\ \mathbf{0} \end{pmatrix}$ and $\begin{pmatrix} \mathbf{0} \\ \mathbf{s}_2 \end{pmatrix}$ be two states partitioned as **A** in (5), having periods $T_1$ and $T_2$, respectively. Then the period of $\mathbf{s} = \begin{pmatrix} \mathbf{s}_1 \\ \mathbf{s}_2 \end{pmatrix}$ is $lcm(T_1, T_2)$.[1]

[1] $lcm(\nu_1, \nu_2, \ldots, \nu_r)$ is the least common multiple of $\nu_1, \nu_2, \ldots, \nu_r$.

*Proof.* If $T$ is the period of $\mathbf{s}$, it is the least integer such that $\mathbf{A}^T\mathbf{s} = \mathbf{s}$ or

$$\begin{pmatrix} \mathbf{A}_1^T \mathbf{s}_1 \\ \mathbf{A}_2^T \mathbf{s}_2 \end{pmatrix} = \begin{pmatrix} \mathbf{s}_1 \\ \mathbf{s}_2 \end{pmatrix} \tag{6}$$

Hence, $T$ is a multiple of $T_1$ and $T_2$. Since (6) holds when $T = lcm(T_1, T_2)$, the assertion follows.

Up to isomorphism, the state graph of $\mathscr{A}$ can be described by its *cycle set*

$$\Sigma = \{N_1[T_1], N_2[T_2], \ldots, N_q[T_q]\} \tag{7}$$

where $N_i$ is the number of cycles of length $T_i$. Each integer pair $N_i[T_i]$ is called a *cycle term.*

Now, consider a matrix $\mathbf{A}$ of the form (5). Suppose the state graph of $\mathbf{A}_1$ has $N_1$ cycles of length $T_1$, and the state graph of $\mathbf{A}_2$ has $N_2$ cycles of length $T_2$. Hence there are $N_1 T_1$ states of the form $\begin{pmatrix} \mathbf{s}_1 \\ \mathbf{0} \end{pmatrix}$, $N_2 T_2$ states of the form $\begin{pmatrix} \mathbf{0} \\ \mathbf{s}_2 \end{pmatrix}$, and thus $N_1 N_2 T_1 T_2$ states of the form $\begin{pmatrix} \mathbf{s}_1 \\ \mathbf{s}_2 \end{pmatrix}$. By Assertion 2, then, the number of cycles of length $lcm(T_1, T_2)$ is given by[1]

$$\frac{N_1 N_2 T_1 T_2}{lcm(T_1, T_2)} = N_1 N_2 gcd(T_1, T_2) \tag{8}$$

Now, define the product of two cycle terms as follows:

$$N_1[T_1] N_2[T_2] = N_1 N_2 gcd(T_1, T_2)[lcm(T_1, T_2)] \tag{9}$$

$\Sigma_1 \Sigma_2$ is defined as the cycle set consisting of all products $a_i b_j$, where $a_i$ is a cycle term of $\Sigma_1$ and $b_j$ is a cycle term of $\Sigma_2$. Thus, we have

**Assertion 3.** If $\mathbf{A}_1$ and $\mathbf{A}_2$ in (5) have the cycle sets $\Sigma_1$ and $\Sigma_2$, respectively, the cycle set of $\mathbf{A}$ is $\Sigma_1 \Sigma_2$.

Generalizing, we have the following result due to Elspas [1]:

**Assertion 4.** Let $d_1(x), d_2(x), \ldots, d_W(x)$ be the elementary divisors of $\mathbf{A}$, and let $\Sigma_i$ be the cycle set of $\mathbf{M}_{d_i(x)}$. Then the cycle set of $\mathbf{A}$ is $\Sigma_1 \Sigma_2 \cdots \Sigma_W$.

The cycle set of each elementary block can be found as follows [1]: If $d_i(x) = [p(x)]^e$, where $p(x)$ is of degree $h$, and if $T_j$ is the least integer $\nu$ such that $[p(x)]^j$ divides $1 - x^\nu$, then

$$\Sigma_i = \left\{1[1], \frac{p^h - 1}{T_1}[T_1], \frac{p^{2h} - p^h}{T_2}[T_2], \ldots, \frac{p^{eh} - p^{(e-1)h}}{T_e}[T_e]\right\} \tag{10}$$

[1] $gcd(\nu_1, \nu_2, \ldots, \nu_r)$ is the greatest common divisor of $\nu_1, \nu_2, \ldots, \nu_r$.

($T_1$ divides $p^h - 1$ and can be found by trial and error; $T_j = p^k T_1$, where $k$ is the least integer such that $p^k \geqslant j$).

## III. Nilpotent Automata

If **A** is nilpotent ($\mathbf{A}^t = 0$ for some $t$), its elementary divisors are all of the form $x^r$. An elementary block of $\mathbf{A}^*$ has the form

$$\mathbf{M}_{x^r} = \begin{pmatrix} 0 & 0 & \cdots & 0 & 0 \\ 1 & 0 & & 0 & 0 \\ 0 & 1 & & 0 & 0 \\ \vdots & & & & \\ 0 & 0 & & 1 & 0 \end{pmatrix} \tag{11}$$

$\mathbf{A}^*$ has the form

$$\mathbf{A}^* = \begin{pmatrix} \mathbf{M}_{x^{r_1}} & \mathbf{0} & \cdots & \mathbf{0} \\ \mathbf{0} & \mathbf{M}_{x^{r_2}} & \cdots & \mathbf{0} \\ \vdots & & & \\ \mathbf{0} & \mathbf{0} & & \mathbf{M}_{x^{r_w}} \end{pmatrix} \tag{12}$$

By writing (12) explicitly and observing what happens to a typical state when successively multiplied by $\mathbf{A}^*$, one can arrive at the following conclusions:

(a) The state graph of **A** is a tree whose root is the null state and whose height $L$ is the largest $r_\nu$.

(b) If $N_i$ denotes the number of states in level $i$, and $m_j$ the number of $j \times j$ elementary blocks in $\mathbf{A}^*$, then

$$N_i = p^{m_1 + 2m_2 + 3m_3 + \cdots + (i-1)m_{i-1} + i(m_i + m_{i+1} + \cdots + m_L)} - (1 + N_1 + N_2 + \cdots + N_{i-1}) \tag{13}$$

(c) The number of states reaching any given state in $i$ steps is either 0 or $1 + N_1 + N_2 + \cdots + N_i$.

The integers $m_1, m_2, \ldots, m_L$, together with these properties, are sufficient to construct the tree for **A** recursively, starting at the root and proceeding towards the top.

## IV. General Automata

In general, the elementary divisors of **A** are of the form $\alpha_0 + \alpha_1 x + \cdots + x^k$, where $\alpha_0 \neq 0$, or $x^k$ (since these divisors are powers of irreducible polynomials). Hence, each elementary block in $\mathbf{A}^*$ is either nonsingular or nilpotent. Thus, we can write

$$\mathbf{A}^* = \begin{pmatrix} \mathbf{A}_0 & \mathbf{0} \\ \mathbf{0} & \mathbf{A}_1 \end{pmatrix} \tag{14}$$

where $\mathbf{A}_0$ is nilpotent and $\mathbf{A}_1$ is nonsingular.

Partitioning states in accordance with $\mathbf{A}^*$ in (14), it is clear that all states of the form $\begin{pmatrix} \mathbf{s}_0 \\ \mathbf{0} \end{pmatrix}$ constitute a tree whose root is $\mathbf{0}$ (called the *null tree* of $\mathbf{A}$), which is the state graph of $\mathbf{A}_0$; all states of the form $\begin{pmatrix} \mathbf{0} \\ \mathbf{s}_1 \end{pmatrix}$ (called *cyclic states*) constitute cycles which are precisely the state graph of $\mathbf{A}_1$.

**Assertion 5.** Every cyclic state in the state graph of $\mathbf{A}$ is the root of a tree isomorphic to the null tree of $\mathbf{A}$.

*Proof.* Let $\begin{pmatrix} \mathbf{0} \\ \boldsymbol{\theta} \end{pmatrix}$ be any cyclic state, and let $\begin{pmatrix} \mathbf{s}_0 \\ \mathbf{0} \end{pmatrix}$ be any state which reaches $\mathbf{0}$ in $\nu$ steps. Establish the following correspondence:

$$\mathbf{s} = \begin{pmatrix} \mathbf{s}_0 \\ \mathbf{0} \end{pmatrix} \rightarrow \bar{\mathbf{s}} = \begin{pmatrix} \mathbf{s}_0 \\ (\mathbf{A}_1^{\nu})^{-1}\boldsymbol{\theta} \end{pmatrix} \tag{15}$$

which is, clearly, one to one. Since

$$\mathbf{s}' = \mathbf{A}^*\mathbf{s} = \begin{pmatrix} \mathbf{A}_0\mathbf{s}_0 \\ \mathbf{0} \end{pmatrix}, \qquad \bar{\mathbf{s}}' = \mathbf{A}^*\bar{\mathbf{s}} = \begin{pmatrix} \mathbf{A}_0\mathbf{s}_0 \\ (\mathbf{A}_1^{\nu-1})^{-1}\boldsymbol{\theta} \end{pmatrix} \tag{16}$$

it follows that $\mathbf{s}'$ and $\bar{\mathbf{s}}'$ also bear this correspondence.

A procedure can now be summarized for constructing the state graph of a general autonomous linear automaton:

a. Find $\mathbf{A}^*$ and partition as in (14).

b. Construct the state graph of $\mathbf{A}_0$ (a tree) and of $\mathbf{A}_1$ (cycles).

c. The state graph of the automaton consists of the cycles of $\mathbf{A}_1$, with the tree of $\mathbf{A}_0$ attached to every state.

## Reference

1. B. Elspas, The theory of autonomous linear sequential networks, *IRE Trans.* **CT-6**, 45–60 (1959).

# Sur Certains Procédés de Définition de Langages Formels

MAURICE GROSS[1]

*Centre National de la Recherche Scientifique*
*Institut Blaise Pascal, Paris, France*

Nous définissons une opération de composition sur des grammaires de Chomsky, linéaires. Les mots engendrés par une telle grammaire servent à définir des dérivations d'une autre grammaire de ce type. Cette composition de grammaires permet d'engendrer une famille de langages qui contient les C-langages. Nous étendrons à cette famille certaines propriétés des C-langages.

## I. Grammaires Linéaires de Chomsky

Rappelons la définition de ce type de C-grammaire ([3], [5]) une C-grammaire linéaire (Cl-grammaire) est définie au moyen de deux alphabets: $V_A$ (alphabet auxiliaire), $V_T$ (alphabet terminal) tous deux finis, et par des règles de réécriture [2] des types

$$A \to xBy \qquad \text{et} \qquad A \to z$$

avec $A, B \in V_A$ et $x, y, z \in F(V_T)$ le monoïde libre engendré par $V_T$. Dans $V_A$ on distinguera un élément: l'axiome. On appellera dérivation une suite

$$f_1, f_2, \ldots, f_k$$

telle que $f_{i+1}$ se déduit de $f_i$ $(1 < i \leqslant k)$ en remplaçant dans $f_i$ un symbole auxiliaire par le second membre d'une règle qui correspond à ce symbole.

Si $f_1$ est l'axiome de la grammaire, le langage engendré par cette grammaire est l'ensemble des $f_k$ terminaux que l'on peut obtenir par application des règles de la grammaire, dans ce cas les $f_i$ ne contiennent qu'un seul symbole auxiliaire; nous écrirons

$$f_1 = S \text{ (axiome)} \Rightarrow f_k \text{ (mot terminal)}: S \text{ engendre } f_k$$

[1] *Present address:* Linguistic Department, University of Pennsylvania, Philadelphia, Pennsylvania.

Exemple

$$G_0: \left| \begin{array}{l} A \rightarrow aAa \\ A \rightarrow bAb \\ A \rightarrow c \end{array} \right| \qquad \begin{array}{l} V_A = \{A\} \quad \text{axiome } A \\ V_T = \{a, b, c\} \end{array}$$

La suite:

$(D_0)$: $A$, $aAa$, $abAba$, $abaAaba$, $abaaAaaba$ est une dérivation dans $G_0$ le langage $L_0$ engendré à partir de $A$ est $L_0 = \{xc\tilde{x}: x \in F(\{a,b\})\}$ où $\tilde{x}$ est l'image miroir de $x$.

A toute règle on peut associer un arbre: Par exemple à $A \rightarrow aAa$ on associe:

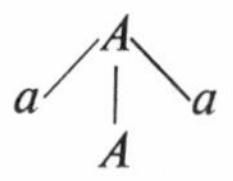

```
   A
 / | \
a  |  a
   A
```

ce qui permet également d'associer un arbre à une dérivation: à $(D_0)$ correspond:

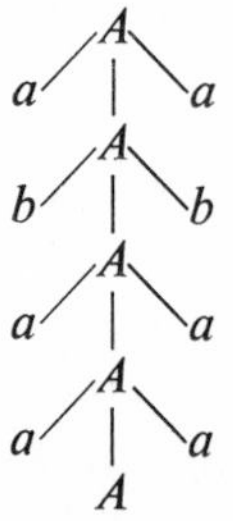

```
   A
 / | \
a  |  a
   A
 / | \
b  |  b
   A
 / | \
a  |  a
   A
 / | \
a  |  a
   A
```

Pour les grammaires nous utiliserons indifféremment cette notation, ou bien la notation sous forme d'équations ([5], [11] á [13]):

Ainsi $(G_0)$ deviendra:

$(EG_0)$: $A = aAa + bAb + c$.

Plus généralement, en regroupant dans une grammaire linéaire quelconque les règles ayant toutes un même premier membre, on obtient un système de type linéaire:

$(EG)$: $\{A_i = \Sigma x_j A_k y_l + \Sigma' z_m\colon 1 \leqslant i \leqslant n\}$ avec $V_A = \{A_i\ 1 \leqslant i \leqslant n\}$, $V_T$, et $x_j, y_l, z_m \in F(V_T)$. Les $\Sigma$ et $\Sigma'$ sont des sommes finies.

$(EG)$ est un système de $n$ équations à $n$ inconnues, sa solution est un $n$-uplets de séries formelles à variates noncommutatives, chaque élément du $n$-uplet correspondant à une variable $A_i$. Si on choisit pour axiome $A_1$, par exemple, le langage engendré par le système est le support de la série formelle associée à $A_1$ [12].

### II. Le Produit $\oplus$ de Deux Equations

Nous définirons un produit noncommutatif de deux équations linéaires noté: $\oplus$, de la manière suivante:

$A_i = \Sigma\alpha$ et $A_j = \Sigma\varphi$ sont deux équations linéaires.
$A_i \oplus A_j$ n'est défini que si au second membre de $A_i = \Sigma\alpha$, figure un monôme $xA_jy$ au moins.

Soit $\Sigma^{(ij)}_{x,y} xA_jy$ la partie du second membre de $A_i = \Sigma\alpha$ qui contient tous les monômes $xA_jy$, alors

$$A_i \oplus A_j = \sum_{x,y}^{(ij)} x(\Sigma\varphi)\,y$$

L'opération $\oplus$ est associative, soit $\Sigma^{(jk)}_{u,v} uA_kv$ la somme partielle de $\Sigma\varphi$ qui contient tous les monômes $uA_kv$ et soit $A_k = \Sigma\psi$ on a

$$A_i \oplus A_j \oplus A_k = \sum_{x,y}^{(i,j)} x\left(\sum_{u,v}^{(j,k)} u(\Sigma\psi)\,v\right)y$$

Nous pouvons décrire l'opération $\oplus$ en termes d'arbres: à $A_i = \Sigma^{(ij)} xA_jy$ nous associerons l'ensemble d'arbres:

$$\sum_{x,y}^{(ij)} \begin{array}{ccc} & A_i & \\ x\diagup & | & \diagdown y \\ & A_j & \end{array}$$

et nous aurons

$$A_i \oplus A_j = \sum_{x,y}^{(ij)} \begin{array}{ccc} & A_i & \\ x\diagup & | & \diagdown y \\ & A_j & \\ & | & \\ & \varphi_l & \end{array} + \cdots + \sum_{x,y}^{(ij)} \begin{array}{ccc} & A_i & \\ x\diagup & | & \diagdown y \\ & A_j & \\ & | & \\ & \varphi_r & \end{array}$$

$$A_i \oplus A_j \oplus A_k = \Sigma \begin{array}{ccc} & A_i & \\ x\diagup & | & \diagdown y \\ & A_j & \\ u\diagup & | & \diagdown v \\ & A_k & \\ & | & \\ & \psi_s & \end{array}$$

Nous appellerons *d*-mot un produit tel que $D = A_{i_1} \oplus A_{i_2} \oplus \cdots \oplus A_{i_m}$ et nous conviendrons que $D$ représente une somme du type

$$\Sigma x_1 x_2 \cdots x_{m-1} f y_{m-1} \cdots y_2 y_1$$

qui peut être terminale ou non suivant la nature de $f$, c'est-à-dire la nature des règles $A_m \to f$; dans les cas où $f$ contient un symbole auxiliaire, $A_1$ par exemple, $A_1$ représente en général une série infinie: $A_1 = \Sigma g$ dans ce cas $D$ représente aussi une série infinie: la série

$$D = \Sigma x_1 x_2 \cdots x_{m-1} (\Sigma g) y_{m-1} \cdots y_2 y_1$$

à laquelle on peut associer un ensemble d'arbres comme ci-dessus.

## III. Composition de Cl-Grammaires

L'opération élémentaire de composition entre deux grammaires $G_1$ et $G_2$ consistera à engendrer des $d$-mots au moyen de $G_1$, et ces $d$-mots seront des dérivations dans $G_2$.

Pour ceci nous noterons la grammaire $G_1$ de la manière suivante: Toute règle $M_i \to XM_j Y$: $M_i, M_j \in V_A^1$; $X, Y \in F(V_T^1)$ avec $V_T^1 = \{A_i: 1 \leqslant i \leqslant n\}$ et $X = A_{i_1} A_{i_2} \cdots A_{i_p}$, $Y = A_{j_1} A_{j_2} \cdots A_{j_q}$ sera remplacée par la règle

$$M_i \to A_{i_1} \oplus A_{i_2} \oplus \cdots \oplus A_{i_p} \oplus M_j \oplus A_{j_1} \oplus A_{j_2} \oplus \cdots \oplus A_{j_q}$$

toute règle $M_i \to Z = A_{k_1} A_{k_2} \cdots A_{k_r}$ sera remplacée par la règle $M_i \to A_{k_1} \oplus A_{k_2} \oplus \cdots \oplus A_{k_r}$, où $\oplus$ est un nouveau terminal ajouté à $V_T^1$. $V_T^1$ sert d'alphabet auxiliaire à $G_2$; $G_1$ engendre des $d$-mots qui contrôlent des dérivations dans $G_2$, ce qui associe aux $d$-mots de $G_1$ des mots de $G_2$. Nous dirons que $G_2$ est connectée à $G_1$.

*Exemple*

$G_1$: $V_A^1 = \{T, S\}$ (axiome $T$); $V_T^1 = \{P, A, B\} \cup \{\oplus\}$;

$$\left| \begin{array}{l} T = S \oplus P \\ S = A \oplus A + B \oplus B + A \oplus S \oplus A + B \oplus S \oplus B \end{array} \right|$$

$G_2$: $V_A^2 = \{P, A, B\}$; $V_T^2 = \{a, b\}$ (on ne choisit pas d'axiome dans $G_2$);

$$\left| \begin{array}{l} A = aAa + bBb + P \\ B = bBb + aAa + P \\ P = e \end{array} \right|$$

($e$ élément neutre pour la concaténation)

Le langage engendré par $G_1$ se compose de $d$-mots de la forme $F \oplus \tilde{F} \oplus P$, ou $F$ est une séquence quelconque de $A$ et de $B$ séparés par l'opérateur $\oplus$; $P$ est un signe de ponctuation qui permet de terminer les dérivations dans $G_2$.

Soit $A \oplus A \oplus A \oplus B \oplus B \oplus A \oplus A \oplus A \oplus P \in L(G_1)$, à ce *d*-mot va correspondre dans $G_1$ la dérivation: *aAa*, *aaAaa*, *aaaAaaa*, *aaabBbaaa*, *aaabbBbbaaa*, *aaabbaAabbaaa*, *aaabbaaAaabbaaa*, *aaabbaaaPaaabbaaa*, *aaabbaaaaaabbaaa*. Il est clair que le système de grammaires $\{G_1, G_2\}$ engendre le langage $L = \{x\tilde{x}x\tilde{x}: x \in F(\{a,b\})\}$.

Plus généralement, nous considérerons des systèmes comportant un ensemble fini de Cl-grammaires, certaines engendrent des *d*-mots, d'autres engendrent des mots terminaux pour le système, ces grammaires sont connectées; l'une d'elles (engendrant des *d*-mots en général) sera choisie comme grammaire axiome et un axiome sera distingué dans l'alphabet auxiliaire. Le langage engendré par un tel système est l'ensemble des mots terminaux (par opposition aux *d*-mots qui ne sont terminaux que par rapport à une *d*-grammaire élément du système) qu'on peut obtenir à partir de l'axiome par dérivations successives dans des grammaires connectées.

Il est possible de représenter un tel système par un graphe orienté dont les sommets sont des grammaires et où une arète entre deux grammaires indique la connection avec son sens; on distinguera un sommet initial: la grammaire axiome, des sommets terminaux: les grammaires engendrant des mots terminaux. Nous conviendrons qu'une grammaire ne peut pas être connectée à elle-même, ceci causerait une confusion entre ses $V_T$ et $V_A$. Une grammaire qui est l'union de *k* grammaires peut donner lieu à des configurations du type (1) (Fig. 1), une même grammaire peut interpréter des *d*-mots de plusieurs grammaires, ceci donne lieu à des configurations du type (2) (Fig. 1).

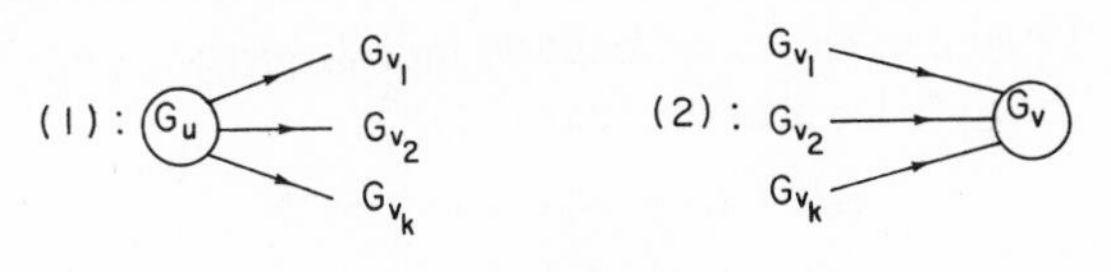


FIG. 1

## IV. Automate Associé à une Cl-Grammaire

Considérons une grammaire élément d'un système et qui soit autre que l'axiome, elle fonctionne à la manière d'un transducteur; en fonction des symboles d'un mot d'entrée elle écrit des symboles en sortie (Fig. 2).

L'automate se compose d'une unité centrale susceptible de prendre un nombre fini d'états: $\{S_i: 1 \leqslant i \leqslant n\}$ associés aux symboles auxiliaires de la grammaire.

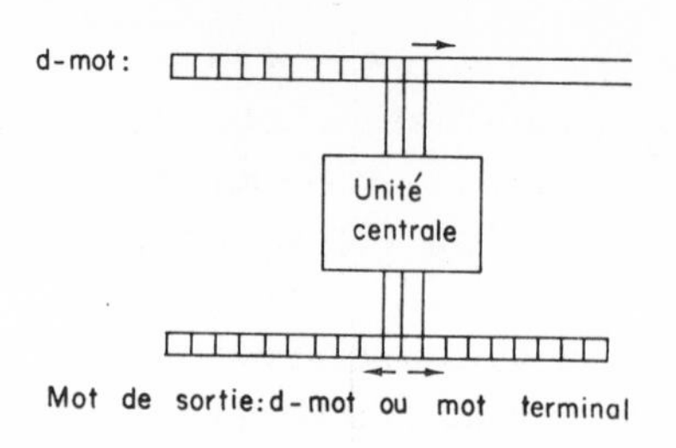


FIG. 2

Une tête de lecture "double" permet de lire à la fois deux symboles d'un *d*-mot inscrit sur une bande qui se déplace de gauche à droite et qui est illimitée à droite.

Une tête d'écriture "double" permet d'écrire des mots simultanément sur deux rubans qui se déplacent l'un vers la droite, l'autre vers la gauche,[1] de plus cette tête procure les quantités de bande nécessaires à l'écriture.

Le fonctionnement de l'automate est décrit par des instructions du type

$$(a): (A_i, A_j; S_i) \rightarrow (S_j; x, y)$$

qui s'interprètent comme suit: l'automate démarre avec la tête de lecture positionnée sur les deux symboles les plus à gauche du *d*-mot d'entrée; soient $A_i$ et $A_j$ deux symboles lus, l'automate passe de l'état $S_i$ à l'état $S_j$, déplace la bande d'entrée d'une case, et écrit $x$ sur la bande de sortie de gauche, $y$ sur la bande de sortie de droite si la grammaire possède la règle $A_i \rightarrow xA_jy$, sinon l'automate se bloque; les bandes de sortie sont déplacées des longueurs de bande correspondant à $x$ et $y$, respectivement.

Quand l'automate se trouve en bout de mot de lecture, il lit $A_k\,\#$, où $\#$ est le blanc, il obéit à des instructions des types

$$(b): (A_k, \#; S_k) \rightarrow (S_f; z)$$
$$(c): (A_k, \#; S_k) \rightarrow (S_r; x, y)$$

qui s'interprètent: (b): $A_k$ est le premier membre d'une règle terminale: $A_k \rightarrow z$, le calcul se termine par l'écriture de $z$ sur une bande (sortie gauche, par exemple) et dans l'état distingué $S_f$, toute la bande d'entrée ayant été lue. (c): $A_k$ est le premier membre d'une règle: $A_k \rightarrow xA_ry$, on a la même action qu'en (a); à la suite d'une telle instruction, l'automate lira $\#\,\#$ et opérera suivant des instructions du type

$$(d): (\#, \#; S_\alpha) \rightarrow (S_\beta; x, y)$$

étant donné que la grammaire contient la règle $A_\alpha \rightarrow xA_\beta y$.

[1] L'associativité du produit $\oplus$ permet certains mouvements de va-et-vient des bandes.

Cet automate est en général non déterministique; suivant la nature du mot d'entrée, il peut correspondre à ce dernier un nombre quelconque (éventuellement nul) de mots de sortie: à chaque situation terminale possible: $(\#, \#; S_f)$ correspond un mot de sortie. Cet automate est en fait, un transducteur associé à un automate à deux bandes ([10], [1]).

## V. Structures et Ambiguité

Nous avons vu qu'à chaque dérivation pouvait être associé un arbre; si le mot engendré est un *d*-mot, il servira de tronc à un nouvel arbre, et ainsi de suite jusqu'au mot terminal. La structure associée à un mot terminal est, en général, un graphe nonplanaire, mais composé d'arbres.

Reprenons l'exemple $\{G_1, G_2\}$ nous avions engendré le *d*-mot:

$$A \oplus A \oplus A \oplus B \oplus B \oplus A \oplus A \oplus A \oplus P$$

qui lui-même engendrait: *aaabbaaaaaabbaaa*, la structure associée est Fig. 3.

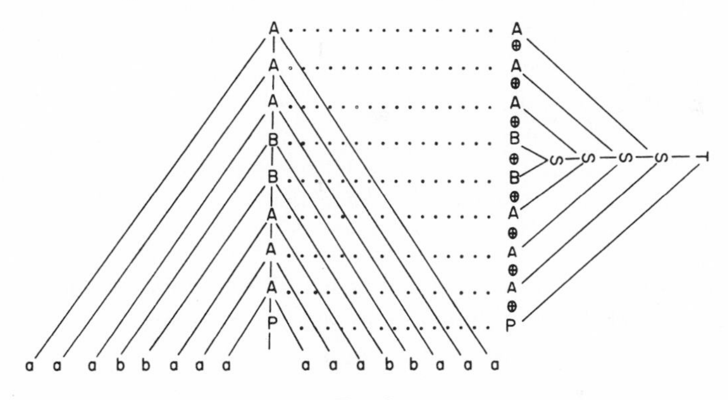


FIG. 3

Comme dans le paragraphe précédent nous avons négligé le symbole $\oplus$, étant donné qu'aucune confusion n'était possible.

Il devient donc possible d'étendre la notion d'ambiguité [2] à ces systèmes, un mot terminal $f$ est ambigu $k$ fois par rapport à un système particulier, si ce système engendre $f$ avec $k$ structures différentes.

On sait [9] que certains C-langages ne peuvent pas être engendrés de manière non-ambigue, il en est ainsi pour

$$L_a = \{a^p b^q a^r : p = q \text{ ou } q = r\}$$

les mots de la forme $a^n b^n a^n$ sont engendrés au moins deux fois, quelque soit la C-grammaire de $L_a$; on supposera $p, q, r > 0$.

Nous allons engendrer $L_a$ de manière non ambigue au moyen d'un système de Cl-grammaires. Nous avons

$$L_a = L_1 \cup L_2 \qquad L_1 = \{a^p b^p a^r : p, r > 0\}$$
$$L_2 = \{a^p b^r a^r : p \neq r\} \qquad L_1 \cap L_2 = \phi$$

$L_1$ est un Cl-langage. Pour engendrer $L_2$, nous engendrerons d'abord les $d$-mots du langage:

$$L_d = \{(A \oplus)^p (B \oplus)^r P : p \neq r\}$$

$L_d$ se sépare en deux Cl-langages:

$$L'_d = \{p > r\} \qquad L''_d = \{p < r\}$$

$L_d$ est donc engendré de manière non-ambigue par le système

$$G'_d: \left| \begin{array}{l} S = T \oplus P \\ T = A \oplus T \oplus B + U \\ U = A \oplus U + A \end{array} \right| \qquad \begin{array}{l} V_A = \{S, T, U\} \quad \text{axiome } S \\ V_T = \{A, B, P\} \\ \end{array}$$

$$G''_d: \left| \begin{array}{l} S' = T' \oplus P \\ T' = A \oplus T' \oplus B + U' \\ U' = U' \oplus B + B \end{array} \right| \qquad \begin{array}{l} V_A = \{S', T', U'\} \quad \text{axiome } S' \\ V_T = \{A, B, P\} \\ \end{array}$$

$$G_t: \left| \begin{array}{l} A = aA + aB \\ B = bBa + bPa \\ P = e \end{array} \right|$$

La question se pose de savoir s'il existe des langages ambigus quels que soient les systèmes d'une classe donnée qui les engendrent.

## VI. Langages de Dyck

Nous allons donner un système de Cl-grammaires qui engendre un langage de Dyck ([5], [12]), où, deux lettres consécutives $x_i x_{-i}$ se réduisant à $e$, on a toujours $i > 0$.

$D_r$ sera défini sur l'alphabet terminal $\{x_{\pm i}: 1 \leqslant i \leqslant n\}$:

$$G_0: \left| \begin{array}{l} T = T_1 + T_2 \\ T_1 = A \oplus P \\ T_2 = B \oplus T_2 + Q \\ A = \sum\limits_{i=n}^{i=1} (A_i \oplus A \oplus A'_i + A_i \oplus A'_i) \end{array} \right| \qquad \begin{array}{l} V_A = \{T, T_1, T_2, A\} \\ \text{axiome } T \\ V_T = \{P, Q, B, A_i, A'_i: \\ 1 \leqslant i \leqslant n\} \text{ et } \oplus \end{array}$$

$G_0$ engendre l'union de deux $d$-langages:

$$L(G_0) = \{(B \oplus)^n Q : n \geqslant 0\} \cup \{F \oplus \tilde{F}' \oplus P\}$$

ou $F$ et $\tilde{F}'$ sont des séquences (par rapport au produit $\oplus$) symmétriques sur les $A_i$ et les $A'_i$, respectivement.

$$G_1: \left| \begin{array}{l} A_i = \sum_{j=1}^{j=n} x_j(A_j + A'_j) \\ A'_i = \sum_{j=1}^{j=n} x_{-j}(A'_j + P) \\ P = T \end{array} \right| \quad \begin{array}{l} V_A = \{P, A_i, A'_i : 1 \leqslant i \leqslant n\} \\ V_T = \{T, x_{\pm i} : 1 \leqslant i \leqslant n\} \end{array}$$

$G_1$ interprétant un $d$-mot $F \oplus \tilde{F}' \oplus P$, engendre un mot $f\tilde{\tilde{f}}T$ ou $f$ et $\tilde{\tilde{f}}$ sont des séquences symmétriques sur les $x_{+i}$ et $x_{-i}$, respectivement, $T$ est l'axiome de $G_0$; en particulier, $G_0$ et $G_1$ engendrent des produits quelconques de mots $f\tilde{\tilde{f}}$, produits terminés par $T$.

$$G_2: \left| \begin{array}{l} B = \Sigma x_i(B + Q)x_{-i} \\ Q = e + T_1 \end{array} \right| \quad \begin{array}{l} V_A = \{B, Q\} \\ V_T = \{T_1, x_{\pm i} : 1 \leqslant i \leqslant n\} \end{array}$$

$G_2$ interprétant un $d$-mot $(B \oplus)^n Q$, engendre un mot $fT_1\tilde{\tilde{f}}$, ou bien un mot $f\tilde{\tilde{f}}$.[1]

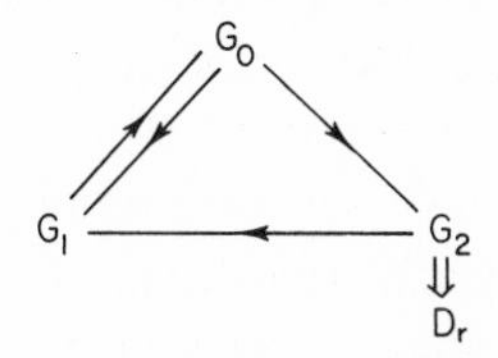


FIG. 4

Le système donne lieu au schéma de Fig. 4 qui engendre $D_r$ de manière non-ambigue.

## VII. Intersection d'un *K*-Langage et d'un Langage Engendré par un Système

Soit un langage de Kleene donné par une grammaire linéaire à droite par exemple [2]; sous forme d'équations on a

$$G_k: \{A_i = \Sigma a_j A_k + \Sigma' a_l\} \; V_{AK} = \{A_i : 1 \leqslant i \leqslant m\} \quad \text{axiome } A_1$$

[1] La manière dont nous dérivons $T$ et $T_1$ à l'intérieur d'une séquence terminale n'a pas été définie, mais il est clair que l'on peut donner un système équivalent qui n'utilise pas cette notation.

On peut toujours s'arranger pour que les $a_j$, $a_1$ soient des symboles terminaux, nous aurons: $V_{TK} = \{a_j, a_l: 1 \leqslant j, l \leqslant n\}$. $G_k$ comporte $m$ équations et les $\Sigma$ et les $\Sigma'$ sont des sommes finies.

Nous considérerons la grammaire $G_k'$ obtenue à partir de $G_k$ en remplaçant les règles terminales $A_i \to a_l$ par les règles $A_i \to a_l R$, où $R$ est un nouveau symbole auxiliaire, et en ajoutant la nouvelle règle $R \to e$; il est clair que $L(G_k') = L(G_k)$.

Soit un langage engendré par un système $S$ de grammaires et défini sur l'alphabet $V_{TS}$. Nous considérerons le système $S'$ obtenu à partir de $S$ par les modifications suivantes:

1. Les $d$-mots engendrés par des $d$-grammaires de $S$ seront marqués en tête: à une $d$-grammaire $G_\alpha$ on associera un marqueur $P_\alpha$ nouvel élément de l'alphabet terminal de $G_\alpha$; on commencera par la grammaire axiome $G_0$, soit $U$ son axiome, $P_0$ son marqueur, on choisira un nouveau symbole $T$ comme axiome et on ajoutera à $G_0$ la règle $T \to P_0 \oplus U$, soit $G_\alpha$ une grammaire connectée à $G_0$ on ajoutera à $G_\alpha$ les règles: $P_0 \to P_\alpha \oplus A_i$ pour tout $A_i$ auxiliaire de $G_\alpha$, la même procédure sera suivie pour les $d$-grammaires connectées à $G_\alpha$ et pour toutes les $d$-grammaires de $S$.

2. Les mots terminaux engendrés par les grammaires terminales seront encadrés entre les marqueurs $Q$ et $R$: on obtiendra ce résultat en considérant les $d$-grammaires $G_\beta$ auxquelles sont connectées les grammaires terminales et en ajoutant à ces dernières les règles $P_\beta \to QB_jR$, pour tous les symboles auxiliaires $B_j$; $Q$ et $R$ sont de nouveaux terminaux.

3. Nous allons maintenant transformer les grammaires terminales en $d$-grammaires, par introduction du symbole $\oplus$ entre les symboles des règles, et nous modifierons ces règles comme suit:

Soit $a_p$ un terminal pour $S$: (a) $a_p \notin V_{TK}$ on laisse $a_p$ inchangé, et (b) $a_p \in V_{TK}$ on remplace $a_p$ par les $A_i$ tels que dans $G_k$ on ait des règles $A_i \to a_p A_k$ dans ce cas toute règle contenant $a_p$ donnera naissance à autant de nouvelles règles qu'il y a de $A_i$ correspondant à $a_p$: (a) $Q$ est remplacé par $A_1$ l'axiome de $G_k'$ et (b) $R$ n'est pas remplacé.

4. $G_k'$ sera la grammaire terminale de $S'$.

Dans ces conditions, *le langage engendré par $S'$ est l'intersection des langages engendrés par $S$ et $G_k$.*

Soit $L(S) \subset F(V_{TS})$ et soit un homomorphisme $\varphi$ de $V_{TS}$ dans un monoïde libre $F'$, nous allons construire un système $S''$ qui engendre le langage $\varphi(L(S))$. $\varphi$ est défini par $a_i \to f_i$; $a_i \in V_{TS}, f_i \in F'$, $1 \leqslant i \leqslant q$.

Par une méthode analogue aux procédures 1 et 2 ci-dessus, nous pouvons engendrer les mots de $S$ avec le marqueur final $R$. Transformons les grammaires terminales en $d$-grammaires (par introduction du symbole $\oplus$) et prenons comme grammaire terminale la grammaire

$$\left| \begin{array}{l} \{a_i = \sum_1^q f_j(a_j + R) \colon 1 \leqslant i \leqslant q\} \\ R = e \end{array} \right| \quad \begin{array}{l} V_T = \{f_j \colon 1 \leqslant j \leqslant q\} \\ V_A = \{R, a_j \colon 1 \leqslant j \leqslant q\} \end{array}$$

Ce systeme $S''$ engendre $\varphi(L(S))$.

Remarquons que si $\bar{\varphi}$ est l'antihomomorphisme associé à $\varphi$, on obtient $\bar{\varphi}(L(S))$ en prenant pour grammaire terminale:

$$\left| \begin{array}{l} \{a_i = \sum_1^q (a_j + R)f_j \colon 1 \leqslant i \leqslant q\} \\ R = e \end{array} \right| \quad \begin{array}{l} V_T = \{f_j \colon 1 \leqslant j \leqslant q\} \\ V_A = \{R, a_j \colon 1 \leqslant j \leqslant q\} \end{array}$$

Nous avons vu qu'il était possible d'engendrer un langage de Dyck au moyen d'un système de Cl-grammaires; nous avons, étant donné que l'exemple $L = \{x\tilde{x}x\tilde{x} \colon x \in F(V_T)\}$ n'est pas un C-langage: la classe des C-langages est proprement incluse dans la classe des langages engendrés par des systèmes de Cl-grammaires. Ceci découle de la caractérisation algébrique des C-langages qui permet d'associer à tout C-langage $L$, un K-langage $\Lambda$, et un homomorphisme $\varphi$ tel que $L = \varphi(\Lambda \cap D_r)$.

## VIII. Propriétés de Fermeture

Nous avons utilisé le fait que la classe des systémes était fermée par union finie, ceci découle du fait que la classe des C-grammaires linéaires a cette propriété.

Nous venons de montrer que la classe des systèmes est fermée par rapport aux opérations: d'intersection avec un K-langage, d'homomorphisme, et d'antihomomorphisme.

Nous venons de voir qu'étant donné un système $S_1$ engendrant un langage $L(S_1)$, il est possible de construire un système $S_1'$ qui engendre le langage $L(S_1)R$, où $R$ nouveau terminal, est un signe de ponctuation.[1]

Considérons un système $S_2$ engendrant le langage $L(S_2)$ et prenons pour axiome de ce système le symbole $R$, le système $S$ qui réunit $S_1$ et $S_2$ engendre le langage produit $L(S_1)L(S_2)$.

[1] Voir note antérieure.

Considérons le système $S_1$ et le système $S'_1$ qui a pour marqueur $R$ l'axiome de $S_1$, le système $S$ qui réunit $S_1$ et $S'_1$ engendre le langage

$$L = L(S_1) \cup L(S_1)^2 \cup \cdots \cup L(S_1)^n \cup \cdots = L(S_1)^*$$

La classe des systèmes est donc fermée par rapport aux opérations produit de langages et étoile * de Kleene [7].

Ces propriétés reposent en fait, sur la possibilité de définir des produits (concaténation) de dérivations $D$ et permettent de généraliser (moyennant certaines précautions) les systèmes au cas où les grammaires élémentaires sont des C-grammaires et non plus des C-grammaires linéaires; cette généralisation n'affecte pas la classe des langages engendrés par systèmes.

Soit un système $S$ qui engendre un langage $L(S)$, on peut construire un système $S'$ qui engendre le langage

$$L(S') = \{\varphi(f)\,\bar{\varphi}(f) : f \in L(S)\}$$

où $\varphi$ et $\bar{\varphi}$ sont, respectivement, un homomorphisme et un antihomomorphisme de l'alphabet terminal $V_{TS}$ de $S$ dans un monoïde libre $F'$.

$S'$ se déduit de $S$ de la manière suivante: (a) $S$ est modifié de manière à engendrer des mots avec le marqueur final $R$, (b) les grammaires terminales de $S$ sont transformées en $d$-grammaires (par introduction de $\oplus$), et (c) la grammaire terminale de $S'$ sera définie par les règles

$$\left| \begin{array}{l} \{a_i = \sum_1^n g_i(a_j + R)\,h_i : 1 \leqslant i \leqslant n\} \\ R = e \end{array} \right|$$

avec

$$V_{TS} = \{a_i : 1 \leqslant i \leqslant n\} \qquad \{g_i, h_i : 1 \leqslant i \leqslant n\} \subset F'$$
$$\varphi : a_i \to g_i \qquad \bar{\varphi} : a_i \to h_i$$

Cette propriété montre que les systèmes de grammaires (ou d'automates) sont capables d'accomplir des opérations que ne peuvent accomplir les C-grammaires (ou les automates à pile de mémoire), en particulier on peut avoir la recopie d'un mot $x$: $x \Rightarrow xx$, et la permutation de deux mots $x$ et $y$: $xy \Rightarrow yx$, qui sont des opérations essentielles dans les grammaires transformationnelles ([4], [6]); un exemple de phrases de langage naturel qu'il n'est pas possible de décrire par C-grammaire, mais pour lesquelles on peut donner une description par système, est le suivant.

Z. S. Harris [6] a remarqué que les phrases formées par conjonction de phrases au moyen de ET, OU, MAIS n'étaient grammaticalement correctes que si certaines contraintes existaient entre les phrases conjointes, ainsi:

1. LE LIVRE QUE J'AI LU HIER M'A PLU, MAIS LE LIVRE QUE

J'AI LU HIER M'A PLU, n'est pas une phrase correcte: elle est la conjonction de deux phrases identiques.

2. LE LIVRE QUE J'AI LU HIER M'A PLU, MAIS LE LIVRE QUE J'AI LU AVANT-HIER M'A PLU, n'est pas une phrase correcte: elle est la conjonction de deux phrases qui sont identiques, à une "différence" près: (HIER, AVANT-HIER).

3. LE LIVRE QUE J'AI LU HIER M'A PLU, MAIS LE LIVRE QUE J'AI LU AVANT-HIER NE M'A PAS PLU, cette phrase est correcte: elle est la conjonction de deux phrases identiques, à *deux* "différences" près: (HIER, AVANT-HIER) et (M'A, NE M'A PAS).

Pour que des phrases reliées par la conjonction MAIS soient correctes, il faut qu'elles présentent au moins une "différence" dans le prédicat, et ceci pour des longueurs de phrase non bornées a priori. Pour la conjonction OU il suffirait d'une seule différence au moins. De nombreuses autres constructions imposent des contraintes de ce type: égalité ou différence de certains segments de phrase dans certaines positions syntaxiques.

La formalisation de ce genre de phénomène peut être illustrée par l'exemple suivant où nous construisons un système qui engendre le complément du langage: $L_c = \{xx: x \in F(\{a,b\})\}$ par rapport à $F(\{a,b\})$.

Le complément de $L_c$ se sépare naturellement en deux langages:

$L_c^1 = \{f: d^0(f) = 2p + 1\}$ (mots de longueur impaire)

$L_c^2 = \{xy: d^0(x) = d^0(y)$, mais $x \neq y\}$ (mots de longueur paire)

mais dont les deux moitiés présentent au moins une "différence": la $k$ième lettre de $x$ est différente de la $k$ième lettre de $y$. $L_c^1$ est un K-langage; nous allons donner un système qui engendre $L_c^2$.

Considérons un mot $f \in L_c^2, f = xy$: $x$ et $y$ se factorisent comme suit:

$$x = f_1 g_1 f_2 g_2 \cdots f_n g_n f_{n+1}$$
$$y = f_1 h_1 f_2 h_2 \cdots f_n h_n f_{n+1}$$

avec $g_i \neq h_i$, $d^0(g_i) = d^0(h_i) \neq 0$, $f_1$ et $f_{n+1}$ peuvent être vides mais pas les autres $f_j$.

Considérons le système

$$G_a: \left| \begin{array}{l} S = T \oplus R \\ T = A \oplus T \oplus A' + B \oplus T \oplus B' + C \oplus U \oplus C' + D \oplus U \oplus D' \\ U = A \oplus U \oplus A' + B \oplus U \oplus B' + C \oplus U \oplus C' + D \oplus U \oplus D' \\ \quad + C \oplus C' + D \oplus D' + V \\ V = A \oplus V \oplus A' + B \oplus V \oplus B' + A \oplus A' + B \oplus B' \end{array} \right|$$

$$V_A = \{S, T, U, V\} \quad \text{axiome } S$$
$$V_T = \{A, A', B, B', C, C', D, D', R\} \cup \{\oplus\}$$

marqueur final $R$, $G_a$ engendre des séquences du type

$$F_1 G_1 F_2 G_2 \cdots G_n F_{n+1} \tilde{F}'_{n+1} \tilde{G}'_n \tilde{F}'_n \cdots \tilde{G}'_2 \tilde{F}'_2 \tilde{G}'_1 \tilde{F}'_1 R$$

Les $F_i$ sont les mots sur $A$, $B$ (séparés par $\oplus$), les $\tilde{F}'_i$ sont des mots sur $A'$, $B'$ "images miroir" des $F_i$ correspondants, seuls $F_1$ et $F_{n+1}$, et par conséquent $\tilde{F}'_1$ et $\tilde{F}'_{n+1}$ peuvent être éventuellement vides; les $G_i$ et $\tilde{G}'_i$, mots

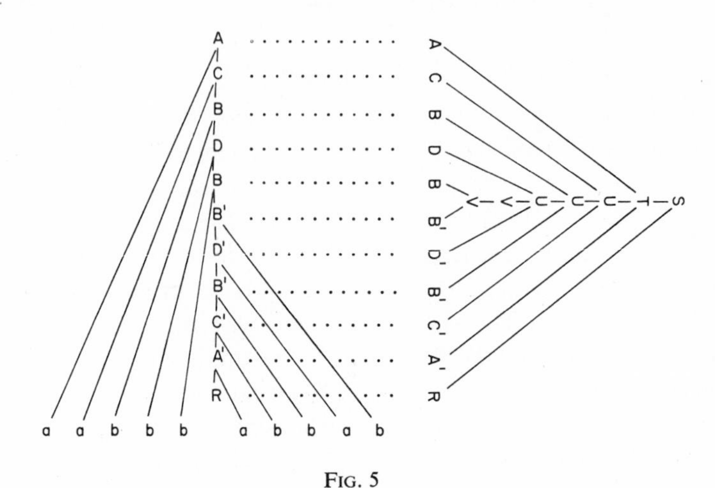


Fig. 5

sur $C, D$ et $C', D'$, respectivement, se correspondent de la même manière et ne sont jamais vides.

$$G_t: \left| \begin{aligned} A &= a(A + B + A' + B' + C + D) \\ B &= b(A + B + A' + B' + C + D) \\ C &= a(A + B + C + D + C' + D') \\ D &= b(A + B + C + D + C' + D') \\ A' &= (A' + B' + C' + D' + R)a \\ B' &= (A' + B' + C' + D' + R)b \\ C' &= (A' + B' + C' + D' + R)a \\ D' &= (A' + B' + C' + D' + R)b \\ R &= e \end{aligned} \right|$$

$$V_A = \{A, A', B, B', C, C', D, D', R\} \qquad V_T = \{a, b\}$$

Le mot *aabbbabbab* dont les deux moitiés présentent deux différences, est engendré avec la structure de Fig. 5.

## IX. Problèmes de Décision et Classification des Systemes

Un certain nombre de problèmes de décision se posent pour les systèmes que nous avons définis:

1. Le langage engendré par un système est-il un langage récursif ou non?
2. Étant donné un système quelconque existe-t-il une procédure générale qui permette de décider si le langage engendré par ce système est vide, fini ou infini?

Remarquons qu'il n'existe pas de procédures générales qui permettraient de décider si le langage engendré par un système est un K-langage ou un C-langage, étant donné que même pour les C-grammaires linéaires qui sont les systèmes les plus simples, il n'existe pas de telles procédures générales [1]. Pour la même raison il n'y a pas de procédure générale qui permette de décider si le langage intersection des langages engendrés par deux systèmes quelconques est un K-langage ou un C-langage.

**Problème 1.** Procédure de décision pour un langage engendré par un système.

Les exemples de systèmes que nous avons donnés précédemment avaient tous la propriété suivante: les règles $A \to f$, où $A$ est un auxiliaire et $f$ un $d$-mot ou un mot quelconque, étaient telles que $d^0(f) \geqslant 2$, autrement dit, l'application d'une règle provoquait toujours l'agrandissement d'un mot (ou d'un $d$-mot), (à des exceptions près pour lesquelles il était toujours possible de modifier le système de façon à avoir un système respectant cette restriction). Dans ces conditions les systèmes engendrent des langages récursifs, l'algorithme trivial consiste à engendrer tous les mots de longueur infèrieure ou égale à la longueur du mot pour lequel se pose le problème de l'appartenance au langage.

Notre définition générale n'implique pas la restriction $d^0(f) \geqslant 2$, en particulier au cours de la dérivation d'un $d$-mot tel que

$$D = A_{i_1} \oplus A_{i_2} \oplus \cdots \oplus A_{i_p}$$

on peut avoir une portion de dérivation de la forme

$$(N)\colon xA_{i_k}y \to xA_{i_{k+1}}y \to \cdots xA_{i_q}y$$

il peut résulter de cette situation qu'un mot obtenu en dérivant $D$ soit plus court que $D$, et l'algorithme trivial de décision peut n'être plus valable, il reste cependant valable si l'on s'est assuré que tout $d$-mot $D$ engendre des mots de longueur supérieure à celle de $D$. Ceci peut être vérifié au moins dans des situations simples.

Dans le cas où l'on utiliserait un système pour formaliser une grammaire transformationnelle, les règles, d'effacement [6] peuvent être formalisées de manière naturelle [au moyen de dérivations du type $(N)$] tout en conservant pour le langage engendré la propriété de récursivité.

**Problème 2.** Cardinalité du langage engendré par un système.

Remarquons qu'étant données deux grammaires connectées: $G_u \to G_v$. $G_v$ n'acceptera que les $d$-mots de $L(G_u)$ susceptibles d'être interprétés par ses propres règles, autrement dit les $d$-mots de $L(G_u)$ devront représenter des chemins dans le graphe des symboles auxiliaires de $G_v$, ce graphe étant défini en joignant des symboles auxiliaires (qui constitueront les sommets) liés par des règles: si $V_i$ et $V_j$ sont deux sommets, et si on a la règle $V_i \to xV_jy$, alors on a l'arête $V_iV_j$. Si nous notons un chemin entre deux sommets par le $d$-mot constitué des noms des sommets successivement rencontrés en parcourant ce chemin ($y$ compris le premier et le dernier), l'ensemble des chemins du graphe constitue un K-langage que nous noterons $K(G_v)$, et $L(G_u) \cap K(G_v)$ représente exactement l'ensemble des $d$-mots qui seront dérivés par $G_v$.

Dans cet ensemble de $d$-mots, on peut distinguer: le sous-ensemble $N_0$ des $d$-mots qui sont réduits à $e$:

$$N_0 = V_{i_1} \oplus V_{i_2} \cdots \oplus V_{i_p}$$

et dans $G_v$ on a les dérivations:

$$V_{i_1} \to V_{i_2} \cdots \to V_{i_p} \to e$$

le sous-ensemble $N_1$ des mots qui contiennent un cycle se réduisant à $e$; ces $d$-mots contiennent un sous-mot de la forme

$$N_e = V_{i_1} \oplus V_{i_2} \cdots V_{i_k} \oplus \cdots V_{i_l}: V_{i_1} \to V_{i_2} \cdots V_{i_k} \to \cdots \to V_{i_l}$$

qui peuvent toujours être détéctés dans une C-grammaire quelconque, [1]; le sous-ensemble $N_2$ des $d$-mots qui se terminent par un symbole $V_d$ à partir duquel il est impossible de dériver un mot terminal de $G_v$.

Soit

$$K^+(G_v) = K(G_v) \cap (F(V_A^v) \setminus (N_0 \cup N_1 \cup N_2))$$

($V_A^v$ est l'alphabet auxiliaire de $G_v$), $L(G_u) \cap K^+(G_v)$ est l'ensemble des $d$-mots engendrés par $G_u$, qui, par dérivation dans $G_v$ fournissent des mots, nonréduits à $e$.

Si $G_u$ est la grammaire axiome et $G_v$ la grammaire terminale, nous avons seulement deux niveaux séparés, cette procédure permet de décider si le langage engendré par un tel système est vide, fini ou infini, puisque l'on pose la question pour le C-langage $L(G_u) \cap K^+(G_v)$. Remarquons que dans ce cas la quantité de mémoire nécessaire pour analyser un mot quelconque du langage est bornée, c'est une fonction linéaire de la longueur du mot: la classe de ces systèmes particuliers est incluse dans la classe des grammaires "context sensitive"; l'inclusion est propre; nous pouvons décider si oui ou non le langage engendré par un tel système est vide par exemple, alors que ceci n'est pas possible pour la classe des cs-grammaires [3, 8].

Une sous-classe intéressante est celle des systèmes dont le graphe est un arbre: les systèmes à deux niveaux en sont un cas particulier; un paramètre de cette famille est la possibilité d'avoir des dérivations libres en fin de *d*-mots, ou, de manière équivalente, la possibilité d'avoir des instructions des types (c) et (d) pour les automates représentant les grammaires; cet effet correspond à la notion de perte d'information dans une transduction.

Cette sous-classe de systèmes, conserve les propriétés des systèmes généraux, à l'exception de la fermeture par rapport à l'opération *, elle ne contient pas tous les C-langages, mais seulement les C-langages méta-linéaires.

La comparaison des différentes familles de systèmes aux machines de Turing et aux cs-grammaires, permet la solution de certains problèmes de décidabilité et d'intersection de langages, que nous n'avons pas considérés ici.[1] Une classification de ces langages devrait également les placer par rapport aux classes des langages rationnels [13] et algébriques [5, 11].

## X. Grammaires Engendrées par *C*-Grammaires

Les systèmes que nous avons considérés précédemment reposent en gros sur l'idée suivante: nous avons deux niveaux, le premier engendre des dérivations qui sont effectuées à un deuxième niveau, cette idée de niveaux peut être utilisée d'une autre manière: un premier niveau engendre des équations définissant des langages; au second niveau, chacune de ces équations engendre un langage.

[1] Tout langage récursivement énumérable peut être engendré par système: à tout système de Post on peut associer un système de Cl-grammaires qui engendre le même langage; ceci prouve que les problèmes que nous avons posés sont récursivement indécidables, pour la classe des systèmes les plus généraux.

*Exemple*

$$\left| \begin{array}{l} S \to Sa \\ S \to A = e + Ab \end{array} \right| \qquad \begin{array}{l} V_A = \{S\} \\ V_T = \{a, b\ A, =, +, e\} \end{array}$$

Les mots engendrés par ce premier niveau sont

$$\{A = e + Aba^n : n \geqslant 0\}$$

Chacune de ces équations engendre le langage $L_n = \{(ba^n)^p : n \text{ fixé } p > 0\}$ et nous pouvons convenir que l'ensemble des deux niveaux engendre le langage $L = \bigcup L_n = \{(ba^n)^p : \{n \geqslant 0\}, p > 0\}$ qui n'est pas un C-langage.

Il est possible de définir cette composition de grammaires, de manière que la classe des langages engendrés soit fermée par union, produit et opération $*$.

## XI. Une Opération sur les Series Formelles

Rappelons brièvement la définition de langages par séries formelles rationnelles [13] ou algébriques ([5], [11]) soient deux C-grammaires $G_1$ et $G_2$; $L(G_1)$ et $L(G_2)$ sont les supports de séries à termes tous positifs effectuons la différence des deux séries, on obtient en général une série dont les termes peuvent être soit positifs soit négatifs, le support de cette série-différence est un langage algébrique, les coefficients qui affectent les mots du support sont les entiers relatifs, Schützenberger [11] a remarqué que ces coefficients pouvaient être définis sur d'autres structures (semi-anneaux, anneaux en caractéristiques $p, \ldots$). Nous donnons un exemple d'une telle méthode.

Un langage algébrique étant défini comme le support d'une série formelle, les coefficients sont affectés d'un signe: soit $+$, soit $-$, notre opération consiste à séparer les mots affectés du signe $+$ des mots affectés du signe $-$.

*Exemples.* Considérons les langages

$$L_0 = a^* b^* c^* \text{ engendré par le système } (E_1): \left| \begin{array}{l} S_0 = aS_0 + aT_0 \\ T_0 = bT_0 + bU_0 \\ U_0 = cU_0 + c \end{array} \right|$$

$$L_1 = \{a^n b^n c^* : n > 0\} \text{ engendré par } (E_2): \left| \begin{array}{l} S_1 = S_1 c + T_1 c \\ T_1 = aT_1 b + ab \end{array} \right|$$

$$L_2 = \{a^* b^m c^m : m > 0\} \text{ engendré par } (E_3): \left| \begin{array}{l} S_2 = aS_2 + aT_2 \\ T_2 = bT_2 c + bc \end{array} \right|$$

$$L_3 = \{a^p b^* c^p : p > 0\} \text{ engendré par } (E_4): \left| \begin{array}{l} S_3 = aS_3 c + aT_3 c \\ T_3 = bT_3 + b \end{array} \right|$$

Chacune des équations ci-dessus a pour solution une série formelle caractéristique (les langages ne sont pas ambigus). Considérons maintenant le langage $L = L_0 - (L_1 + L_2 + L_3)$ engendré par le système $(E)$ d'équations, formé de l'équation $S = S_0 - (S_1 + S_2 + S_3)$ et de la réunion des systèmes $(E_1)$, $(E_2)$, $(E_3)$, $(E_4)$.

La solution de $E$ est une série formelle à coefficients positifs et négatifs: (a) les coefficients positifs sont tous égaux à 1 et affectent les mots $a^p b^q c^r$: $p \neq q \neq r \neq p$, et (b) les coefficients négatifs sont tous égaux à $-2$ et affectent les mots $a^n b^n c^n$.

Le langage $\{a^p b^q c^r : p \neq q \neq r \neq p\}$ est rationnel et n'est pas un C-langage et le langage $\{a^n b^n c^n\}$ n'est pas algébrique [Schützenberger, communication personnelle].

De même, soient $L_4 = \{a^p b^q c^* : p \leqslant q\}$ et $L_5 = \{a^* b^q c^r : q \leqslant r\}$, considérons le langage algébrique $L_0 - L_4 - L_5$ et séparons la partie positive de la partie négative.

le coefficient $+1$ affecte les mots du langage: $\{a^p b^q c^r : p > q > r\}$
le coefficient $-1$ affecte les mots du langage: $\{a^p b^q c^r : p \leqslant q \leqslant r\}$

Ces deux langages ne peuvent pas être engendrés par des équations algébriques (et de manière non-ambigue).

## Références


1. Y. Bar-Hillel, M. Perles, and E. Shamir, On formal properties of simple phrase structure grammars, *Z. Phonetik, Sprachwiss. und Kommunikationsforsch.* **14**[2], 143–172 (1961).
2. N. Chomsky, On certain formal properties of grammars, *Inform. and Control* **2**, 137–167 (1959).
3. N. Chomsky, Formal properties of grammars, in *Handbook of Mathematical Psychology* (R. D. Luce, R. R. Busch, and E. Galanter, eds.), Vol. II, Wiley, New York, 1963.
4. N. Chomsky, *Syntactic Structure*, Mouton & Co., La Haye, 1957.
5. N. Chomsky and M. P. Schützenberger, The algebraic theory of context-free languages, *in Computer Programming and Formal Systems* (P. Braffort and D. Hirschberg, eds.), North-Holland, Amsterdam, 1962, pp. 118–161.
6. Z. S. Harris, The Elementary Transformations, *T.D.A.P.* 54, Univ. Pennsylvania, Philadelphia, 1964.
7. S. C. Kleene, Representation of events in nerve nets and finite automata, in *Automata Studies* (C. E. Shannon and J. McCarthy, eds.), Princeton University Press, Princeton, N.J., 1956.
8. S. Y. Kuroda, Classes of languages and linear-bounded automata, *Inform. and Control* **7**, 207–223 (1964).

9. R. Parikh, Language-generating devices, *R.L.E. Quart. Progr. Rept.* **60**, M.I.T. Cambridge, Mass., 1961, pp. 199–212.
10. M. O. Rabin and D. Scott, Finite automata and their decision problems, *IBM J. Res. Develop.* **3**, 115–125 (1959).
11. M. P. Schützenberger, Certain elementary families of automata, in *Mathematical Theory of Automata*, (J. Fox, ed.), Polytechnic Institute of Brooklyn, Brooklyn, New York, 1963, pp. 139–153.
12. M. P. Schützenberger, On context-free languages and pushdown automata, *Inform. and Control* **6**, 246–264 (1963).
13. M. P. Schützenberger, *Un problème de la théorie des automates*, Séminaire Dubreil-Pisot, Institut Henri Poincaré, Paris, 1959.

# Brain Models and Thought Processes

ERICH M. HARTH

*Department of Physics*
*Syracuse University*
*Syracuse, New York*

## I. Introduction

Any attempt to devise a physical model of thought processes is faced at the outset with the problem that these processes are not *observables* in the physicist's sense, since their observation can be carried out by one person only—the owner of the brain. Not only can the measurements (that is to say, the results of these observations) not be subjected to verification by other observers, but there even appear to be some fundamental difficulties in communicating them. This fact will be discussed again at the end of this paper.

The alternative of restricting the discussion to the limited variety of output forms, i.e., the overt behavior of the individual, thereby avoiding the epistemological dilemma, is of course open to us, and has been adopted by many. We shall make an attempt here to admit introspection as a legitimate tool for carrying out measurements upon one's own thought processes. The latter we assume to be homologous with the complex spatial and temporal configurations of neural activity in the cortex or subcortical regions of the brain. In this framework it becomes meaningful to require a brain model to be more than a decision-making machine which exhibits the correct response to each of a given set of inputs.

The physical system described below represents a very tentative first step. We hope to be able to omit a number of the restrictive features (e.g., the absence of inhibitories) in later extensions of the present work. What we wish to stress in this paper is an approach to the simulation of mental processes, including those accessible to us only through introspection.

It may be thought presumptuous to look in a primitive model like ours for the so-called higher functions of the brain. But this would assume that these functions require a high order of structural delicacy in addition to the large volume of operational units; we are used to seeing complex structure and complex tasks go hand-in-hand in man-made devices. Whether or not this rule holds also for the brain is still an open question. It may be significant, however, that the higher functions of brain activity are generally assigned to the relatively unstructured association areas of the cortex, which was shown many years ago by Lashley [for a recent compilation of his work see Lashley (1963)] to be remarkably unimpaired by injury and to perform more or less in proportion to the volume left intact.

## II. Model of the Neural Net

The specific assumptions underlying subsequent discussions will now be described. The model is based, on the one hand, on the McCulloch-Pitts concept of a neural net [McCulloch and Pitts (1943)] composed of many identical, interconnected logical units, the neurons; on the other, it incorporates elements of randomness [first introduced by Shimbel and Rapoport (1948)] based on arguments of limited information in genetic coding, relative insensibility to injury, and observation of the microstructure of the brain. This is not to deny the fact that considerable structuring into many different functional units does exist, and that even the cortex is neither homogeneous nor isotropic. The assumption of random connections makes for a close resemblance between our model and the perceptron [Rosenblatt (1962)]. Our model differs from the latter, however, in one important respect: While the perceptron is equipped with output units which integrate over the states of many associator neurons to give dichotomic answers, we shall have occasion to consider the more complex *internal* states of the system. Moreover, our model is not designed to perform particular cognitive tasks, but, observing its performance, we shall remain alert to any processes analogous to psychological aspects of brain function.

### A. Neurons

The properties of individual neurons[1] are taken to conform as much as possible to the known properties of real neurons [see, for example the

[1] We retain here the names of the biological counterparts, although we are referring of course to an artificial system.

recently published Nobel lectures—Eccles (1964a), Hodgkin (1964) and Huxley (1964)]. In the schematic shown in Fig. 1 the neuron body $B$ receives pulses from any number of afferent connections $a, b, c, \ldots$ via the

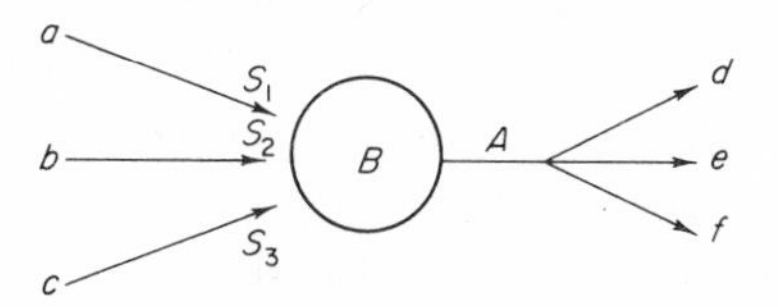


FIG. 1. Schematic diagram of neuron: ($A$) axon, ($B$) neuron body; ($a$), ($b$), ($c$) afferent connections; ($S_1$), ($S_2$), ($S_3$) afferent synapses; ($d$), ($e$), ($f$) efferent connections.

synapses $S_1, S_2, S_3, \ldots$, and emits a pulse along the efferent axon $A$ whenever the sum of the signals received at $B$ exceeds a threshold $t$. The pulse along $A$ is of standard height and travels without attenuation. The same pulse height appears also at all ramifications $d, e, f, \ldots$ of the axon. We shall take this pulse height as unity. However, at the synapses, where the axonal endings connect to another neuron, an attenuation occurs which we describe by a coupling coefficient. It is assumed further that there are no time delays in the transmission of signals across synapses or along axons, and that there is no delay between the excitation and the firing of a neuron.

## B. Structure of the Net

The connectivity of the network is shown in Fig. 2. The only structure introduced here is a distinction between sensors and associator neurons. The sensors, or $S$-units, denoted by $s_1 \cdots s_j \cdots s_S$ are triggered by transducers

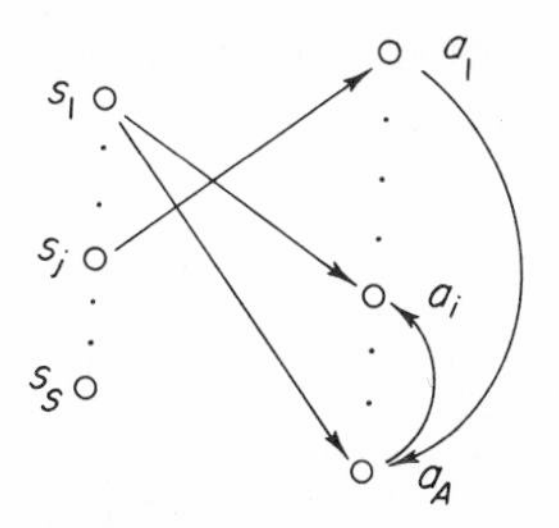


FIG. 2. Connectivity assumed in network. Neurons are shown by circles, connections by arrows. The set $s_1 \cdots s_S$ represents the sensory net ($S$-units); the set $a_1 \cdots a_A$ represents the associator net ($A$-units).

of a particular sensory modality. For the sake of illustration we may think of the sensors as forming a retinal grid. The total number of sensors is

$S$. The associators $a_1 \cdots a_i \cdots a_A$ form a larger network, the total number of neurons in this portion being $A$.

Axonal connections are of two types: (a) those carrying pulses from an $S$-unit to an $A$-unit, and (b) those carrying pulses from one $A$-unit to another. We assume that the connectivity of the net does not change with time.

Connections are chosen at random, subject only to parameters $\bar{m}$ and $\bar{\mu}$, which specify the average number of connections of type (a) and (b), respectively, terminating on one $A$-unit.

## C. Coupling Coefficients

The continuity of neural pathways is interrupted at the synapses. Transmission of signals across the synaptic gap is believed to be mediated by chemical action [Eccles (1964b)], possibly by the release of quantized amounts of transmitter substance from the so-called synaptic vesicles located at the axonal terminals. The postsynaptic excitation produced by the arrival of a presynaptic (standard) signal thus appears to be variable. It will be described in our model by a coupling coefficient having two indices, which denote the postsynaptic and presynaptic neuron, respectively.

We shall use two types of coupling coefficients, according to whether the presynaptic neuron is an $S$-unit or an $A$-unit. The first will be denoted by $c_{ij}$ (synapse leading from the $j$th $S$-unit to the $i$th $A$-unit); the second type is called $k_{ij}$ (synapse leading from the $j$th $A$-unit to the $i$th $A$-unit). The absence of a connection between neurons is denoted by a zero coupling coefficient. The totality of coupling coefficients is thus given by a matrix of dimensionality $(S+A)(S+A)$.

The structure of this matrix reflects all the structure we have assumed in the net. It can be written

**K**=

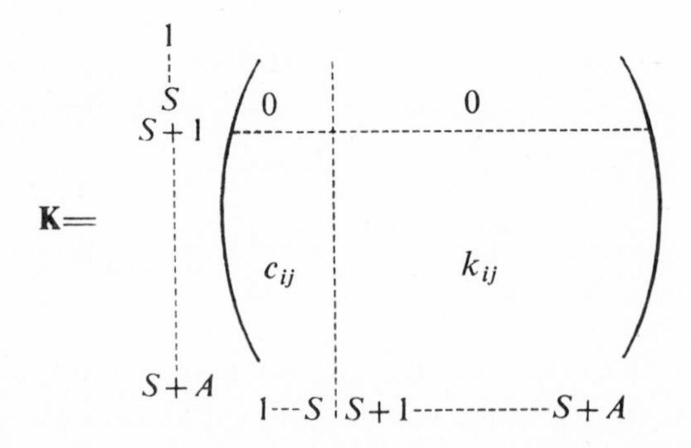

Note that the elements of the first $S$ rows are zero, since no axons terminate on $S$-units; also all diagonal elements are zero, since no neuron connects to itself.

Choice of the values for the matrix elements $c_{ij}$ and $k_{ij}$ will to a large extent determine the performance of the system. The parameters $\bar{m}$ and $\bar{\mu}$ fix the number of nonvanishing elements, assumed to be randomly distributed over the matrices, apart from the avoidance of diagonal elements in $k_{ij}$. In the computations that have been carried out thus far, nonvanishing elements of the $\mathbf{c}$ matrix were taken to be constant and all equal to $c = 0.5$. Different choices of $k_{ij}$ have been tried. To complete the nomenclature we denote by *stimulus* or *input*, $\mathbf{s}$, the complete specification of those $S$-units which are simultaneously firing. Denoting the firing state by a 1 and the inactive state by 0, a stimulus is written as a column matrix of $S$ rows:

$$\mathbf{s} = \begin{pmatrix} s_1 \\ \vdots \\ s_S \end{pmatrix} \qquad s_i = 0 \text{ or } 1$$

Similarly by *output* we mean the specification of the firing state of all $A$-units, and write for the output

$$\mathbf{a} = \begin{pmatrix} a_1 \\ \vdots \\ a_A \end{pmatrix} \qquad a_i = 0 \text{ or } 1$$

## D. Learning

The passage of stimuli (with their consequent outputs in the associator system) must produce permanent or semipermanent changes in the network, if the system is to have the capability of learning. We assume the changes to affect only the coupling coefficients $k_{ij}$. The changes due to learning an output pattern $\mathbf{a}$ will consist of incrementing by a fixed amount $\delta$ all those coefficients $k_{ij}$ for which both $a_i$ and $a_j$ were active $A$-units in the output pattern $\mathbf{a}$. For all other cases the coupling coefficients remain unchanged. Formally,

$$k'_{ij} = k_{ij} + \delta_{ij}$$

$$\delta_{ij} = \begin{cases} \delta & \text{if } a_i = a_j = 1, k_{ij} \neq 0 \\ 0 & \text{otherwise} \end{cases} \tag{1}$$

The condition $k_{ij} \neq 0$ in (1) ensures that no new connections are made, since we assumed $k = 0$ to mean the absence of a connection.

The increments $\delta$ may be constants; alternatively they may depend on the value of $k_{ij}$, or they may have an exponential time decay. We shall assume them to be constants in this paper.

This type of *synaptic learning* has been suggested by Hebb (1949), Eccles (1953), and others. There is now some experimental evidence [De Robertis and Franchi (1956)] from electron microscopy, showing that the size of presynaptic vesicles decreases with disuse of the junction.

## III. Performance of the Model

With the assumptions made above, the output **a** is unique for any given stimulus and internal state (**k**-matrix) of the system. Furthermore, these outputs may be computed for reasonably small systems, as shown below.

A fundamental difficulty arises with the description of the outputs. A complete specification of the state of a system comparable in size with the human cortex is out of the question, since the communication of $10^{11}$ bits —the specification of but a single output state—would require the continuous recital at a rate of 3 bits per second, lasting for about 1000 years. Evidently, the description must confine itself to the uncovering of parameters which turn out to be meaningful in the light of known cognitive functions.

### A. Computation of Outputs

The assumption of zero time delays causes each stimulus **s** to be accompanied by an output **a**. We now wish to devise a scheme of calculating **a** for any **s**, given the complete matrix **K** of coupling coefficients.

Let $I_i$ be the total signal intensity at the $i$th $A$-unit. We can write

$$I_i = \sum_{j=1}^{S} c_{ij} s_j + \sum_{l=1}^{A} k_{il} a_l \tag{2}$$

Equation (2) presupposes knowledge of the firing states of all neurons; hence it is not directly useful. Instead, we define an input ${}^0I_i$ due to connections of type (a) only:

$${}^0I_i = \sum_{j=1}^{S} c_{ij} s_j \tag{3}$$

The $A$-units triggered as a result of $^0\mathbf{I}$ alone are expressed by the matrix $^0\mathbf{a}$, where

$$^0a_i = \begin{cases} 1 & \text{if } ^0I_i \geqslant t \\ 0 & \text{if } ^0I_i < t \end{cases}$$

and where $t$ is the threshold for triggering. The knowledge of $^0\mathbf{a}$ may now be used to generate the next iteration of signal intensity $^1I_i$:

$$^1I_i = {^0I_i} + \sum_{j=1}^{A} k_{ij} {^0a_j} \tag{4}$$

Again,

$$^1\mathbf{a}_i = \begin{cases} 1 & \text{if } ^1I_i \geqslant t \\ 0 & \text{if } ^1I_i < t \end{cases}$$

In general,

$$^nI_i = {^{n-1}I_i} + \sum_{j=1}^{A} k_{ij}({^{n-1}a_j} - {^{n-2}a_j}) \tag{5}$$

Equation (5) reflects the fact that the signal intensity corresponding to the $n$th iteration differs from the preceding one only by the contribution of those $A$-units which were made active during the $(n-1)$ iteration. It follows that, if no $A$-units were triggered during the $(n-1)$ iteration (i.e., if $^{n-1}a_j - {^{n-2}a_j} = 0$ for all $j$), then $^nI_i = {^{n-1}I_i}$, and hence no new $A$-units will be triggered during the $n$th iteration. By induction we see that no further changes will therefore take place; hence we have succeeded in obtaining the output pattern $\mathbf{a}$. It must be emphasized that the quantities $^nI_i$, $^na_i$ are artificial; they are introduced for the sake of computation only, but do not correspond to physical states.

## B. Specific Excitation

The number of simultaneously active neurons involved in both the sensory and the associator nets will be of interest. We therefore define a *specific input size* $\sigma$ and a *specific excitation* $\alpha$ by

$$\sigma = \frac{1}{S} \sum_{i=1}^{S} s_i; \qquad \alpha = \frac{1}{A} \sum_{i=1}^{A} a_i$$

The quantity $^0\alpha$ we define as the fraction of $A$-units triggered directly by the sensors; thus

$$^0\alpha = \frac{1}{A} \sum_{i=1}^{A} {^0a_i}$$

The expectation values $\overline{{}^0\alpha}$ were computed as a function of specific input size $\sigma$ and for different values of $\bar{m}$. The results are shown in Fig. 3 together with the results of Monte Carlo calculations done on a digital computer for $\bar{m} = 1.7$ and $\bar{m} = 3.4$. Other parameters of the net were $c = 0.5$, $t = 1.0$. Similarly, the expectation values $\bar{\alpha}$ for a variety of choices of the coefficients[1] $k_{ij}$ were computed in a series of computer runs (Fig. 4), using the parameters $\bar{m} = 1.7$, $\bar{\mu} = 3.8$, $c = 0.5$, $t = 1.0$.

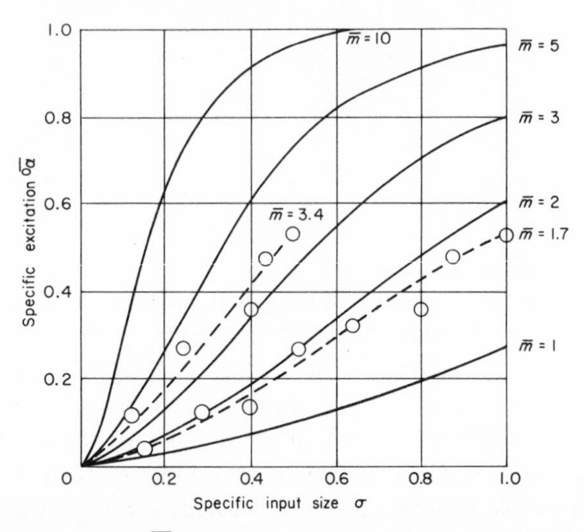


FIG. 3. Specific excitation $\overline{{}^0\alpha}$ (expectation values) vs. specific stimulus size $\sigma$ for different multiplicities $\bar{m}$ of connections from $S$-units to $A$-units. The curves correspond to the coefficients $k_{ij}$ being zero for all $i,j$. Other parameters of the net were $c = 0.5$, $t = 1.0$. The circles correspond to values obtained in computer runs using a simulated net of 25 $S$-units and 100 $A$-units.

The convenience of the quantity $\alpha$ stems from the fact that it is independent of the size of the neural net (number of sensors and $A$-units), but depends only on such quantities as the specific input size $\sigma$ (fraction of sensory neurons active), the multiplicities $m$ and $\mu$ of the connections, the coupling coefficients, and the assumed threshold.

The curve marked $\bar{k} = k = 0$ in Fig. 4 is of course identical with the curve marked $\bar{m} = 1.7$ in Fig. 3, since it represents the values for $\bar{\alpha}$ under the assumption of vanishing coupling coefficients between $A$-units. The differ-

[1] It should be noted that in four of the curves in Fig. 4 all nonvanishing coefficients $k_{ij}$ were taken to be equal, which is denoted by $\bar{k} = k$. In one curve, marked $\bar{k} = 0.5$, $0.1 \leqslant k \leqslant 0.9$, the nonvanishing values of $k_{ij}$ were between 0.1 and 0.9 with a flat distribution.

ence between this curve and the others in Fig. 4 thus shows the effect of the cross connections on the specific excitation of the net. We note in particular the tendency of the net to saturate as $\bar{k}$ is increased.

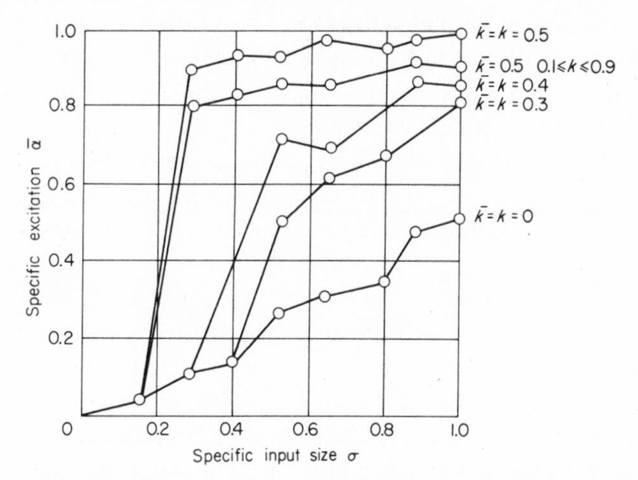


FIG. 4. Specific excitation $\bar{\alpha}$ vs. specific stimulus size $\sigma$ for a computer simulated net, using $S = 25$, $A = 100$, $c = 0.5$, $t = 1.0$, $\bar{m} = 1.7$, and $\bar{\mu} = 3.8$, for different distributions of coupling coefficients $k_{ij}$.

While very little is known at present about the comparable numbers in actual neural nets, the very high specific excitations probably occur only under very unusual circumstances (such as epileptic seizures.) It is hoped that, in the future, multielectrode measurements of brain activity may allow direct comparisons to determine in this way the values of some of the pertinent parameters. In this connection we may mention the experiments on neural activity (averaged over a few neurons) of a cat vs. click intensity, reported by Rosenblith (1959), which bear a striking resemblance to the curves in Figs. 3 and 4.

## C. Pattern Completion

We shall now discuss the effect of the learning rules on the outputs. The changes in the $k$-matrix due to Eq. (1) will in general produce changes in the mapping from a stimulus to its corresponding output. Assume that the system "learned" the output **a** to a stimulus $\mathbf{s}_1$ and that another stimulus $\mathbf{s}_2$ produced the output **b** before **a** was learned. Let the output due to $\mathbf{s}_2$ after **a** was learned be **b**′. We distinguish between the following possibilities:

1. $\mathbf{s}_1 = \mathbf{s}_2$. This also implies $\mathbf{b} = \mathbf{a}$. Consider an $A$-unit, say $a_i$, which was not active in **a**. According to the learning rule, none of the connections terminating on $a_i$ have been changed as a result of learning **a**; hence $k'_{ij} = k_{ij}$ for all $j$ provided $a_i$ was not active in **a**. From Eq. (4) we see that ${}^1I'_i = {}^1I_i$, since ${}^0\mathbf{a}$ is never affected by learning; hence ${}^1\mathbf{a}$ and all subsequent iterations remain unchanged. It follows that in general the output **a** to a stimulus $\mathbf{s}_1$ remains unchanged after learning **a**.

2. Consider the case in which **b** and **a** have no active $A$-units in common. We denote this by $\mathbf{a} \cap \mathbf{b} = 0$. The same arguments used in 1 above lead to the conclusion that after learning **a** the output to $\mathbf{s}_2$ remains unchanged, or $\mathbf{b}' = \mathbf{b}$.

3. Finally, we consider the general case $\mathbf{b} \neq \mathbf{a}$, $\mathbf{a} \cap \mathbf{b} \neq 0$. The two output states are not equal but have some active $A$-units in common. Now consider an $A$-unit which was active in **a** but was not active in **b**; let this unit be $b_i$ in the matrix **b**. There may exist $A$-units $b_j$ such that $b_j = 1$, $a_j = 1$, i.e., $A$-units that were active in both **a** and **b**. Under these circumstances all nonvanishing connections $k_{ij}$ are reinforced and the signal intensity reaching $b_i$ will have been augmented, which may cause $b_i$ to fire. For a large system and output states involving many $A$-units the expectation value of $\mathbf{b}' \cap \mathbf{a}$ will in general be larger than $\mathbf{b} \cap \mathbf{a}$, provided the learning parameter $\delta$ is sufficiently large. This effect we call *pattern completion.*

The following practical situations arise:

(a) Sensory fragments. Under our assumptions, a portion $\mathbf{s}_2$ of a stimulus $\mathbf{s}_1$ (such that $\mathbf{s}_2 \subset \mathbf{s}_1$) will always produce an output $\mathbf{b} \subseteq \mathbf{a}$. In the case of the inequality we have the situation described in 3 above. Therefore, having learned the complete pattern **a**, there will subsequently be the tendency to complete the pattern in response to a sensory fragment.

(b) Association of two stimuli. Let two stimuli $\mathbf{s}_1$ and $\mathbf{s}_2$ be presented simultaneously to the network, producing an output $\mathbf{a}_{12}$ which is reinforced according to the learning rules. Also, let $\mathbf{a}_1$ and $\mathbf{a}_2$ be the outputs corresponding to the stimuli $\mathbf{s}_1$ and $\mathbf{s}_2$ shown separately. The effect of learning $\mathbf{a}_{12}$ on the output to $\mathbf{s}_2$ will be a tendency to include a portion of $\mathbf{a}_1$ in the output $\mathbf{a}'_2$. This follows from the fact that we may consider $\mathbf{s}_1 + \mathbf{s}_2$ as a stimulus and $\mathbf{s}_2$ as a corresponding sensory fragment. It is seen, therefore, that the original patterns $\mathbf{a}_1$ and $\mathbf{a}_2$ are now linked by the effect of pattern completion. This will be true even if $\mathbf{a}_1$ and $\mathbf{a}_2$ had no $A$-units in common. The model thus exhibits the classical conditioned reflex.

(c) Chance overlaps of two outputs. An output state may be produced for instance by the spontaneous firing of a number of randomly distributed

*A*-units. If the output **b** generated by these firings has an overlap with an output state **a** previously learned, then there will again be the tendency to complete the pattern of state **a**. Thus any endogenous activity which in the untutored brain may produce random, hence meaningless patterns, will in the experienced brain evoke responses similar to previously formed output states.

The property of pattern completion which is characteristic to our model bears a striking resemblance to a physiological model for simple conditioned responses proposed by John (1962), based on the concept of dominant foci [Ukhtomski (1926)]. John describes the concept in these words: "When a number of central nervous system neurons are active repeatedly during the same period of time, they become organized into a system that is characterized by a tendency for its constituent neurons to discharge as a group." The author also cites several experimental findings supporting this concept.

## D. Computer Simulation of Small Systems

The above arguments were tested in a number of runs on a digital computer. The property of pattern completion was strikingly demonstrated in all cases. In Fig. 5 we show the results of a run simulating situation c above.

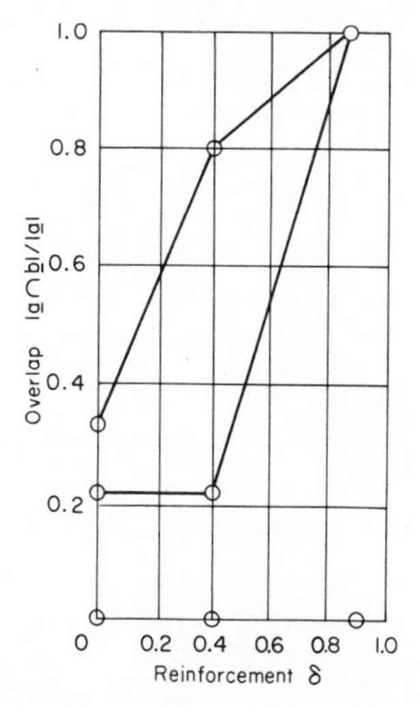


Fig. 5. Pattern completion following spontaneous triggering of *A*-units. Here **a** is a specific, reinforced output and **b** are various outputs generated by triggering 5 out of 25 sensors selected at random. The fractional overlap $|\mathbf{a} \cap \mathbf{b}|/|\mathbf{a}|$ is plotted against the learning parameter $\delta$. Three curves correspond to initial overlaps (at $\delta = 0$) of 0, 22% and 32%.

Outputs **b** were computed, starting not from a stimulus but from a set of five randomly chosen active $A$-units. These outputs were then compared with an output **a**, which was actually generated by a stimulus. The fractions of **a** excited by **b** in various trials are plotted in Fig. 5. The three points at $\delta = 0$ correspond to three chance overlaps before **a** was learned by the system. If **a** is now reinforced, the fractions of **a** covered will be increased depending on the original overlap and on the learning parameter $\delta$. With no overlap originally, no amount of learning will produce an overlap. Hence the curve that goes through the origin at $\delta = 0$ is the abscissa. A learning parameter of $\delta = 0.9$ produced 100% pattern completion for original overlaps of above 22%. The system studied here had $S = 25$, $A = 100$, $t = 1.0$, $\bar{m} = 1.7$, $\bar{\mu} = 3.8$, $c = 0.5$, $\bar{k} = 0.5$, $0.1 \leqslant k \leqslant 0.5$.

## E. Lattices

We shall now adopt another representation of the behavior of the network, which will have applicability beyond some of the limiting assumptions of this model. Consider the set of all possible output states of the associator net. This is a partially ordered set, since we can define an inclusion relation $\mathbf{a}_1 \subset \mathbf{a}_2$ which is reflexive, antisymmetric, and transitive. This relation we define as valid whenever every active $A$-unit in $\mathbf{a}_2$ is also active in $\mathbf{a}_1$. Further, for any two members of the set of all outputs, there exists a unique least upper bound (written $\mathbf{a}_1 \cup \mathbf{a}_2$) and a unique greatest lower bound ($\mathbf{a}_1 \cap \mathbf{a}_2$), defined in the usual way. Also it can be shown that the distributive laws are satisfied and that for every member **a** there exists a complement $\mathbf{a}^*$ such that $\mathbf{a} \cup \mathbf{a}^* = \mathbf{e}$ and $\mathbf{a} \cap \mathbf{a}^* = \mathbf{0}$, where $\mathbf{x} \subseteq \mathbf{e}$ and $\mathbf{0} \subseteq \mathbf{x}$ for all members $x$ of the set. With these conditions satisfied, the output states form a complemented distributive lattice.

Before continuing the description in terms of lattices, we wish to take a look at the information content at various stages of the processing. Some exceedingly interesting data on the flow of information in the human brain were presented at this conference by George Zopf. We are told that in the optic nerve alone there are about $2 \times 10^6$ fibers entering the brain; the number of photoreceptors in the retina is even higher, by two orders of magnitude. This is to be contrasted with a total output of only between $10^5$ and $10^6$ fibers which control all of man's motor and glandular system. That portion of the output which makes up the communication channel, i.e., speech, can sustain an *information current* of only about 3 bits per second, while the vast associator system lying between the sensory input and the information output is potentially capable of processing perhaps $10^{11}$ bits per second, assuming only 10 pattern changes per second. This situation is shown schematically in Fig. 6. If thought processes occupy a substantial

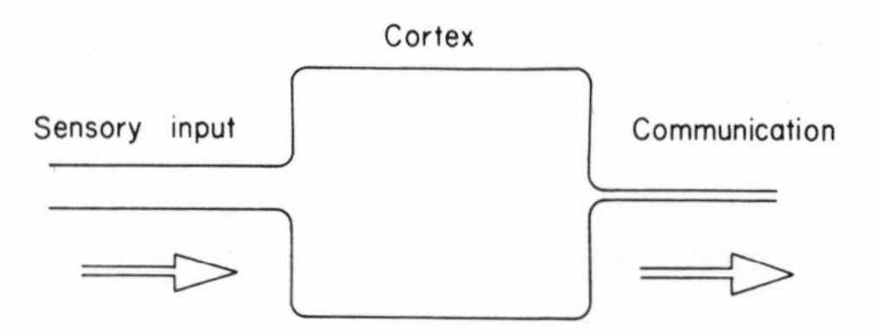


FIG. 6. Channel capacities of neural system.

portion of the large central channel, the difficulty in *verbalizing* what goes on in the mind can be explained as being due to the mismatch in channel capacity on the output side.

But for the moment we wish to focus our attention on the first vertex, i.e., the input to the cortex. We have adopted the point of view that relevant information is contained in the momentary pattern of active $A$-units. Instead of allowing any number of $A$-units to be active, we may ask, as a matter of economy, what is the smallest number of active $A$-units with which we can code all the information contained in the input state. Since the latter is $S$ bits, we have the relation

$$2^S = \frac{A!}{(A-a)!\,a!}$$

Letting $\alpha$ again denote the specific excitation $a/A$ and setting $\Sigma = S/A$ we obtain

$$\Sigma \approx \frac{1}{\ln 2}\left[\alpha \ln \frac{1}{\alpha} - (1-\alpha)\ln(1-\alpha)\right]$$

Here $\Sigma$ denotes the *specific information content* of the associator net (in *bits per A-unit*). We have plotted $\Sigma$ against $\alpha$ in Fig. 7. The curve is seen to have a maximum $\Sigma \approx 1.0$ at $\alpha = 0.5$, i.e., with half of the $A$-units active.

We return now to the lattice description of output states. This is sketched in Fig. 8. There are $A + 1$ rows in the lattice running from the lower apex point 0 (no active $A$-units) to the point $e$ (all $A$-units active). We have also labeled the number of lattice points and the information content of some of the rows. The maximum lateral extension of the lattice occurs at $a = A/2$, where the information content is $A$ bits, which corresponds, of course, to the peak of the curve in Fig. 7.

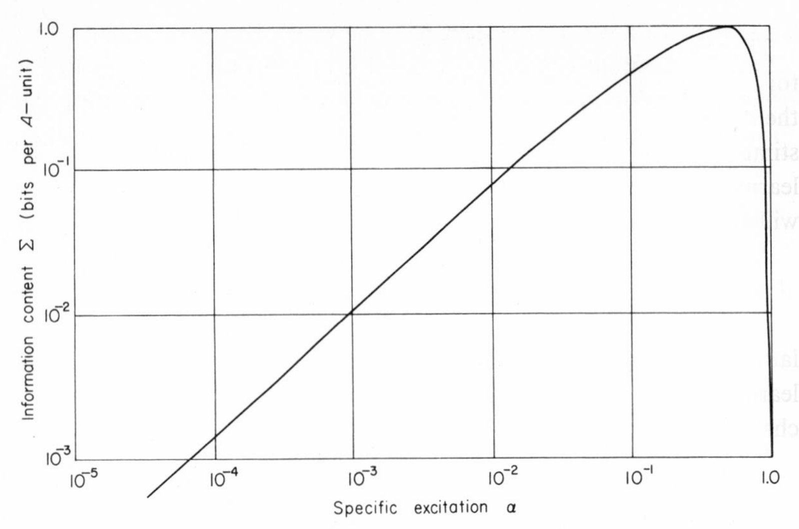


FIG. 7. Specific information content $\Sigma$ vs. specific excitation $\alpha$. It is assumed here that the fraction $\alpha$ of active $A$-units is specified.

The output state of the net corresponding to a given stimulus is now characterized by a single point in the lattice, which, making the assumption of economy, is as low in the lattice as is compatible with the information

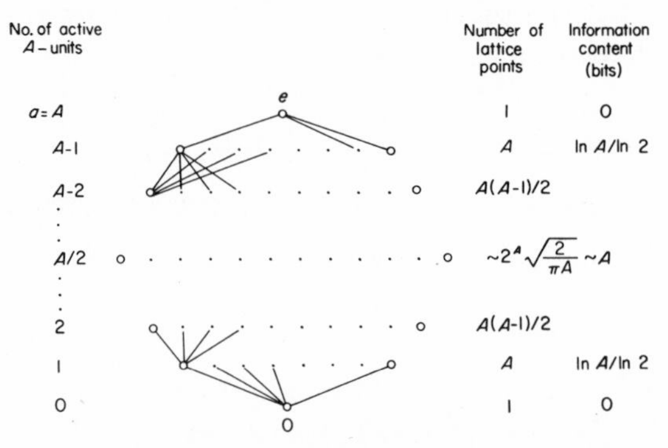


FIG. 8. Lattice diagram of outputs of neural net. Each point in the lattice specifies a particular output state. Lines represent *links* connecting lattice points.

contained in the stimulus. We now ask: What will be the dynamics of points in the lattice; specifically, how will the lattice point corresponding to a given stimulus move as the result of intervening learning? With our assumption of no inhibitory signals, the trajectories are clearly ascending *chains* in the diagram; i.e., every later output $\mathbf{b}'$ to a given stimulus is related to an earlier output $\mathbf{b}$ to the same stimulus by $\mathbf{b}' \supseteq \mathbf{b}$.

Thus, to each of the totality of possible stimuli will correspond a trajectory[1] in the lattice of output states. These trajectories depend, of course, on the *experience* of the system, by which we mean the particular history of stimuli presented. As an output **a** becomes reinforced through repeated learning, trajectories of other outputs having nonvanishing overlaps with **a** will be affected in a predictable manner.

As an example, consider an output state $\mathbf{a}_0$ due to a stimulus $\mathbf{s}_1$, and assume that $\mathbf{a}_0$ is being reinforced according to our learning rules. Another stimulus $\mathbf{s}_2$ produces initially an output $\mathbf{b}_0$. The two states are shown in the lattice together with the points $\mathbf{a}_0 \cup \mathbf{b}_0$ and $\mathbf{a}_0 \cap \mathbf{b}_0$ (Fig. 9). The effect of learning $\mathbf{a}_0$ on the outputs **b** will be to cause **b** to evolve along an ascending chain toward the union $\mathbf{a}_0 \cup \mathbf{b}_0$. Conversely, learning of $\mathbf{b}_0, \mathbf{b}_1, \ldots$ will cause

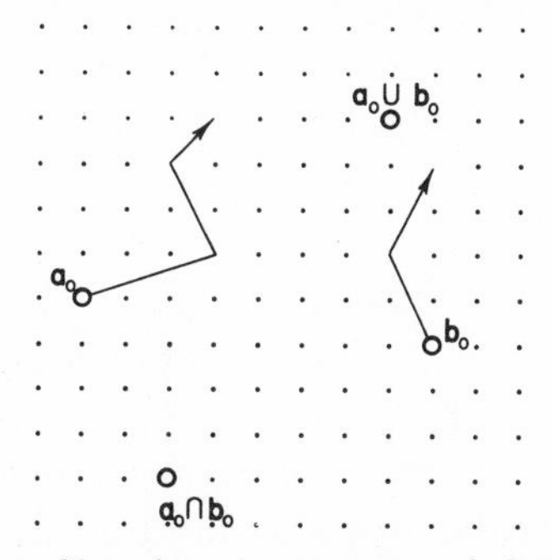


FIG. 9. Effect of learning on output states in lattice diagram.

the trajectory of $\mathbf{a}_0$ to evolve in the general direction of $\mathbf{a}_0 \cup \mathbf{b}_0$. The same is true of the trajectory of $\mathbf{b}_0$, as $\mathbf{a}_0$ (or one of the states superseding $\mathbf{a}_0$) is learned. It appears therefore that *neighboring* trajectories will attract each other if the stimulus corresponding to one of them is reinforced. Thus, if the set of outputs corresponding to all possible stimuli is originally a diffuse cloud in the lattice, experience in which certain select stimuli occur with great frequency (and are reinforced accordingly) may cause a condensation of lattice points into many clusters; these may be likened to what John (1962) calls *representational systems.*

Consideration of inhibitory impulses would make both up and down motions possible in the lattice diagram. The general attraction between trajectories would be expected to hold also in this more general case. A further study of the dynamics of lattice points under different sets of assumptions promises to be of great interest.

[1] We can speak of the trajectory of outputs even though the stimulus that generates these outputs may never actually be presented to the system.

## IV. Some Speculations regarding Thought Processes

We ask, finally, to what extent parallels may be drawn between the physical properties of models like ours, on the one hand, and mental processes, on the other.

One of the features that emerged almost immediately in our model was the property we called *pattern completion*. We have already noted its counterpart in certain psychological theories. If we take the analogy seriously, we may ask just what happens "in our mind" when the neural net reproduces a substantial fraction of a previously learned pattern. At what point do we become *aware* of its presence? If the stimulus is a sensory fragment, at what point do we *recognize* the whole of which we have perceived a part? Is recognition a threshold phenomenon, requiring activation of, say, 70% or more of the original pattern in the associator net? What happens when an output state overlaps more than one previously learned state?

We have no firm answers to any of these questions but will allow ourselves a few speculations at this point. Only an unbending behaviorist would deny that thinking may take place at many different levels of consciousness. But anyone attempting to define consciousness is immediately face to face with the formidable mind-body problem. It is perhaps safe to say, though, that at least a necessary condition for conscious thought is that it must be communicable, i.e., capable of fitting into the communication channel. Rado (1949) speaks of the mind on the "reporting" and "nonreporting" level.

At the outset we have identified thoughts (or mental states) with the spatio-temporal configurations of neural activity in certain portions of the brain. In analogy to the simple model we have described, a neural state may have varying degrees of overlap with many dominant foci at the same time. Owing to its complexity and high information content, such a state could not correspond to a conscious thought. To be communicable it would have to contract perhaps to something like a single dominant focus, and the speed of temporal development of one state from another would have to be drastically curtailed in order not to exceed the capacity of the communication channel. We don't know the mechanism for this *fixation*, but may consider the act of rendering a thought conscious, as performing a measurement upon one's own thought processes. Such a measurement cannot be carried out without disturbing the state that is being measured, in much the same way that the states of atomic and subatomic systems are changed by the act of observation. We may thus look for a principle of complementarity in the description of thought processes. Such extensions of the principle beyond the confines of quantum mechanics had in fact been suggested long ago by Bohr (1955).

In further work along these lines, it is hoped that more of the already established physiological data can be incorporated in the model. This is particularly true of the known threshold changes which occur in a neuron subsequent to its excitation, and the synaptic and axonal delays. At the same time, much of the crucial information is still lacking. Of particular interest will be the outcome of time-correlation studies of neural activity like those initiated by Braitenberg, from which should also emerge information on the total number of neurons active at any one time. Finally, the as-yet-unknown mechanisms linking the association areas to the various output channels may hold the key to the interplay between conscious and subconscious thought processes.

## Acknowledgments

The author wishes to thank Mr. P. Hagerty for writing the computer programs used here, and the Computing Center of Syracuse University for making their facilities available for this work.

## References

Bohr, N. (1955), *Discussions with Einstein*, W. Kohlheimer, Stuttgart.

DeRobertis, E. D. P., and C. M. Franchi (1956), *J. Biophys. Biochem. Cytol.* **2**, 307.

Eccles, J. C. (1953), *The neurophysiological basis of mind, The Principles of Neurophysiology*, Clarendon Press, Oxford.

Eccles, J. C. (1964a), Ionic mechanism of postsynaptic inhibition, *Science* **145**, 1140.

Eccles, J. C. (1964b), *The Physiology of Synapses*, Springer, Berlin.

Hebb, D. O. (1949), *The Organization of Behavior*, Wiley, New York.

Hodgkin, A. L. (1964), The ionic basis of nervous conduction, *Science* **145**, 1148.

Huxley, A. F. (1964), Excitation and conduction in nerve: qualitative analysis, *Science* **145**, 1154.

John, E. R. (1962), Some speculations on the psychophysiology of mind, in *Theories of the Mind* (J. Scher, ed.), Free Press, New York.

Lashley, K. S. (1963), *Brain Mechanisms and Intelligence*, Dover, New York.

McCulloch, W. S., and W. Pitts (1943), A logical calculus of the ideas immanent in nervous activity, *Bull. Math. Biophys.* **5**, 115.

Rado, S. (1949), Mind, unconscious mind and brain, *Psychosomat. Med.* **15**, 165.

Rosenblatt, F. (1962), *Principles of Neurodynamics*, Spartan Books, Washington, D.C.

Rosenblith, W. A. (1959), Some quantifiable aspects of the electrical activity of the nervous system, *Rev. Mod. Phys.* **31**, 532.

Shimbel, A., and A. Rapoport (1948), A statistical approach to the theory of the central nervous system, *Bull. Math. Biophys.* **10**, 41.

Ukhtomski, A. A. (1926), *Novoev refleksologii i fiziologii nervnoi sistemy* **2**, 3; abstr. in *Psychol. Abstr.* 2388.

# Universal Spaces: A Basis for Studies of Adaptation[1]

JOHN H. HOLLAND

*Department of Communication Sciences, The University of Michigan*
*Ann Arbor, Michigan*

The first objective of these lectures is to present a definition of automata appropriate to studies of construction and adaptation. This entails the development, in the context of automata theory, of three general ideas:

1. Structure, particularly that part of the concept relevant to connected sets of components having an organization presentable in terms of a hierarchy of block diagrams.
2. Computation, especially the computation procedures which can be realized by finite automata.
3. Simulation, the representation of details of the behavior of one device by appropriately constraining (programming) the behavior of another.

In what follows, the formal counterparts of these ideas will be designated "compositions," "uniform computation procedures," and "embeddings," respectively. Only a résumé of these ideas is presented here; a full development appears in [6].

In terms of these definitions, we can carry out the second step of the development: definition and investigation of the class of universal embedding spaces. Each such space will be defined in terms of a countably infinite, connected set of automata and will have the following properties:

1. Ability to represent both structure and behavior.
2. Homogeneity, in the sense that if an automaton has a representation in the space it has the same representation everywhere in the space.
3. Universality, in the sense that all computation procedures can be represented in the space (by embedding an appropriate composition).

Again only a résumé is given; see [6] for a more complete development.

[1] The work reported here was supported in part by the National Institutes of Health under Grant GM-12236-01.

The last of the lectures will give a formal outline of the use of these notions in the study of adaptive systems.

I shall begin with the notion of a composition. The concept is developed first by defining a "free" product automaton, which is simply a collection of noninteracting automata treated as a single automaton. Constraints are then applied to the product automaton by identifying (connecting) selected inputs with outputs. Formally, the latter process amounts to adding a set of constraining equations to the set of equations which defines the product automaton. The major difficulty will be that of assuring the consistency of the resulting set of simultaneous equations. The set of compositions will be the set of all consistently constrained product automata over finite or countably infinite sets of automata. Thus, corresponding to each finite automaton there will be an infinite class of compositions (structural representatives). Compositions over a countably infinite set of automata are an extension of the notion of finite automaton, and it is from them that we shall draw the universal embedding spaces.

A word of motivation: Although it would be impossible to present (by a state diagram, say) or deal directly with a transition function defined over an unstructured set of 1,000,000 states, that same transition function may easily be comprehended in terms of a connected set of 20 two-state devices. By the same token, though a state reduction from 1,000,000 states to 500,000 states looks impressive, it amounts to the elimination of only one two-state device from the connected set. In some sense the only way of understanding complex devices (even a small digital computer will have in excess of $10^{10^4}$ states) is to present them in terms of a hierarchy of block diagrams—a diagram at level $k$ being expanded into, say, 10 diagrams at level $k - 1$, the diagrams at level 0 consisting then of the basic components. In this way one can quickly investigate the behavior of any part of a device with $10^{10}$ basic components (for two-state devices, $2^{10^{10}}$ states) using only 10 levels in the diagram hierarchy. In what follows, the hierarchy of block diagrams will have as their formal counterpart a hierarchy of subcompositions: the quintuple characterizing a subcomposition, at any given level, being structured in terms of the quintuples of subcompositions at the next lower level.

Compositions will be defined for any indexed set of elements $\{a_\alpha \ni \alpha \in A\}$ satisfying the following conditions:

$A$ is a countable ordered set

$$a_\alpha = \langle I_\alpha, S_\alpha, O_\alpha, f_\alpha, u_\alpha \rangle$$

where $I_\alpha = \prod_{i=1}^{m_\alpha} I_{\alpha,i}$, where each $I_{\alpha,i}$ is a finite set

$S_\alpha$: a finite set

$O_\alpha = \prod_{j=1}^{n_\alpha} O_{\alpha,j}$, where each $O_{\alpha,j}$ is a finite set

$f_\alpha: I_\alpha \times S_\alpha \to S_\alpha$

$u_\alpha: I_\alpha \times S_\alpha \to O_\alpha$

Each quintuple constitutes one of the standard definitions of a finite automaton, with $f_\alpha$ and $u_\alpha$ being interpreted as the transition and output functions, respectively. $f_\alpha$ and $u_\alpha$ can be extended in the usual way to two families of functionals, $F_\alpha$ and $U_\alpha$, on infinite input sequences:

$$F_\alpha: I_\alpha^N \times S_\alpha \to S_\alpha^N$$
$$U_\alpha: I_\alpha^N \times S_\alpha \to O_\alpha^N$$

where $N = \{0, 1, 2, \ldots\}$ and $I_\alpha^N = \{\mathbf{I}_\alpha \ni \mathbf{I}_\alpha: N \to I_\alpha\}$, etc.

An *unrestricted* (*product*) *composition* $\mathbf{A}$ on $\{a_\alpha\}$ is a quintuple $\langle I_\mathbf{A}, S_\mathbf{A}, O_\mathbf{A}, f_\mathbf{A}, u_\mathbf{A}\rangle$ such that

$$S_\mathbf{A} = \prod_{\alpha \in A} S_\alpha = \{s: A \to \bigcup_\alpha S_\alpha \ni \alpha \in A \text{ and } s(\alpha) \in S_\alpha\}$$

Similarly,

$$I_\mathbf{A} = \prod_{\alpha \in A} \prod_{i=1}^{m_\alpha} I_{\alpha,i} = \{i: X \to \bigcup_x I_x \ni x \in X \text{ and } i(x) \in I_x\}$$

where $X = \{(\alpha, i) \ni \alpha \in A \text{ and } 1 \leqslant i \leqslant m_\alpha\}$ and

$$O_\mathbf{A} = \prod_{\alpha \in A} \prod_{j=1}^{n_\alpha} O_{\alpha,j} = \{o: Y \to \bigcup_y O_y \ni y \in Y \text{ and } o(y) \in O_y\}$$

where $Y = \{(\alpha, j) \ni \alpha \in A \text{ and } 1 \leqslant j \leqslant n_\alpha\}$.

$f_\mathbf{A}: I_\mathbf{A} \times S_\mathbf{A} \to S_\mathbf{A}$ satisfies the requirement

$$f_\mathbf{A}(i, s)(\alpha) = s'(\alpha) = f_\alpha(i(\alpha), s(\alpha))$$

where $i \in I_\mathbf{A}$, $s$, $s' \in S_\mathbf{A}$ and $i(\alpha) = (i(\alpha, 1), \ldots, i(\alpha, m_\alpha))$.

$u_\mathbf{A}: I_\mathbf{A} \times S_\mathbf{A} \to O_\mathbf{A}$ satisfies

$$u_\mathbf{A}(i, s)(\alpha) = o(\alpha) = u_\alpha(i(\alpha), s(\alpha)).$$

Each composition over $\{a_\alpha\}$ will be defined in terms of a *composition function* $\gamma$ satisfying the conditions:

(1) $\gamma: Y' \to X'$ from $Y' \subset Y$ 1 to 1 onto $X' \subset X$

(2) $O_y \subset I_{\gamma(y)}$

$\gamma$ induces a set of equations of the form

$$U_y(\mathbf{I}_\alpha, s) = \mathbf{I}_{\gamma(y)} \qquad (*)$$

This set of constraining equations combined with the defining equations for the $U_y$ gives us a set of simultaneous equations for which we require a unique solution. (That is, if such a solution exists we can go on to find a quintuple corresponding to the product automaton constrained by $\gamma$.) To assure consistency of the equations (*), $\gamma$ must satisfy a further requirement of "local effectiveness":

$\gamma$ will be called *consistent* with respect to $s \in S_\mathbf{A}$ if for each $\alpha \in A$, there is an integer $l_{s,\alpha}$ such that every connected sequence of output indices (defined as usual, see [3]) to $\alpha$ of length $l_{s,\alpha}$ contains an element $y_h = (\delta, j)$ such that

$$(i_1, i_2 \in I_\mathbf{A})\,[i_1 | X - X' = i_2 | X - X' \Rightarrow u_{\delta,j}(i_1(\delta), s(\delta)) = u_{\delta,j}(i_2(\delta), s(\delta))]$$

That is, for state $s$, $u_{\delta,j}$ does not depend on any of its constrained inputs. Define

$$I_{\gamma,\mathbf{A}} = \{i | X - X' \ni i \in I_\mathbf{A}\} \quad \text{and} \quad O_{\gamma,\mathbf{A}} = \{o | X - X' \ni o \in O_\mathbf{A}\}$$

calling these *composition input* (*output*) *states*.

Modifying an algorithm of Burks and Wright [3], one can prove the following

**Lemma.** If $\gamma$ is consistent with respect to $s \in S_\mathbf{A}$, then there is a unique extension $\mu_s$: $I_{\gamma,\mathbf{A}} \to I_\mathbf{A}$ satisfying equations (*).

$\gamma$ will be called a locally effective composition function (LECF) if: (1) $\gamma$ is consistent for some computable $s \in S_\mathbf{A}$, (2) $\gamma$ is consistent for $s \in S_\mathbf{A}$ $\Rightarrow$ for every $i \in I_{\gamma,\mathbf{A}}$ $\gamma$ is consistent with respect to $f_\mathbf{A}(\mu_s(i), s)$.

For each LECF $\gamma$ and unrestricted composition $\mathbf{A}$, the *composition* $\mathbf{A}_\gamma$ is defined by the quintuple

$$\langle I_{\gamma,\mathbf{A}}, S_{\gamma,\mathbf{A}}, O_{\gamma,\mathbf{A}}, f_{\gamma,\mathbf{A}}, u_{\gamma,\mathbf{A}}\rangle$$

where $I_{\gamma,\mathbf{A}}$ and $O_{\gamma,\mathbf{A}}$ are as above
$S_{\gamma,\mathbf{A}} = \{s \in S_\mathbf{A} \ni \gamma$ is consistent w.r.t. $s$ and $s$ is computable$\}$
$f_{\gamma,\mathbf{A}}(i, s) = f_\mathbf{A}(\mu_s(i), s)$
$u_{\gamma,\mathbf{A}}(i, s) = u_\mathbf{A}(\mu_s(i), s)$ for $i \in I_{\gamma,\mathbf{A}}$, $s \in S_{\gamma,\mathbf{A}}$

(The subscript **A** will be dropped where no confusion can arise.) Thus the set $\{\mathbf{A}_\gamma \ni \mathbf{A}$ is an unrestricted composition and $\gamma$ is LECF over $\mathbf{A}\}$ will be the set of all compositions.

**Lemma.** Given any $\mathbf{A}_\gamma$, $\alpha \in A$, and $t \in N$: $\mathbf{S}_\gamma(t)|\alpha$ can be calculated from $\mathbf{S}_\gamma(o)|B(\alpha,t)$ and $\mathbf{I}_\gamma(o)|B(\alpha,t),\ldots,I_\gamma(t)|B(\alpha,t)$, where $B$ is a computable function and $B(\alpha,t)$ is a finite subset of $A$ containing $\alpha$.

**Theorem.** The property LECF is decidable for all $\gamma$ over finite $\mathbf{A}$ but not for all $\gamma$ over all $\mathbf{A}$.

The following definitions are useful:

$\{a_1,\ldots,a_k\}$ will be called a set of *generators* for $\mathbf{A}_\gamma$ if $\{a_\alpha \ni \alpha \in A\}$ consists only of copies of elements of $\{a_1,\ldots,a_k\}$.

$\mathbf{B}_\zeta$ over $\{b_\beta \ni \beta \in B\}$ will be called a *subcomposition* of $\mathbf{A}_\gamma$ over $\{a_\alpha \ni \alpha \in A\}$ if: (1) $\{b_\beta\} \subset \{a_\alpha\}$, (2) $\zeta = \gamma | Y_B$, where $Y_B = \{y \in Y' \ni \mathrm{proj}_1\, y \in B$ and $\mathrm{proj}_1\, \gamma(y) \in B\}$.

For any composition $\mathbf{A}_\gamma$ one can construct a hierarchy of subcompositions corresponding exactly to any set of block diagrams describing the composition.

The idea of computation, for compositions, will be developed for functions $\Gamma$: $\Sigma_i \to \Sigma_j$, where $\Sigma_i = \{\sigma\colon N \to N_i \ni N = \{0,1,2,\ldots\}$ and $N_i = \{0, 1,2,\ldots,i\}\}$. $\mathbf{A}_\gamma$ with initial state $s$ will be said to compute $\Gamma$ *b*-uniformly if: After any arbitrary "start-up" time $\tau$, and a fixed "processing delay" $c$, $\mathbf{A}_\gamma$ produces successive values of $\Gamma(\sigma)$ every $b$ units of time when the input sequence $\mathbf{I}_\gamma$ presents successive values of $\sigma$ at the same rate. More formally,

$$(\exists c \in N)(\exists \Omega \in I_\gamma)(\forall \sigma \in \Sigma_i)(\forall n \in N)(\forall \tau \in N)$$

$$\left[ U_\gamma(\mathbf{I}_\gamma, s);\, (t+c) = \begin{cases} \Gamma\sigma(n) & \text{when } t = bn + \tau \\ \Omega & \text{otherwise} \end{cases} \right.$$

$$\left. \text{when } \mathbf{I}_\gamma(t) = \begin{cases} \sigma(n) & \text{for } t = bn + \tau \\ \Omega & \text{otherwise} \end{cases} \right]$$

$\Omega$ plays the role here of a "no-signal" condition. (Actually this definition should be weakened to allow the input and output sets, $I_\gamma$ and $O_\gamma$, to contain coded representations of elements of $N_i$ and $N_j$ rather than only the elements themselves.)

In what follows it will be assumed that, whatever notion of computation is employed, the set of computable $\Gamma$ will contain the set of *b*-uniformly computable $\Gamma$.

It is worth noting that, interpreting the sequences $\sigma$ as expansions of real numbers, the uniformly computable $\Gamma$ are continuous although often undefined at various points—several interesting questions arise, but they will not be followed up here.

**Lemma.** If $\Gamma$ is finitely computable in the sense of Burks [2] then $\Gamma$ is uniformly computable.

**Lemma.** If $\mathbf{A}_\gamma$ and $\mathbf{A}'_{\gamma'}$ $b$-uniformly compute $\Gamma$ and $\Gamma'$, respectively, and if $\Gamma\Gamma'$ (the composition of the functions) is defined, then $\mathbf{A}_\gamma$ and $\mathbf{A}'_{\gamma'}$ can be connected to form a new composition such that

$$U_\gamma(U_{\gamma'}(\mathbf{I}_\gamma, s), s') = \Gamma(\Gamma'(\sigma)) \text{ when } \mathbf{I}_\gamma(t) = \begin{cases} \sigma(n) & \text{for } t = bn + \tau \\ \Omega & \text{otherwise} \end{cases}$$

Third in the lineup of underlying ideas is that of simulation. To specify the manner in which one device simulates another is to supply a mapping whereby actions in the image device can be reinterpreted as actions of the object being simulated. The formal counterpart of this will be an embedding map defined as follows:

Let $A$, $X$, $Y$ and $S_\gamma$, $I_\gamma$, $O_\gamma$ be the index and state sets, respectively, of the object composition $\mathbf{A}_\gamma$, and let $B$, $X_1$, $Y_1$ and $S_{\gamma_1}$, $I_{\gamma_1}$, $O_{\gamma_1}$ be the corresponding sets for the image composition $B_{\gamma_1}$. A mapping $\varphi$ from the sets $A$, $X$, $Y$, $S_\gamma$, $I_\gamma$, $O_\gamma$ to subsets of $B$, $X_1$, $Y_1$, $S_{\gamma_1}$, $I_{\gamma_1}$, $O_{\gamma_1}$, respectively, will be called a *strict embedding* if:

1. Distinct {indices, states} map onto distinct {sets of indices, states}:

$$\alpha \neq \alpha_1 \Rightarrow \varphi(\alpha) \cap \varphi(\alpha_1) = \text{null set, etc.}$$

2. Each index of a {free, bound} {input, output} of a given element maps onto corresponding indices of the image subset:

$$\text{proj}_1\, \varphi(x) \subset \varphi(\text{proj}_1\, x),\ x \in X - X' \Rightarrow \varphi(x) \subset X_1 - X_1'$$

and similarly for $y$.

3. If $x = \gamma(y)$ then the same must hold for all indices in $\varphi(x)$:

$$\varphi(\gamma(y)) = \gamma_1(\varphi(y))$$

4. If two states of $\mathbf{A}_\gamma$ assign the same state to an element, then the images of these states must assign the same state to the images of the element:

$$s(\alpha) = s_1(\alpha) \Rightarrow \varphi(s)|\varphi(\alpha) = \varphi(s_1)|\varphi(\alpha)$$

and similarly for $i, i_1 \in I_\gamma$, $o, o_1 \in O_\gamma$.

5. When the state of $\mathbf{B}_{\gamma_1}$ is the image $\varphi(s)$ of a state $s$ of $\mathbf{A}_\gamma$, then $f_{\gamma_1}$ does not depend upon the states of unassigned inputs:

$$i|\varphi(X - X') = i_1|\varphi(X - X') \Rightarrow f_{\gamma_1}(i, \varphi(s)) = f_{\gamma_1}(i_1, \varphi(s))$$

where $i, i_1 \in I_{\gamma_1}$.

6. The successor states of the element images must be the images of the successor states:

$$f_{\varphi(\alpha)}(\varphi(i)|\varphi(\alpha), \varphi(s)|\varphi(\alpha)) = \varphi f_\alpha(i|\alpha, s|\alpha)$$

where $f_{\varphi(\alpha)}$ is the transition function of the subcomposition indexed by $\varphi(\alpha)$.

Conditions 5 and 6 assure that the transformations, $F_{\varphi(\alpha)}$ and $U_{\varphi(\alpha)}$ of the image subcompositions can be restricted so as to be the same as $F_\alpha$ and $U_\alpha$.

The requirements on $\varphi$ can be weakened in a natural way to yield weak and $b$-slow embeddings or, briefly, *embeddings*:

[weak] (1) $\mathbf{A}_\gamma$ can be partitioned into disjoint subcompositions which are then embedded as elements, only over-all behavior of the subcompositions being preserved (thus, for example, $\gamma$ need not be preserved in the subcompositions).

[slow] (2) A $b$-slow embedding yields an image with a time scale $t' = bt$, where $t$ is the time index of $\mathbf{A}_\gamma$. This can be accomplished in a natural way by mapping input states of the object composition into strings of input states in the image. That is, input sequences to the object composition are "slowed" in the image by the "insertion" of $b-1$ "no-signal" states between signals, cf. McNaughton [9].

The characterization of homogeneity for compositions, which I shall discuss next in conjunction with universal compositions, depends upon three definitions:

An *isomorphic embedding* $\varphi$ of $\mathbf{A}_\gamma$ on $\mathbf{B}_{\gamma_1}$ is a strict embedding such that $\alpha \simeq \varphi(\alpha)$, $x \simeq \varphi(x)$, $y \simeq \varphi(y)$, $S_\alpha \simeq S_{\varphi(\alpha)}$, $I_x \simeq I_{\varphi(x)}$, and $O_y \simeq O_{\varphi(y)}$.

Two embeddings, $\varphi_1$ and $\varphi_2$, of $\mathbf{A}_\gamma$ in $\mathbf{C}_{\gamma_2}$ {on a single generator} will be called *identical* {*identically oriented*} if:

1. There is an isomorphic embedding $\theta$ of the subcomposition indexed by $\varphi_1(A)$ on the subcomposition indexed by $\varphi_2(A)$ such that $\theta\varphi_1 = \varphi_2$.

2. For all $\alpha, \alpha' \in A$ and any connected sequence $\rho$ from $\varphi_1(\alpha)$ to $\varphi_1(\alpha')$ {or from $\varphi_1(\alpha)$ to $\varphi_2(\alpha)$}, there exists a connected sequence $\rho'$ from $\varphi_2(\alpha)$ to $\varphi_2(\alpha')$ {from $\varphi_1(\alpha')$ to $\varphi_2(\alpha')$} such that $\text{proj}_2\,\rho = \text{proj}_2\,\rho'$ [where $\text{proj}_2\,\rho = (i_1, i_2, \ldots, i_l)$ just in case $y_h = (\beta_h, i_h)$, $1 \leq h \leq l$].

A composition $\mathbf{V}_\nu$ will be called *universal and locally homogeneous* for (uniformly) computable $\Gamma$ if:

1. For each (uniformly) computable $\Gamma$ there is an embedding $\varphi$, into $\mathbf{V}_\nu$, of a composition $\mathbf{A}_\gamma$ capable of (uniformly) computing $\Gamma$.
2. If $\varphi_1$ embeds $\mathbf{A}_\gamma$ in $\mathbf{V}_\nu$ then, given arbitrary $\alpha \in A$, $\xi \in \varphi(\alpha)$, and $\xi' \in V$, there exists $\varphi_2$ embedding $\mathbf{A}_\gamma$ in $\mathbf{V}_\nu$ identically so that $\theta(\xi) = \xi'$.

**Lemma.** Necessary conditions for $\mathbf{V}_\nu$ to be universal and locally homogeneous are:

1. $\mathbf{V}_\nu$ must be generated by a single element.
2. $V$ must be countably infinite.

If condition 2 of the definition is modified to require identical orientation (since in either case $\mathbf{V}_\nu$ must be generated by a single element) we obtain a third necessary condition:

3. Strings over output indices are "commutative"; i.e., if $\rho$ is a connected sequence from $\alpha$ to $\alpha'$, $\sigma = \text{proj}_2\ \rho$ and $\sigma'$ is any permutation of $\sigma$, then there exists a connected sequence $\rho'$ such that $\text{proj}_2\ \rho' = \sigma'$.

Compositions satisfying the modified definition will be called universal and homogeneous or, simply, *computation-universal.* It is a consequence of the third part of the lemma that computation-universal spaces can be "coordinatized" on a discrete (integer) cartesian $k$-dimensional grid ($k \leqslant n_\alpha$). In these terms the second part of the definition assures that all "translations" of an image are also images of the same object. As a consequence, properties of the image, such as its connection scheme, can be made independent of the "location" of the image.

Let $U$ denote the class of computation-universal compositions. If part 1 of the definition of computation-universal is modified to read: "Given any finite composition $\mathbf{A}_\gamma$ there exists an embedding $\varphi$ of $\mathbf{A}_\gamma$ in $\mathbf{V}_\nu$," then a natural subclass $U_c$ of $U$ is defined—the class of *composition-universal* compositions. Another natural subclass, $U_d$, is defined by: $U_d = \{\mathbf{V}_\nu \ni \mathbf{V}_\nu$ is computation-universal with a Moore (lag time $\geqslant 1$) automaton as generator$\}$.

Elements of $U_d$ are the most natural generalizations of von Neumann's "logical-universal" space [11] because each exhibits the "propagation delay" which plays an important part in his study of self-reproduction. In fact, von Neumann's detailed example establishes the existence of $U_d$ and hence of $U$. It can also be shown that there exist elements in $U_c$. (The class of iterative circuit computers [5] contains a subset of composition-universal compositions.)

It can be established that $U_d$ and $U_c$ are disjoint—a result which has important consequences for the study of construction and adaptation via universal compositions.

**Theorem.** Given any $\mathbf{V}_\nu \in U_d$, any set of automata $G$, containing at least one automaton with two input dependent outputs, and $b \in N$, there exists a finite composition $\mathbf{A}_\gamma$ generated by $G$ which cannot be $b$-slow embedded in $\mathbf{V}_\nu$. [In fact, for each $\mathbf{V}_\nu$, $G$, and $b$ there exists a constant $c$ and a function $e(l)$ such that the theorem is true for any $\mathbf{A}_\gamma$ containing subcomposition "trees" with at least $e(l)$ elements, $l \geqslant c$; $e(l)$ and $c$ are such that "almost all" $\mathbf{A}_\gamma$ over $G$ satisfy the condition. The theorem turns on the failure of Kleene's representation theorem [8] for the embedded compositions.]

Thus the elements of $U_d$ are not composition-universal; it follows at once that the generating element of any composition of type $U_c$ must be a Mealy (lag time zero for some states) automaton.

**Corollary.** Given any finite composition $\mathbf{A}_\gamma$ and any $b$-slow embedding of $\mathbf{A}_\gamma$ in a composition $\mathbf{V}_\nu \in U_d$, "almost all" compositions containing $\mathbf{A}_\gamma$ as a subcomposition cannot be $b$-slow embedded in $\mathbf{V}_\nu$.

Thus, given any finitely computable $\Gamma$, "almost none" of the compositions capable of computing $\Gamma$ can be embedded in $\mathbf{V}_\nu \in U_d$. Moreover, given a set of computation procedures with a common "subroutine," it will in general be impossible to embed them in $\mathbf{V}_\nu$ so as to preserve the common subroutine. Or, again:

**Corollary.** Given $\mathbf{V}_\nu \in U_{d}$, any $b \in N$, and any set of generators $G$, as above, there exist $\Gamma_1, \Gamma_2, \ldots, \Gamma_j, \ldots$ such that

1. Each $\Gamma_j$ is $b$-uniform computable by some $[\mathbf{A}_j]_{\gamma_j}$ over $G$.
2. $[\mathbf{A}_j]_{\gamma_j}$ can at best be $b_j$-slow embedded in $V_\nu$, where $b_j > b_{j-1}$, $b \in N_j$.

Since $\lim_j b_j = \infty$, the computation rates of the images approach zero.

I would say that the above results argue strongly for the use of spaces of type $U_c$, rather than $U_d$, in studies of construction and adaptation. Though one may question how "realistic" such spaces are in allowing propagation of signals with negligible delay, no mathematical difficulty ensues, because the spaces $U_c$ are compositions and hence satisfy strong local effectiveness conditions (see the lemma following the definition of composition).

I shall turn now to adaptive systems. By way of motivation, note that there is a problem of adaptation only when some aspects of the environment are initially unknown to the adaptive system. If we think of the system as attempting to model the environment, then its model is incomplete. The system cannot predict the consequences of some of its responses; in terms of its model the system may be facing any of several environments determined by the possible alternatives (substitution instances) for unknown aspects. In what follows this will be formalized by designating a class $\mathscr{E}$ of admissible (or possible) environments.

In a similar vein, it is necessary to specify the techniques or models available to the adaptive system before one has a clearly defined problem of adaptation. The class of devices which the system can bring to bear through rearrangement of its structure will be designated $\mathscr{A}$.

For present purposes both $\mathscr{E}$ and $\mathscr{A}$ will be taken to be possibly infinite collections of compositions (the elements of $\mathscr{A}$ being restricted to finite compositions). An adaptive strategy, then, can be thought of as a set of trajectories through the set $\mathscr{A}$, parametrized by the elements of $\mathscr{E}$. That is, the strategy will dictate successive reorganizations of the adaptive system (the trajectory) according to the information (inputs) it receives from the environment, $\mathbf{E} \in \mathscr{E}$, confronting the system.

In greater detail:

Let $\mathscr{E} = \{\mathbf{E}_b \ni \mathbf{E}_b = \langle I_b, S_b, f_b, s, q_b, \mu_b \rangle$ with $b \in B\}$

$s \in S_b$ and $B$ an ordered index set

Let $\mathscr{A} = \{\mathbf{A}_d \ni \mathbf{A}_d = \langle I_d, S_d, f_d, q_d \rangle$ with $d \in D\}$

$D$ an ordered index set

$I_b, S_b, f_b$ and $I_d, S_d, f_d$ will be defined as for compositions and $q_b$ will be defined as a map

$$q_b\colon \bigcup_{d \in D} (I_d \times S_d) \to I_b$$

Under interpretation, $q_b$ determines the input (response) to environment $\mathbf{E}_b$ for any complete state of any admissible device in $\mathscr{A}$. Similarly,

$$q_d\colon \bigcup_{b \in B} S_b \to I_d$$

$q_d$ corresponds to the symbolization of the environment (cues, etc.) used by $\mathbf{A}_d$. It is worth noting that even if $\mathbf{A}_{d_1}$ differs from $\mathbf{A}_{d_2}$ only because $q_{d_1} \neq q_{d_2}$ (that is, as automata, $\mathbf{A}_{d_1}$ and $\mathbf{A}_{d_2}$ are essentially the same), the adaptability of $\mathbf{A}_{d_1}$ may be greatly different from that of $\mathbf{A}_{d_2}$. The amount of information $\mathbf{A}_d$ receives from the environment depends critically on $q_d$; changes in $q_d$ may be an essential part of the system's adaptation to the environment.

Finally, $\mu_b$ is a utility function over the states $S_b$ of $\mathbf{E}_b$, $\mu\colon S_b \to$ reals. In this formulation, each state of the environment is assumed to yield some payoff (possibly zero) to the adaptive system (cf. the corresponding formulation in the theory of games, interpreting states as outcomes).

An adaptive strategy $\tau$ will be a map

$$\tau\colon D \times [\bigcup_{d \in D} I_d] \times [\bigcup_{d \in D} S_d] \to D$$

which determines for every device and every complete state of that device what admissible device is to succeed it. That is, the device employed by the adaptive system at time $t+1$ is determined from the complete state of the device employed at time $t$:

$$d(t+1) = \tau(d(t), i(t), s(t)) \qquad \text{where } i(t) \in I_{d(t)}, s(t) \in S_{d(t)}$$

Given a device $\mathbf{A}_{d(0)}$ and its initial state, an environment, and an adaptive strategy $\tau$, the over-all behavior of the system is determined by the following recursions:

$$\begin{aligned} I(t) &= q_{d(t)}(S_b(t)) & I(t) &\in I_{d(t)} \\ I_b(t) &= q_b(I(t), S(t)) & S(t) &\in S_{d(t)} \\ S_b(t+1) &= f_b(I_b(t), S_b(t)) & S_b(0) &= s \\ d(t+1) &= \tau(d(t), I(t), S(t)) \\ S'(t+1) &= f_{d(t)}(I(t), S(t)) \end{aligned}$$

[$S(t+1)$ is determined from $S'(t+1)$ by deleting those components of $S'(t+1)$ corresponding to components deleted by $\tau$ and adding components corresponding to the initial states of components added by $\tau$. For example, if $\mathbf{A}_{d(t+1)}$ is a subcomposition of $\mathbf{A}_{d(t)}$, indexed by $A_1 \subset A$, then $S(t+1) = S'(t+1)|A_1$.]

If the devices produced by strategy $\tau$ are embedded in a universal space $\mathbf{V}_\nu$, then a natural restriction on the "amount of construction per unit time" results:

Let $B(S(t), \alpha)$ be the set of all elements in $\mathbf{V}_\nu$ which can affect the state of element $a_\alpha$ at time $t+1$, given the state assignment $S(t) \in S_\nu$ [cf. the definition: $\nu$ consistent with respect to $S(t)$]. Let $V(t)$ be the index set of elements in the subcomposition which is the image of $A_{d(t)}$ in $\mathbf{V}_\nu$ and let $\bar{V}(t) = \{\alpha \ni B(S(t), \alpha) \text{ contains } \beta \in V(t)\}$. Require $V(t+1) \subseteq \bar{V}(t)$. That is, $\tau$ at any given time can only add elements which, in the embedding, lie within the radius of immediate action (unit delay) of the extant image. When $\tau(d(t), I(t), S(t)) \neq d(t)$, this must be achieved by the image of $I(t), \varphi(I(t))$, causing changes in the dependencies of the subcomposition indexed by $\bar{V}(t)$ so that $f_{V(t+1)}(\varphi(I(t)), \varphi(S(t))) = \varphi(f_{d(t+1)}(I(t), S(t)))$, whereas $f_{V(t)} = \varphi f_{d(t)}$ before.

From this point on it will be assumed that all strategies begin with some fixed device $\mathbf{A}_{d(0)}$ in state $S_{d(0)}(0)$. Under this assumption, $\tau$, when confronted by any environment $E_b$, will determine a unique environmental sequence $S_b(1), S_b(2), \ldots, S_b(t), \ldots$. This in turn will determine a sequence of payoffs $\mu(S_b(1)), \mu(S_b(2)), \ldots$. Let $\mu_{\tau,E_b}(t)$ designate the payoff so determined by $\tau$ at $t$.

$\tau_0$ will be called *$\epsilon$-near-optimal* if

$$(\forall E_b \in \mathscr{E})\ (\text{almost all admissible } \tau) \left[ \lim_{T\to\infty} \frac{\Sigma_0^T \mu_{\tau_0,\, E_b}(t)}{\Sigma_0^T \mu_{\tau,\, E_b}(t)} > \epsilon \right]$$

Note that the subset of $\{\tau\}$ for which the condition need not be met may vary from one element of $\mathscr{E}$ to another without destroying the near-optimality of $\tau_0$. The motivation for this definition lies in its consequences: If such a $\tau_0$ exists for a pair $(\mathscr{E}, \mathscr{A})$ then, given any $E_b \in \mathscr{E}$, almost no other strategy can force $\tau_0$ into gambler's ruin. [The exceptions are those enumerative strategies which happen to produce a device, early in the sequence $\mathbf{A}_{d(t)}$, which is optimal for $E_b$; if the strategy *is* enumerative, however, it will perform poorly over almost all other elements of $\mathscr{E}$, assuming $\mathscr{E}$ is at all large.] Stated another way, if the payoff determines the duplication rate of an entity employing strategy $\tau$, then an $\epsilon$-near-optimal strategy will escape extinction against almost all other strategies in any environment of $\mathscr{E}$.

The definition may be strengthened to *strictly-$\epsilon$-near-optimal* by substituting "$\forall\tau$" for "almost all $\tau$." The difficulty of finding interesting pairs $(\mathscr{E}, \mathscr{A})$ for which such strategies exist is accordingly increased.

The necessity for definitions of optimality, like the above, which involve "rate of accumulation" or "efficiency," is shown by the trivial way in which "convergence to an optimal rate" can be established: One need only apply a diagonal procedure to an enumeration of Turing machines to eventually arrive at the optimal device (optimal payoff rate) for any effectively solvable environment. Such procedures are of no interest in studies of adaptation because the corresponding "times of convergence" are in general many orders of magnitude greater than that required by other possible strategies. (Applied to real adaptive systems, such strategies entail extinction.)

It can be shown that near-optimal strategies exist for a class of environments $\mathscr{E}$, which includes a rich class of normalized game trees (cf. von Neumann and Morgenstern [12]). No systematic study over a structured family of pairs $(\mathscr{E}, \mathscr{A})$ exists, and the existence of strictly near-optimal strategies over any interesting pair $(\mathscr{E}, \mathscr{A})$ is still an open question. Studies under way indicate that an interesting class of near-optimal strategies results if one produces successive sets of strings [corresponding to recursive definition of $\mathbf{A}_{d(t)}$] through recombination of fragments of duplicates of extant strings (duplication rate determined by payoff)—a translation into this context of the genetic process of crossover with epistatic effects (see Kimura [7]). It can be shown that the techniques employed by Samuel [10], Friedberg [4], and Bledsoe and Browning [1] (among others) are essentially special cases of this class.

## References


1. W. W. Bledsoe and I. Browning, Pattern recognition and reading by machine, *Proc. Eastern Joint Computer Conf.*, 225–232 (1959).
2. A. W. Burks, Computation, behavior and structure in fixed and growing automata, *Self-Organizing Systems*, Pergamon Press, London, 1960, pp. 282–311.
3. A. W. Burks and J. B. Wright, Theory of logical nets, *Proc. IRE* **41**, 1357–1365 (1953).
4. R. M. Friedberg, A learning machine: part 1, *IBM J. Res. Develop.* **2**, 2–13 (1958).
5. J. H. Holland, Iterative circuit computers, *Proc. Western Joint Computer Conf.* 259–265 (1960).
6. J. H. Holland, Universal embedding spaces for automata (forthcoming in a festschrift for Norbert Weiner).
7. M. Kimura, On the change of population fitness by natural selection, *Heredity* **12**, 145–167 (1958).
8. S. C. Kleene, Representation of events in nerve nets and finite automata, in *Automata Studies*, (C. E. Shannon and J. McCarthy, eds.), Princeton University Press, Princeton N.J., 1956, pp. 3–41.
9. R. McNaughton, On nets made up of badly timed elements, I, *Summer Conference Notes on Parallel Computers, Automata and Adaptive Systems*, University of Michigan, Ann Arbor, 1962.
10. A. L. Samuel, Some studies in machine learning, using the game of checkers, *IBM J. Res. Develop.* **3**, 210–229 (1959).
11. J. von Neumann, in *The Theory of Automata: Construction, Reproduction, and Homogeneity* (A. W. Burks, ed.), to be published by Univ. Illinois Press, Urbana.
12. J. von Neumann and O. Morgenstern, *Theory of Games and Economic Behavior*, Princeton University Press, Princeton, N.J., 1947.

# Graphes de Transfert des Réseaux Neuroniques

H. KOREZLIOGLU[1]

*Istituto di Fiscia Teorica,*
*Naples, Italy*

Dans le présent travail, sont considérés des réseaux constitués d'éléments bistables à seuil et qui ont été proposés comme modèles de réseaux neuroniques ([1], [2]).

Le signal de sortie d'un élément bistable à seuil est égal à 1, si son signal d'entrée ne dépasse pas la valeur de son seuil; autrement, il est égal à 0. Le signal d'entrée de chacun des éléments d'un réseau du type considéré est la somme pondérée des signaux de sortie de tous les éléments du réseau. Par conséquent, le schéma de transfert d'un tel réseau peut être défini par un nombre de fonctions booléennes linéairement séparables, égal au nombre d'éléments contenus dans le réseau.

Certaines propriétés des schémas de transfert de ces réseaux sont étudiées ici, par la linéarisation des inégalités qui définissent les fonctions booléennes.

## I. Fonctions Booléennes Linéairement Séparables

Nous allons désigner par $F(x_1, x_2, \ldots, x_n)$, une fonction booléenne à $n$ variables $x_1, x_2, \ldots, x_n$. Le domaine de définition de $F$ est l'ensemble $[0,1]^n$, $n$-ième puissance cartésienne de l'ensemble $[0,1]$ contenant seulement les éléments 0 et 1. A chaque sommet du cube unité dans $R^n$ correspond biunivoquement un élément de l'ensemble $[0,1]^n$. Par conséquent, il n'y aura pas d'ambiguité à désigner le cube par $[0,1]^n$ et à considérer l'ensemble de ses sommets comme domaine de définition de $F$.

A tout sommet $X_j (0 \leqslant j \leqslant 2^n - 1)$ dont les composantes sont $x_{j,1}, x_{j,2}, \ldots,$ $x_{j,n}$, sera attribué le nombre

$$j = \sum_{i=1}^{n} 2^{i-1} \cdot x_{j,i}$$

Le vecteur qui a pour extrémité le sommet $X_j$ et pour origine, l'origine des axes cartésiens dans $R^n$ sera désigné par $\mathbf{X}_j$. Les indices considérés ici seront tous des entiers.

[1] *Present address:* Institut Henri Poincaré, Paris, France.

**Définition 1.** Soient

$$M_0 = \{X_j; F(X_j) = 0\}$$
$$M_1 = \{X_j; F(X_j) = 1\}$$

$F$ est dite linéairement séparable, s'il existe un hyperplan dans $R^n$, qui sépare $M_0$ et $M_1$.

Réciproquement, étant donné dans $R^n$, un hyperplan

$$\sum_{i=1}^{n} a_i x_i = s \tag{1}$$

il est possible de définir une fonction booléenne, séparable par ce plan, de la manière suivante:

$$\sum_{i=1}^{n} a_i x_{j,i} - s \begin{cases} \geqslant 0 \\ < 0 \end{cases} \Rightarrow F(X_j) = \begin{cases} 1 \\ 0 \end{cases} \tag{2}$$

Pour tout sommet du cube $[0,1]^n$, on peut déduire de (1) et de (2), les relations

$$\sum_{i=1}^{n} a_i x_{j,i} = s + b_j, \qquad 0 \leqslant j \leqslant 2^n - 1 \tag{3}$$

qui donnent, pour les sommets $\{X_j; j = 0 \text{ et } j = 2^i; 0 \leqslant i \leqslant n-1\}$

$$-s = b_0 \qquad \text{et} \qquad a_i = s + b_{2^{i-1}} \tag{4}$$

En remplaçant $s$ et $a_i$ dans (3) par (4), on trouve

$$\sum_{i=1}^{n} b_{2^{(i-1)}} \cdot x_{j,i} = b_0(\|j\| - 1) + b_j, \qquad 0 \leqslant j \leqslant 2^n - 1 \tag{5}$$

où $\|j\|$ est le nombre des 1 dans l'expression binaire de $j$.

Le système de relations linéaires (5) est équivalent au système d'inégalités (2), étant donné que

$$b_j \begin{cases} \geqslant 0 \\ < 0 \end{cases} \Rightarrow F(X_j) = \begin{cases} 1 \\ 0 \end{cases} \tag{6}$$

**Propriété 1.** Si $X_k$, $X_l$, $X_m$, $X_n$ forment les quatre sommets d'un rectangle du cube $[0,1]^n$, tels que $X_k$, $X_l$ se trouvent sur l'une des diagonales du rectangle et $X_m$, $X_n$ sur l'autre diagonale, on a:

$$b_k + b_l = b_m + b_n$$

En effet, pour deux couples de tels sommets, nous avons:

$$x_{k,i} + x_{l,i} = x_{m,i} + x_{n,i}, \qquad 1 \leqslant i \leqslant n$$

Les relations (5) donnent immédiatement le résultat.

Cette propriété entraine une propriété des fonctions booléennes linéairement séparables.

**Propriété 1′.** Si une fonction booléenne linéairement séparable prend la valeur $\alpha$ sur deux sommets diagonalement opposés d'un rectangle du cube et si elle prend la valeur $\bar{\alpha}$ (complément de $\alpha$) sur l'un des sommets de l'autre diagonale; alors, elle prend la valeur $\alpha$ sur le quatrième sommet.

### A. Remarque sur la Réalisabilité

Cette propriété des rectangles qui est nécessaire pour la séparabilité des fonctions booléennes n'est pas suffisante pour $n > 5$ (cf. [3]). Nous ne connaissons pas de propriétés géométriques simples qui permettent d'éviter le calcul du plan de séparation des deux ensembles $M_0$ et $M_1$ ou bien celui des coefficients $b$ des relations (5). Le problème de la séparabilité linéaire exprimé par les relations (5) et (6) peut toujours se ramener au problème bien connu de la compatibilité des inégalités linéaires avec des variables positives (cf. [4]). Posons:

$$b_k = \alpha_j \cdot \beta_j$$

avec

$$\alpha_j = \begin{cases} 1 & \text{si } b_j \geqslant 0 \\ -1 & \text{si } b_j < 0 \end{cases}$$

Les relations (5) deviennent

$$\sum_{i=1}^{n} \alpha_{2^{(i-1)}} \beta_{2^{(i-1)}} x_{j,i} = \alpha_0 \beta_0(\|j\| - 1) + \alpha_j \beta_j, \qquad 0 \leqslant j \leqslant 2^n - 1 \tag{7}$$

Nous avons:

$$\sum_{i=1}^{n} \alpha_j \alpha_{2^{(i-1)}} \beta_{2^{(i-1)}} x_{j,i} - \alpha_j \alpha_0 \beta_0(\|j\| - 1) \geqslant 0, \qquad 0 \leqslant j \leqslant 2^n - 1 \tag{8}$$

Etant donnée une fonction booléenne, les coefficients $\alpha_j \alpha_0$ et $\alpha_j \alpha_{2^{(i-1)}}$ des inégalités ci-dessus sont connues. Par conséquent, la fonction booléenne est réalisable si et seulement si les $2^n - (n+1)$ contraintes correspondant à $j \neq 0$ et $j \neq 2^i$ $(0 \leqslant i \leqslant n-1)$ dans (8) sont compatibles avec l'existence des $(n+1)$ variables non négatives $\beta_0, \beta_1, \ldots, \beta_{2^i}, \ldots, \beta_{2^{(n-1)}}$.

## II. Graphes de Transfert des Réseaux à Eléments à Seuil

Soient donnés $n$ hyperplans $P_1, P_2, \ldots, P_n$ dans $R^n$

$$\sum_{i=1}^{n} a_{k,i} x_i = s_k, \qquad 1 \leqslant k \leqslant n \tag{9}$$

auxquels correspondent $n$ fonctions booléennes $F_1, F_2, \ldots, F_n$ linéairement séparables. Si la valeur de $F_j$ est considérée comme étant la $j$-ième composante des sommets du cube $[0, 1]^n$, l'ensemble des fonctions $F_1, F_2, \ldots, F_n$ définit une application de $[0, 1]^n$ dans lui-même.

Considérons maintenant un réseau à éléments à seuil. L'état de chaque élément est connu par la valeur de sa sortie, c'est-à-dire par la valeur de la fonction booléenne qu'il réalise. Supposons que le nombre des éléments à seuil contenus dans le réseau soit égal à $n$ et attribuons à chacun d'eux un indice allant de 1 jusqu'à $n$. L'état du réseau peut donc être décrit par un mot binaire de longueur $n$, dont la composante de poids $i$ est la sortie du $i$-ième élément du réseau. En associant ainsi à tout élément la fonction booléenne qu'il réalise, la transition d'états du réseau peut être décrite par le graphe suivant:

**Définition 2.** Les sommets du graphe coïncident avec ceux du cube $[0, 1]^n$; il existe un arc allant de $X_j$ à $X_k$, si

$$\begin{aligned} F_1(X_j) &= x_{k,1} \\ F_2(X_j) &= x_{k,2} \\ &\cdots \\ F_n(X_j) &= x_{k,n} \end{aligned} \tag{10}$$

Le graphe ainsi défini sera appelé graphe de transfert du réseau.

Remarquer que de tout sommet sort un seul arc, puisque le réseau ne peut pas se trouver dans deux états en même temps.

Comme nous avons fait pour la séparabilité linéaire des fonctions booléennes, substituons au système (9), les relations

$$\sum_{i=1}^{n} \mathbf{b}_{2(i-1)} \cdot x_{j,i} = \mathbf{b}_0(\|j\| - 1) + \mathbf{b}_j, \qquad 0 \leqslant j \leqslant 2^n - 1 \tag{11}$$

déduites des relations (5) en remplaçant les coefficients scalaires $b$ par des vecteurs à $n$ dimensions $\mathbf{b}$.

**Propriété 2.** Les extrémités des vecteurs $\mathbf{b}_j$ $(0 \leqslant j \leqslant 2^n - 1)$ forment les sommets d'un parallélépipède dans $R^n$.

*Démonstration.* Il suffit de montrer que, pour tout rectangle de sommets $X_i$, $X_j$, $X_k$, $X_l$ de $[0, 1]^n$, les extrémités de $\mathbf{b}_i$, $\mathbf{b}_j$, $\mathbf{b}_k$, $\mathbf{b}_l$ sont les sommets d'un parallélogramme. La relation $\mathbf{b}_i + \mathbf{b}_j = \mathbf{b}_k + \mathbf{b}_l$ est toujours valable pour quatre sommets $X_i$, $X_j$, $X_k$, $X_l$ d'un rectangle tels que $i + j = k + l$.

Considérons maintenant, le cube $[-1, 1]^n$ qui est homothétique au cube $[0, 1]^n$ dans le rapport 2, le sommet $X_{2^n-1}$ étant le centre d'homothétie et associons à tout sommet de $[-1,1]^n$ le même numéro que le sommet de $[0,1]^n$ dont il est déduit par homothétie.

Cette numérotation peut être considérée comme une numérotation de quadrants de $R^n$, dans le système de coordonnées cartésiennes, en donnant à chaque quadrant le numéro du sommet de $[-1,1]^n$ qu'il contient. Nous allons désigner par $0_j$ le $j$-ième quadrant ainsi défini. Soit $\mathbf{c}_k$ le vecteur dont l'origine coïncide avec l'origine des axes dans $R^n$ et l'extrémité avec le sommet $k$ de $[-1,1]^n$. Un vecteur $\mathbf{b}$ a son extrémité dans $0_k$, si et seulement si le produit de Hadamard de $\mathbf{b}$ avec $\mathbf{c}_k$ est nonnégatif. Nous supposons ici que tout semi-axe cartésien positif est fermé à gauche.

**Propriété 3.** Le graphe de transfert possède un arc allant de $X_j$ à $X_k$ si et seulement si l'extrémité de $\mathbf{b}_j$ se trouve dans $0_k$.

*Démonstration.* S'il existe un arc allant de $X_j$ à $X_k$, les relations (10) sont vérifiées. Par conséquent, nous avons:

$$x_{k,i} = \begin{cases} 1 \\ 0 \end{cases} \Rightarrow b_{j,i} \begin{cases} \geqslant 0 \\ < 0 \end{cases} \text{et } c_{k,i} = \begin{cases} 1 \\ -1 \end{cases}$$

pour $1 \leqslant i \leqslant n$, où $b_{j,i}$ et $c_{k,i}$ sont respectivement les $i$-ièmes composantes de $\mathbf{b}_j$ et $\mathbf{c}_k$. Puisque $b_{j,i}$ et $c_{k,i}$ ont le même signe, l'extrémité de $\mathbf{b}_j$ se trouve dans le quadrant $0_k$. Réciproquement, si l'extrémité de $\mathbf{b}_j$ se trouve dans $0_k$, il existe un arc allant de $X_j$, à $X_k$, puisque l'implication ci-dessus est réversible.

Il est clair qu'il existe une certaine réciprocité entre les $n$ hyperplans $P_1, P_2, \ldots, P_n$ définis par (9) et le parallélépipède déduit des relations (11) à partir des vecteurs $\mathbf{b}_j$. En effet, le graphe de transfert correspondant peut aussi être défini de la manière suivante. Posons

$$(M_0)_k = \left\{ j;\ \sum_{i=1}^{n} a_{k,i} x_{j,i} - s_k < 0 \right\}$$

$$(M_1)_k = \left\{ j;\ \sum_{i=1}^{n} a_{k,i} x_{j,i} - s_k \geqslant 0 \right\}$$

L'ensemble des indices de sommets reliés à $X_j$ avec un arc incident à $X_j$ est donné par

$$\bigcap_{i=1}^{n} (M_{x_{j,i}})_i$$

où $x_{j,i}$ prend la valeur 0 ou 1. S'il n'y a aucun arc incident à $X_j$, cet ensemble est vide.

Supposons que les coefficients $a_{k,i}$ dans les équations (9) soient tels que le vecteur ayant pour composantes $a_{k,1}, a_{k,2}, \ldots, a_{k,n}$ qui est orthogonal à $P_k$ soit unitaire pour tout $k$ ($0 \leqslant k \leqslant n$). Alors, $b_{j,k}$ est la distance du sommet $X_j$ au plan $P_k$. $b_{j,k} \geqslant 0$, si $X_j$ est du côté du plan $P_k$ défini par la direction positive de la normale ou si $X_j$ est sur le plan même et $b_{j,k} < 0$ autrement.

Nous avons attribué le nombre $j$ au sommet du parallélépipède qui coïncide avec l'extrémité de $\mathbf{b}_j$. Soit $Q_k$ l'hyperplan des coordonnées défini par $x_k = 0$ dans $R^n$. Posons

$$(M'_0)_k = \{j;\ b_{j,k} < 0\}$$
$$(M'_1)_k = \{j;\ b_{j,k} \geqslant 0\}$$

**Propriété 4.** Pour $\alpha$ égal à 0 ou à 1 et pour tout $k$, ($1 \leqslant k \leqslant n$), on a:

$$(M'_\alpha)_k = (M_\alpha)_k$$

*Démonstration.* L'ensemble

$$\bigcap_{i=1}^{n} (M'_{x_{k,i}})_i$$

est l'ensemble des sommets du parallélépipède se trouvant dans $0_k$. Alors,

$$\bigcap_{i=1}^{n} (M_{x_{k,i}})_i = \bigcap_{i=1}^{n} (M'_{x_{k,i}})_i$$

Nous déduisons

$$(M_\alpha)_j = \bigcup_{k'} \bigcap_{i=1}^{n} (M_{x_{k,i}})_i = \bigcup_{k'} \bigcap_{i=1}^{n} (M'_{x_{k,i}})_i = (M'_\alpha)_j$$

où $k'$ prend toutes les valeurs de $k$ pour lesquelles $x_{k,j} = \alpha$.

En résumé, les sommets du parallélépipède séparés par $Q_k$ et ceux du cube $[0,1]^n$ séparés par $P_k$ ont les mêmes indices. Il est facile de démontrer, d'après cette propriété et la remarque que $b_{j,k}$ est la distance de $X_j$ à $P_k$, la propriété suivante.

**Propriété 5.** La transformation linéaire correspondant à

$$\mathbf{X}_j \rightarrow \mathbf{b}_j \qquad 0 \leqslant j \leqslant 2^n - 1$$

applique respectivement les hyperplans $P_1, P_2, \ldots, P_n$ aux plans de coordonnées $Q_1, Q_2, \ldots, Q_n$.

Etant donné un parallélépipède, nous attribuons le numéro 0 à un de ses sommets, les numéros $1, 2, \ldots, 2^i, \ldots, 2^{(n-1)}$ aux sommets adjacents à 0 (peu importe l'ordre) et après, nous numérotons les autres sommets suivant la règle des rectangles comme s'il s'agissait d'un cube. Nous pouvons résumer, alors, de la manière suivante la condition de réalisabilité d'un graphe de transfert donné sur $[0,1]^n$. Il suit des Propriétés 2 et 3, qu'il existe un réseau à éléments bistables à seuil qui admet ce graphe comme graphe de transfert, si et seulement s'il existe des vecteurs $\mathbf{b}_0, \mathbf{b}_1, \ldots, \mathbf{b}_{2^n-1}$ dont les extrémités sont les sommets d'un parallélépipède dans $R^n$ respectant la numérotation ci-dessus, tels que le sommet qui est l'extrémité de $b_j$ porte le numéro $j$ et que si le graphe possède un arc allant de $X_j$ à $X_k$, le sommet $j$ du parallélépipède se trouve dans le quadrant $0_k$. Inversement, à tout parallélépipède dans $R^n$ avec les sommets numérotés suivant la règle donnée correspond le graphe de transfert d'un réseau à éléments à seuil réalisable. Une application intéressante de ce fait est le cas où le parallélépipède coïncide avec le cube $[-1,1]^n$.

**Définition 3.** Soit $\Gamma$, l'application de graphe sur $[0,1]^n$. Nous dirons que $\Gamma$ est complète si l'ensemble de sommets $\{X_j\} = \{\Gamma X_j; 0 \leqslant j \leqslant 2^n - 1\}$ coïncide avec l'ensemble des sommets de $[0,1]^n$. Dans ce cas, à tout sommet du graphe rentre un seul arc.

**Définition 4.** Nous dirons qu'une numérotation des sommets du cube $[-1,1]^n$ suivant la règle donnée, est une application du cube sur lui-même, si l'on fait correspondre le numéro de chaque sommet à celui du quadrant dans lequel il se trouve.

**Propriété 6.** A toute application du cube $[-1,1]^n$ sur lui-même correspond un réseau à éléments à seuil réalisable, ayant un graphe de transfert complet.

Mais les applications du cube sur lui-même ne sont pas suffisantes pour engendrer tous les graphes de transfert complets réalisables. Par ailleuss, remarquant que, d'après les Propriétés 4 et 5 le parallélépipède correspondant à un graphe de transfert complet peut avoir son centre de gravité à l'origine des axes dans $R^n$, nous avons la condition nécessaire suivante de la réalisabilité.

**Propriété 7.** Pour qu'un graphe de transfert soit complet, il est nécessaire que deux arcs sortant de deux sommets diagonalement opposés de $[0,1]^n$ aillent respectivement à deux sommets diagonalement opposés.

Ceci implique que les fonctions booléennes réalisées par les éléments du réseau doivent être self-duals (cf. [5]). Toutes les permutations des diagonales du cube dans toutes les directions donnent $2^n!$ graphes de transfert complets qui ne sont pas tous réalisables. Parmi ceux-ci, il y en a $(n!)2^n$ qui sont les applications du cube sur lui-même qui, d'après la Propriété 6, sont réalisables.

Nous citons aussi, pour terminer, la propriété suivante qui est déduite des propriétés de réciprocité 4 et 5.

**Propriété 8.** Si un graphe de transfert complet est réalisable, le graphe obtenu en inversant l'orientation de tous les arcs est aussi réalisable.

### Bibliographie


1. W. S. McCulloch and W. Pitts, *Bull. Math. Biophys.* **5**, 115 (1943).
2. E. R. Caianiello, *J. Theoret. Biol.* **2**, 204–235 (1961).
3. R. O. Winder, R.C.A. Labs., Princeton, N.J., 1962.
4. K. Fan, *Linear Inequalities and Related Systems*, Princeton University Press, Princeton, N.J., 1956.
5. S. Muroga, *IBM J. Res. Develop.* **7** (1963).

# Sur Certaines Chaines de Markov Nonhomogènes

J. Larisse

*CETIS–EURATOM*
*Ispra, Italy*

et M. P. Schützenberger

*Institut Blaise Pascal*
*Paris, France*

Considérons un ensemble $\{m_1 m_2 \cdots m_k\}$ $(k \leqslant \infty)$ de matrices stochastiques $I \times I$. Une séquence infinie arbitraire $m_{i_1} m_{i_2} \cdots$ constitue une chaîne de Markov nonhomogène sur les états $I$. D'une manière équivalente nous pouvons définir cette chaîne comme une représentation $\mu$ du monoïde libre $F$ [1] dans le monoïde $M$ des $I \times I$ matrices stochastiques. Soit $X = \{x_1 x_2 \cdots x_k\}$ $(k \leqslant \infty)$ l'ensemble générateur de $F$, nous nous proposons dans cet exposé d'étudier les propriétés limites de $\mu f = \mu x_{i_1} \cdot \mu x_{i_2} \cdots \mu x_{i_n}$ pour $n \to \infty$ ; le cas homogène se ramenant à celui du sous-monoïde engendré par l'élément unique $\mu f$, nous aurions alors à étudier les propriétés asymptotiques de $\mu f_n$ pour $n \to \infty$.

Un résultat de J. Wolfowitz [2] montre que si $\{A_1, A_2, \ldots, A_k\}$ est un ensemble fini ou infini de matrices stochastiques carrées de même ordre tel que tout produit $B$ de la forme $A_{i_1} A_{i_2} \cdots A_{i_n}$ est apériodique et indécomposable, c'est-à-dire que

$$\lim_{n \to \infty} B^n = Q$$

où $Q$ a toutes ses lignes égales, alors en définissant

$$\delta(B) = \max_j \max_{i_1 i_2} |b_{i_1 j} - b_{i_2 j}|$$

nous pouvons pour $\epsilon$ arbitrairement petit donné trouver $n(\epsilon)$ tel que

$$\delta(B) < \epsilon \text{ dès que } |B| = n > n(\epsilon) \tag{1}$$

En d'autres termes soit $M_1$ l'ensemble des matrices stochastiques ayant une racine simple de module un (ce qui est équivalent à l'hypothèse d'apériodicité et d'indécomposabilité), définissant

$$\text{norme } \mu f = \|\mu f\| = \max_{i \in I} \sum_{j \in I} |\mu f|_{ij}$$

$$\bar{\mu} f = \lim_{n \to \infty} \mu f^n \qquad \text{pour } \mu f \in M_1$$

On a

$$\|\mu f_1 f_2 - \bar{\mu} f_2\| < \epsilon \text{ dès que } |f_2| > n(\epsilon) \text{ et quel que soit } f_1$$

En effet, pour $|f_2| > n(\epsilon)$ on peut écrire

$$\mu f_2 = m + E$$

où $m \in M_1$ a toutes ses lignes égales, $E$ est une matrice quelconque avec $|\epsilon_{ij}| < \epsilon$ pour $i, j \in I$. Dès lors,

$$|(\mu f f_2)_{ij} - (\mu f_2)_{ij}| = |\sum_{k \in I} (\mu f)_{ik}(m_{.j} + \epsilon_{kj}) - m_{.j} - \epsilon_{ij}|$$

$$= |\sum_{k \in I} (\mu f)_{ik}\, \epsilon_{kj} - \epsilon_{ij}| < 2\epsilon$$

$$\|\mu f f_2 - \mu f_2\| < 2I\epsilon$$

ceci étant vérifié pour $\mu f$ stochastique quelconque, faisons $\mu f = \mu f_1$ et $\mu f = \bar{\mu} f_2$ on a

$$\|\mu f_1 f_2 - \bar{\mu} f_2\| \leqslant \|\mu f_1 f_2 - \mu f_2\| + \|\mu f_2 - \bar{\mu} f_2\|$$
$$= \|\mu f_1 f_2 - \mu f_2\| + \|\bar{\mu} f_2 \cdot \mu f_2 - \mu f_2\| \leqslant 4I\epsilon$$

d'où

$$\lim_{|f_2| \to \infty} \|\mu f_1 f_2 - \bar{\mu} f_2\| = 0 \tag{2}$$

Pour assurer dans la suite de l'exposé (Remarque 2) une convergence uniforme nous imposerons à la plus petite entrée positive $\omega x$ des $\mu x$, $x \in X$ la condition suffisante qu'il existe $\bar{\omega} > 0$ tel que $\omega x > \bar{\omega}$, $x \in X$. Nous poserons $\omega x = 0$ si les éléments positifs de $\mu x$ sont tous égaux à 1. La donnée de $\mu$ déterminant d'une façon univoque l'homomorphisme $\omega$ de $F$ dans le groupe additif des réels nous définirons

$$F_z = \{f \in F;\ \omega f > z\}$$

ce qui entrainera en particulier que $\mu f \in P$ (sous-monoïde des matrices d'application de $I$ dans $I$) pour tout $f \in F \setminus F_0$. Avec ces notations (1) s'écrit donc

$$(W_1) \cdot \lim_{z \to \infty} \{\|\mu f_1 f_2 - \bar{\mu} f_2\| : f_1 \in F, f_2 \in F_z\} = 0$$

Considérons maintenant le cas où les $\mu f \in M_r$ (ensemble des matrices stochastiques $I \times I$ ayant $r$ classes ergodiques). La forme la plus générale de telles matrices est (Fig. 1; [3])

$g_i\, i \in [1, m]$: blocs indécomposables de classes ergodiques cycliques $r_{ik}$
$t_j j \in [1, p]$: groupements transitoires

Il est clair que la propriété pour une matrice $\mu f$ d'avoir $r$ classes ergodiques ne dépend pas de la valeur particulière des entrées mais de la

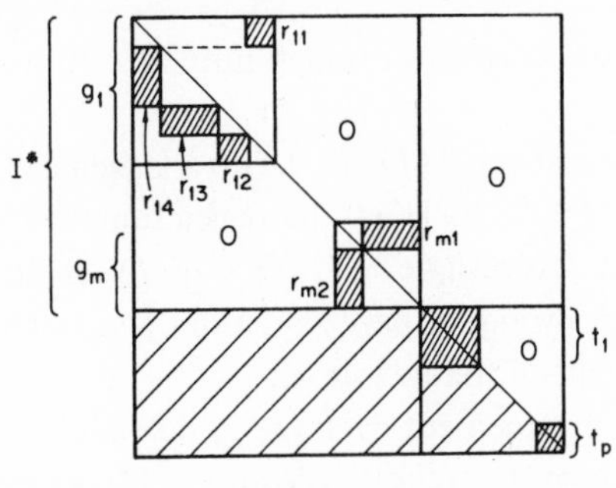


FIG. 1

distribution des éléments nuls. Nous associerons donc à chaque $\mu f$ sa matrice de support $\beta\mu f$ définie de la manière suivante:

$$(\beta\mu f)_{ij} = 1 \quad \text{si } (\mu f)_{ij} \neq 0$$
$$= 0 \quad \text{si } (\mu f)_{ij} = 0$$

Avec les lois d'addition et de multiplication booléennes on voit aisément que $\beta$ est un homomorphisme du monoïde $\{\mu f; f \in F\}$ dans le sous-monoïde des matrices de support:

$$\beta(\mu f_1)\cdot\beta(\mu f_2) = \beta(\mu f_1 \cdot \mu f_2) = \beta(\mu f_1 f_2)$$

En remarquant, d'autre part que

La $i$ème ligne de $\beta(\mu f_1 f_2) = \bigcup_k \{k$ième ligne de $\beta\mu f_2;\, k \in \beta\mu f_1\}$

on vérifie immédiatement que:

Si $\beta_i \mu f_1$ est un élément minimal de la famille $\{\beta_j \mu f_1; j \in I\}$

ordonnée par inclusion, $\beta_i \mu f_1 f_2$ est un élément minimal de la famille $\{\beta_j\, \mu f_1 f_2; j \in I\}$.

Si $\beta_i \mu f_1 f_2 \cap \beta_{i'} \mu f_1 f_2 = \phi$ alors, d'une part $\beta_i \mu f_1 \cap \beta_{i'} \mu f_1 = \phi$, d'autre part $\beta_j \mu f_2 \cap \beta_{j'} \mu f_2 = \phi$ pour tout $j \in \beta_i \mu f_1$ et $j' \in \beta_{i'} \mu f_1$. Il découle de ces dernières relations que si $\Delta(\mu f)$ est la cardinalité maximale d'un ensemble de lignes de $\mu f$ ayant leurs supports deux à deux disjoints, on a pour tout $\mu f_1, \mu f_2 \in M$.

$$\Delta(\mu f_1 f_2) \leqslant \{\Delta(\mu f_1), \Delta(\mu f_2)\}$$

Le sous-monoïde des supports étant fini il existe un $n \geqslant (\mathbf{Card\ I})!$ et un $q$ tels que

$$(\beta\mu f)^n = (\beta\mu f)^{n+q}$$

La propriété est alors vraie pour une infinité de $n$ et nous dirons que $(\beta\mu f)^n$ est cyclique.

En réservant la notation $I_j^*(f)$ $(j \in [1, r])$ à la $j$ième classe ergodique et en posant $I^*(f) = \cup\{I_j^*(f); j \in [1, r]\}$ la restriction à $I_j^*(f) \times I$ de $\beta\mu f$ est contenue dans un "rectangle" $I_j^*(f) \times I_{j'}^*(f)$ et elle est égale à ce rectangle si $\beta\mu f$ est cyclique, parce qu'alors les sous-matrices $r_{ij}$ (Fig. 1) n'ont que des éléments différents de zéro.

D'autre part, le groupement cyclique $g_i$ possédant $r_i$ classes ergodiques est isomorphe au groupe cyclique d'ordre $r_i$ [4], et $r!$ étant divisible par $r_1 r_2 \cdots r_m$ $(r = r_1 + \cdots r_m)$ il s'ensuit que $(\mu f)^{r!}$ est apériodique et la limite $\bar{\mu} f = \lim_{k \to \infty} \mu f^{kr!+1}$ existe.

$\bar{\mu} f$ est une matrice stochastique dont toutes les lignes dans $I^*(f) \times I$ ayant même support sont égales et dont les autres lignes sont des combinaisons linéaires à coefficients nonnégatifs des premières [3]. Il s'ensuit que la restriction à $I \times I^*(f)$ du support de $\mu f$ est contenue dans $\beta\bar{\mu} f$ et $\beta\bar{\mu} f$ est égale à la restriction à $I \times I^*(f)$ du support de $\mu f$ quand $\beta\mu f$ est cyclique.

Ces notions étant rappelées, définissons $R$ comme la fermeture convexe du sous-ensemble $P_r \subset P$ des matrices représentant une application $I \to I$ telle que l'image $I_p$ de $I$ ait au plus $r$ éléments. A chaque $f \in F$ nous associons $\chi f \in [0, 1]$, $\mu_R f \in R$ et $m \in M$ par les relations suivantes:

$$\mu f = (1 - \chi f)\,\mu_R f + \chi f m$$
$$\chi f = \min\{\chi \in [0, 1]: \mu f = (1 - \chi) m + \chi m'; m \in R, m' \in M\}$$

Enfin soit $F_+$ l'ensemble des $f \in F$ tel qu'il existe au moins un $g \in F_0$ de support cyclique et une paire $f', f'' \in F$ satisfaisant $\beta\mu f = \beta\mu f' g f''$.

**Remarque 1.** Pour chaque $f \in F_+$ on a $\chi f < 1$ et $\beta\mu_R f \subset \beta\bar{\mu} f$.

*Vérification.* Il est clair que $PP_r P \subset P_r$ et que le support de tout $m \in M$ est une union de supports d'applications $p' \in P$. Il en résulte immédiatement que $\chi ff' \leqslant \chi f \cdot \chi f'$ pour tout $f, f' \in F$. En effet,

$$\begin{aligned} \mu f &= (1 - \chi f)\mu_R f + \chi f m \\ \mu f' &= (1 - \chi f')\mu_R f' + \chi f' m' \\ \mu f \cdot \mu f' = \mu ff' &= (1 - \chi f)(1 - \chi f')\mu_R f \cdot \mu_R f' + \chi f'(1 - \chi f)\mu_R f m' \\ &\quad + \chi f(1 - \chi f') m \cdot \mu_R f' + \chi f \cdot \chi f' m m' \end{aligned}$$

Etudions les produits $\mu_R f \cdot \mu_R f'$, $\mu_R f \cdot m'$, $m\mu_R f'$, et $mm'$. La fermeture convexe de l'ensemble $P_r$ étant égale à l'ensemble des combinaisons linéaires convexes de $P_r$ on a

$$\mu_R f \cdot \mu_R f' \in R$$

D'autre part,

$$m \cdot \mu_R f' = \sum_{k=1}^{n} \alpha_k' m r_k' \qquad \mu_R f \cdot m' = \sum_{k=1}^{n'} \alpha_k r_k m'$$

$$\sum_{k=1}^{n} \alpha_k' = \sum_{k=1}^{h'} \alpha_k = 1$$

On vérifie aisément que $mr_k' \in R$, et que $r_k m'$ est une matrice stochastique dont toutes les lignes de même support dans $I^* \times I$ sont identiques, les autres étant des combinaisons linéaires à coefficients nonnégatives des premières, donc $r_k m' \in R$. Comme $mm' \in M$ on peut écrire:

$$\begin{aligned} (1 - \chi f)(1 - \chi f')\mu_R f \cdot \mu_R f' + \chi f'(1 - \chi f)\mu_R f \cdot m' + \chi f(1 - \chi f') m \cdot \mu_R f' \\ = (1 - \chi f \cdot \chi f')\mu_R ff' \qquad \text{avec } \mu_R ff' \in R \end{aligned}$$

puis

$$\mu ff' = (1 - \chi f \cdot \chi f')\mu_R ff' + \chi f \cdot \chi f' m''$$

ce qui montre que $\chi ff' \leqslant \chi f \cdot \chi f'$.

Considérons $g \in F_0$ de support cyclique. Si $I' \subset I$ a un et un seul élément en commun avec chacune des classes ergodiques $I_j^*(g)$, le fait que pour chaque $i \in I$ la ligne $\beta_i \mu g$ contienne au moins un $I_j(g)$ montre qu'il existe au moins un $p \in P_r$ tel que $I' = Ip$ et $\beta p \subset \beta \mu g$. Donc $\chi g < 1$ et par conséquent $\chi f' g f'' < 1$ pour tout $f', f'' \in F$. Comme la propriété $\chi m < 1$ ne dépend en fait que de $\beta m$, l'inégalité $\chi f < 1$ pour $f \in F_+$, est établie.

Soit maintenant $\beta p \subset \beta \mu f$ où $p \in P_r$ et $f \in F_+$. Si $I' = Ip$, l'union des supports des colonnes de $\mu f$ d'indice $i \in I'$ est égale à $I$, et il en est de même pour toute matrice de la forme $\mu f' f$. Prenant $f' = f^n$ tel que $\beta \mu f' f$ soit cyclique, on en conclut que $I'$ doit avoir un (et un seul) élément en commun avec chacune des classes ergodiques $I_j^*(f)$ et qu'en particulier $I' \in I^*(f)$. Comme $\beta p \subset \beta \mu f$ et comme la restriction de $\beta \mu f$ à $I \times I^*(f)$ est contenue dans $\beta \bar{\mu} f$, la remarque est entièrement vérifiée.

Il résulte de $\beta\mu\ f \subset \beta\bar{\mu}f$ que chaque classe $I_j^*(f)$ admet un sous-ensemble minimal $I_j'^*(f)$ tel que $I^*(f) \times I_j'^*(f)$ contienne la restriction à $I^*(f) \times I_j^*(f)$ du support de $\mu_R f$. De même, il existe un sous-ensemble maximal $I_j''^*(f)$ contenant tous les $i \in I$ tels que $\beta_i \mu_R f \subset I_j'^*(f)$.

*Exemple*

$$\mu f = \begin{array}{c|c|c} & \overbrace{\quad}^{I_1^*}\ \overbrace{\quad}^{I_2^*} & \\ & \overbrace{\quad}^{I_1'^*}\ \overbrace{\quad}^{I_2'^*} & \\ \hline I_1''^* \left\{ I_1^* \right. & \begin{array}{ccccc} . & . & . & x & x \\ . & . & . & x & x \\ . & . & . & x & x \end{array} & \begin{array}{ccc} . & . & . \\ . & . & . \\ . & . & . \end{array} \\ I_2^* \left\{ I_2''^* \right. & \begin{array}{ccccc} x & x & x & . & . \\ x & x & . & . & . \end{array} & \begin{array}{ccc} . & . & . \\ . & . & . \end{array} \\ \hdashline & \begin{array}{ccccc} x & x & . & . & . \end{array} & \begin{array}{ccc} . & . & x \end{array} \\ \{ & \begin{array}{ccccc} . & . & . & x & x \\ x & x & x & x & x \end{array} & \begin{array}{ccc} . & . & . \\ x & x & x \end{array} \end{array}$$

$$\mu_R f = \begin{array}{cccccccc} . & . & . & x & x & . & . & . \\ . & . & . & x & x & . & . & . \\ . & . & . & x & x & . & . & . \\ x & x & . & . & . & . & . & . \\ x & x & . & . & . & . & . & . \\ x & x & . & . & . & . & . & . \\ . & . & . & x & x & . & . & . \\ x & x & . & x & x & . & . & . \end{array}$$

$$\bar{\mu}f = \begin{array}{cccccccc} . & . & . & x & x & . & . & . \\ . & . & . & x & x & . & . & . \\ . & . & . & x & x & . & . & . \\ x & x & x & . & . & . & . & . \\ x & x & x & . & . & . & . & . \\ x & x & x & . & . & . & . & . \\ . & . & . & x & x & . & . & . \\ x & x & x & x & x & . & . & . \end{array}$$

**Remarque 1'.** Si $f, f' \in F_+$ il correspond à chaque $j \in [1, r]$ un et un seul $j' \in [1, r]$ tel que $I_j'^*(f) \subset I_{j'}''^*(f')$.

*Vérification.* Soit $f \in F_+$ on a $\Delta(\mu f) \leqslant \Delta(\mu g) = r$ puisque $f$ admet $g$ comme facteur. D'autre part nous savons que pour $n \geqslant$ (**Card I**)! $\mu f^n$ est cyclique donc $r = \Delta(\mu f^n) \leqslant \Delta(\mu f)$, il s'ensuit que $\Delta(\mu f) = r$.

Considérons maintenant le cas particulier de l'énoncé où $\beta\mu f$ et $\beta\mu f'$ sont cycliques. La relation $\Delta(\mu f f') = r$ montre que pour chaque $i \in I_j^*(f)$, le support $\beta_i \mu f'$ doit avoir une intersection nonvide avec une seule classe $I_{j'}^*(f)$. Le cas général s'en déduit immédiatement: en effet, $I_j'^*(f) \subset I_j^*(f)$ et les seuls $i \in I$ tels que $\beta_i \mu f'$ n'intersecte qu'une seule classe $I_{j''}^*(f')$, appartiennent à l'union $I''^*(f')$ des ensembles disjoints $I_j''^*(f')$.

Nous écrivons désormais pour abréger lim au lieu de $\lim_{z\to\infty}$ max et nous désignons par $f_z$ et $f_z'$ des variables liées par la condition $f_z, f_z' \in F_z$.

**Remarque 2.** $\mathrm{Lim}\|\mu f_z - \mu_R f_z\| = 0$.

*Vérification.* Soit $B = \{\beta\mu f; f \in F_0\}$. Si un élément $b \in B$ appartient à une $\mathscr{D}$-classe régulière [5], il existe un élément $b' \in B$ tel que $b'^2 = b'$ et $b' b = b$. Donc si $B_+$ est l'idéal de $B$ engendré par les $D$-classes régulières, l'image inverse de $B_+$ par $\beta^{-1}$ appartient à $F_+$.

Soit $h$ le nombre des $\mathscr{D}$-classes de $B$, $B$ étant fini on a $\mathscr{D} = \mathscr{J}$ et dans le monoïde $B^1 = B \cup e$ la relation d'inclusion sur les idéaux bilatères principaux $B^1 a B^1 \subseteq B^1 b B^1$, $a, b \in B^1$ induit une relation d'ordre partiel sur les $\mathscr{J}$-classes donc sur les $\mathscr{D}$-classes. Autrement dit les idéaux bilatères principaux forment un semi-treillis dont l'élément minimal, idéal minimum de $B$, est une $\mathscr{D}$-classe régulière (plus précisément un sous-demi-groupe complètement simple). Or nous savons [6] que si $b', b''$ et $b' b''$ appartiennent à la même $\mathscr{D}$-classe celle-ci est régulière, autrement la $\mathscr{D}$-classe de $b' b''$ est telle que

$$\mathscr{D}_{b'b''} \leqslant \mathscr{D}_{b'} \qquad \mathscr{D}_{b'b''} \leqslant \mathscr{D}_{b''}$$

On peut alors montrer que tout produit $b_1 b_2 \cdots b_{\bar{h}}$ de $\bar{h} = 2^{h-1}$ éléments de $B$ a au moins un facteur nonvide appartenant à une $\mathscr{D}$-classe régulière de $B$ donc appartient lui-même à $\beta F_+$. Ceci est trivial pour $h = 1$ puisque dans ce cas $B$ a une seule $\mathscr{D}$-classe qui est nécessairement régulière. On peut donc supposer le résultat vérifié quand $B$ a moins de $h > 1$ $\mathscr{D}$-classes, et naturellement, on peut aussi supposer qu'aucun des $b_{k'}$ ($k' = 1, 2 \ldots, \bar{h} = 2^{h-1}$) n'appartient lui-même à une $\mathscr{D}$-classe régulière. Le sous-monoïde engendré par les $2^{h-2}$ produits $b_1 b_2, b_3 b_4, \ldots, b_{\bar{h}-1} b_{\bar{h}}$ a au plus $h - 1$ $\mathscr{D}$-classes et le résultat découle de l'hypothèse d'induction.

Soit maintenant $F_+' = F_+ \backslash F \times F_+ \times F$. Le résultat qui vient d'être vérifié montre que tout $f \in (F_0)^{n\bar{h}}$ a au moins $n$ facteurs dans $F_+'$. Faisant intervenir l'hypothèse selon laquelle $\omega x = 0$ ou $\omega x > \bar{\omega} > 0$ pour tout $x \in X$ on voit que $\omega f > \bar{\omega}^{\bar{h}}$, $\chi f < 1 - \omega f < 1 - \bar{\omega}^{\bar{h}}$ pour tout $f \in F_+'$ et par suite $\chi f < (1 - \bar{\omega}^{\bar{h}})^n$ pour tout $f \in (F_0)^{n\bar{h}}$ ce qui entraine lim $\chi f_z = 0$.

Soit $m \in M$ et définissons [7]

$$\lambda(m) = 1 - \min_{i_1 i_2} \sum_j \min(m_{i_1 j}, m_{i_2 j})$$

on a $0 \leqslant \lambda(m) \leqslant 1$ avec

$$\lambda(m) = 0 \quad \text{si et seulement si } m \text{ a toutes ses lignes égales}$$
$$\lambda(m) = 1 \quad \text{si et seulement si } \beta m \text{ a deux lignes disjointes}$$

$0 < \lambda(m) < 1$ définiera une "scrambling matrix," c'est-à-dire que quelles que soient les deux lignes $i_1 i_2$ il existe une colonne $j$ telle que $m_{i_1 j}, m_{i_2 j} > 0$.

On démontre que $\delta(m_1 m_2) \leqslant \delta(m_1)$ et qu'un produit de matrices stochastiques dont un facteur est "scrambling" est lui-même scrambling. Cette propriété est identique à celle des matrices positives ayant une colonne d'éléments nonnuls et aux matrices $\mu f \in F_+$.

Soit $V$ l'ensemble des $I$-vecteurs $v$ à coordonnées nonnégatives tels que $\Sigma_{i \in I} v_i = 1$. Pour $(v, v') \in V \times V$ et $m \in M$ nous pouvons poser

$$\delta_{vv'} m = 1 - \sum_{i \in I} \min\{(vm)_i, (v'm)_{i'}\}$$

Par définition: $\delta_{vv'} m = \lambda(m_v m')$ où $m_v$ est une matrice stochastique dont les deux premières lignes sont identiques aux vecteurs $v$ et $v'$, les autres étant, par exemple, identique à $v$ (ou $v'$). On a donc pour tout $m' \in M$

$$0 = \delta_{vv'} mm' \leqslant \delta_{vv'} m \leqslant 1 \qquad \text{avec } \delta_{vv'} m = 0 \text{ (resp. } = 1)$$

si et seulement si $vm = vm'$ (resp. $\beta vm \cap \beta v'm = \phi$). Quand $\mu$ et $\mu'$ sont deux applications de $F$ dans $M$ telles que $\lim \|\mu f_z - \mu' f_z\| = 0$ on a évidemment $\lim |\delta_{vv'} \mu f_z - \delta_{vv'} \mu' f_z| = 0$.

Nous considérons maintenant un sous-ensemble fixe $K$ de $I$ ayant $r$ éléments et nous définissons la $I \times I$ matrice $e_k$ par $(e_k)_{i,i'} = 1$ si $i = i' \in K$; $= 0$, autrement. Pour abréger, nous écrivons $m' \in M'$ (resp. $m'' \in M''$) si $m' = m \cdot e_k$ (resp. $m'' = e_k \cdot m$ pour au moins un $m \in M$) et si $m'$ contient $r$ lignes ayant des supports disjoints telles que toute autre ligne soit une combinaison linéaire à coefficients nonnégatifs de ces dernières (resp. et si $m''$ a $r$ lignes ayant des supports disjoints nonvides).

**Remarque 3.** Il existe deux applications $\mu'\colon F \to M'$ et $\mu''\colon F \to M''$ telles que $\lim \|\mu f_z - \mu' f_z \cdot \mu'' f_z\| = 0$.

*Vérification.* Nous utilisons les notations de la Remarque 1'. Le support de la restriction de $\mu_R f_z$ à $I''^*(f_z) \times I$ est une union de $r$ rectangles disjoints

$I_j''(f_z) \times I_{j'}'(f_z)$. Comme $\mu_R f_z$ appartient à la fermeture convexe $R$ de $Pr$ ceci entraîne que deux lignes quelconques de cette matrice soient égales quand leurs supports sont identiques. Il existe donc une matrice $\mu'' f_z \in M''$ dont les lignes nonnulles sont égales aux $r$ lignes distinctes de la restriction de $\mu_R f_z$ à $I''^*(f_z) \times I$.

Soit $f_z'$ un autre élément de $F_z$. D'après la Remarque 1', chacun des ensembles $I_{j'}'^*(f_z')$ est contenu dans un et un seul ensemble $I_j''(f_z)$ et $\mu_R f_z'$ est identique à la somme de ses restrictions à $I \times I_{j'}'^*(f_z)(j' \in [1, r])$. Donc deux lignes quelconques nonnulles de la restriction à $I \times I_j'(f_z)$ de $\mu_R f_z' \cdot \mu_R f_z$ sont proportionnelles et l'on peut trouver une application $\nu' = F \times F \to M'$ telle que l'on ait $\mu_R f_z' \cdot \mu_R f_z = \nu'(f_z', f_z) \cdot \mu'' f_z$ identiquement. D'après la Remarque 2,

$$\lim \| \mu f_z' f_z - \mu_R f_z' f_z \| = 0$$

Par conséquent,

$$\lim \| \mu f_z' f_z - \nu'(f_z', f_z) \mu'' f_z \| = 0$$

ce qui entraîne la validité de la Remarque 3.

**Remarque 3'.** Si les applications $\mu' : F \to M'$; $\nu = F \times F \times F \to M$ et $\mu'' : F \to M''$ satisfont la relation $\lim \| \mu f_z f f_z' - \mu' f_z \nu(f_z, f, f_z') \cdot \mu'' f_z' \| = 0$, il existe trois applications $\bar{\mu}' = F \to M'$; $\rho : F \times F \times F \to M$ et $\bar{\mu}'' : F \to M''$ telles que

$$\begin{aligned} \lim \| \mu' f_z - \bar{\mu}' f_z f f_z' \| &= \lim \| \nu(f_z, f, f_z') - \rho(f_z, f, f_z' \| \\ &= \lim \| e_k \nu(f_z, f, f_z') \mu'' f_z' - \bar{\mu}'' f_z f f_z' \| = 0 \end{aligned}$$

et qu'en outre, d'une part la restriction de $\rho(f_z, f, f_z')$ à $K \times I$ représente une permutation de $K$, d'autre part, pour tout $f' \in F_0$, $\bar{\mu} f' = \bar{\mu}' f' \cdot \bar{\mu}'' f'$.

*Vérification.* Deux lignes de même support de la restriction à $I^*(f) \times I$ de $\bar{\mu} f'$ étant égales, les autres étant des combinaisons linéaires à coefficients nonnégatifs des précédentes, il est clair que l'existence d'applications $\bar{\mu}' : F \to M'$ et $\bar{\mu}'' : F \to M''$ satisfaisant $\bar{\mu} f' = \bar{\mu}' f' \cdot \bar{\mu}'' f'$ est triviale et que toutes les paires d'applications satisfaisant ces conditions sont équivalentes sur $F_0$ à une permutation de $K$ près.

Désignons maintenant par $\lambda^i m$ la plus grande entrée de la $i$ème colonne de $m$. Il est bien connu que $\lambda^i m' m < \lambda^i m$ identiquement. Donc pour tout $i \in I$ et $(f_z, f, f_z') \in F \times F \times F$ on a

$$\lambda^i \bar{\mu} f_z f f_z' = \lambda^i \bar{\mu}'' f_z f f_z' \leqslant \lambda^i \mu f_z f f_z'$$

et

$$\lambda^i [\mu' f_z \cdot \nu(f_z f f_z') \cdot \mu'' f_z'] \leqslant \lambda^i [\nu(f_z f f_z') \cdot \mu'' f_z'] \leqslant \lambda^i \mu'' f_z'$$

Les hypothèses impliquent que

$$\lim \|\lambda^i(\mu' f_z \cdot \nu(f_z, f, f'_z) \cdot \mu'' f'_z) - \lambda^i \mu f_z f f'_z\| = 0$$

et comme $\bar{\mu}'' f_z f f'_z$ et $\mu'' f'_z$ appartiennent à $M''$, on a

$$\sum_{i \in I} \lambda^i \bar{\mu}'' f_z f f'_z = \sum_{i \in I} \lambda^i \mu'' f'_z = r$$

Donc, pour chaque $i \in I$

$$\lim |\lambda^i \bar{\mu}'' f_z f f'_z - \lambda^i(\nu(f_z f f'_z) \cdot \mu'' f'_z| = \lim |\lambda^i(\nu(f_z f f'_z) \cdot \mu'' f'_z) - \lambda^i \mu'' f'_z = 0$$

et

$$\lim \sum_{i \in I} \lambda^i(\nu(f_z, f, f'_z) \cdot \mu'' f'_z) = r$$

ce qui montre l'existence de $\rho$: $F \times F \times F \to M$, identique à $\nu$ sur $(I \setminus K) \times I$ se réduisant à une permutation de $K$ sur $K \times I$ et satisfaisant

$$\lim \|\nu(f_z f f'_z) - \rho(f_z f f'_z)\| = 0$$

D'après la première de ces relations on peut choisir $\bar{\mu}''$: $F \to M''$ telle que

$$\lim \|e_k \cdot \rho(f_z f f'_z) \mu'' f'_z - \bar{\mu}'' f_z f f'_z\| = 0$$

De façon analogue, pour tout $(v, v') \in V \times V$ on a

$$\delta_{v,v'} \bar{\mu}' f_z f f'_z = \delta_{v,v'} \bar{\mu} f_z f f'_z \leqslant \delta_{v,v'} \mu f_z f f'_z$$

et

$$\lim \delta_{v,v'} \mu f_z f f'_z < \lim \delta_{v,v'} \mu' f_z$$

Comme l'ensemble des $(v, v') \in V \times V$ telles que $\delta_{v,v'} \bar{\mu}' f_z f f'_z$ (resp. $\delta_{v,v'} \mu' f_z$) est 0 ou 1 détermine $\bar{\mu}'$ (resp. $\mu'$) à une permutation près de $K$ et comme le support de la restriction de $\mu f_z f f'_z$ à $I \times I^*(f_z f f'_z)$ est contenu dans $\beta \bar{\mu} f_z f f'_z$, la vérification est achevée.

**Propriété 1.** Si $\mu$: $F \to M$ est telle que pour chaque $f \in F_0$ la chaine de Markov $\{\mu f^n : n \in N\}$ a exactement $r$ classes ergodiques, il existe une application $\pi$ de $F$ dans un sous-ensemble fini de $M$ telle que

$$(W_r) \cdot \lim \|\mu f_z f f'_z - \bar{\mu} f_z \cdot \pi f \cdot \mu f'_z\| = 0$$

Si en outre toutes les chaines $\{\mu f^n : n \in \mathbf{N}\}$ $(f \in F_0)$ sont apériodiques, on peut écrire

$$(W_r^*) \cdot \lim \|\mu f_z f f'_z - \bar{\mu} f_z \cdot \bar{\mu} f'_z\| = 0$$

*Vérification.* D'après la Remarque 3, il existe deux applications $\mu'$: $F \to M'$ et $\mu''$: $F \to M''$ telle que $\lim \|\mu f_z - \mu' f_z \cdot \mu'' f_z\| = 0$. Prenant une application $\nu$ de $F \times F \times F$ sur la matrice unité $e_I$ et employant la Remarque 3′ on a $\lim\|\mu f_z f_z - \mu' f_z \cdot \mu'' f_z\| = 0$, ceci montre que $\lim\|\bar{\mu} f_z - \mu f_z\| = 0$. En effet, quel que soit $\epsilon$ petit on peut trouver $z(\epsilon)$ tel que pour tout $z > z(\epsilon)$ on a

$$\|\mu f_z - \mu' f_z \cdot \mu'' f_z\| < \epsilon \qquad \text{et} \qquad \|\mu f_z \cdot \mu f_z - \mu' f_z \cdot \mu'' f_z\| < \epsilon$$

d'où

$$\|\mu f_z \cdot f_z - \mu f_z\| \leqslant \|\mu f_z \cdot f_z - \mu' f_z \cdot \mu'' f_z\| + \|\mu' f_z \cdot \mu'' f_z - \mu f_z\| < 2\epsilon$$

D'autre part on voit par récurrence que

$$\|\mu f_z^{p+1} - \mu f_z^p\| \leqslant \|\mu f_z\| \, \|\mu f_z^p - \mu f_z^{p-1}\| \leqslant 2\epsilon$$

et en particulier,

$$\|\mu f_z^{kr!+1} - (\mu f_z)^{kr!}\| < 2\epsilon$$

donc en sommant

$$\|\mu f_z^{kr!+1} - \mu f_z\| < \sum_{p=1}^{kr!} \|\mu f_z^{p+1} - \mu f_z^p\| < kr!\, 2\epsilon$$

De plus,

$$\|\bar{\mu} f_z - \mu f_z\| \leqslant \|\bar{\mu} f_z - \mu f_z^{kr!+1}\| + \|\mu f_z^{kr!+1} - \mu f_z\|$$

et on sait que si on se donne $\epsilon'$ petit on peut trouver $k(\epsilon')$ tel que pour $k > k(\epsilon')$ on aura

$$\|\bar{\mu} f_z - \mu f_z\| \leqslant 2r!\, k\epsilon + \epsilon'$$

On peut donc se donner $\epsilon, \epsilon', \epsilon'', k(\epsilon')$ tels que pour tout $z > z(\epsilon)$ on aura

$$\|\bar{\mu} f_z - \mu f_z\| \leqslant \epsilon'' \text{ par suite } \lim\|\bar{\mu} f_z - \mu f_z\| = 0$$

Il n'y aura donc aucune diminution de généralité à supposer désormais que $\mu' = \bar{\mu}'$ et $\mu'' = \bar{\mu}''$, c'est à dire que $\mu' f \cdot \mu'' f = \bar{\mu} f$ pour tout $f \in F_0$.

Le premier de ces résultats donne

$$\lim\|\mu f_z f f'_z - \bar{\mu} f_z \cdot \mu f \cdot \bar{\mu} f'_z\| = \lim\|\bar{\mu} f_z f f'_z - \bar{\mu} f_z \cdot \mu f \cdot \bar{\mu} f'_z\| = 0$$

Comme

$$\bar{\mu} f_z \cdot \mu f \cdot \bar{\mu} f'_z = \mu' f_z \cdot \nu(f_z, f, f'_z) \cdot \mu'' f'_z$$

où maintenant $\nu$ est une application quelconque de $F \times F \times F$ dans $M$ telle que $e_K \cdot \nu(f_z, f, f'_z) = \mu'' f_z \cdot \mu f \cdot \mu' f'_z$, on peut appliquer de nouveau la Remarque 3′ qui montre cette fois l'existence d'une application $\rho$ de $F \times F \times F$ dans $M$ telle que $e_K \cdot \rho$ soit une permutation de $K$ et que

$$\lim\|\mu'' f_z \cdot \mu f \cdot \mu' f'_z - e_K \cdot \rho(f_z, f, f'_z)\| = 0$$

D'après l'hypothèse faite plus haut,

$$\mu' f_z \cdot \mu'' f_z = \bar{\mu} f_z \qquad \text{et} \qquad \mu' f'_z \cdot \mu'' f'_z = \bar{\mu} f'_z$$

On en conclut que $\mu'' f_z \cdot \mu f \cdot \mu' f_z'$ est elle-même, pour tout $(f_z, f, f_z') \in F \times F \times F_0$, une matrice ayant son support contenu dans $K \times K$ et représentant une permutation de cet ensemble.

Puisque les matrices $\mu' f_z$, $\mu f$, et $\mu' f_z'$ ont des entrées nonnégatives, ceci entraîne $\mu'' f_z \cdot \mu f \cdot \mu' f_z' = \mu'' f_z \cdot \pi f \cdot \mu' f_z'$ quelque soit l'application $\pi : F \to M$ telle que $\beta\mu f = \beta\pi f$. Par conséquent, sous cette hypothèse $\bar{\mu} f_z \cdot \mu f \cdot \bar{\mu} f_z' = \bar{\mu} f_z \cdot \pi f \cdot \bar{\mu} f_z'$ ce qui achève la vérification de $(W_r)$ puisque le monoïde $\{\beta\mu f : f \in F\}$ est fini.

Supposons maintenant que toutes les chaînes $\{\mu f^n : n \in \mathbf{N}\}$ soient apériodiques, c'est-à-dire que $\bar{\mu} f = \bar{\mu} f^2$ pour tout $f \in F_0$, c'est-à-dire encore (dans les notations de la Remarque 2') que $I_j'^*(f) \subset I_j''^*(f)$ pour tout $j \in [1, r]$. La Remarque 1' montre que l'on peut choisir l'indexage des classes ergodiques des différentes chaînes $\{\mu f^n : n \in \mathbf{N}\}$ $(f \in F_0)$ de telle sorte que $I_j'^*(f) \subset I_j''^*(f')$ pour tout $f, f' \in F_+$ et $j \in [1, r]$. Ceci entraîne que $\mu'' f_z \cdot \mu' f_z' = e_K$ identiquement quand $f_z, f_z' \in F_+$. La propriété est entièrement vérifiée.

*Note:* Cet exposé est un développement de l'article "Sur certaines chaînes de Markov non-homogènes" par J. Larisse et M. P. Schützenberger, Publications de l'Institut de Statistique de l'Université de Paris, Vol. XIII, fasc. 1, 1964.

## Références


1. C. Chevalley, *Fundamental Concepts of Algebra*, Academic Press, New York, 1956.
2. J. Wolfowitz, Products of indecomposable, aperiodic stochastic matrices, *Proc. Am. Math. Soc.* **14**, 733–737 (1963).
3. J. L. Doob, *Stochastic Processes*, Wiley, 1953.
4. M. Hall, Jr., *The Theory of Groups*, Macmillan, 1959.
5. A. H. Clifford et G. B. Preston, *Algebraic Theory of Semi-Groups*, Vol. 1, Am. Math. Soc., 1961.
6. J. A. Green, On the structure of semi-groups, *Ann. Math.* **54**, 163–172 (1951).
7. J. Hajnal, Weak ergodicity in non-homogeneous Markov chains, *Proc. Cambridge Phil. Soc.* **54**, 233–246 (1958).

# Explicability of Sets and Transfinite Automata

LARS LÖFGREN

*Lund Institute of Technology*
*Lund, Sweden*

## I. Introduction

One of the basic questions of set theory refers to the membership relation. For a given set $S$ we may ask if a given element belongs to $S$ or not, or if the question is undecidable. However, in order to make the question meaningful, the domain of inquiry has itself to be characterized as a set.

In this paper we want to investigate the problem of characterizing a set in terms of those properties of its elements that make them distinct. The minimal number of monadic predicates, needed to distinguish between the elements of a set $S$ of a given cardinality, is said to constitute the predicate set $P$ for $S$.

In the transfinite case, card $P$ is shown to be the amount of information that is needed to select an element out of $S$, or again the amount of information that is produced when an element is selected and the only, *a priori* knowledge concerning the outcome is that the element belongs to $S$. It should be noticed that a straightforward extension of the corresponding finite information measure will not be defined for all transfinite sets. However, card $P$ is defined for all such sets $S$ and is shown to satisfy the information equation in the whole transfinite region.

If card $P$ is less than card $S$, we have an explicable information model of $S$, and $S$ is said to be explicable. On the other hand, if card $P$ is equal to card $S$, the information model does not explain $S$, and $S$ is here said to be inexplicable.

Considering explicability of explicability and so forth, together with its reverse, a production process, we are led to the notions of effectively explicable sets and strongly inexplicable sets. Strong inexplicability turns out to be equivalent with Tarski's notion of strong inaccessibility, a concept introduced to set theory in a different context.

In Section IV the preceding concepts are applied to the notion of a deterministic automaton. Such an automaton shall have the ability to accept the information measure of its configuration set and to determine its next state and output herefrom. Accordingly, the preceding explicability notions permit us to conclude upon the determinism of transfinite automata. The discussion is limited to automata of a fixed structure. Thus Turing machines, which are finite but growing automata, are not dealt with.

At the end of the paper there is a list of symbols, axioms, and theorems used in the development. These axioms and theorems are referred to with Roman numerals. Proofs of Theorems V and VI are found in Bachmann (1955). Theorem VII is proved in Fraenkel and Bar-Hillel (1958). It is recommended that this list of explanations be read before the paper is penetrated.

## II. An Information Measure of a Set

The elements $x_i$ of a set $S$, say $\{x_1, x_2, x_3, x_4\}$, are by definition distinct. Let the distinguishing properties be expressed by four predicates $Q_1(x)$, $Q_2(x)$, $Q_3(x)$, $Q_4(x)$ such that the proposition $Q_1(x_1)$ is true but $Q_2(x_1)$, $Q_3(x_1)$, $Q_4(x_1)$ are all false; $Q_2(x_2)$ is true but $Q_1(x_2)$, $Q_3(x_2)$, $Q_4(x_2)$ are all false; and so on. In most cases, however, the set $Q$ of distinguishing predicates does not have to be as large as this, i.e., need not contain as many predicates as there are elements of $S$.

For the example at hand, the four predicates can be generated by only two predicates $P_1(x)$ and $P_2(x)$:

$$\begin{aligned} Q_1(x) &\mathrel{.\equiv.} \quad P_1(x) \,.\, \quad P_2(x) \\ Q_2(x) &\mathrel{.\equiv.} \quad P_1(x) \,.\, \neg P_2(x) \\ Q_3(x) &\mathrel{.\equiv.} \neg P_1(x) \,.\, \quad P_2(x) \\ Q_4(x) &\mathrel{.\equiv.} \neg P_1(x) \,.\, \neg P_2(x) \end{aligned}$$

A set $P = \{P_1(x), P_2(x), \ldots\}$ is called a *minimal predicate set* (*predicate set* for short) for a set $S$ if $P$ does not contain more elements, generative predicates, than what is necessary for a distinction between all the elements of $S$.

We are primarily interested in the cardinal $p$ ($=$ card $P$) of the predicate set for $S$ and in its relation to $s$ ($=$ card $S$). Obviously (compare the above example), the largest set $S$ that can be characterized with a predicate set $P$ corresponds one-to-one to the set of mappings of $P$ into $\{\neg\neg, \neg\}$. Because

$$\vdash . \operatorname{card} \{\neg\neg, \neg\}^P = 2^p \tag{1}$$

we obtain the following condition on $p$ and $s$:

$$2^p \geqslant s \tag{2}$$

If for a given $s$, a cardinal $p$ is chosen such that condition 2 is fulfilled and such that there does not exist a smaller cardinal $q$ $(q < p)$ fulfilling (2), then $p$ is the cardinal of the predicate set for $S$. We denote this relation by $R$. In other words, $pRs$ reads: $p$ is the cardinal of a predicate set for $S$. The relation $R$ is thus defined by

$$R =_{\text{def}} \{\langle p,s\rangle ; (p,s,q) \in V_c \,.\, 2^p \geqslant s \,.\, \neg : \exists q \,.\, q < p \,.\, 2^q \geqslant s\} \tag{3}$$

The following theorems for $R$ will prove useful.

$$\vdash_1 . \; R = \{\langle p,s\rangle ; (p,s,q) \in V_c \,.\, 2^p \geqslant s \,.\, \forall q : q < p \,.\Rightarrow .\, 2^q < s\} \tag{4}$$

$$\vdash_1 . \; R = \{\langle p,s\rangle ; (p,s,q) \in V_c \,.\, 2^p \geqslant s \,.\, \forall q : 2^q \geqslant s \,.\Rightarrow .\, p \leqslant q\} \tag{5}$$

$$\vdash_1 . \; \text{Fnc}(R) \tag{6}$$

$$\vdash . \; \neg \; \text{Fnc}\,(\breve{R}) \tag{7}$$

$$\vdash_1 . \; d\text{‘}R = V_c \tag{8}$$

$$\vdash_2 . \; r\text{‘}R = V_c \tag{9}$$

*Proof of Theorems 4, 5, 6, 7, 8, and 9*

$$A_s =_{\text{def}} \{p ; p \in V_c \,.\, 2^p \geqslant s\} \tag{10}$$

$[\vdash_1 . \text{III} \Rightarrow 11]$

$$\begin{aligned} &\neg : \exists q \,.\, q < p \,.\, 2^q \geqslant s : \\ &\equiv : \forall q : q \geqslant p \,.\vee .\, 2^q < s : \\ &\equiv : \forall q : q < p \,.\Rightarrow .\, 2^q < s : \\ &\equiv : \forall q : 2^q \geqslant s \,.\Rightarrow .\, p \leqslant q \end{aligned} \tag{11}$$

$[\vdash_1 : 11 . 3 . \Rightarrow . 4 . 5]$ which completes the proof of (4) and (5).

$[\vdash : \text{I} . 10 . \Rightarrow . 12]$ $\quad \forall s \,.\, s \in A_s \quad (12)$

$[\vdash . 12 \Rightarrow 13]$ $\quad \forall s \,.\, A_s \neq \phi \quad (13)$

$[\vdash_1 : \text{III} . 13 . \Rightarrow . 14]$ $\quad \forall s :: \exists ! p :. p \in A_s \,.\, \forall q : q \in A_s \,.\Rightarrow .\, p \leqslant q \quad (14)$

$[\vdash_1 : 5 . 14 . \Rightarrow . 15]$ $\quad \forall s : \exists ! p \,.\, pRs \quad (15)$

$[\vdash_1 . 15 \Rightarrow 16]$ $\quad \text{Fnc}\,(R) \quad (16)$

$[\vdash_1 . 16 \Rightarrow 6]$ which completes the proof of (6).

| | | |
|---|---|---|
| $[\vdash_1 . 15 \Rightarrow 17]$ | $d`R = V_c$ | (17) |
| $[\vdash_1 . 17 \Rightarrow 8]$ | which completes the proof of (8). | |
| $[\vdash 18]$ | $(\forall p, q) : q < \aleph_0 . q < p . \Rightarrow . 2^q < 2^p$ | (18) |
| $[\vdash_2 : \text{IV} . \text{I} . \Rightarrow . 19]$ | $(\forall p, q) : p > \aleph_0 . q \geqslant \aleph_0 . q < p . \Rightarrow . 2^q \leqslant p . p < 2^p$ | (19) |
| $[\vdash_2 : 18 . 19 . \Rightarrow . 20]$ | $(\forall p, q) : q < p . \Rightarrow . 2^q < 2^p$ | (20) |
| $[\vdash_2 : 4 . 20 . \Rightarrow . 21]$ | $\forall p : \exists ! s . s = 2^p . pRs$ | (21) |
| $[\vdash_2 . 21 \Rightarrow 22]$ | $r`R = V_c$ | (22) |
| $[\vdash_2 . 22 \Rightarrow 9]$ | which completes the proof of (9). | |
| $[\vdash . 3 \Rightarrow 23]$ | $\vdash : 0R0 . 0R1$ | (23) |
| $[\vdash . 23 \Rightarrow 7]$ | which completes the proof of (7). | |

It should be noted that if the proposition $s = 2^p$ is deleted from (21), then $\exists ! s$ of (21) has to be replaced by $\exists s$.

In the proof of (20) we have used the aleph hypothesis IV. However, should there exist[1] a pair of cardinals $p$ and $q$ such that $q < p$ and $2^q = 2^p$ (which implies that the aleph hypothesis is not true), we could conclude that $p$ does not belong to the range of $R$ [cf. (3)]. In other words, (22) would not be true. Because of theorem (6) we can write $Rs$ (or $R(s)$) for the unique $p$ that according to (15) corresponds to the argument $s$.

Let us discuss $Rs$ in connection with information measures of the set $S$. Our notion of information measure is explained as follows. Consider a process that selects an element from a set $S$. Let the process be observed by a mathematician who abstracts from all properties of the selected elements except those that distinguish the elements from each other. If the only *a priori* knowledge of the process is that the outcome will be an element of $S$, then a particular outcome gives to the observer a certain amount of information $Fs$, i.e., a function of the cardinal $s$, where $s = \text{card}(S)$. Conversely,

[1] In A. Lévy, Indépendance conditionnelle de $V=L$ et d'axiomes qui se rattachent au système de M. Gödel, *Compt. Rend.* **245** (1957), pp. 1582–1583, there is a discussion on the nonprovability of the statement $(\forall \alpha, \beta) : \alpha < \beta . \Rightarrow . 2^{\aleph_\alpha} < 2^{\aleph_\beta}$ in relation to the nonprovability of the generalized continuum hypothesis. It would seem that a corollary of this discussion and Paul Cohen's result on the independence of the continuum hypothesis is the following. Our result (20) is nonprovable in ZF1 (but provable, as demonstrated, in ZF2). Theorem (9) can be sharpened by saying that the corresponding statement is nonprovable in ZF1.

if the observer restricts his activity to selections of elements from $S$, he can, at the expense of $Fs$, force the process to select a particular element.

Furthermore, if two selections are going on, one from a set $S_1$ and the other from a set $S_2$, the observer feels that a particular outcome gives him the information $Fs_1 + Fs_2$. He realizes, however, that what he is doing is nothing but observing the selection of one element from the set $S_1 \times S_2$, whose cardinal is $s_1 \cdot s_2$. The information-measure function $F$ should therefore satisfy

$$F(s_1 \cdot s_2) = Fs_1 + Fs_2 \tag{24}$$

As is well known [Fadiev (1956)], the validity of (24) for all finite $s_1$ and $s_2$ determines the function $F$ up to a constant $b$:

$$Fs = {}^b\log s \tag{25}$$

(If $s$ is the cardinal of a finite set containing $n$ elements, the integer $n$ is as usual taken as a representative of $s$.)

Hence, if the domain of $F$ is the set of all natural numbers, its range is not included in the set of all integers but contains real numbers as well. The choice $b = 2$ will obviously give to the range of $F$, which corresponds to a domain of naturals, a larger number of integers than any other choice would. Let us denote this function by $M$:

$$2^{Ms} = s \tag{26}$$

Table 1 compares $Ms$ of (26) with $Rs$ of (3). In the transfinite case, comparisons for ZF1 are made separate from those for ZF2. For ZF1 we have indicated several alternatives for the value of $Rs$ for particular arguments $s$. Of course, this does not mean that $Rs$ is not a function, but only that ZF1 is open for certain further choices. For example $R\aleph_2 = \aleph_0$ if $2^{\aleph_0} = \aleph_2$ or $2^{\aleph_0} > \aleph_2$, but $R\aleph_2 = \aleph_1$ if $2^{\aleph_0} < \aleph_2$ (and $\aleph_2 \leqslant 2^{\aleph_1}$). ZF1 is open for any one of these three alternatives concerning $2^{\aleph_0}$ and $\aleph_2$, but not for more than one at the same time ($<$ is a total ordering relation in ZF1).

For all finite cardinals $s$ of the form $s = 2^\nu$ (where $\nu$ is an integer) $Rs$ is equal to $Ms$. For all other finite cardinals $s$ such that $2^{\nu-1} < s < 2^\nu$, we have $Rs = \nu$, whereas $Ms = \nu - \epsilon(s)$, where $\epsilon(s)$ is a number such that $0 < \epsilon(s) < 1$.

In the transfinite case, $Rs$ and $Ms$ are equal for all arguments $s$ such that $Ms$ is defined. There are, however, cardinals for which $Ms$ is not defined, whereas $Rs$ is defined for all cardinals [compare (8)]. $\aleph_0$ is such a cardinal. For if $p$ is finite, $2^p$ is finite and hence less than $\aleph_0$. Again if $p$ is transfinite, i.e., $p \geqslant \aleph_0$, we have by (I): $2^p > \aleph_0$. Hence there exists no cardinal $p$ such that $2^p = \aleph_0$. As is seen from Table 1, $Ms$ may also be undefined for $s = \aleph_1, \aleph_2, \ldots$ in ZF1 (which does not contain the aleph hypothesis IV).

TABLE 1

| | $s\,(=\text{card } S)$ | $Rs$; see (3) | $Ms$; see (26) | |
|---|---|---|---|---|
| $s$ finite | 0 | 0 | | |
| | 1 | 0 | 0 | |
| | 2 | 1 | 1 | |
| | 3 | 2 | log 3 | |
| | 4 | 2 | 2 | |
| | $\vdots$ | $\vdots$ | $\vdots$ | |
| | $s;\ (2^{\nu-1} < s < 2^{\nu})$ | $\nu$ | $\nu - \epsilon(s);\ (0 < \epsilon(s) < 1)$ | |
| | $s;\quad (s = 2^{\nu})$ | $\nu$ | $\nu$ | |
| ZF2 | $\aleph_0$ | $\aleph_0$ | undefined | |
| | $\aleph_1$ | $\aleph_0$ | $\aleph_0$ | |
| | $\aleph_2$ | $\aleph_1$ | $\aleph_1$ | |
| | $\aleph_3$ | $\aleph_2$ | $\aleph_2$ | |
| | $\aleph_4$ | $\aleph_3$ | $\aleph_3$ | $R\aleph_\nu$ exists for all $\aleph_\nu$. For all those $\aleph_\nu$ for which $M\aleph_\nu$ exists, we have: $M\aleph_\nu = R\aleph_\nu$ |
| | $\vdots$ | $\vdots$ | $\vdots$ | |
| ZF1 | $\aleph_0$ | $\aleph_0$ | undefined | |
| | $\aleph_1$ | $\aleph_0$ | $\aleph_0$ if $2^{\aleph_0} = \aleph_1$; undefined otherwise | |
| | $\aleph_2$ | $\aleph_0$ if $\aleph_2 \leqslant 2^{\aleph_0}$; $\aleph_1$ if $2^{\aleph_0} < \aleph_2 \leqslant 2^{\aleph_1}$ | $\aleph_0$ if $2^{\aleph_0} = \aleph_2$; $\aleph_1$ if $2^{\aleph_1} = \aleph_2$ | |
| | $\vdots$ | $\vdots$ | $\vdots$ | |
| | $\aleph_\nu$ | $R\aleph_\nu$ always exists | $\aleph_\mu$ if $2^{\aleph_\mu} = \aleph_\nu$; undefined otherwise | |

In the transfinite case, $Rs$ is an extension of $Ms$ in the sense that $Rs$ here satisfies the functional equation (24) (and for all transfinite cardinals $s$ such that $Ms$ is defined, we have $Ms = Rs$):

$$\vdash_1 :: (\forall s_1, s_2) :.\ s_1 > 0 \,.\, s_2 \geqslant \aleph_0 \,.\vee.\, s_2 > 0 \,.\, s_1 \geqslant \aleph_0 : \;\Rightarrow .\ R(s_1 \cdot s_2) = Rs_1 + Rs_2 \qquad (27)$$

For the proof of (27) we need the following lemma, (28), and its corollary, (29):

$$\vdash_1 :.\ (\forall s_1, s_2) : s_1 \leqslant s_2 \,.\Rightarrow.\, Rs_1 \leqslant Rs_2 \qquad (28)$$

$$\vdash_1 :.\ (\forall s) : s \geqslant \aleph_0 \,.\Rightarrow.\, Rs \geqslant \aleph_0 \qquad (29)$$

*Proof of 28 and 29*

$[\vdash_1 : 5 . 8 . \Rightarrow . 30]$ $$(\forall s_1, s_2) :: p_1 R s_1 . p_2 R s_2 . s_1 \leqslant s_2 :. \Rightarrow :. \forall q : 2^q \geqslant s_1 . \Rightarrow . p_1 \leqslant q :. 2^{p_2} \geqslant s_2 \geqslant s_1 :. \Rightarrow :. p_1 \leqslant p_2 \tag{30}$$

$[\vdash_1 . 30 \Rightarrow 28]$ which completes the proof of (28).

$[\vdash . 3 \Rightarrow 31]$ $$R\aleph_0 = \aleph_0 \tag{31}$$

$[\vdash_1 : 28 . 31 . \Rightarrow . 32]$ $$\forall s : s \geqslant \aleph_0 . \Rightarrow . Rs \geqslant R\aleph_0 = \aleph_0 \tag{32}$$

$[\vdash_1 . 32 \Rightarrow 29]$ which completes the proof of (29).

*Proof of Theorem 27*

$[\vdash_1 : 28 . 29 . \text{V} . \text{VI} . \Rightarrow . 33]$ $$(\forall s_1, s_2) : 0 < s_1 \leqslant s_2 . s_2 \geqslant \aleph_0 . \Rightarrow . Rs_2 \geqslant \aleph_0 . Rs_2 \geqslant Rs_1 . (s_1 \cdot s_2) = s_2 . \Rightarrow . R(s_1 \cdot s_2) = Rs_1 + Rs_2 \tag{33}$$

$[\vdash_1 : 28 . 29 . \text{V} . \Rightarrow . 34]$ $$(\forall s_1, s_2) : s_1 \geqslant s_2 \geqslant \aleph_0 . \Rightarrow . Rs_1 \geqslant Rs_2 \geqslant \aleph_0 . (s_1 \cdot s_2) = s_1 . \Rightarrow . R(s_1 \cdot s_2) = Rs_1 + Rs_2 \tag{34}$$

$[\vdash_1 : 33 . 34 . \Rightarrow . 27]$ which completes the proof of (27).

The above comparison between $Ms$ and $Rs$ can be summarized as follows. For all nonzero, finite cardinals $s$, the information measure $Ms$ equals $Rs$ as soon as $Ms$ is an integer. If $Ms$ is not an integer, $Rs$ is the smallest integer that is larger than $Ms$ ($Rs = Ms + \epsilon(s)$, where $0 < \epsilon(s) < 1$).

In the transfinite case, $Ms$ does not exist for all cardinals. $Rs$ exists, however, for all cardinals $s$ [compare (8)]. For all those $s$ for which $Ms$ exists, we have $Ms = Rs$. Furthermore, $Rs$ satisfies the functional equation (24) in the whole transfinite region [compare (27)] and is thus an extension of $Ms$ in the transfinite region.

Since our prime interest is in the transfinite region, the following treatment will be based on $Rs$ as the information measure; in the finite case, $-\epsilon(s)$ has to be appended to $Rs$ if $s$ is a natural number such that $s \neq 2^\nu$.

## III. Explicable and Inexplicable Sets

### A. Explicable and Simply Inexplicable Sets

If $S$ is a set such that $Rs < s$, we have, according to Sec. II, an information model that generates any element of $S$, although the predicate set $P$ that is needed for the generation is smaller than $S$: card$(P) <$ card$(S)$ $[p = Rs < s]$. The model is in this case said to be an *explicable information model* for $S$ in the sense that it explains $S$ in terms of a set of smaller cardinality. In the same sense, the set $S$ is said to be *explicable*.

On the other hand, if $S$ is a set such that $Rs = s$, we need for the generation of any element of $S$ a predicate set $P$ that is equivalent with $S[p = Rs = s]$. Clearly we cannot now conclude on the existence of $S$ by the (single) information model. The existence of $S$ has to be assured by other means, for example by an axiom. The information model is in this case said to be a (*single*) *inexplicable information model* and $S$ a *simply inexplicable* set.

Accordingly, we define the predicates $E(s)$: "a set with cardinal $s$ is explicable" and $IE(s)$: "a set with cardinal $s$ is simply inexplicable" as follows:

$$E(s) \,.\!=_{\text{def}}.\, Rs < s \tag{35}$$

$$IE(s) \,.\!=_{\text{def}}.\, Rs \geqslant s \tag{36}$$

Concerning (36), we can make the following assertions:

$$\vdash : IE(s) \,.\!\equiv.\, Rs = s \tag{37}$$

$$\vdash_1 :. \forall s : \neg\, IE(s) \,.\!\equiv.\, E(s) \tag{38}$$

*Proof of 37 and 38*

$[\vdash : 3 \,.\, \text{I} \,.\Rightarrow.\, 39]$

$$\begin{aligned} &\forall s :. p = Rs \geqslant s : \\ &\equiv : p \geqslant s \,.\, 2^s > s \,.\, 2^p \geqslant s \,. \\ &\neg : \exists q \,.\, q < p \,.\, 2^q \geqslant s : \\ &\equiv : p = s = Rs \end{aligned} \tag{39}$$

$[\vdash : 36 \,.\, 39 \,.\Rightarrow.\, 37]$ which completes the proof of (37).

$[\vdash_1 : 8 \,.\, \text{III} \,.\, 36 \,.\, 35 \,.\Rightarrow.\, 40]$

$$\begin{aligned} &\forall s : \neg\, IE(s) \,.\!\equiv.\, \neg \,.\, Rs \geqslant s \,. \\ &\equiv.\, Rs < s \,.\!\equiv.\, E(s) \end{aligned} \tag{40}$$

$[\vdash_1 \,.\, 40 \Rightarrow 38]$ which completes the proof of (38).

For the cardinal region $0 \leqslant s \leqslant \aleph_\omega$ we can make the following assertions:

$$\vdash IE(0) \tag{41}$$

$$\vdash IE(\aleph_0) \tag{42}$$

$$\vdash_2 IE(\aleph_\omega) \tag{43}$$

$$\vdash :. \forall s : 0 < s < \aleph_0 \,.\Rightarrow.\, E(s) \tag{44}$$

$$\vdash_1 :. \forall s : \aleph_0 < s < \aleph_\omega \,.\Rightarrow.\, E(s) \tag{45}$$

(41) and (42) have already been asserted [compare (37) and Table 1]. Again, (44) is an easy consequence of the relations listed in Table 1.

*Proof of 43 and 45*

$[\vdash . \mathrm{I} \Rightarrow 46]$ $\qquad \forall\alpha . \aleph_\alpha < \aleph_{\alpha+1} \leqslant 2^{\aleph_\alpha}$ (46)

$[\vdash_1 : 4 . 46 . \Rightarrow . 47]$ $\qquad \forall\alpha :. pR\aleph_{\alpha+1} :$
$\Rightarrow : 2^p \geqslant \aleph_{\alpha+1} . \forall q : q < p . \Rightarrow . 2^q < \aleph_{\alpha+1} :$
$\Rightarrow : p \leqslant \aleph_\alpha < \aleph_{\alpha+1}$ (47)

$[\vdash_1 : 47 . 35 . \Rightarrow . 45]$ which completes the proof of (45).

$[\vdash 48]$ $\qquad \forall\alpha : \alpha < \omega . \Rightarrow . \alpha + 1 < \omega$ (48)

$[\vdash_2 : 48 . \mathrm{IV} . \Rightarrow . 49]$ $\qquad \forall\alpha : \aleph_\alpha < \aleph_\omega . \Rightarrow . \aleph_{\alpha+1} = 2^{\aleph_\alpha} < \aleph_\omega$ (49)

$[\vdash_2 : 4 . 49 . \Rightarrow . 50]$ $\qquad pR\aleph_\omega : \Rightarrow : 2^p \geqslant \aleph_\omega . \forall q : q < p . 2^q < \aleph_\omega :$
$\Rightarrow : p = \aleph_\omega$ (50)

$[\vdash_2 : 50 . 37 . \Rightarrow . 43]$ which completes the proof of (43).

A corollary of the proof of (45) is that also $E(\aleph_{\omega+1})$, $E(\aleph_{\omega+2})$, and so forth.

In the whole cardinal region $s < \aleph_\omega$ there are only two simply inexplicable cardinals, namely, 0 and $\aleph_0$.

## B. Explicability Chains

Clearly our notion of explicability is a relative one. For example, $\aleph_1$ is explicable with respect to $\aleph_0$, which is inexplicable. To study this relativism we define the notion of an *explicability chain*, $C(s)$, for the set $S$, as the set of the distinct elements of the simply ordered sequence: $s > Rs > R^2 s > R^3 s > \cdots$. The notation $R^n$ means the $n$th relative product of $R$. With $R^0$ for equivalence we can write $R^0 s$ for the first element $s$ of the chain. The chain stops at $R^n s$ if $R^n s$ is inexplicable.

$$C(s) =_{\mathrm{def}} \{R^\nu s ; 0 \leqslant \nu \leqslant n . IE(R^n s) . \forall \nu : \nu < n . \Rightarrow . E(R^\nu s)\} \quad (51)$$

We can make the following assertions for $C(s)$:

$$\vdash_1 : \forall s . \exists ! C(s) \quad (52)$$

$$\vdash_1 :. \forall s : s < \aleph_\omega . \Rightarrow . 0 < \mathrm{card}\ C(s) < \aleph_0 \quad (53)$$

*Proof of 52 and 53*

$[\vdash_1 : 6 . 8 . \Rightarrow . 54]$ $\forall \nu :. \forall s : \exists ! p . pR^\nu s$ (54)

$[\vdash_1 : 54 . 38 . \Rightarrow . 55]$ $\forall \nu :. \forall s : E(R^\nu s) . \vee . IE(R^\nu s)$ (55)

$[\vdash_1 : 51 . 54 . 55 . 37 . 35 . \Rightarrow . 52]$ which completes the proof of (52).

$[\vdash_1 : 54 . 44 . 41 . 51 . \Rightarrow . 56]$ $\forall s : 0 \leqslant s < \aleph_0 . \Rightarrow . 0 \in C(s)$ (56)

$[\vdash_1 : 51 . 56 . \Rightarrow . 57]$ $\forall s : 0 \leqslant s < \aleph_0 .$
$\Rightarrow . \aleph_0 > 1 + s \geqslant \text{card } C(s) > 0$ (57)

$[\vdash_1 : 54 . 45 . 42 . 29 . 51 . \Rightarrow . 58]$ $\forall s :. \aleph_0 \leqslant s < \aleph_\omega :$
$\Rightarrow : \aleph_0 \in C(s) .$
$\forall q : q < \aleph_0 . \Rightarrow . \neg . q \in C(s)$ (58)

$[\vdash_1 : 51 . 58 . \Rightarrow . 59]$ $\forall s :. \aleph_0 \leqslant s = \aleph_\alpha < \aleph_\omega :$
$\Rightarrow : (\exists ! \beta, \gamma, ., 0) : \omega > \alpha > \beta > \gamma > \cdot > 0 .$
$C(s) = \{\aleph_\alpha, \aleph_\beta, \aleph_\gamma, ., \aleph_0\} :$
$\Rightarrow : 0 < \text{card } (C(s)) < \aleph_0$ (59)

$[\vdash_1 : 57 . 59 . \Rightarrow . 53]$ which completes the proof of (53).

Theorem (53) says that for any cardinal $s$ in the region $s < \aleph_\omega$, the explicability chain $C(s)$ is *finite* even though the cardinal $s$ itself may be transfinite. Furthermore, a corollary of (53) and (44) is that, for every $s$ in the region under consideration, $C(s)$ itself is an explicable set (indeed an effectively explicable set; compare Sec. III.D).

For all finite $s$, we see from (56) that the explicability chains $C(s)$ all end in the simply inexplicable cardinal 0. Again, for all transfinite cardinals $s$ in the region $\aleph_0 \leqslant s < \aleph_\omega$, we see from (58) that all $C(s)$ end in the simply inexplicable cardinal $\aleph_0$.

## C. Productions

We have seen that, for example, $\aleph_0$ is an inexplicable cardinal. Its existence therefore has to be ensured by an axiom. In ZF the axiom of infinity serves this purpose. In ZF1 the axiom of choice furthermore ensures the existence of a choice function for its transfinite sets.

Let us examine what further cardinals could be produced within ZF1 from a predicate set of cardinality $\aleph_0$. Within a first production step we reach a set of cardinality $2^{\aleph_0}$ [compare (2)] or a subset thereof. Hence we have at our disposal a new predicate set, equivalent with this produced set, i.e., a predicate set of cardinality $2^{\aleph_0}$. Again this predicate set produces (characterizes) a set of cardinality $2^{(2^{\aleph_0})}$, and another predicate set of this cardinality is at our disposal for a further production, and so on.

Notice, however, that for this production process we have to select new representatives for the successive predicate sets. To explain this point, let us return to the example given at the beginning of Section II. If we here tried to use the produced predicates $Q_1(x)$, $Q_2(x)$, $Q_3(x)$, $Q_4(x)$ directly as generative predicates for a next step, we should find this impossible because $\neg . Q_1(x) . Q_2(x) . Q_3(x) . Q_4(x)$ for all $x$, and so forth. However, a predicate set that is equivalent with $\{Q_1(x), Q_2(x), Q_3(x), Q_4(x)\}$, but disjoint from this set, permits a further production step.

Let us return to the denumerable predicate set from which we started the production process. Its cardinal is $\aleph_0$. The first production step will produce (characterize) a set of cardinality $2^{\aleph_0}$. The abstraction from explicable constructivism that permitted us to start off from $\aleph_0$ again permits us to select a new predicate set, equivalent with that produced but disjoint from it such that it can serve as a predicate set for a next production step. In fact, we have at our disposal a totality of $2^{\aleph_0} + \aleph_0$ predicates and are thus even permitted to select the new predicate set with this cardinality. Even further, the abstraction mentioned permits us to select an uncountable ($2^{\aleph_0}$) number of sets, each of cardinality $2^{\aleph_0}$ or less. At this stage the cardinal of the thus-selected total predicate set will, however, not be larger than $2^{\aleph_0}$ ($2^{\aleph_0} 2^{\aleph_0} = 2^{\aleph_0}$; compare V).

Since we started the production process from $\aleph_0$, the corresponding abstraction from explicable constructivism permits us to consider $\aleph_0$ production steps. In general, having reached the cardinal $s$ by the production process, we have at our disposal for a further production step a number of $\sigma_s$ predicates, where $\sigma_s$ is the largest cardinal that meets with (62):

[Prod. process impl. $s$] $$\exists X . \mathrm{card}\,(X) \leqslant s \tag{60}$$

[$s$ and $X$ from 60] $$\forall x :. \exists p_x : x \in X . \Rightarrow . p_x \leqslant s \tag{61}$$

[$X$ from 60, $p_x$ from 61] $$\sigma_s =_{\mathrm{def}} \sum_{x \in X} p_x \tag{62}$$

(With each member $x$ of a set $X$ such that card $(X) \leqslant s$ a cardinal $p_x$ is associated, such that $p_x \leqslant s$. Each $p_x$ is the cardinal of a particular predicate set.

At most, $s$ such predicate sets are allowed for the next production step, i.e., a totality of $\sigma_s$ predicates is allowed).

Are there now any cardinals of ZF1 which cannot be reached by such a production process from $\aleph_0$? Let us examine $\aleph_\omega$ which, by the aid of IV, was shown to be simply inexplicable [compare (43)]. Since $\aleph_1 \leqslant 2^{\aleph_0}$, $\aleph_2 \leqslant 2^{(2^{\aleph_0})}$, and so forth, it is clear that any cardinal $\aleph_\alpha$ such that $\aleph_\alpha < \aleph_\omega$ (i.e., $\alpha < \omega$) can be reached by the production process. But then, by VII and (62), a $\sigma_s$ can be reached that equals $\aleph_\omega$. Hence, contrary to what might have been expected, $\aleph_\omega$ can be reached by a production process from $\aleph_0$.

Starting from a finite cardinal, however, the production process only generates finite cardinals, i.e., $\aleph_0$ cannot be reached. Since the production process is defined under the assumption that at least one predicate exists, we should here start from cardinal number 1. This number generates $2^1 = 2$, 2 generates $2^2 = 4$, and so forth. But for any finite cardinal $s$, $\sigma_s$ is finite; i.e., the next produced cardinal will again be finite and $\aleph_0$ is not reached.

## D. Effectively Explicable and Strongly Inexplicable Sets

A production process that starts from the cardinal number 1 is *effectively constructive* in the sense that it could be mechanized such that no inexplicable steps would be involved. Any explicable (and hence nonempty) set $S$ that is a subset (proper or improper) of a set $Q$ that is generated by such an effectively constructive process will therefore be said to be *effectively explicable*:

> $s$ ( = card $S$) is by definition *effectively explicable* iff $s$ is explicable and $S$ is a subset (proper or improper) of a set $Q$ that is generated by a production process from 1 such that (62) is fulfilled at each step of the process. (63)

Thus, since all nonempty, finite sets are both explicable [compare (44)] and effectively producible, they are all effectively explicable. No transfinite cardinal, however, is effectively explicable, because no production process that starts from 1 and fulfills (62) can generate $\aleph_0$ (compare Sec. III.C).

As we have seen in Sec. III.C, an inexplicable cardinal may or may not be reached by a production process from a smaller cardinal. An inexplicable cardinal $s$ that cannot be reached by a production process from a smaller cardinal will be said to be *strongly inexplicable*, $IE_{\text{str}}(s)$:

$$IE_{\text{str}}(s) \,.\!=_{\text{def}} : IE(s) \,.\, \forall q : q < s \,.\Rightarrow .\forall \sigma_j \,.\, \sigma_q < s \qquad (64)$$

Obviously 0 is strongly inexplicable. Since the inexplicable cardinal $\aleph_0$ cannot be produced by a smaller cardinal (compare Sec. III.C) it is also strongly inexplicable:

$$\vdash . IE_{\text{str}}(0) \tag{65}$$

$$\vdash . IE_{\text{str}}(\aleph_0) \tag{66}$$

A corollary of the preceding results is that 0 and $\aleph_0$ are the only two strongly inexplicable cardinals in the whole cardinal region considered so far, i.e., $0, 1, 2, \ldots, \aleph_0, \aleph_1, \aleph_2, \ldots, \aleph_\omega, \aleph_{\omega+1}, \aleph_{\omega+2}, \ldots$.

## E. Inaccessible Cardinals

The inaccessible cardinals are central to the foundations of set theory. We shall remind on their definition and see that one type of them, the Tarski cardinals, are equivalent to the strongly inexplicable cardinals.

Inaccessible cardinals are usually considered to be of two kinds, the Tarski and the Kuratowski inaccessible cardinals. Within the cardinal range considered above, the two kinds are identical and we shall here give only the definition of the Tarski inaccessible cardinals. Let us use the predicate $IA(s)$ for "the cardinal $s$ is a Tarski inaccessible cardinal" and $B(s)$ for "the cardinal $s$ is regular" in the sense of Tarski:

$$B(s) \,.\!=_{\text{def}} : (\forall X, p_x) : \text{card}\,(X) < s \,.\, p_x < s \,.\Rightarrow .\, s > \sum_{x \in X} p_x \tag{67}$$

$$IA(s) \,.\!=_{\text{def}} : B(s) \,.\, \forall q : q < s \,.\Rightarrow .\, 2^q < s \tag{68}$$

To see the equivalence between $IA(s)$ and $IE_{\text{str}}(s)$ we need only the following lemma:

$$\vdash_1 :. IE(s) \,.\equiv : \forall q : q < s \,.\Rightarrow .\, 2^q < s \tag{69}$$

*Proof of 69*

$[\vdash_1 : 37 . 4 . I . \Rightarrow . 70]$ $\quad IE(s) \,.\equiv : p = s \,.\, pRs :$

$$\equiv : p = s \,.\, 2^p \geqslant s \,.\, \forall q : q < p \,.\Rightarrow .\, 2^q < s :$$

$$\equiv : \forall q : q < s \,.\Rightarrow .\, 2^q < s \tag{70}$$

$[\vdash_1 . 70 \Rightarrow 69]$ $\quad$ which completes the proof of (69).

As a corollary of (64), (70), (62) and (68) we obtain

$$\vdash_1 . IE_{\text{str}}(s) \equiv IA(s) \tag{71}$$

The question whether there exists inaccessible cardinals (and hence strongly inexplicable cardinals) larger than $\aleph_0$ cannot be decided upon within ZF (or ZF1 or ZF2). Tarski (1938) has introduced additional axioms for the existence of inaccessible cardinals larger than $\aleph_0$.

## IV. Applications to Transfinite Automata

A characteristic feature of a deterministic automaton is that it determines its next state (and output) from its present state and input. Let us denote by $S$ the configuration set of the automaton, i.e., the cartesian product of the state set and set of inputs. Since the automaton is supposed to act by itself, it has at each stage to determine the present element of $S$. On the basis of such a determination the next state will be caused. Let us, however, restrict our attention to the basic element determination.

Let us first assume that the deterministic automaton has a *fixed structure* in the sense that it has a sequential-net representation. The net must thus be able to accept the information $Rs$, where $s$ is the cardinal of the configuration set. Or, in the terminology of Sec. I, the net must contain an information model of $S$. Now, if $S$ is strongly inexplicable, the sequential-net representation of the automaton will be a strongly inexplicable model.

The previous analysis of the explicability concept thus shows that the existence of a deterministic automaton of fixed structure and with a strongly inexplicable configuration set cannot be derived from the existence of finite automata but has to be axiomatized. The important point is that if this axiomatization is done along the lines of ZF, then the deterministic behavior of such an automaton has to be axiomatized also.

To support this point let us reason as follows. Suppose that there were a theory of transfinite cardinals such that all transfinite cardinals were effectively explicable. This would mean that we had an effectively explicable information model for the selection of elements out of every transfinite set. In particular we would have an effectively explicable model for the choice function of the axiom of choice, II. The axiom of choice could therefore be derived in such a theory, because II excludes selections from the only finite, strongly inexplicable set, namely, the empty set.

However a theory of transfinite cardinals must contain $\aleph_0$, and $\aleph_0$ is strongly inexplicable [compare (66)]. In other words, the information model for the selection of elements from a set of cardinality $\aleph_0$ is strongly inexplicable and, in particular, the existence of a choice function has to be axiomatized; compare ZF with ZFI.

Accordingly, if the existence of an automaton of fixed structure with $\mathrm{card}(S) = \aleph_0$ is axiomatized along the lines of ZF, then we have also to axiomatize its capability of determining an element out of $S$, i.e., its deterministic behavior. Again, since no transfinite cardinal is effectively explicable, the same argument goes through for any transfinite, fixed automaton, i.e., its deterministic behavior cannot be derived on the basis of ZF but has to be axiomatized.

However, the usual meaning of a deterministic automaton (computer) is intimately connected with effective explicability. A support for this opinion is, for example, the following quotation from Davis (1958): "If an algorithm for performing a task exists, then, at least in principle, a computing machine for accomplishing this task can be constructed. Such a computing machine is *deterministic* in the sense that, while it is in operation, its entire future is completely specified by its status at some one instant."

Hence, since the determinism of a fixed automaton with a transfinite configuration set has to be axiomatized, surely this *axiomatization of the determinism* means that we have to go beyond the above-mentioned meaning of determinism.

Indeed, such an axiomatization of the determinism would imply that the automaton could produce numbers that a Turing machine cannot. A Turing machine produces "computable" numbers, and the set of computable numbers is denumerable. An axiomatized determinism, on the other hand, permits the transfinite, fixed automaton to produce a nondenumerable amount of numbers. Our conclusions are thus that the notion of a transfinite, fixed, deterministic automaton does not conform with the usual sense of determinism.

However, the situation is different for growing automata. Such an automaton, although deterministic in the effectively explicable sense, can no doubt be thought of as having a *potentially infinite* configuration set. A Turing machine belongs to this kind of automata. The potentially infinite tape of a Turing machine is, for example, mentioned in Kleene (1952) and Davis (1958), and Burks (1960) provides a description of a tape-extension mechanism.

The step from automata with computation behaviors to automata with construction behaviors was taken first by von Neumann. We want to mention that the ideas of the present paper are of special interest in connection with the constructive automata of the von Neumann tessellation type. They lead rather directly to the consideration of an effectively explicable hierarchy of potentially infinite tessellation spaces, one space being a configuration on the subsequent space. However, these questions will be dealt with in another paper.

In formalizing automata theory it is of course very tempting to make abstractions as they are usually made in mathematics. However, it is important not to abstract away from what is effectively explicable because, as we have argued, this leads away from the very essence of automata theory. Also the abstractions made, that permit the consideration of exorbitant large sets, are themselves explained by finite means in the sense that all books on set theory contain a finite number of words [compare the Skolem paradox; see Kleene (1952) and Fraenkel and Bar-Hillel (1958)].

In deriving the explicability notions we started off from the notion of information measure. Again the notion of information originates with a Gedanken experiment of Szilard (1929), where he, in order to explain an observed physical law, associates a basic mental activity to the Maxwell demon. This is mentioned because it points towards the cybernetic view of thought processes as physical (and chemical) processes. On the other hand, physical (and chemical) theories are products of thought processes. A true recognition of such a mutual dependency is likely to shed new light on the abstraction processes of transfinite set theory. Besides, it will probably result in a fruitful rapprochement of disciplines which are now considered entirely independent.

## List of Symbols, Axioms, and Theorems Used

ZF — denotes the Zermelo-Fraenkel (see Fraenkel 1961) set theory without the axiom of choice (II) and without the aleph hypothesis (IV), which is also called the generalized continuum hypothesis.

ZF1 — denotes the Zermelo-Fraenkel set theory without the aleph hypothesis (IV) but with the axiom of choice (II) included. (The continuum hypothesis has recently been proved to be independent of ZF1; Cohen (1963)).

ZF2 — denotes the Zermelo-Fraenkel set theory with the aleph hypothesis (IV) included (and thus also with the axiom of choice included).

$\vdash P$ — means that the proposition $P$ has been asserted within ZF.

$\vdash_1 P$ — means that the proposition $P$ has been asserted within ZF1.

$\vdash_2 P$ — means that the proposition $P$ has been asserted within ZF2.

. : :. :: — and so forth are the dot symbols of Whitehead and Russell (1962). They are used for brackets and for the logical connective &. The scope of a bracket indicated by dots is explained by dividing them in three groups, (a), (b), and (c). (a) consists of dots adjoining a sign of implication ($\Rightarrow$) or of equivalence ($\equiv$) or of disjunction ($\vee$). Group (b) consists of dots following the negation sign $\neg$ (not so in *Principia Mathematica*, however) and of dots following the quantifier expressions $\forall x$, $\exists x$, $\exists ! x$. Group (c) consists of dots which stand between propositions in order to indicate the logical product (&). Group (a) is of greater force than group (b), group (b) than group (c). The scope of the bracket indicated by any collection of dots extends backwards or forwards beyond any *smaller* number of dots, or any *equal* number from a group of less force, until we reach either the end of the proposition or a *greater* number of dots or an *equal* number belonging to a group of equal or superior force. Dots indicating a logical product have a scope which works both backwards and forwards; the other dots only work away from the adjacent sign of disjunction, implication, or equivalence or forward from the adjacent symbol of one of the other kinds enumerated in group (b). As an example, the proposition

$\vdash :. \neg : \neg p . q . \vee . \neg . p . q : \equiv . p . q$

reads: "the proposition $(\neg(((\neg p) \,\&\, q) \vee (\neg(p \,\&\, q)))) \equiv (p \,\&\, q)$ is asserted." We use the abbreviated form $(a < b < c)$ for $(a < b . b < c)$.

| | |
|---|---|
| $\forall$ | the universal quantifier. |
| $\exists$ | the existential quantifier. |
| $\exists ! x . P(x)$ | "there exists a unique $x$ such that $P(x)$." |
| $V_c$ | the class of all cardinals. |
| $\omega_0$ | the smallest limit ordinal (also denoted $\omega$). |
| $\omega_0 + 1$ | the ordinal that follows $\omega_0$. |
| $\omega_1$ | the smallest nondenumerable limit ordinal (between $\omega_0$ and $\omega_1$ there are ordinals like $\omega + \nu$, $\omega\nu$, $\omega^2$, $\omega^\nu$, $\omega^\omega$, $(\omega^\omega)^\omega$, and so forth; they are all denumerable). |
| $\omega_{\alpha+1}$ | the smallest limit ordinal that comes after the limit ordinal $\omega_\alpha$. |
| $\aleph_0$ | the smallest transfinite cardinal. |
| $\aleph_{\alpha+1}$ | the smallest cardinal that is larger than $\aleph_\alpha$ ($\omega_\alpha$ is the smallest ordinal among all those ordinals whose cardinal is $\aleph_\alpha$). |
| $\aleph_\omega$ | Ordered by magnitude the cardinals come in the order $\aleph_0, \aleph_1, \aleph_2, \ldots, \aleph_\omega, \aleph_{\omega+1}, \aleph_{\omega+2}, \ldots, \aleph_{\omega 2}, \aleph_{\omega 2+1}, \ldots.$ |
| $\{x; P(x)\}$ | the set of all $x$ such that $P(x)$. |
| $\phi$ | the empty set. |
| $s = \text{card}\,(S)$ | $s$ is the cardinal of the set $S$. |
| $\breve{R}$ | the converse of the relation $R$ $(x\breve{R}y . \Rightarrow . yRx)$. |
| $\text{Fnc}\,(R)$ | $R$ is a function $(pRs . qRs . \Rightarrow . p = q)$. |
| $d\text{'}F$ | the domain of the function $F$. |
| $r\text{'}F$ | the range of the function $F$. |

I The Cantor inequality:

$\vdash :. \forall s : s \in V_c . \Rightarrow . s < 2^s$

II The axiom of choice: For each set $S$ there exists a choice function $F$ whose domain is the collection of nonempty subsets of $S$ and, for every $X \subseteq S$ with $X \neq \phi$, $F(X) \in X$.

III The law of trichotomy:

$\vdash_1 :: (\forall x, y) :. (x, y) \in V_c . \Rightarrow : x < y . \vee . x = y . \vee . x > y$

IV The aleph hypothesis (or the generalized continuum hypothesis):

$\vdash_2 : \forall \aleph_\alpha . 2^{\aleph_\alpha} = \aleph_{\alpha+1}$

(by the previous explanation of $\aleph_{\alpha+1}$, the aleph hypothesis implies that $\vdash_2 :: \forall \aleph_\alpha :. \neg : \exists c . \aleph_\alpha < c < 2^{\aleph_\alpha}$)

V The Hessenberg theorem

$\vdash : (\forall \aleph_\alpha, \aleph_\beta) . \aleph_\alpha + \aleph_\beta = \aleph_\alpha \cdot \aleph_\beta = \aleph_{\max(\alpha, \beta)}$

VI A modification of V:

$\vdash :. (\forall s, \aleph_\alpha) : 0 < s < \aleph_0 . \Rightarrow . s + \aleph_\alpha = s \cdot \aleph_\alpha = \aleph_\alpha$

VII $\vdash_1 . \sum_{\alpha < \omega} \aleph_\alpha = \aleph_\omega$

## References


Bachmann, H. (1955). *Transfinite Zahlen*, Springer, Berlin.

Burks, A. W. (1960). Computation, behavior and structure in fixed and growing automata, in *Self-Organizing Systems* (Yovits and Cameron, eds.), Pergamon Press, New York.

Cohen, P. (1963). "The independence of the continuum hypothesis," *Proc. Natl. Acad. Sci. U.S.A.* **50**, 1143–1148, and **51**, 105–110.

Davis, M. (1958). *Computability and Unsolvability*, McGraw-Hill, New York.

Fadiev, D. (1956). On the notion of entropy of a finite probability space (in Russian). *Usp. Mat. Nauk*, **11**, 227–231.

Fraenkel, A. (1961). *Abstract Set Theory*, North-Holland, Amsterdam.

Fraenkel, A. and Y. Bar-Hillel (1958). *Foundations of Set Theory*, North-Holland, Amsterdam.

Kleene, S. C. (1952). *Introduction to Metamathematics*, Van Nostrand, Princeton, N.J.

Szilard, L. (1929). Über die Entropieverminderung in einem thermodynamischen System bei Eingriffen intelligenter Wesen, *Z. Phys.* **53**, 840–856.

Tarski, A. (1938). Über unerreichbare Kardinalzahlen, *Fundamenta Mathematicae* **30**, 68–89.

von Neumann, J. *The Theory of Automata: Construction, Reproduction, and Homogeneity* (A. W. Burks, ed.). To be published by Univ. Illinois Press, Urbana.

Whitehead, A. N., and B. Russell (1962). *Principia Mathematica*, Cambridge University Press, New York.

# Introduction to the Problem of the Reticular Formation[1]

WARREN S. MCCULLOCH
in collaboration with
WILLIAM L. KILMER

*Research Laboratory of Electronics*
*Massachusetts Institute of Technology*
*Cambridge, Massachusetts*

## I. Historical Note

Although the construction of automata to handle information began with Ramon Lull 750 years ago, theoretical consideration goes back no farther than Leibnitz' universal characteristic and the nineteenth paragraph of his *Monadology*, and Descartes' eight years of dissection of brains in Leiden, which led him to postulate the nervous impulse, to propose inverse feedback to regulate the behavior of muscles, and to state the first clear notion of coding, in which spatial forms were transformed into temporal sequences. In those days the physical means of realizing the proposed computations were, and were long to remain, inadequate.

Some 30 years ago the hardware began to be available, and the theory of automata grew up with Turing's computer, Shannon's relay device, von Neumann's JONIAC, and Pitts' and my work on the logical calculus to describe how ideas could be immanent in nervous activity. It was our intent to show that a proper net, with circles for memory and for control, could, given a tape, compute any number that a Turing machine could compute.

[1] This work was supported in part by the U.S. Army, Navy, and Air Force under Contract DA36-039-AMC-03200(E); and in part by the National Institutes of Health (Grants NB-04985-01 and MH-04737-04), the National Science Foundation (Grant GP-2495), the U.S. Air Force [ASD Contract AF33(615)-1747], and the National Aeronautics and Space Administration (Grant NsG-496). The work of W. L. Kilmer was supported in part by U.S. Air Force Cambridge Research Laboratories Contract AF19(628)-3807 (administered by Montana State College).

For that purpose, we proposed neurons with few afferents, each having a fixed threshold, enjoying summation of excitations and an inhibition that was total. No neuron was then known to be, as they say, "spontaneously" active, and we proposed none. For our purpose, that is, to account for such computations as real nervous systems produce, those assumptions were sufficiently realistic. These impoverished neurons proved inadequate in 1947, when we began to attempt to account for the reliability of the performance of nets with local perturbations of thresholds, of strength of signals, and even of the details of synapsis. It was at that time that "spontaneously" active neurons were plentifully demonstrated and that, in terms of their actions, it became realistic to propose embodiments of Sheffer's stroke functions.

It was these, and other equally realistic, considerations which for some years had troubled him, that led von Neumann to his *Toward a Probabilistic Logic*. From its appearance in 1952, I worked with Manuel Blum, who cleaned up the problem of logical stability of circuit action under common shift of threshold; with Leo Verbeek, who worked out the best ways of combating the scattered fits and deaths of neurons; and with Jack Cowan and Sam Winograd, who demonstrated the possibility, and the price, of an information-theoretic capacity in computation with noisy components.

Their results, and our progress in understanding perception, have now released me from these tasks to turn, with William L. Kilmer, toward the central problem of coordinate nervous activity—namely, the functional organization of the core of the reticular formation.

## II. A More Realistic Neuron

For ultimate solution of this central problem I believe we shall have to regard every neuron as a highly nonlinear oscillator. Unfortunately, the mathematical methods for handling complicated circuit actions of coupled oscillators leave much to be desired. It may be many years before we are capable of such a verisimilitude in matching our fancy to the facts. But, thanks largely to Jerry Lettvin, we have at least one better notion relating structure to function.

In our work on what the frog's eye tells the frog's brain, we were able to assign, on the basis of connectivity, one of five functions to each of the five varieties of dendritic arbors of ganglion cells of the retina. Further consideration of these relations, together with a novel conception of the physics of nerve membranes, gave us some of the increasingly realistic notions required for analysis of the reticular formation.

Figure 1 is a diagram of a neuron with soma *S*, showing a representative branched dendrite, $D_1 D_2$, to which are applied excitatory, *E*, and inhibitory, *I*, synapses. The trigger point is on the axon hillock, *A*, with a threshold $\theta$. At each *E* a pulse of current, carried by $Na^+$, is injected, while at each *I* a shunt operated by $K^+$ is provided. To a crude first approximation, the tendency for the axon to fire is given by the Euclidean algorism, which

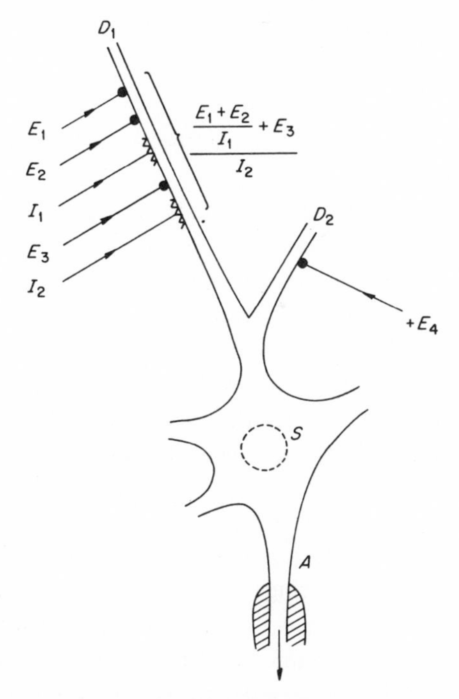


FIG. 1. Lettvin model of a neuron.

(for every dendrite) sums adjacent excitations and divides the result by the sum of inhibitions next nearer to *A* (see Fig. 1). At junction points of dendrites effects add. This principle allows the neuron, according to its total dendritic input at a given time, to be able to compute any Boolian function of its input, not merely those of threshold logic, and hence to give a succession of spikes in its output, determined by the large capacity of the cell membrane, by the voltage at the trigger point, and by the threshold $\theta$.

The axon is to be conceived of as a distributed repeater, having a distributed capacity, distributed resistance, and distributed source of power.

Hence each nervous impulse is independent of the strength of the stimuli that evoked it but is determined by local conditions, local factors of capacity and resistance, and local sources and sinks of current provided by neighboring structures.

The effects of taper and of branch points of axons need not concern us here, although we know much about their blocking of conduction; nor need we consider the inherent thermal noise affecting threshold most in final branches, for we are primarily interested in understanding how the reticular formation, under the most favorable circumstances, can achieve those functions that we know it performs.

## III. Delineation of the Term "Reticular Formation"

Our ancestors believed that the brain and spinal marrow were jelly in which fibers precipitated, forming a net or reticulum: so the word originally referred to the whole central nervous system. Vertebrates, including man, have evolved from linear systems composed of segments, each of which had its own input over afferent peripheral neurons and its own output over efferent peripheral neurons. Within each segment these were connected to each other by the reticular cells, and the segments themselves were connected to each other by the reticular cells to coordinate the whole system from end to end.

With increasing delineation of brain structure came special names for specialized portions which have manifestly evolved from the reticulum's originally simple structure, leaving the core almost unchanged. Let us forget all elaborate specializations out of the reticular formation, such as the cerebrum and the colliculi for analysis of inputs yielding the universals and particulars of perception, the basal ganglia for programming movements to be executed by half-centers for antagonistic motor activities, and the cerebellum for interval timing and correlation of signals. Their problems are specialities and their activities are parochial questions of circuit actions.

In higher vertebrates the incoming afferent peripheral neuron, besides supplying the reticulum of its own and adjacent segments, divided, sending a long branch forward and a long branch backward, to end on the reticulum of remoter segments, or to be relayed by specialized groups derived from it. The reticular system itself developed a four-layered receptive structure to sort out information received over the afferent peripheral neuron. Rexed has described these layers and P. D. Wall of our group has worked this out—

the so-called secondary sensory complex—in the spinal cord (of the cat). Near the innermost of these layers lies the dorso-lateral reticular nucleus, apparently chiefly concerned with forward-going relays of information. More ventral lies the lateral reticular nucleus, apparently concerned with programmed interactions of reflexes in each segment and between adjacent segments, affecting the same general part of the body. Finally, around the efferent peripheral neuron lies another relatively specialized portion of the reticular formation, its ventral nucleus, which is probably most important in inhibiting activity over a few segments on behalf of over-all organization. On the other hand, the core of the reticular formation, especially in the mid-brain, has probably remained relatively unchanged throughout vertebrate phylogeny.

## IV. The Reticular Core

The cells of which the reticular core is composed are probably least specialized. They are chiefly of medium size, say, 20 or 30 microns in diameter of cell body. Their dendrites are long and thin with few branches, or hooks, fanning out through almost half a circle at right angles to the neuraxis, and reaching to the periphery (Fig. 2a). Their axons typically grow diametrically away from the dendritic fan; then they divide, sending one branch forward, the other backward. Those reticular neurons with soma farthest forward have the longer axonal branch to the rear, and vice versa. The axon very frequently has a recurrent branch, which ascends among the dendritic branches of its cell-of-origin and neighboring dendritic branches of neighboring cells, presumably inhibiting them, for this direction of approach usually produces a sink of current among the dendrites and leaves a source of current on the cell body. The main, bifurcated axon typically has branchlets at right angles (Fig. 2b), which end on the four-layered secondary sensory cortex or on adjuvant reticular structures, such as the lateral and ventral reticular moities; but the main branches themselves usually terminate on reticular cells without angulating. There are minor local modifications; for example, ventral cells of the core fan out their dendrites through narrower angles ($\sim 60°$), and tend to have larger cell bodies and thicker caudal branches.

To appreciate these relationships at the head end, one has to be careful to cut the brain at the proper angles because its stem bends in the mid-brain. I think the leading anatomists now working on the reticular system would all agree on the foregoing general description: the Scheibels and Valverde, using Golgi stains; Nauta, working out details of connections by small lesions and staining dead or dying axons; Brodal, employing the modified Gudden method; and Droogleever Fortuyn, cutting the brainstem at

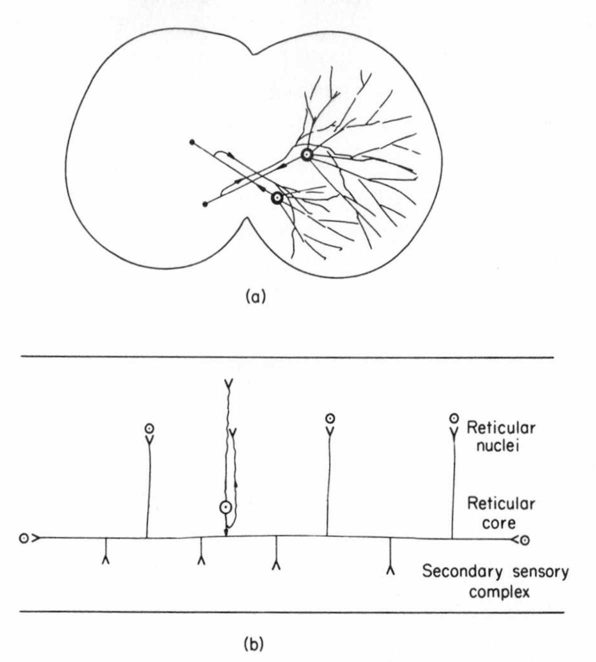


FIG. 2. (a) Reticular core neurons in top section of brainstem. (b) Reticular core neurons in lateral section.

optimum angles for Nissl information. There is comparable agreement as to the constancy, among species, of the number of cells in the core, it being of the same order as the number of afferent peripheral neurons or of efferent peripheral neurons. The core has apparently neither multiplied in number nor changed significantly in structure from frog to man.

## V. Résumé

Let me summarize it thus: The core of the reticular formation is an iterative net certainly at the segmental level, and probably, from the flattening of the dendritic field, at an even finer level. Looked at in cross section, it is a computer, which is very wide but only one cell deep. Only its longitudinal structure gives it effective depth. This is such that whatever segment has the most urgent information can take command of the whole organism; it can, locally and generally, set the filters and command the computers on the sensory side and select the program of motor performance on the outgoing side. The anatomy provides us with the requisite circuit connections, and the gross physiology assures us of the facts of performance. Neither helps us much in the invention of an appropriate theory of these automata.

## VI. Physiological Clues

We look for guidance, therefore, to the detailed physiology. We find it still very partial. I believe Amassian was the first to get beautiful records of the responses of single neurons of the reticular core, and his work has been confirmed and amplified by others. Such a cell may respond to many and diverse inputs, say a flash, a click, and a touch of one hind leg. The typical response is a short series of spikes. Repetition of the stimulus produces rapid adaptation, spikes decreasing in number and often ceasing. Next, these cells show prompt conditioning. When, say, an electric shock is given to that hind leg to which the cell responds, there is a large burst of impulses. Repetition of a click before each shock causes an increasing response to the click and a marked diminution of the response to the shock. It takes hours for this conditioning to disappear to such an extent that it cannot be reconstituted by a few recouplings of the stimuli; but this may depend upon other parts of the system specialized for longer retention of traces.

Next, we note that whereas two electrodes recording from neighboring neurons, say, in the cerebral cortex, show a high probability of either cell firing within a few milliseconds of its neighbor, in the reticular core there is a very low probability of such a relation. This strongly strengthens the supposition that the recurrent collaterals of reticular neurons are inhibitory.

Again, whereas gross electrical stimulation to the reticular formation by single shocks over large inset electrodes fails to produce observed outputs, a train of six or more pulses at a rate of two or three hundred per second is most effective. Bursts at three to four per second produce spike-and-dome waves in the frontal cortex. This fits well with other evidence—that it takes approximately a third of a second for the reticular core to take the organism from one mode of response into another. Since the fastest reticular axons conduct at $\sim$ 100 meters per second and run the whole length of the spinal cord, this leaves time for only a dozen or so transits of signals to operate a decision to change from mode to mode. If the animal be in one stable mode of behavior and the system then be thrown out of balance by some input requiring change of mode, the transient disturbance must not persist longer than a third of a second before the new mode is stabilized.

We can simplify the conception of what is meant by a mode of behavior if we consider, for instance, one of Rioch's or Bard's animals with everything in front of the mid-brain removed. It can (1) sleep or awake, (2) eat, (3) drink, (4) defecate, (5) urinate, (6) copulate, (7) engage in one mode of escape, or (8, 9) perform either of two modes of fighting, or (10) one mode of surrender; but it can pursue no two of these activities at the same time. They are, like breathing and swallowing, incompatibles. Again, if, in the newborn puppy, the spinal cord is cut completely across in the middle of the back and he is allowed to grow up unhampered, the hind quarters can be set into one mode or another by the fore quarters. Thus the hind quarters can work against gravity or else relax, they can stand still or else progress, and any combination of these either symmetrically or asymmetrically. There are thus, in these puppies, three vectors of decisive import which can be organized only by the reticular formation below the cut. Moreover, the lowest part of the cord, the conus, still having nervous connection to this part of the cord, can produce micturition, defecation, and copulation, with their appropriate postures and motions.

The foregoing data from lesions show in simplified form the ability of the reticular core to commit the remainder of the whole organism, or the isolated fragment, to one mode of behavior. When we turn from these cripples to the whole organism, even to man, and ask how many inherited, or innate, incompatible modes of behavior he may enjoy, we may agree as to whether there are, say, 14 or 18, but scarcely that there are 30. Thus the job of the reticular formation is, on receipt of signals from within the organism and the world around it, to discover promptly how to classify the event as a case under one or another of its few inherited diagnostic categories for which it has a repertoire of appropriate rules of conduct.

We have sought a way of thinking about this redundancy of potential command in which urgent information constitutes authority. The requisite theory must ensure that whatever part of the reticular core is in receipt of that urgent information can take the whole of the core promptly into a new stable mode. Since this is an iterated net of computers at the segmental level, and perhaps at even thinner slices, we looked first to the theory of iterated nets as elaborated by Hennie and Kilmer, but discovered after more than a year of work that one could prove that almost every question we desired to settle was recursively undecidable, and hence, no doubt, practically undecidable also. A brief look at the more appropriate theory of multiple coupled nonlinear oscillators convinced us that the necessary mathematics for that approach does not yet exist.

At this point, Rabin's theory of probabilistic automata appeared, with a possibility of looking at actual automata requiring fewer states per module and yielding the stability theorems that we required. But the effect of this was only to increase the generality of the iterative net formulation. So to avoid unsolvability, we particularized the iterative net to consist of a richly interconnected, linearly ordered set of computing modules, each containing two ranks of threshold elements interconnected to compute arbitrary Boolian functions stably. It is in these terms that we are at present thinking, but until and unless we succeed, we may turn to other notions.

This is the present stage of the problem of the function of the reticular formation, which is the last place where the homunculus hides, between the most elaborate analysis of sensory input and the most complicated coordination of motor output. By comparison with this problem, all other neurophysiological problems seem truly parochial.

# Eléments de la Théorie Générale des Codes

MAURICE NIVAT

*Centre National de la Recherche Scientifique*
*Institut Blaise Pascal*
*Paris, France*

## I. Définition

Considérons deux monoïdes libres $X^*$ et $Y^*$ engendrés respectivement par les alphabets $X$ et $Y$, que nous supposerons finis et possédant au moins deux éléments. Un monomorphisme de $Y^*$ dans $X^*$ est un *codage*. Rappelons qu'un tel monomorphisme, soit $\eta$ est défini par la donnée de l'ensemble $\{\eta(y_i) | y_i \in Y\}$ c'est-à-dire l'ensemble des images des générateurs de $Y^*$. En effet on a alors

$$\eta(y_1 y_2 \cdots y_n) = \eta(y_1)\, \eta(y_2) \cdots \eta(y_n)$$

$\eta$ étant un codage, l'ensemble $\eta(y_i)$ est un *code*.

On peut ainsi donner la définition suivante.

Un code sur $X$, soit $A$, est une partie du monoïde $X^*$ telle qu'il existe un ensemble non vide $Y$ et une bijection $\eta$ de $Y$ sur $A$, qui puisse être étendue en un monomorphisme de $Y^*$ dans $X^*$.

La théorie algébrique du codage se propose la caractérisation de ceux des sous-ensembles de $X^*$ qui sont des codes, c'est à dire en d'autres termes de ceux des sous-ensembles de $X^*$ qui engendrent un sous-monoïde libre (comme étant isomorphe à $Y^*$).

Ce sont aussi ceux des sous-ensembles de $X^*$ qui possèdent la propriété dite d'unique déchiffrabilité à savoir.

$A \subset X^*$ possède la propriété d'unique déchiffrabilité $\Leftrightarrow$

$$a_{i_1}, a_{i_2}, \ldots, a_{i_n}, a_{j_1}, a_{j_2}, \ldots, a_{j_p} \in A$$

et

$$a_{i_1} a_{i_2} \cdots a_{i_n} = a_{j_1} \cdots a_{j_p} \Rightarrow a_{i_1} = a_{j_1}$$

*Exemple*

Soit $X = \{a, b\}$ et $A = \{aa, ab, ba, bb\}$: $A$ est un code. En effet soit $Y = \{x, y, z, t\}$ et $\eta$ la bijection de $Y$ sur $A$.

$$\eta(x) = aa \quad \eta(y) = ab \quad \eta(z) = ba \quad \eta(t) = bb$$

$\eta$ s'étend en une application de $Y^*$ dans $X^*$: ainsi $\eta(xxytz) = aaaaabbbba$. C'est un homorphisme. Il est aisé de voir que c'est un monomorphisme à savoir $\forall g \in A^*$ $\exists f \in Y^*$ tel que $\eta(f) = g \cdot$ par ailleurs $f$ est unique. Déterminer $f$ connaissant $g$ est résoudre le problème du décodage.

## II. Une Condition Nécessaire et Suffisante de Codicité

Rappelons tout d'abord les conditions de F. Lévi, nécessaires et suffisantes pour qu'un monoïde $M$ soit un monoïde libre [1].

1. $\exists$ un homorphisme $\lambda$ de $M$ sur $N$ ensemble des entiers positifs, avec $\lambda^{-1}(0) = e$ (élément neutre de $M$).

2. Quelque soit $f_1, f_2, f_3, f_4 \in M$ tels que $f_1 f_2 = f_3 f_4$ on a l'une des deux situations suivantes:

$$- \exists f_5 \in M \qquad f_1 = f_3 f_5 \quad \text{et} \quad f_5 f_2 = f_4$$
$$- \exists f_6 \in M \qquad f_1 f_6 = f_3 \quad \text{et} \quad f_2 = f_6 f_4$$

Ces conditions sont évidemment vérifiées dans $X^*$, monoïde libre engendré par $X$, dont les éléments s'identifient aux suites finies d'éléments de $X$. L'homorphisme $\lambda$ associe à un élément de $X^*$ (ou mot) sa "longeur" (ou degré total). Nous pouvons ainsi démontrer la propriété suivante due à Schützenberger [2] et établie indépendamment par divers auteurs [3, 4]. On consultera aussi [5].

Pour que $A \subset X^*$ soit un code il faut et suffit que

$$\forall f \in X^* \qquad \left.\begin{matrix} A^* f \cap A^* \neq \phi \\ f A^* \cap A^* \neq \phi \end{matrix}\right\} \Rightarrow f \in A^* \tag{1}$$

Supposons que $A$ vérifie la condition (1) et que $A$ ne soit pas un code. Il existe $a_{i_1}, \ldots, a_{i_n}, a_{j_1} \cdots a_{j_p} \in A$ tels que $a_{i_1} \cdots a_{i_n} = a_{j_1} \cdots a_{j_p}$ avec $a_{i_1} \neq a_{j_1}$. On peut toujours supposer qu'il n'existe pas $n' < n$ et $p' < p$ tels que $a_{i_1} \cdots a_{i_{n'}} = = a_{j_1} \cdots a_{j_{p'}}$ et que $a_{j_1} = a_{i_1} h$, $h \in X^*$. J'ai alors $A^* h \cap A^* \neq \phi$ puisque $a_{i_1} h = a_{j_1}$ mais aussi $hA^* \cap A \neq \phi$ puisque de $a_{i_1} h a_{j_2} \cdots a_{j_p} = a_{i_1} a_{i_2} \cdots a_{i_n}$ on peut déduire $h a_{j_2} \cdots a_{j_p} = a_{i_2} \cdots a_{i_n}$. Or $h \notin A^*$ ce qui contredit la condition (1).

Réciproquement, supposons que $A$ ne vérifie pas la condition (1). Il existe alors $f \notin A$ tel que

$$a_{i_1} \cdots a_{i_m} f = a_{j_1} \cdots a_{j_n} \qquad a_{i_1} \neq a_{j_1}$$

et

$$f a_{k_1} \cdots a_{k_p} = a_{l_1} \cdots a_{l_q}$$

Mais alors

$$a_{i_1} \cdots a_{i_m} f a_{k_1} \cdots a_{k_p} = a_{j_1} \cdots a_{j_n} a_{k_1} \cdots a_{k_p} = a_{i_1} \cdots a_{i_m} a_{l_1} \cdots a_{l_q}$$

avec $a_{i_1} \neq a_{j_1}$ et ceci entraîne que $A$ n'est pas un code.

**Remarque 1.** On peut mettre la condition (1) sous la forme plus compacte suivante

$$\forall f \in X \qquad A^* f \cap f A^* \cap A^* \neq \phi \Rightarrow f \in A^* \tag{2}$$

en effet

$$A^* f \cap f A^* \cap A^* \neq \phi \Rightarrow f A^* \cap A^* \neq \phi \qquad \text{et} \qquad A^* f \cap A^* \neq \phi$$

réciproquement de

$$\left.\begin{array}{l} f a_1 = a_2 \\ a_3 f = a_4 \end{array}\right\} a_1, a_2, a_3, a_4 \in A^*$$

On déduit $f a_1 a_4 = a_2 a_4 = a_2 a_3 f$ donc $a_2 a_4 \in A^* f \cap f A^* \cap A$ qui est ainsi nonvide.

2. A partir de la condition de (1) on peut déduire la caractérisation suivante: $A'$ étant une partie de $X^*$ on construit la suite d'ensemble $A_0, A_1, A_2, \ldots, A_n, \ldots$ telle que

(a) $A_0 = A$
(b) $f \in A_{i+1} \Leftrightarrow \exists g, a,$ tels que $g \in A_i, a \in A$ et $gf = a$ ou $af = g$

On a alors: $A$ est un code $\Leftrightarrow \forall i \geqslant 1, A_i \cap A = \phi$. Ceci fournit une procédure automatique pour décider si un ensemble fini de mots est un code: en effet,

$$\forall f \in A_i, |f| < \max_{h \in A \cup A_i} |h| \qquad (|f| \text{ est la longueur de } f)$$

et par suite il n'y a qu'un nombre fini de $A_i$ distincts. Cette procédure est connue sous le nom d'algorithme de Sardinas et Patterson qui l'ont proposée dans [6]. Une nouvelle démonstration est donnée dans [7].

3. Il est intéressant de remarquer que la condition (1) caractérise les sous-groupes d'un groupe. Si $G$ est un groupe et $H$ un sous-groupe de $G$ il est clair en effet que

$$\forall f \in G \qquad \left.\begin{array}{l} Hf \cap H \neq \phi \\ fH \cap H \neq \phi \end{array}\right\} \Rightarrow f \in H \tag{3}$$

Réciproquement si une partie $H$ de $G$ vérifiie (3) on a

$e \in H$, $e$ élément neutre de $G$
$h \in H \Rightarrow h^{-1} \in H$ puisque $hh^{-1} = e$ et $h^{-1} h = e$
$h_1, h_2 \in H \Rightarrow h_1 h_2 \in H$ puisque $h_1^{-1} h_1 h_2 = h_2 \in H$ et $h_1 h_2 h_2^{-1} = h_1 \in H$

4. Enfin, anticipant un peu sur le suite, soit $\varphi$ un homorphisme de $X^*$ sur un monoïde quelconque $M$. Posons $M' = \varphi(A^*)$ et supposons $A^* = \varphi^{-1}(M')$. On vérifie aisèment que dans ces conditions

$$\forall m \in M \qquad \left.\begin{array}{l} mM' \cap M' \neq \phi \\ M'm \cap M' \neq \phi \end{array}\right\} \Rightarrow m \in M'$$

## III. Monoïde Quotient

Définissons sur le monoïde $X^*$ la relation d'équivalence

$$f\mathscr{R}_A g \Leftrightarrow \forall h_1, h_2 \in X^*(h_1 f h_2 \in A^* \Leftrightarrow h_1 g h_2 \in A^*)$$

autrement dit pour tout *contexte* $h_1, h_2$ tel que $h_1 f h_2$ soit dans $A^*$, $h_1 g h_2$ est aussi dans $A^*$ et réciproquement. $f$ et $g$ sont encore équivalents si il n'existe pas de contexte $h_1, h_2$ tel que $h_1 f h_2 \in A$ ni de contexte $k_1, k_2$ tel que $k_1 g k_2 \in A$. Il est facile de voir que $\mathscr{R}_A$ est une congruence, qui permet donc de définir un monoïde quotient $M$ et une application canonique $\varphi$ de $X^*$ sur $M$. On a de plus si $M' = \varphi(A) = \{\varphi(f) : f \in A\}$,

$$A^* = \varphi^{-1}(M') = \{f \in X^* : \varphi(f) \in M'\}$$

Autrement dit $A^*$ est une union de classes d'équivalence pour la relation $\mathscr{R}_A$. $\mathscr{R}_A$ est un cas particulier d'une congruence dont l'existence, et les propriétés essentielles ont été établies dans un cadre général en [8]. Une propriété impotante est la suivante: si $A$ est un code fini, $\mathscr{R}_A$, est d'index fini et par suite $M$ est un monoïde fini.

En effet à une classe d'équivalence correspond un sous-ensemble de $X^* \times X^*$, à savoir l'ensemble des contextes $h_1, h_2$ tels que si $f$ est un élément de cette classe $h_1 f h_2 \in A^*$. On remarque toutefois que si $A$ est fini et si $d = \max_{a \in A} |a|$ on peut se borner à considérer les contextes $h_1, h_2$ où $|h_1| \leqslant d$ et $|h_2| \leqslant d$ car si $h_1 f h_2 \in A^* \exists h_1', h_2'$ tels que $h_1' f h_2' \in A^*$ et $|h_1'| \leqslant d\, |h_2'| \leqslant d$. A une classe on fait alors correspondre un sous-ensemble de $X^d \times X^d$. Mais $X^d$ étant fini, il ne peut y avoir qu'un nombre fini de classes et ceci établit le propriété.

**Remarque.** La réciproque est fausse à savoir il peut exister des codes infinis, tels que la congruence associée soit d'index fini. On se reportera à une théorie des $K$-langages (ou évènements réguliers) dans laquelle on établit une caractérisation algébrique des ensembles dont la congruence est d'index fini, par exemple [9] ou [10].

## IV. Codes Complets

**Définition.** Un code $A$ sur $X$ est dit complet si et seulement si il n'existe pas de partie $A' \neq A$ de $X^*$, contenant $A$ et qui soit elle même un code.

Etablissons la propriété [11]: L'ensemble des messages d'un code complet $A$ sur $X$ intersecte tous les idéaux bilatères de $X^*$: autrement dit $\forall f \in X^* \; \exists f_1, f_2 \in X^*$ tels que $f_1 f f_2 \in A^*$.

Supposons en effet que $A \cap X^* f X^* = \phi$. Si de plus $f$ n'est pas une sequipuissance, i.e., si $\nexists u, v \in X^*, u \neq e$ tels que $f = uvu$ alors $A' = A \cup \{f\}$ est un code.

Considérons $x_{i_1}, x_{i_2}, \ldots, x_{i_m}, x_{i_1}, \ldots, x_{j_p} \in A'$ tels que

$$x_{i_1} x_{i_2} \cdots x_{i_m} = x_{i_1} \cdots x_{j_p} \tag{4}$$

Ou bien:

1. Pour aucun $l \leqslant m$ et aucun $l \leqslant p$ on n'a $x_{i_k} = x_{j_l} = f$. Alors comme $A$ est un code $m = p$ et $x_{i_1} = x_{j_1}$.

2. Supposons $x_{i_k} = f$. Je dis qu'alors $\exists l \leqslant p$ tel que $x_{j_l} = f$ en effet si ce n'était le cas on aurait $A^* \cap X^* f X^* \neq \phi$. Donc on a

$$x_{j_1} \cdots x_{i_{k-1}} f x_{i_{k+1}} \cdots = x_{j_1} \cdots x_{i_{l-1}} f x_{j_{l+1}} \cdots \tag{5}$$

et l'on peut supposer que

$$\begin{array}{ll} \forall k' < k & x_{i_{k'}} \neq f \\ \forall l' < l & x_{i_{l'}} \neq f \end{array}$$

Supposons alors $x_{i_1} \cdots x_{i_{k-1}} \neq x_{j_1} \cdots x_{j_{l-1}}$, par exemple,

$$x_{i_1} \cdots x_{i_{k-1}} = x_{j_1} \cdots x_{j_{l-1}} h$$

L'hypothèse $h = ff'$ est exclue car on aurait $A^* \cap X^* f X^* \neq \phi$ donc $f = hf'$. Mais alors

$$x_{i_1} \cdots x_{i_{k-1}} f' = x_{j_1} \cdots x_{i_{l-1}} f \qquad \text{d'où } f = f' h'$$

Or $f = hf' = f' h'$ entraîne que $f$ est une sesqui-puissance. D'après notre hypothèse $f$ n'en est pas une, par suite

$$x_{i_1} \cdots x_{i_{k-1}} = x_{j_1} \cdots x_{j_{l-1}} \qquad \text{soit } x_{i_1} = x_{j_1} \cdots$$

On peut dans l'égalité (5) simplifier à gauche par $x_{i_1} \cdots x_{i_{k-1}} f = x_{j_1} \cdots x_{j_{l-1}} f$ et recommencer. $A'$ est bien un code.

Maintenant si $f$ est une sesqui-puissance considérons la première "lettre" de $f$ soit $a \in X, f = af'$ et soit $b \neq a, b \in X$. Le mot $g \in X^*$, $g = fb^{|f|}$ n'est pas une sesqui-puissance et $X^*gX^* \cap A \neq \phi$. La propriété est établie (cf [7]). Le lecteur étendra sans peine cette démonstration pour établir la propriété légèrement plus forte:

(a) Si $A$ est complet, $\forall f \in X^*$, $A^* \cap A^*fX^* \neq \phi$. C'est cette propriété qui va vous servir à établir.

(b) Si $A$ est un code complet fini (ou plus généralement un $k$-langage) alors $\exists \mathbf{a} \in A^*$ tel que

$$\forall f \in X^*, \exists f' \in X^*, \mathbf{a}ff' \in A^*$$

Supposons que ce ne soit pas le cas autrement dit $\forall a \in A^*$, $\exists f \in X^*$ tel que $\sigma(af) = \phi$ en appelant $\sigma(g) = \{g' \in X^* | gg' \in A^*\}$ et établissons qu'alors $\exists g \in X^*$ tel que $\forall a \in A^*$, $\sigma(ag) = \phi$ ce qui contredit (5).

La relation d'équivalence compatible à droite $\sigma f_1 = \sigma f_2$ étant d'index fini si $\mathscr{R}_A$ est d'index fini on peut prendre un représentant dans chacune de celles de ces classes qui sont contenues dans $A^*$ soit $a_1, \cdots, a_s$. $\exists a_1'$ tel que $\sigma(a_1 a_1') = \phi$. Considérons $a_2 a_1'$ ou bien $\sigma(a_2 a_1') = \phi$ au quel cas on prendra $a_2' = a_1'$ ou bien prenons $a_2''$ tel que $a_2 a_1' a_2'' \in A^*$ et $a_2'''$ tel que $\sigma(a_2 a_1' a_2'' a_2''') = \phi$. $a_2'''$ existe par hypothèse. En ce cas on prendra $a_2' = a_1' a_2'' a_2'''$. Dans les deux cas $\sigma(a_1 a_2') = \sigma(a_2 a_2') = \phi$. On poursuit la construction: $a_s'$ jouit de la propriété voulue. Nous appellerons *quasi-compact* un tel code.

La propriété établie au début de ce paragraphe l'a été pour la première fois dans [11]. La réciproque nécessite au moins l'hypothèse de finitude du code comme le montre l'exemple du code $A = \{b^{2+|f|}af | f \in X^*\}$ qui intersecte tous les idéaux bilatères mais n'est pas complet $A \cup \{ba\}$ est encore un code. Mais il semble qu'il faille faire également d'autres hypothèses (par exemple; le monoïde image $\mathscr{R}_A$ se compose d'une seule $\mathscr{D}$-classe).

## V. Décodage—Automates Finis

Si $A$ est un code fini nous avons vu que la congruence $\mathscr{R}_A$ était d'index fini, ainsi d'ailleurs que l'équivalence compatible à droite $\sigma f_1 = \sigma f_2$. Ceci nous permet de construire un automate fini qui lisant un mot $g \in X^*$ (de gauche à droite) décide si oui ou non $g \in A^*$. La construction est standard (cf. [10]).

Considérons $K$, ensemble de tous les facteurs droits propres des mots de $A$, $e$ (élément neutre de $X^*$) étant considéré un tel facteur. Nous associons à un mot $g$, le sous ensemble $\sigma' g$ de $K$ tel que

$$k \in \sigma' g \Leftrightarrow gk \in A$$

$\sigma' g_1 = \sigma' g_2$ est une relation d'équivalence compatible à droite (de fait c'est la même que l'équivalence $\sigma g_1 = \sigma g_2$).

Identifions les différents ensembles $\sigma' g$ avec les états d'un automate dont les transitions seront données par

$$\sigma' g \cdot x = \sigma'(gx) \qquad \forall x \in X$$

Il est immédiat que l'automate commençant sa lecture dans l'état $\sigma' e$, et lisant le mot $g$, celui-ci appartient à $A^*$ si et seulement si en fin de lecture l'automate se trouve dans l'état $\sigma' g$ tel que $e \in \sigma' g$. Prenons un exemple sur $X = \{x,y\}$:

$$A = \{x, xxy, yxy, yy\}$$

d'où $K = \{e, y, xy\}$. Tableau 1 suivant permet de construire les $\sigma' g$.

TABLE 1

| | $e$ | $y$ | $xy$ | Etats de l'automate |
|---|---|---|---|---|
| $e$ | × | | | $t_1$ |
| $x$ | × | | × | $t_2 - t_2 = t_1 x$ |
| $y$ | | × | × | $t_3 - t_3 = t_1 y$ |
| $xx$ | × | × | × | $t_4 - t_4 = t_2 x$ |
| $xy$ | | × | × | $t_3 - t_3 = t_2 y$ |
| $yx$ | | × | | $t_5 - t_5 = t_3 x$ |
| $yy$ | × | | | $t_1 - t_1 = t_3 y$ |
| $xxx$ | × | × | × | $t_4 - t_4 = t_4 x$ |
| $xxy$ | × | × | × | $t_4 - t_4 = t_4 y$ |
| $xyx$ | | × | | $t_6 - t_6 = t_5 x$ |
| $xyy$ | × | | | $t_1 - t_1 = t_5 y$ |

Notre automate peut être représenté par Fig. 1. Les états *finaux* contenant $e$ sont $\{t_1, t_2, t_4\}$. Ainsi si $g = xyxyxxyxyx$ l'automate prendra la suite d'états 2, 5, 3, 1, 2, 4, 4, 4, 4, 4 et comme $t_4$ est un état final on peut conclure $g \in A^*$.

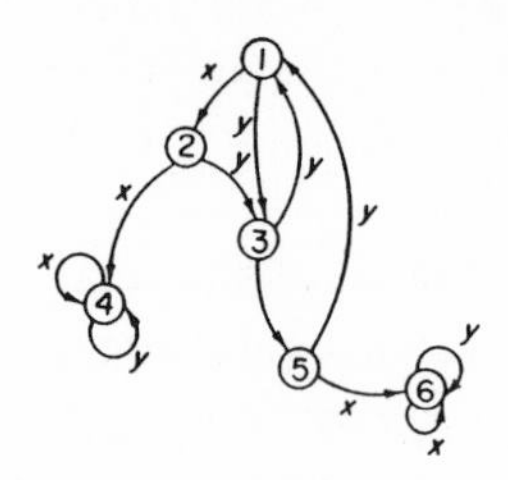


FIG. 1

Il y a quelque arbitraire à considérer un automate de gauche à droite et cette construction peut se répéter identiquement pour donner naissance à un automate de droite à gauche. On considèrera $H$, l'ensemble des facteurs gauches propres, $e$ compris et l'équivalence compatible à gauche définie par

$$\lambda' g_1 = \lambda' g_2 \qquad \text{où} \qquad \lambda' g = \{h \in H \,|\, hg \in A^*\}$$

Les états de l'automate seront identifiés avec les ensembles $\lambda' g$ et les transitions seront données par

$$\forall x \in X \qquad x \cdot \lambda' g = \lambda'(xg)$$

Imaginons maintenant que les deux automates fonctionnent simultanément et que $g$ ait été factorisé en

$$g = g_1 g_2 \qquad \text{avec } e \in \sigma' g_1 \text{ et } e \in \lambda' g_2$$

Alors on peut affirmer que si $g_1$ qui appartient à $A^*$ se factorise en $a_{i_1} \cdots a_{i_m}$, $a_{i_1}, a_{i_2}, \ldots, a_{i_m} \in A$ et $g_2$ se factorise en $a_{j_1} \cdots a_{j_p}, a_{i_1}, \ldots, a_{i_p} \in A$, alors $g = a_{i_1} \cdots a_{i_m} a_{j_1} \cdots a_{j_p}$. C'est ce double automate qui permet le *décodage* proprement dit à savoir: $Y$ étant donné et $\eta$ surjection de $Y$ sur $A$ on peut grâce à ces deux automates déterminer pour un $g$ donné, $g \in A^*$, le mot $f \in Y^*$ tel que $\eta(f) = g$. On trouvera en [12] une définition et quelques propriétés des transducteurs finis bilatères, qui résultent de la fusion de deux automates lisant de gauche à droite et de droite à gauche et qui sont les machines les plus propres à résoudre le problème du décodage.

## VI. Automates à Bandes

Toutefois il est intéressant de pouvoir décoder en n'effectuant qu'une lecture de gauche à droite, ne serait-ce que pour pouvoir décoder un message en cours de transmission. Pour cela nous allons reprendre l'automate fini de gauche à droite dont l'ensemble des états s'identifie à $\{\sigma' g | g \in X^*\}$ et nous le doterons d'un certain nombre de *bandes*.

Supposons que cette machine au moment de lire la lettre $x$ du mot $g = g' x g''$ ait déjà enregistré sur un certain nombre de bande les mots $f_i \in Y^*$ tels que

$$\eta(f_i) = g'_i \text{ ou } g' = g'_i h'_i \qquad h'_i \in H$$

A chaque $h'_i$ correspond un ou plusieurs $k \in K$ tel que $h'_i k \in A$. Un tel $k$, est bien évidemment un élément de $\sigma' g'$. Très exactement

$$\sigma' g' = \{k \in K | \exists h_i, h_i k \in A\}$$

Par suite le nombre de bandes, chaque bande correspondant à un $h'_i$, est borné par *card* $\sigma' g'$.

Que se passe-t-il au moment où l'on lit $x$? On examine toutes les bandes et l'on opère de la façon suivante:

1. Si $h_i x \notin A$, $h_i x \notin H$ on efface la bande.
2. Si $h_i x \notin A$, $h_i x \in H$ on ne fait rien.
3. Si $h_i x \in A$, $h_i x \notin H$ on écrit sur la bande la lettre $y \in Y$ telle que $\eta(y) = h_i x$. Si bien qu'il y a alors sur la bande le mot $f_i y$ avec $\eta(f_i y) = g' x$. La bande est désormais indicée par $e$ (qui est un élément de $H$).
4. Si $h_i x \in A$, $h_i x \in H$ on dédouble la bande. Autrement dit on recopie $f$ sur une bande, bande qui est alors indicée par $h_i x$. Sur la bande contenant primitivement $f_i$ on opère comme en 3.

Enfin l'automate passe dans l'état $\sigma' g' \cdot x = \sigma'(g' x)$.

*N.B.*: *On pourrait de fait utiliser comme ensemble des états un ensemble isomorphe à l'ensemble des* $h'_i$ *avec les transitions*

$$\{h'_i\} \cdot x = \begin{cases} \{h'_i x\} & \text{si } \{h'_i x\} \cap A = \phi \\ \{h'_i x\} \setminus A \cup \{e\} & \text{si } \{h'_i x\} \cap A \neq \phi \end{cases}$$

Il est assez clair qu'à un moment donné il existe au plus une bande indicée par $e$, si $A$ est un code. En particulier si $g \in A^*$ après lecture de la dernière lettre de $g$ une bande et une seule est indicée par $e$: c'est celle-ci qui contient le mot $f$ tel que $\eta(f) = g$.

## VII. Codes à Délai Borné

Imaginons la machine précédemment décrite en train de fonctionner c'est à dire recevant un message $g$. Les divers déchiffrages possibles (à un moment donné) s'inscrivent sur des bandes dont on sait a priori borner le nombre. Ceci ne signifie toutefois pas que la "quantité de mémoire" nécessaire soit bornée: en effet il peut se faire que la longueur de plusieurs bandes croisse en même temps que la longueur de $g$. Pour s'en convaincre il suffira de considérer l'exemple suivant:

$$Y = \{x, y, z\},\ X = \{a, b\}$$

$$\eta(x) = a,\ \eta(y) = ab,\ \eta(z) = bb$$

$g = abb \ldots bb \ldots$. Pendant toute la durée de la lecture deux bandes seront utilisées sur lesquelles seront écrits les mots $xzz \ldots z \ldots$ et $yzz \ldots zz \ldots$, respectivement.

Il faut attendre la lecture de la dernière lettre de $g$ pour savoir que

(a) Si $g = ab^{2p}$ à la fin de l'opération c'est la bande $xzz\ldots$ qui est indicée par $e$ donc $f = \eta^{-1}(g)$ est le mot $xz^p$.

(b) Si $g = ab^{2p+1}$ à la fin c'est la bande $yzz\ldots$ qui est indicée par $e$ et par suite $\eta^{-1}(g) = yz^p$.

On ne peut donc a priori borner la mémoire nécessaire au déchiffrement sauf si le code jouit de la propriété suivante: il existe un entier $p$ tel que si à un moment donné une bande contient plus de $p$ caractères, mettons $q$, le mot $f$ formé des $q-p$ premiers caractères est tel que $\eta^{-1}(g) = ff'$. Cette propriété est dite propriété de délai borné (de gauche à droite): elle entraîne qu'il suffit pour décoder d'avoir à sa disposition des bandes (en nombre inférieur à $\max_{g \in X^*} (card\,(\sigma' g))$) de longueur égale à $p$.

Nous allons voir en reformulant cette condition tout son intérêt.

**Définition.** Nous dirons que $A$ est à délai borné de gauche à droite si et seulement si

$$\exists p \in N \qquad \text{tel que } \forall a \in A^*, \forall a' \in A^p, \forall f \in X^* \qquad aa'f \in A^* \Rightarrow a'f \in A^* \tag{6}$$

Pour $p = 0$ (6) se formule de la façon suivante

$$\forall a \in A^*, af \in A^* \Rightarrow f \in A^* \tag{6'}$$

Les codes correspondants jouent un rôle prépondérant. On dit aussi qu'ils sont préfixes (de gauche à droite).

Etablissons ici une propriété: $A$ est un délai borné $p$ si et seulement si le code $B = A^p$ est à délai borné 1.

En effet considérons $b_1 \in B^*, b_2 \in B, f \in X^*$ et supposons $b_1 b_2 f \in B^*$. $A$ étant à délai borné $p$ on a $b_2 f \in A^*$. Il suffit alors d'appliquer le lemme évident

$$\left.\begin{matrix} ab \in B^* \\ a \in B, b \in A^* \end{matrix}\right\} \Rightarrow b \in B^*$$

pour conclure $b_2 f \in B^*$ ce qui démontre la première implication.

Réciproquement supposons $B$ à délai borné 1 et soit

$$aa_1 \cdots a_p f \in A^* \qquad \text{où} \qquad a \in A^*, a_1, \ldots, a_p \in A, f \in X^*$$

Il existe $a' \in A^*$ tel que $a' a \in B^*$. Il existe $f' \in A^*$ tel que $a' aa_1 \cdots a_p ff' \in B^*$. On peut alors conclure du fait que $B$ est à délai 1, $a_1 \cdots a_p ff' \in B^*$ ou encore $a_1 \cdots a_p ff' \in A^*$. Rapprochant alors $a_1 \cdots a_p ff' \in A^*$ et

$aa_1 \cdots a_p f \in A^*$, la condition de codicité implique
$a_1 \cdots a_p f \in A^*$ ce qui achève la démonstration

Par ailleurs il découle immédiatement de la définition et du fait que $A$ est un code fini complet à délai borné $p$ de gauche à droite que

$$\forall a \in A^p, \forall f \in X^*, \exists f' \in X, aff' \in A^* \tag{7}$$

En effet nous savons qu'il existe alors un élément $\mathbf{a} \in A^*$ tel que $\forall f \in X^*$, $\exists f' \in X^*$, $\mathbf{a}ff' \in A^*$, en particulier $\forall a \in A^p$, $\forall f \in X^*$, $\exists f' \in X^*$, $\mathbf{a}aff' \in A^*$. Le délai borné entraîne alors $aff' \in A$

On peut évidemment définir une motion de délai borné de droite à gauche: $A$ est à délai borné $p$ de droite à gauche $\Leftrightarrow$

$$\forall b \in A^*, \forall b' \in A^p, \forall f \in X^*$$

$$fb' b \in A^* \Rightarrow fb' \in A^*$$

On transpose aisément les deux propriétés énoncées plus haut.

L'importance pratique des codes à délai borné donne au problème de leur construction un certain intérêt. De fait nous venons plus loin qu'il n'est pas difficile de construire les codes préfixes. Par ailleurs en 1957 Gilbert et Moore [13] ont posé la question de savoir si un code peut être à la fois fini complet non préfixe et à délai borné des deux côtés. A. A. Markov [14] (voir aussi [15]) a énoncé un théorème plus fort: Il n'existe pas de code fini complet, nonpréfixe et à délai borné (d'un seul côté).

La démonstration s'appuie sur deux lemmes.

1. Si $A$ est fini, complet sur $X$, pour tout $x \in X$, $\exists n \in N$ tel que $x^n \in A$. En effet $A$ est quasi-compact et $\forall k \in N$, $\exists f \in X^*$ tel que $\mathbf{a}x^k f \in A^*$. En prenant $k$ assez grand, la longueur des mots de $A'$ étant bornée, on démontre le lemme.

2. Si $A$ est nonpréfixe mais à délai borné, de gauche à droite par exemple il existe $v \in X^*$ tel que $vX^* \cap A^* = \phi$. En effet supposons que $\forall f \in X^*$, $fX^* \cap A^* \neq \phi$ et considérons $f_1, f_2 \cdots f_n$ tels que

$$a_2 = a_1 f_1 \qquad \text{avec } a_1, a_2 \in A$$
$$f_2 \in f_1 X^* \cap A^*$$
$$f_i \in f_{i-1} X^* \cap A^*$$

Il est assez clair que pour $i$ assez grand le mot $a_1 f_1 \cdots f_i$ contredit au délai borné de $A$.

De ces deux lemmes et de la quasi-compacité Markov conclut que pour un certain $n' : x^{n'} vX^* \cap A^* = \phi$ or ceci n'est point vrai si $x^n fX^* \cap A^* \neq \phi$ pour tout $f \in X^*$ (propriété qui découle du fait que $A$ est un délai borné 1).

Bornons nous à signaler que néanmoins le théorème est vrai. Une démonstration en a été donnée par M. P. Schützenberger [16].

## VIII. Codes Préfixes

L'intérêt des codes préfixes est considérablement accru par ce théorème qui affirme qu'un code complet fini est soit préfixe soit à délai nonborné (dans chaque sens). Par ailleurs le décodage d'un code préfixe est immédiat puisqu'il suffit d'une seule bande.

Revenons sur la définition: $A$ est un code préfixe de gauche à droite $\Leftrightarrow$

$$\forall a \in A, \forall f \in X^*, af \in A^* \Rightarrow f \in A^*$$

La proposition que voici est immédiate.

1. Pour qu'une partie $A$ de $X^*$ soit un code préfixe de gauche à droite il faut et suffit qu'aucun mot de $A$ ne soit facteur gauche d'un autre mot de $A$. En effet si $af \in A^*$, $a \in A$ on peut écrire $af = a_{i_1} \cdots a_{i_n}$ et la condition entraîne $a = a_{i_1}$ d'où $f = a_{i_2} \cdots a_{i_n} \in A$. $A$ est donc un code puisque $A^* f \cap A^* \neq \phi \Rightarrow f \in A^*$ par répétition du même argument.

Un code préfixe $A$ est dit complet $\Leftrightarrow$ il n'existe pas de mot $f \in X^*$ tel que $A \cup \{f\}$ soit un code préfixe.

Une caractérisation immédiate est la suivante:

2. Pour qu'un code $A$ préfixe de gauche à droite soit complet il faut et il suffit que tout $f \in X^*$ ait au moins un facteur gauche dans $A$ (ou soit facteur gauche d'un mot de $A$).

C'est suffisant car quelque $f$ que l'on essaye de rajouter à $A$ pour former le code $A \cup \{f\}$ celui-ci n'est pas préfixe. C'est nécessaire: supposons en effet qu'il existe un $f$ qui ne remplisse pas la condition ci-dessus $A \cup \{f\}$ est alors une partie de $X^*$ qui satisfait à proposition 1 et $A$ n'est pas préfixe complet. Il suit de (2) que

$$\forall f \in X^*, \exists f' \in X^*, ff' \in A^*$$

On peut représenter un code préfixe, sur un alphabet $X$, au moyen d'un arbre. Considérons en effet l'arbre ci-contre et désignons chaque sommet pendant par le chemin qui le relie à la racine, $a$ désignant une arête "gauche," $b$ une arête "droite." On obtient ainsi pour l'arbre [Fig. 2(a)]

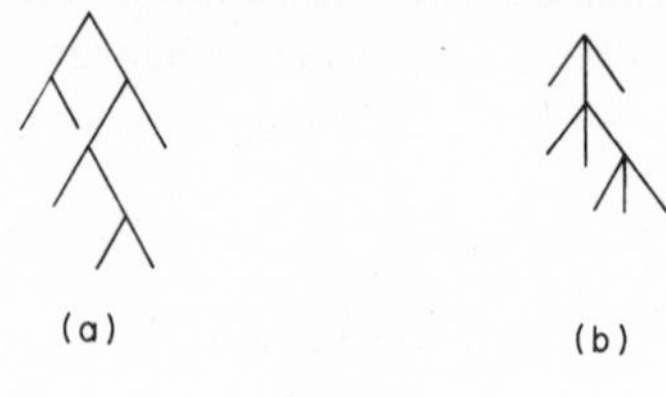

FIG. 2.

$$\{aa, ab, baa, baba, babb, bb\}$$

Figure 2(b) correspond au code

$$\{a, ba, bb, bcb, bcc, c\}$$

Il est clair qu'à un code complet correspond un arbre saturé en ce sens que de tout sommet autre que pendant, part le nombre maximum d'arêtes (à savoir $card(X)$). On a donc là un moyen de construire tous les codes préfixes (dans un sens ou dans l'autre). Ceci ne signifie pourtant pas que la structure de ces codes soit sans mystère comme nous allons le voir.

## IX. Composition des Codes

Considérons $X^*$, $Y^*$, $Z^*$ et $A$ (resp. $B$) un code sur $X$ (resp. $Y$). La bijection $\lambda$ (resp. $\mu$) de $Y$ sur $A$ (resp. $Z$ sur $B$) s'étend en monomorphisme de $Y^*$ dans $X^*$ (resp. $Z^*$ dans $Y^*$) $\eta = \mu \circ \lambda$ est un monomorphisme de $Z^*$ dans $X^*$ donc un codage. Le code correspondant est un code $C$ sur $X$ obtenu en prenant les images par $\lambda$ des mots de $B$, c'est à dire en codant les mots de $B$ au moyen de $A$. C'est ce qui fait que l'on parle parfois de *surcodage*. Nous obtenons $C = B \otimes A$.

*Exemple*

$$X = \{a, b\} \qquad A = \{a, ba, bb\}$$

$$Y = \{u, v, w\} \qquad \lambda\mu = a, \lambda v = ba, \lambda w = bb$$

$$B = \{u, uv, vv, wv, w\}$$

Le code $C = B \otimes A$ est le code

$$\{a, aba, baba, bb, bbba\}$$

Il est intéressant de constater sur cet exemple que en composant deux codes préfixes, l'une de gauche à droite l'autre de droite à gauche l'on obtient un code qui n'est préfixe d'aucun coté.

Par contre supposons $A$ comme ci-dessus et

$B' = \{u, vu, vv, vw, w\}$ qui est préfixe de gauche à droite

$B \otimes A = \{a, baa, baba, babb, bb\}$ est également un code préfixe de gauche à droite

On a la propriété.

Si $A$ et $B$ sont préfixes, de même côté, $B \otimes A$ est préfixe. En effet aucun mot de $B \otimes A$ ne peut être facteur gauche (ou droit selon le cas) d'un autre mot de $B \otimes A$ puisque $A$ étant préfixe à gauche

$$\forall a_1, a_2 \in (B \otimes A)^*, \forall f \in X^* \qquad a_1 f = a_2 \Rightarrow f \in A^*$$

donc $(\lambda^{-1} a_1)(\lambda^{-1} f) = \lambda^{-1} a_2$ qui contredit le fait que $B$ est lui aussi préfixe à gauche.

Si de plus $A$ et $B$ sont complets, $B \otimes A$ l'est aussi. En effet $\forall f \in X^*$ a au moins un facteur gauche dans $B \otimes A$ (ou bien un facteur gauche d'un mot de $B \otimes A$). Le lecteur s'en convaincara aisèment.

Dans le cas général si on ne peut sans hypothèses supplèmentaires démontrer que $B \otimes A$ est complet si $A$ et $B$ le sont on remarque du moins que $A, B$ complets $\Rightarrow$ $B \otimes A$ intersecte tous les idéaux bilatères. En effet soit $f \in X^*$, $A$ étant complet $\exists f_1, f_2 \in X^*, f_1 f f_2 \in A^*$, mais alors si $g = \lambda^{-1}(f_1 f f_2)$, $g \in Y$:*

$$\exists\ g_1, g_2 \in Y^* \text{ tels que } g_1 g g_2 \in B^*$$

$$\lambda(g_1 g g_2) = \lambda(g_1) f_1 f f_2 \lambda(g_2) \in (B \otimes A)^*$$

## X. Conjectures sur la Structure des Codes

**Définition.** Un code $A$ sur $X$ est dit *maximal* si et seulement si il n'existe pas de code $B$ sur $X$, $B \neq X$, $B \neq A$ tel que $A^* \subset B^*$. Un code maximal est évidemment complet.

Réciproquement il existe des codes complets nonmaximaux c'est le cas des codes complets composés. Très généralement on a en effet $(B \otimes A)^* \subset A^*$. Considérons un code fini complet nonmaximal $B$, $B^* \subset A^*$, inclusion stricte. $A$ est fini complet. En effet $B^* \subset A^* \Rightarrow \forall b \in B : b \in A^*$.

Appelons $A'$ l'ensemble

$$A' = \{a \in A \mid \exists b \in B, b \in A^* a A^*\}$$

$A'$ est fini puisque $\forall a \in A'$, $|a| \leqslant \max_{b \in B} |b|$. C'est un code puisque $A' \subset A$.

Enfin $A'$ est complet puisque s'il existait un $f \in X^*$ tel que $A' \cup \{f\}$ soit un code à fortiori $B \cup \{f\}$ serait un code (remarquer $B^* \subset A'^*$). D'où $A' = A$ qui est bien fini complet.

Soit par ailleurs $Y$ un ensemble fini, $\lambda$ une bijection de $Y$ sur $A$, $\lambda$ désignant aussi le monomorphisme de $Y^*$ sur $A^*$ défini par cette bijection. A tout $b \in B$ on peut associer $\lambda^{-1}(b)$ défini puisque b $\in A^*$.

Soit $B' = \lambda^{-1}(B) = \{\lambda^{-1}(b) | b \in B\}$, $B'$ est un code sur $Y$. En effet s'il existait $f \in Y^*$ tel que $B'^* f \cap f B'^* \cap B'^* \neq \phi, f \notin B'^*$, on aurait

$$B^* \lambda f \cap \lambda f B^* \cap B \neq \phi \qquad \text{avec } \lambda f \notin B^*$$

$B'$ est par ailleurs complet.

Comme il est clair que $B = B' \otimes A$ on peut énoncer: Tout code fini complet nonmaximal est composé de deux codes finis complets. Supposons $B = B' \otimes A$ et $A$ lui-même composé $A = A' \otimes C$. $B = B' \times (A' \otimes C)$ est aussi égal à $(B' \otimes A') \otimes C$. (Bien que noté différemment la composition des codes jouit des mêmes propriétés d'associativité que celle des monomorphismes qu'ils définissent.) Par ailleurs remarquons que si $B = B' \otimes A$

$$\sum_{b' \in B'} |b'| < \sum_{b \in B} |b| \qquad \text{et} \qquad \sum_{a \in A} |a| < \sum_{b \in B} |b|$$

Par suite le processus de décomposition se termine et l'on a: Tout code fini complet nonmaximal est composé d'un nombre fini de codes maximaux finis.

Les conjectures annoncés dues essentiellement à M. P. Schützenberger portent sur la structure des codes maximaux finis:

*Conjecture.* Tout code maximal fini possède l'une des propriétés suivantes:

1. $A$ est préfixe de gauche à droite, en outre $A^*$ contient un idéal à gauche de $X^*$ (i.e., $\exists \mathbf{a} \in X, X^* \mathbf{a} \subset A^*$). $A$ contient un mot $a'$ tel que $fa' \in A^* \Rightarrow f \in A^*$.
2. Identique à (1) en inversant le sens.
3. $A$ est *bipréfixe*. Ceci peut se caractèriser par $\forall f \in X^*, A^* f A^* \cap A^* \neq \phi \Rightarrow f \in A^*$.

## XI. Codes Synchronisant Bilatères

**Définition.** Un code $A$ est dit synchronisant bilatère si et seulement $\exists a_1, a_2 \in A$ tels que

$$f_1 a_2 a_2 f_2 \in A \Rightarrow f_1 a_1 \in A^* \qquad \text{et} \qquad a_2 f_2 \in A^*$$

Un code préfixe de gauche à droite, contenant un idéal à gauche de $X^*$ est synchronisant bilatère. En effet si $\mathbf{a}$ est tel $X^* \mathbf{a} \subset A^*$ l'on a $\mathbf{a} \in A$.

Pour tout $b \in A$ considérons $f_1 \mathbf{a} b f_2 \in A^*$. On sait que $f_1 \mathbf{a} \in A^*$ mais aussi $b f_2 \mathbf{a}$ donc

$$A^* b f_2 \cap A^* \neq \phi$$
$$b f_2 A^* \cap A^* \neq \phi$$

et ceci entraîne $bf_2 \in A^*$. Ainsi quelque soit $b \in A$ le couple $(\mathbf{a}, b)$ synchronise. De même un code préfixe de droite à gauche contenant un idéal à droite est synchronisant bilatère.

On remarque d'ailleurs que si $A$ est préfixe de gauche à droite (resp. de droite à gauche) la condition d'être synchronisant bilatère entraîne qu'il contient un idéal à gauche (resp. à droite). Au contraire un code $A$ sur $X$ bipréfixe ne peut étre synchronisant bilatère s'il est complet et distinct de $X$. En effet supposons qu'il existe un couple synchronisant $a_1, a_2$.

Soit $f \in X^*, f \notin A^*$. $A$ étant préfixe de gauche à droite, complet

$$\exists f' \in X^*, f a_1 a_2 f' \in A^*$$

d'où $fa_1 \in A^*$ mais ceci implique $A'$ étant bipréfixe $f \in A^*$ contradiction. Montrons enfin que $B, A$ synchronisant bilatère $\Leftrightarrow B \otimes A$ synchronisant bilatère si $B$ est complet. Supposons que $b_1, b_2$ synchronisent dans $B$, $a_1, a_2$ synchronisent dans $A$.

Considérons le couple $\lambda(b_1)\lambda(b_2)a_1 a_2 \lambda(b_1), \lambda(b_2)a_1 a_2 \lambda(b_1)\lambda(b_2)$ et remarquons tout d'abord que ces deux éléments sont des $(B \times A)^*$. En effet $B$ intersectant tous les idéaux bilatères $\exists y_1, y_2$ tels que $y_1 b_1 b_2 \lambda^{-1}(a_1)\lambda^{-1}(a_2)$ $b_1 b_2 y_2 \in B^*$ d'où $b_2 \lambda^{-1} a_1 \lambda^{-1} a_2 b_1 \in B^*$.

Par ailleurs soit

$$f_1 \lambda(b_1)\lambda(b_2)a_1 a_2 \lambda(b_1)\lambda(b_2)a_1 a_2 \lambda(b_1)\lambda(b_2) f_2 \in (B \times A)^*$$

comme $(B \times A)^* \subset A^*$ on a

$$f_1 \lambda(b_1)\lambda(b_2)a_1 \in A^* \text{ d'où } \exists g_1 \in Y^*, f_1 \lambda(b_1)\lambda(b_2)a_1 = \lambda(g_1)$$
$$a_2 \lambda(b_1)\lambda(b_2) f_2 \in A^* \text{ d'où } \exists g_2 \in Y^*, a_2 \lambda(b_1)\lambda(b_1) f_2 = \lambda(g_2)$$

Par suite on a

$$g_1 \lambda^{-1}(a_2) b_1 b_2 \lambda^{-1}(a_1) g_2 \in B^*$$

soit

$$g_1 \lambda^{-1}(a_2) b_1 \in B^* \qquad \text{et} \qquad b_2 \lambda^{-1}(a_1) a_2 \in B^*$$

Mais ceci signifie que $f_1 \lambda(b_1)\lambda(b_2)a_1 a_2 \lambda(b_1) \in (B \otimes A)^*$ et $\lambda(b_2)a_1 a_2 \lambda(b_1)$ $\lambda(b_2) f_2 \in (B \otimes A)^*$ ce qui montre que $B \otimes A$ est synchronisant bilatère.

Réciproquement si $B \otimes A$ est synchronisant bilatère, $B$ et $A$ ($B$ complet) sont synchronisants soient $c_1, c_2$ tels que $f_1 c_1 c_2 f_2 \in (B \otimes A)^* \Rightarrow$

$$f_1 c_1 \in (B \otimes A)^* \qquad \text{et} \qquad c_2 f_2 \in (B \otimes A)^*$$

Il est immédiat que le couple $\lambda^{-1}(c_1)$, $\lambda^{-1}(c_2)$ synchronise dans $B$.

Considérons $f_1, f_2$ avec $f_1 c_1 c_2 f_2 \in A^*$. $B$ étant complet $\exists g_1, g_2$ avec $\lambda(g_1) f_1 c_1 c_2 f_2 \lambda(g_2) \in (B \times A)^*$ d'où $\lambda(g_1) f_1 c_1 \in A^*$ et $c_2 f_2 \lambda(g_2) \in A^*$. On a ainsi $A^* f_1 c_1 \cap A^* \neq \phi$ et $f_1 c_1 A^* \cap A^* \neq \phi$ puisque $f_1 c_1 c_2 f_2 \lambda(g_2) \in A^*$ d'où $f_1 c_1 \in A^*$ de même $c_2 f_2 \in A^*$. $A$ est bien synchronisant bilatère.

Ainsi si les conjectures du Sec. X sont vérifiées on aura:

Un code complet fini est synchronisant bilatère si et seulement si il est composé de codes préfixes synchronisant bilatère, c'est-à-dire si dans sa décomposition n'entre aucun code bipréfixe.

## Références


1. F. W. Levi, *Bull. Calcutta Math. Soc.* **36**, 191 (1944).
2. M. P. Schützenberger, On an application of semi-group methods to some problems in coding, *IRE Trans. Inform. Theory* **II.2**, 47–60 (1956).
3. L. N. Ševrin, On subsemigroups of free semi-groups (en russe), *Dokl. Akad. Nauk SSSR* **133**, 537–539 (1960).
4. M. L. Dubreil-Jacotin, Sur l'immersion d'un demi-groupe dans un groupe, *Comp. Rend.* **225**, 787–788 (1947).
5. P. M. Cohn, On subsemigroups of free semi-groups, *Proc. Am. Math. Soc.* **13**, 347–351 (1962).
6. A. A. Sardinas et C. W. Patterson, A necessary and sufficient condition for the unique decomposition of coded messages, *IRE Intern. Conv. Recd.* **8**, 104–108 (1953).
7. G. Bandyopadhyay, A simple proof of the decipherability criterion of Sardinas and Patterson, *Inform. and Control* **6**, 331–336 (1963).
8. M. Teissier, Sur les équivalences régulières dans les demi-groupes, *Comp. Rend.* **232**, 1987–1989 (1951).
9. J. C. Shepherdson, The reduction of two-way automata to one-way automata, *IBM J. Res. Develop.* **3**, 198–200 (1959).
10. M. O. Rabin et D. Scott, Finite automata and their decision problems, *IBM J. Res. Develop.* **3**, 114–125 (1959).
11. R. S. Markus et M. P. Schützenberger, Full decodable code word sets, *IRE Trans. Inform. Theory* **II.5**, 12–15 (1959).
12. C. C. Elgot and J. E. Metzgei, Two-sided finite-state transductions, *IBM Res. Paper RC*-1017, Juin 1963.
13. E. N. Gilbert et E. F. Moore, Variable length binary encodings, *Bell System Tech. J.* **38**, 933–967 (1959).
14. A. A. Markov, Conditions of completeness for irregular codes (en russe), *Problemy kibernitiki No.* 9 (traduit en anglais dans J.P.R.S. livraison du 14 Oct. 1963).
15. A. A. Markov, On alphabet coding (en russe), *Dokl. Akad. Nauk SSSR* **139**, 560–561 (1961).
16. M. P. Schützenberger, Sur certains monoïdes libres (à paraître).

# Organigrammes et Machines de Turing

L. Nolin

*Institut Blaise Pascal*
*Paris, France*

Dans presque toutes les disciplines scientifiques l'accroissement des connaissances tend à scinder l'ensemble des spécialistes en deux groupes, les "praticiens" et les "théoriciens". Chaque chercheur s'agrège alors à l'un ou à l'autre suivant sa tournure d'esprit. Tel est le cas des "programmeurs" et des "théoriciens des automates".

Il serait fâcheux, à mon sens, que cette division du travail fasse oublier aux uns et aux autres que les outils qu'ils façonnent ou les objets qu'ils étudient sont en un certain sens identiques. Je me propose tout d'abord de rappeler cette vérité quelque peu oubliée. Certains programmeurs trop enclins à négliger l'aspect théorique de la question seront peut-être amenés, de ce fait, à réviser leur opinion. Et pour jouer jusqu'au bout mon rôle de conciliateur—ou de perturbateur, c'est selon—j'essaierai de montrer que les théoriciens peuvent trouver leur pâture dans ces procédés que les programmeurs ont tendance à considérer comme des "astuces", et qui ne sont, au fond, qu'un traitement approprié de notions fondamentales.

## Part I

Comme le mot "machine" est pris en des acceptions différentes par les programmeurs et par les théoriciens, j'appellerai *calculateur de Turing* une machine à calculer ainsi composée: sa mémoire est une bande de papier

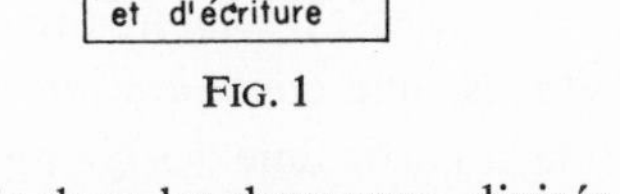

Fig. 1

indéfiniment prolongeable dans les deux sens, divisée en cases qu'une tête de lecture et d'écriture peut explorer à raison d'une case et d'une seule à un instant donné; chacune de ces cases contient l'un ou l'autre des objects $B$ ("blanc") ou $N$ ("noir") (Fig. 1).

J'appellerai *file* la suite des objets contenus dans les cases:

$$\cdots BNNNNBNNNB \cdots$$

et *configuration* le couple formé par la file et un *index* qui permet de repérer la case explorée:

$$\cdots BN\underset{\uparrow}{N}NNBNNNB \cdots$$

Un calculateur de Turing est capable de modifier une telle configuration lorsqu'on lui demande d'effectuer l'une des quatre opérations suivantes:

$\rightarrow$
(explorer la case située à la droite de la case explorée)

$\leftarrow$
(explorer la case située à la gauche de la case explorée)

$B$
(effacer le contenu de la case explorée et lui substituer $B$)

$N$
(effacer le contenu de la case explorée et lui substituer $N$)

Un *algorithme* est un ensemble partiellement ordonné de telles opérations. La première opération à effectuer est nommément désignée. Après chaque opération, l'opération à exécuter est précisée, soit par la relation d'ordre partiel, soit par le résultat d'un test concernant la nature de l'objet **ob** contenu dans la case explorée: le calculateur exécute l'opération $\alpha$ si **ob** est $B$ et l'opération $\beta$ si **ob** est $N$ (Fig. 2).

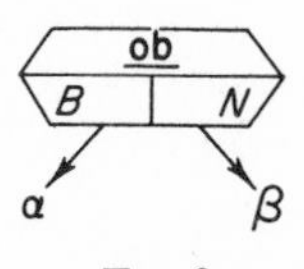


FIG. 2

En général, un algorithme est associé à une fonction: à partir d'une configuration d'une certaine classe il tend à faire construire au calculateur, en un nombre fini d'étapes, une configuration appartenant à une autre classe. Dans ce cas, seule la partie finie des configurations qui se trouve au voisinage de l'index est modifiée par l'exécution de l'algorithme.

Ainsi, on peut imaginer que la configuration décrite plus haut représente le nombre 4 (quatre $N$) suivi du nombre 3 (trois $N$), séparés l'un de l'autre et isolés du reste de la file par des $B$, et on peut envisager de faire construire au calculateur la différence de ces deux nombres, soit 1 (un seul $N$). Plus généralement, à partir de la configuration

$$\cdots B\overbrace{N\cdots N}^{m}B\overbrace{N\cdots N}^{n}B\cdots$$
$$\uparrow$$

où $m$ est $> n$, on envisage de construire la configuration

$$B\overbrace{N\cdots N}^{m-n}B\cdots$$
$$\uparrow$$

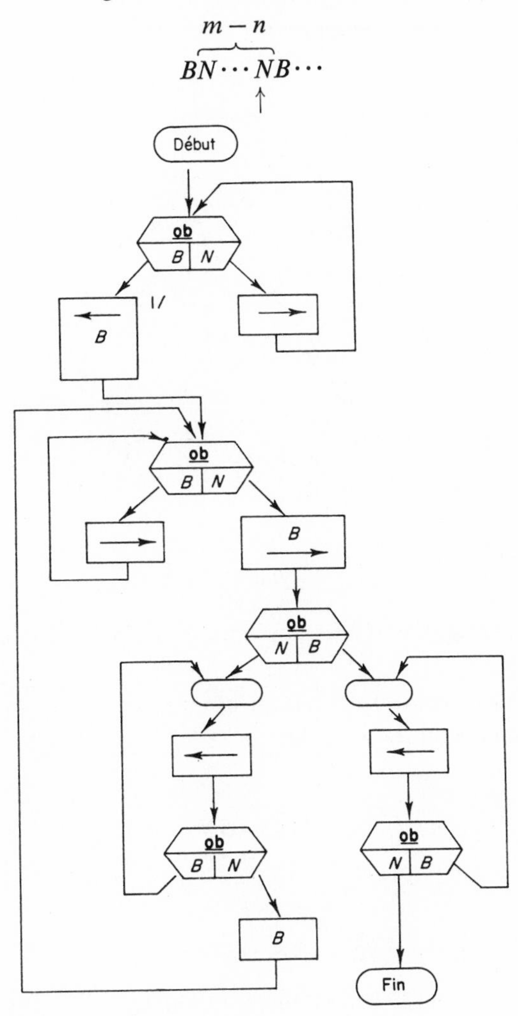


Fig. 3

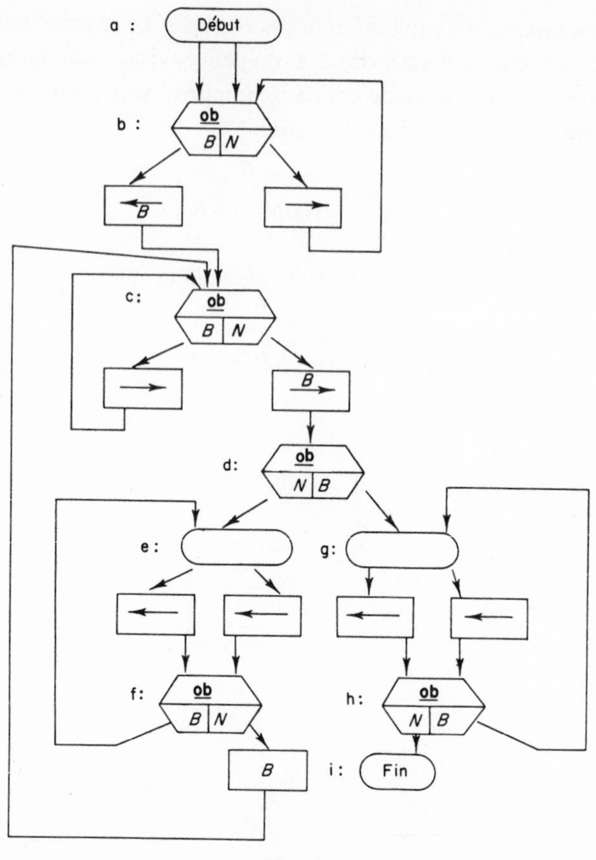


FIG. 4

L'un des algorithmes possibles peut être décrit par l'organigramme de la Fig. 3.

Il conduit à construire un certain nombre de configurations dont les plus importantes sont les suivantes:

$$\cdots B\overbrace{N\cdots N}^{m-1}\overbrace{B\cdots B}^{3}\overbrace{N\cdots N}^{n-1}B\cdots$$

$$\cdots$$

$$\cdots B\overbrace{N\cdots N}^{m-n}\overbrace{B\cdots B}^{2n+1}B\cdots$$

L'organigramme précédent est un multigraphe, c'est à dire une structure

$$\mathscr{G} = \langle \mathscr{E}, \mathscr{N}, \mathscr{V}, \psi \rangle$$

où $\mathscr{E}$ est l'ensemble des sommets, $\mathscr{N}$ l'ensemble $\{B, N\}$, $\mathscr{V}$ l'ensemble dont les éléments sont **un**, **zéro** (absence d'arc), et les $K$-uplets d'éléments de $\{B, N, \rightarrow, \leftarrow\}$, $\psi$ enfin, une application de $\mathscr{E} \times \mathscr{E} \times \mathscr{N}$ dans $\mathscr{V}$.

Si on l'écrit sous forme canonique (Fig. 4), on peut lui associer une sorte de matrice d'incidence aux origines des arcs (Table 1).

TABLE 1

| | $a$ | $b$ | $c$ | $d$ | $e$ | $f$ | $g$ | $h$ | $i$ |
|---|---|---|---|---|---|---|---|---|---|
| $B$ | $a$ **un** $b$ | $b \leftarrow Bc$ | $c \rightarrow c$ | $d$ **un** $g$ | $e \leftarrow f$ | $f$ **un** $e$ | $g \leftarrow h$ | $h$ **un** $g$ | $i$ **zéro** |
| $N$ | $a$ **un** $b$ | $b \rightarrow b$ | $cB \rightarrow d$ | $d$ **un** $e$ | $e \leftarrow f$ | $fBc$ | $g \leftarrow h$ | $h$ **un** $i$ | $i$ **zéro** |

On peut lui donner aussi une forme plus concise (Table 2).

TABLE 2

| | $a$ | $b$ | $c$ | $d$ | $e$ | $f$ | $g$ | $h$ | $i$ |
|---|---|---|---|---|---|---|---|---|---|
| $B$ | $b$ | $\leftarrow Bc$ | $\rightarrow c$ | $g$ | $\leftarrow f$ | $e$ | $\leftarrow h$ | $g$ | **zéro** |
| $N$ | $b$ | $\rightarrow b$ | $B \rightarrow d$ | $e$ | $\leftarrow f$ | $Bc$ | $\leftarrow h$ | $i$ | **zéro** |

Ce n'est rien d'autre qu'une façon de décrire une *machine de Turing*.

## Part II

Les *calculateurs* usuels dérivent des calculateurs de Turing par un certain nombre d'extensions qui sont destinées à les rendre, sinon plus "puissants", du moins plus "maniables". Quelques-unes d'entre elles sont bien connues des théoriciens. La première consiste à admettre comme contenu d'une case $n$ objets au lieu de deux seulement ($B$ et $N$); une autre, à multiplier les files et par voie de conséquence, les index.

Cette dernière extension est particulièrement importante. Pour s'en convaincre, il suffit d'essayer d'adapter l'algorithme d'Euclide pour la construction du p.g.c.d. de deux entiers $m$ et $n$, au calculateur décrit plus haut.

Pour faciliter les choses, j'emploierai un calculateur à deux bandes; **ob1** et **ob2** désigneront les contenus des cases explorées sur la bande 1 et la bande 2, respectivement. Les opérations permises seront ici

| | | |
|---|---|---|
| $\rightarrow 1$ | et | $\rightarrow 2$ |
| $\leftarrow 1$ | et | $\leftarrow 2$ |
| $B1$ (ou **ob1**$: = B$) | et | $B2$ (ou **ob2**$: = B$) |
| $N1$ (ou **ob1**$: = N$) | et | $N2$ (ou **ob2**$: = N$) |

et on pourra tester à tout moment la nature de **ob1** et de **ob2**.

A partir d'une configuration telle que

$$\text{file 1: } B\overbrace{N\cdots N}^{m}B$$
$$\uparrow$$

$$\text{file 2: } B\overbrace{N\cdots N}^{n}B$$
$$\uparrow$$

l'exécution de l'organigramme $A$ ci-dessous conduira par une suite de soustractions à la configuration

$$\text{file 1: } B\overbrace{N\cdots N}^{p}B$$
$$\uparrow$$

$$\text{file 2: } B\overbrace{N\cdots N}^{n}B$$
$$\uparrow$$

où $p$ est le reste de $m$ modulo $n$ $(0 \leqslant p < n)$ (Fig. 5).

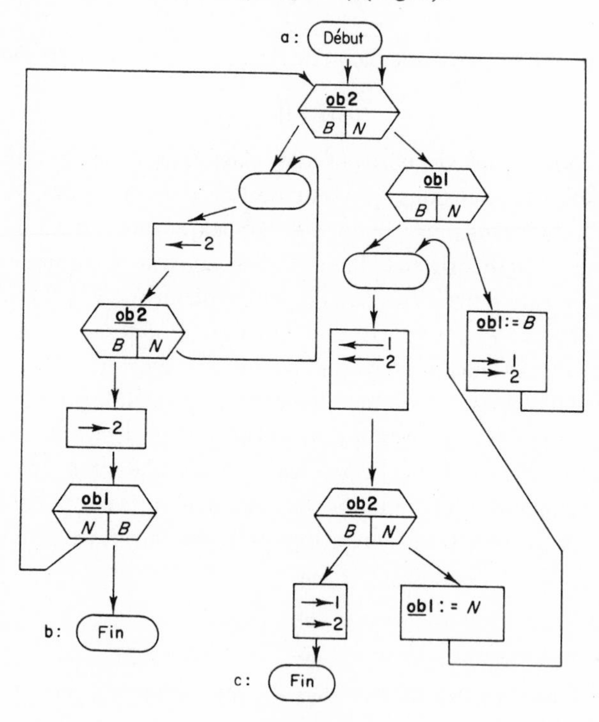


FIG. 5

Si l'exécution s'arrête en $b$, c'est que $p = 0$; dans ce cas, le p.g.c.d. de $m$ et de $n$ est en file 2.

Si l'exécution s'arrête en $c$, c'est que $p$ est $\neq 0$. Il faut donc appliquer une seconde fois au moins l'algorithme *en échangeant les rôles des files* 1 et 2.

Il y a bien des manières de réaliser cette opération.

1. Soit $A$ l'organigramme qu'on déduit de $A$ en permutant

$\rightarrow 1$ et $\rightarrow 2$
$\leftarrow 1$ et $\leftarrow 2$
**ob1** et **ob2**

L'algorithme d'Euclide sera traduit par l'organigramme suivant (Fig. 6).

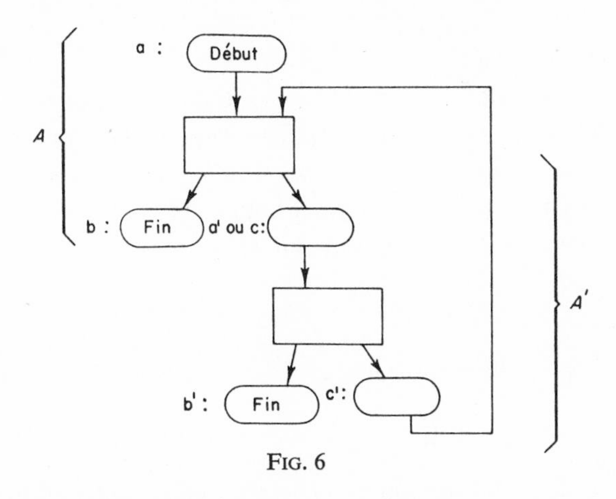


FIG. 6

Même si cette solution satisfaisait les théoriciens, elle ne manquerait pas d'horrifier les programmeurs.

2. Soit $B$ un organigramme exprimant l'algorithme:

"permuter les *contenus* des files 1 et 2"

L'algorithme d'Euclide peut être traduit par l'organigramme de la Fig. 7.

Cette solution présente les mêmes défauts que la précédente, car l'organigramme $B$ est en réalité constitué par une chaîne de trois organigrammes qui traduisent les algorithmes suivants:

"placer en file 3[1] le contenu de la file 1"
"placer en file 1 le contenu de la file 2"
"placer en file 2 le contenu de la file 3"

[1] File crée pour les besoins de la cause.

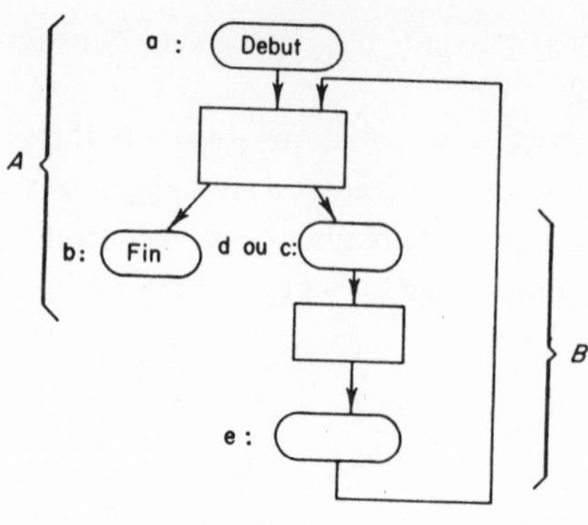


FIG. 7

Elle est à rejeter pour les mêmes raisons.

3. La seule solution raisonnable consiste donc à permuter les **noms** des files 1 et 2 ou tout au moins ceux des objets contenus dans les cases explorées. Soient $\alpha$ et $\beta$ les contenus de deux cases situées sur de nouvelles bandes. $\alpha$ et $\beta$ seront des **noms**, et, tout d'abord, le **nom** $\ulcorner$**ob1**$\urcorner$ et le **nom** $\ulcorner$**ob2**$\urcorner$, respectivement. Autrement dit, on posera, au début:

$$\alpha := \ulcorner \mathbf{ob1} \urcorner \qquad \text{et} \qquad \beta := \ulcorner \mathbf{ob2} \urcorner$$

Par définition, on aura, de ce fait:

$$[\alpha] = \mathbf{ob1} \qquad \text{et} \qquad [\beta] = \mathbf{ob2}$$

Ainsi $[\alpha]$ et $[\beta]$ seront des objets au sens où nous l'entendions jusqu'ici, à savoir $B$ ou $N$ suivant les circonstances.

Pour unifier la notation, on emploiera enfin

$$AV(\alpha) \qquad \text{et} \qquad AR(\alpha)$$

pour

$$\rightarrow 1 \qquad \text{et} \qquad \leftarrow 1$$

lorsque $\alpha = \ulcorner$**ob1**$\urcorner$, et pour

$$\rightarrow 2 \qquad \text{et} \qquad \leftarrow 2$$

lorsque $\alpha = \ulcorner$**ob2**$\urcorner$.

On emploiera de la même façon $AV(\beta)$ et $AR(\beta)$.

L'organigramme qui exprime l'algorithme d'Euclide pourra alors s'écrire très simplement (Fig. 8).

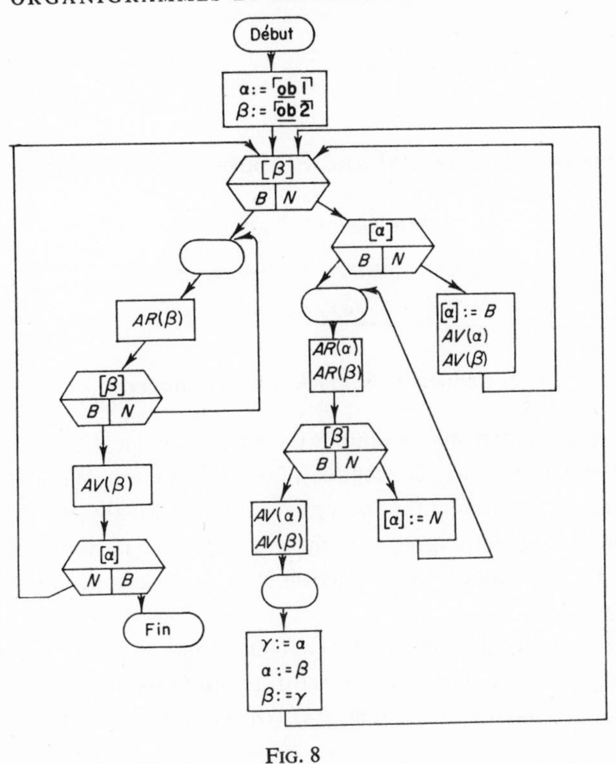


FIG. 8

C'est certainement cette solution qu'on adoptera *en pratique*. Sur le plan *théorique* elle conduit à une généralisation du concept de machine de Turing qui permet de définir et d'étudier une opération beaucoup plus complexe que la simple "composition", à savoir la "substitution".

# Lectures on Classical and Probabilistic Automata[1]

MICHAEL O. RABIN

*Department of Mathematics*
*Hebrew University, Jerusalem, Israel*

## I. Introductory Remarks about Automata

In these remarks we shall examine the methodological considerations leading to the mathematical concept of a finite automaton. We shall briefly discuss the algebraization of the theory of automata. Finally, we shall show how the abstract algebraic approach helps in proving a result about machines, namely, the theorem concerning reduction of two-way automata to one-way automata.

Let $\Sigma$ be a finite alphabet (*input alphabet*) and let $Y=\{0,1\}$ (*output alphabet*). By $S^*$ we shall denote the set of all finite sequences of elements of the set $S$. If $x=x_1x_2\cdots x_n$, then $l(x)=n$ will denote the *length* of the sequence $x$.

We are interested in transformations $\phi:\Sigma^* \rightarrow Y^*$ of input sequences to output sequences. Nothing of interest can be said about general transformations of this sort. We therefore impose some limiting assumptions.

We assume that $\phi$ is realized by a physical apparatus (black box, BB), that the input $x=\sigma_1\cdots\sigma_n$ is entering BB symbol by symbol at discrete time moments, and that after receiving the $i$th input symbol $\sigma_i$ of $x$, the BB produces the $i$th output symbol $\epsilon_i$ of the output $\phi(x)=y=\epsilon_1\cdots\epsilon_n$. Thus, in particular, *$\phi$ preserves length.*

Furthermore, a machine (e.g., sequential circuit or neural net) is *not* endowed with the power of prophecy: the $i$th output $\epsilon_i$ depends only on past inputs, i.e., there exists a function $f_i$ such that

$$f_i(\sigma_1\cdots\sigma_i)=\epsilon_i$$

Thus $\phi$ leads to a sequence $f_1, f_2,\ldots$ of functions describing it piecewise. The mapping $\phi$ is therefore completely determined by the inputs $x\in\Sigma^*$ for which the output at the end of the sequence $x$ is 1.

[1] Preparation of these notes was supported, in part, by ONR Contract N62558-3882 through the European Branch of the U.S. Office of Naval Research.

Hence we need only consider the problem of classifying, by means of a physical apparatus, input sequences $x \in \Sigma^*$ into those leading to output 1 (we shall call them *accepted* by the machine) and those leading to output 0 (*rejected* by the machine). From this point of view, the apparatus is used to define a set $T \subseteq \Sigma^*$, namely,

$$T = \{x | x \textit{ accepted by apparatus } \mathrm{BB}\}$$

Whatever we can say about sets $T$ of this form carries over to machine-realizable transformations $\phi : \Sigma^* \to Y^*$ and vice versa.

We must now go into somewhat greater detail in describing the apparatus BB. We abstract from the finer structure of BB, be it a nerve net or a circuit, and try to describe by a single *state* $s$, the sum total of physical characteristics which at any given moment are significant for the calculation performed by it. This notion of an abstract state is the cornerstone of the mathematical theory of automata and was first formulated by Kutti (see *Sequential Machines* (E. F. Moore, ed.), Addison-Wesley, Reading, Mass., 1964).

**Assumption 1.** The classification of inputs (or the transformation $\phi$) is realized by an apparatus (automaton) with just a finite number of states.

**Assumption 2.** If the automaton is in a state $s$ and has input symbol $\sigma$, then it will move into a new state which depends (is a function of) only on $s$ and $\sigma$.

So a finite automaton $\mathfrak{A}$ over $\Sigma$ can be defined mathematically as a system $\mathfrak{A} = \langle S, M, s_0, F \rangle$ where $S$ is a finite set (the set of states), $M$ is a function $M : S \times \Sigma \to S$ (the table of moves), $s_0 \in S$ (the initial state), and $F \subseteq S$ (the designated final states). When presented with an input sequence $x = \sigma_1 \sigma_2 \cdots \sigma_n \in \Sigma^*$, $\mathfrak{A}$ will start in $s_0$. Under input $\sigma_1$ it will go into state $s_1 = M(s_0, \sigma_1)$ under input $\sigma_2$ it will go into state $s_2 = M(s_1, \sigma_2)$, and so on until a state $s_n$ is reached at the end of $x$.

**Definition.** $\mathfrak{A}$ *accepts* $x$ if $s_n \in F$. The set of all those $x \in \Sigma^*$ which are accepted by $\mathfrak{A}$ is denoted by $T(\mathfrak{A})$ and called the *set defined by* $\mathfrak{A}$.

As remarked before, we can also associate with $T(\mathfrak{A})$ a transformation $\phi : \Sigma^* \to Y^*$.

Why should one be interested in the theory of automata? There is no doubt that the application of automata-theory concepts and techniques to practical problems is confined to systems with a relatively small number of states (this number can be, say, at most in the thousands). There are practical situations in which this limitation on size is met. The sequential circuits which are the basic components of computers are specified by the input-output transformation which they have to realize. The designer starts by describing the circuit's operation in terms of states, and the number of states, since it is humanly manageable, cannot be too large. In fact, modern books on computer design often contain a chapter on automata, state minimalization procedures, and the like. The same considerations apply to possible future computing devices which will be organized as big iterative arrays. The basic component of the array will be a circuit with a small number of states.

On a more global and abstract level, we observe that a computer program is first expressed by means of a flow diagram. The flow diagram consists of a number of boxes, which can be viewed as states. At each box there is a number of possible *outcomes* of the computation under progress, and the box, together with the outcome, determine transition to another box (state). The possible outcomes are taken to be the elements of $\Sigma$ so that the flow diagram is a finite automaton over $\Sigma$. Again the system is of manageable size. One can define an appropriate notion of equivalence of programs (flow diagrams), and studies are now under way to see whether this point of view will produce results concerning programming.

Finally, it is of course true that a digital computer is a finite automaton. But the number of states may be of the order of $2^{100000}$ and hence render application of automata theory to whole computers unrealistic. Here the application goes, in a sense, the other way round. We have the notion of an automaton which is modelled on the finite-state physical machine. In developing the mathematical theory of automata, we rely on our intuitive concept of finite-state actual machines. It is this speaker's personal bias that whatever generalization of the finite automaton concept we may want to consider, it ought to be based on some intuitive notion of machines. This is probably the best guide to fruitful generalizations and problems, and our intuition about behavior of machines will then be helpful in conjecturing and proving theorems.

## II. Algebraization of Automata

The basic problem of theory of automata is the following: given a set $T \subseteq \Sigma^*$, to find a necessary and sufficient condition for the existence of an automaton $\mathfrak{A}$ such that $T = T(\mathfrak{A})$. A set $T$ such that $T = T(\mathfrak{A})$ for some automaton is called a *regular event* or a *definable set*.

We introduce some notations. If $E$ is an equivalence relation on $\Sigma^*$, then we denote by *index* $(E)$ the number of equivalence classes of $\Sigma^*$ by $E$. If $x$ and $y$ are finite sequences, then $xy$ will denote the result of concatenating these sequences. Note that $\Sigma^*$ with this operation $xy$ is a semigroup.

**Definition.** An equivalence relation $E$ on $\Sigma^*$ is called *right-invariant* if for all $x, y, z \in \Sigma^*$, $xEy$ *implies* $xzEyz$. The notion of *left-invariance* is similarly defined.

**Definition.** An equivalence relation $E$ on $\Sigma^*$ is called a *congruence* if $E$ is left-invariant and right-invariant.

There is a natural, well-known, one-to-one correspondence between congruence relations on $\Sigma^*$ and homomorphisms $\psi: \Sigma^* \to M$ of $\Sigma^*$ into semigroups $M$. Thus to the homomorphism $\psi$ there corresponds the congruence $E$ defined by

$$xEy \qquad \textit{if and only if } \psi(x) = \psi(y)$$

**Theorem.** $T \subseteq \Sigma^*$ is a regular event if and only if $T$ is the union of equivalence classes of a congruence relation $E$ (on $\Sigma^*$) such that the *index* $(E)$ is finite.

In semigroup language, the above condition has the following form: There exists a homomorphism $\psi: \Sigma^* \to M$ of $\Sigma^*$ onto a finite semigroup such that $\psi^{-1}\psi(T) = T$.

The above theorem is somewhat too general because, given $T$, we do not know how to produce an $E$ to prove that $T$ is regular. We can, however, consider the following relation:

**Definition.** $x \equiv_T y$, by definition, if and only if for all $u, v \in \Sigma^*$, $uxv \in T$ if and only if $uyv \in T$.

The relation $\equiv_T$ is a congruence on $\Sigma^*$ and $T$ is always the union of equivalent classes of $\equiv_T$.

**Theorem.** $T$ is a regular event if and only if the *index* $(\equiv_T)$ is finite.

The characterization of regular events by means of homomorphisms into finite semigroups is of interest because it points the way toward defining special classes of regular events, on the one hand, and generalizations of the concept of regular event, on the other. We may look at the cases where the semigroup $M$ is commutative, or is in fact a group, and see what special regular events are obtained in this way. We can also try to relax the finiteness condition on the semigroup in various ways and see whether this leads to interesting generalizations of the notions of finite automaton and regular event.

A somewhat different characterization of regular events can be given in terms of right-invariant relations.

**Definition.** Let $T \subseteq \Sigma^*$. Define a relation $E_T$ by $xE_Ty$ if and only if for all $z \in \Sigma^*$, $xz \in T$ if and only if $yz \in T$.

$E_T$ is a right-invariant equivalence relation and $T$ is the union of equivalence classes of $E_T$.

**Theorem.** $T$ is a regular event if and only if the *index* $(E_T)$ is finite. If $T$ is indeed regular, then this (finite) *index* $(E_T)$ is the least number $k$ such that there exists an automaton $\mathfrak{A}$ with $k$ states and $T = T(\mathfrak{A})$.

This last result has the advantage that it gives us precise information on the number of states needed to define $T$.

## III. Two-Way Automata

Let us now generalize the notion of a finite automaton in that we shall allow it to return to past inputs in order to determine whether to accept a sequence $x$. The mathematical definition runs as follows.

**Definition.** A two-way automaton $\mathfrak{A}$ over $\Sigma$ is a system $\mathfrak{A} = \langle S, M, s_0, F \rangle$, where $S, s_0, F$ are as in the previous definition of an automaton and $M$ is a function $M: S \times \Sigma \to S \times \{-1, 1, 0\}$.

We assume that the input sequence $x = \sigma_1 \sigma_2 \cdots \sigma_n$ is given on a linear tape divided into $n$ squares, $\sigma_1$ occupying the first square of the tape, $\sigma_2$ occupying the second square, and so on. $\mathfrak{A}$ can move across the tape and read the contents of the tape squares. Let $\mathfrak{A}$ be in state $s \in S$ and read $\sigma \in \Sigma$; let $M(s, \sigma) = (s_1, e)$; then $\mathfrak{A}$ will enter state $s_1$ and move on the tape one square to the left, one square to the right, or not at all, according to whether $e = -1, 1, 0$, respectively. This action will be called an *atomic move*.

Given a sequence (tape) $x$ we shall say that $\mathfrak{A}$ *accepts* $x$ if when started in state $s_0$ on the left end of $x$ (i.e., on $\sigma_1$), it will go through a sequence of its atomic moves and get off the right end of $x$ in a designated state $s \in F$. The set of all sequences accepted by $\mathfrak{A}$ will again be denoted by $T(\mathfrak{A})$.

The following theorem was first proved by complicated constructions involving machines. Here we give a rather simple proof, due essentially to

Shepherdson, which is based on the algebraic characterization of regular events. Our theorem answers the natural question whether two-way automata are actually stronger than the usual automata.

**Theorem.** If $\mathfrak{A}$ is a two-way automaton over $\Sigma$ then $T(\mathfrak{A})$ is a regular event; i.e., there exists a one-way automaton $\mathfrak{B}$ such that $T(\mathfrak{A}) = T(\mathfrak{B})$.

*Proof.* Denote $T(\mathfrak{A})$ by $T$. We shall show that the *index* $(E_T)$ is finite. Let $\mathfrak{A} = \langle S, M, s_0, F\rangle$ and let $d$ be an element not in $S$. Let $H$ be the set of all functions $f: S \to S \cup \{d\}$.

With each $x \in \Sigma^*$ associate a function $f_x \in H$ as follows. If, when started on the right end of $x$ in state $s \in S$, $\mathfrak{A}$ does eventually (after a sequence of one or more atomic moves) get off the right end of $x$ in some states $s_1$, then set $f_x(s) = s_1$; if $\mathfrak{A}$ never gets off the right end of $x$, then set $f_x(s) = d$. Thus $f_x$ is defined for every $s \in S$ and $f_x(s) \in S \cup \{d\}$. Hence $f_x \in H$.

Furthermore we associate with $x$ a unique element $s(x) \in S \cup \{d\}$. If, when started on the left end of $x$ in the initial state $s_0$, $\mathfrak{A}$ gets off the right end of $x$ and is then in a state $s$, then put $s(x) = s$; if $\mathfrak{A}$ does not get off the right end of $x$, then put $s(x) = d$.

We contend that if for $x, y \in \Sigma^*$, $f_x = f_y$ and $s(x) = s(y)$ then $xE_Ty$. Let $z \in \Sigma^*$ and assume $xz \in T$, we have to show that $yz \in T$. Since $\mathfrak{A}$ accepts $xz$ it will get off the right-end square $E$ of $x$ if started on the left in state $s_0$. Assume the state at that time to be $s_1$, in fact $s_1 = s(x)$. $\mathfrak{A}$ will then move for a while on $z$ and perhaps return to $E$; call the state at that time $r_1$. If so, then $\mathfrak{A}$ must eventually move again off $E$ to the right in a state $s_2$; in fact $s_2 = f_x(r_1)$. In this way the motion of $\mathfrak{A}$ on $xz$ produces a sequence $s_1, r_1, s_2, r_2, \ldots, s_p$ of states, where $s_p$ is the state of $\mathfrak{A}$ when it gets off $E$ for the last time ($p = 1$ is possible). We have a similar sequence $s_1', r_1', \ldots, s_q'$ for $yz$. Now $s_1 = s(x) = s(y) = s_1'$. This means that $\mathfrak{A}$ gets for the first time onto the $z$ portion of $xz$ and $yz$ in the same state $s_1 = s_1'$. But this implies $r_1 = r_1'$. Now $s_2 = f_x(r_1) = f_y(r_1) = s_2'$, and so on. Hence $p = q$ and $s_p = s_q'$. Since $xz$ was accepted by $\mathfrak{A}$ this implies that $yz$ is accepted by $\mathfrak{A}$.

Thus the number of equivalence classes of $E_T$ is smaller than the number of pairs $(f, s)$, where $f \in H$, $s \in S$, and hence is finite. This completes the proof.

## IV. Probabilistic Automata

We consider a generalization of the notion of automata obtained by introducing probabilities into the system. Aside from the fact that we get in this way a neat mathematical generalization, we are also motivated by the desire to formulate a mathematical model for sequential circuits with random malfunctioning, i.e., with random errors. Some of our results will bear upon problems of reliability of sequential circuits.

The automaton again has a finite set $S$ of states. When in state $s \in S$ and under input $\sigma \in \Sigma$ the automaton is not assumed, as before, to move into a definite state, but rather may move into any one of the states of $S$ with a certain probability. Note that we are again adopting the point of view of general automata theory in dealing with unanalyzed states and the transitions between them.

**Definition.** A *probabilistic automaton* (p.a.) over the alphabet $\Sigma$ is a system $\mathfrak{A} = \langle S, M, s_0, F \rangle$, where $S = \{s_0, \ldots, s_n\}$ is a finite set (the set of states), $M$ (the transition probabilities table) is a function such that for $s \in S$, $\sigma \in \Sigma$,

$$M(s, \sigma) = (p_0(s, \sigma), \ldots, p_n(s, \sigma))$$
$$0 \leqslant p_i(s, \sigma), \qquad \sum_i p_i(s, \sigma) = 1$$

$s_0 \in S$ (the initial state), and $F \subseteq S$ (the set of designated final states).

Probabilistic automata are models for systems (such as sequential circuits) capable of a finite number of states $s \in S$. The system may receive inputs $\sigma \in \Sigma$. When in state $s$ and if the input is $\sigma$, the system can go into any one of the states $s_i \in S$ and the probability of going into $s_i$ is the $(i + 1)$th coordinate of $M(s, \sigma)$. These transition probabilities $p_i(s, \sigma)$ are assumed to remain fixed and be independent of time and previous inputs. Thus the system also has definite transition probabilities for going from state $s_i$ to state $s_j$ by a sequence $x \in \Sigma^*$ of inputs. These probabilities are calculated by means of products of certain stochastic matrices which we shall now define.

**Definition.** For $\sigma \in \Sigma$ and $x = \sigma_1 \cdots \sigma_m$ define the $n + 1$ by $n + 1$ matrices $A(\sigma)$ and $A(x)$ by

$$A(\sigma) = [p_j(s_i, \sigma]_{0 \leqslant i, j \leqslant n}$$
$$A(x) = A(\sigma_1) \cdots A(\sigma_m) = [p_j(s_i, x)]_{0 \leqslant i, j \leqslant n}$$

An easy calculation (involving induction on $m$) will show that the $(i + 1, j + 1)$ element $p_j(s_i, x)$ is the probability of $\mathfrak{A}$ for moving from state $s_i$ to state $s_j$ by the input sequence $x$.

**Definition.** If $\mathfrak{A} = \langle S, M, s_0, F \rangle$ and $F = \{s_{i_0}, \ldots, s_{i_r}\}$, $I = \{i_0, \ldots, i_r\}$, define

$$p(x) = \sum_{i \in I} p_i(s_0, x)$$

$p(x)$ clearly is the probability for $\mathfrak{A}$, when started in $s_0$, to enter into a state which is a member of $F$ by the input sequence $x$.

A p.a. $\mathfrak{A}$ may be used to define sets of tapes in a manner similar to that of deterministic automata except that now the set of tapes will depend not just on $\mathfrak{A}$ but also on a parameter $\lambda$.

**Definition.** Let $\mathfrak{A}$ be p.a. and $\lambda$ be a real number, $0 \leqslant \lambda < 1$. The set of tapes $T(\mathfrak{A}, \lambda)$ is defined by

$$T(\mathfrak{A}, \lambda) = \{x | x \in \Sigma^*, \lambda < p(x)\}$$

If $x \in T(\mathfrak{A}, \lambda)$, we say that $x$ is *accepted* by $\mathfrak{A}$ with cut point $\lambda$; $T(\mathfrak{A}, \lambda)$ will also be called *the set defined by* $\mathfrak{A}$ with cut point $\lambda$.

Deterministic automata can be considered as a special case of p.a. Namely, if $M(s, \sigma) = s_i$, we can view this as if $\mathfrak{A}$ will enter state $s_i$ with probability 1. Thus in rewriting the deterministic automaton as a p.a., the stochastic vectors $M(s, \sigma) = (p_0, \ldots, p_n)$ will have exactly one coordinate 1 and all others 0. It is readily seen that in this case $p(x) = 1$ for $x \in \Sigma^*$, if and only if $x \in T(\mathfrak{A})$. Hence for any $0 \leqslant \lambda < 1$, we have $T(\mathfrak{A}, \lambda) = T(\mathfrak{A})$. Thus every set definable by a deterministic automaton is trivially definable by some p.a. We shall see that the converse is not true and that therefore p.a. give a strictly larger class of definable sets.

The following matrices were suggested by E. F. Moore:

$$P_0 = \begin{bmatrix} 1 & 0 \\ \frac{1}{2} & \frac{1}{2} \end{bmatrix} \qquad P_1 = \begin{bmatrix} \frac{1}{2} & \frac{1}{2} \\ 0 & 1 \end{bmatrix}$$

It can be readily verified that if

$$P_{\delta_1} P_{\delta_2} \cdots P_{\delta_n} = \begin{bmatrix} m & p \\ q & r \end{bmatrix}, \qquad \delta_i \in \{0, 1\}$$

then $p = .\delta_n \cdots \delta_1$, where $p$ is written in binary expansion.

**Theorem.** Let $\mathfrak{A} = \langle S, M, s_0, F \rangle$ be an automaton over $\Sigma = \{0, 1\}$ such that $S = \{0, 1\}$, $A(0) = P_0$, $A(1) = P_1$, $F = \{s_1\}$. There exists a $0 \leqslant \lambda < 1$ such that $T(\mathfrak{A}, \lambda)$ is not definable by a deterministic automaton (is not a regular event).

*Proof.* If $x = \delta_1 \cdots \delta_n$ then, by the above, $p(x) = .\delta_n \cdots \delta_1$. The values $p(x)$ are dense in the whole interval $[0, 1]$. This implies that if $0 \leqslant \lambda < \lambda_1 < 1$ then $T(\mathfrak{A}, \lambda_1) \subset T(\mathfrak{A}, \lambda)$, where the inclusion is proper. The sets $T(\mathfrak{A}, \lambda)$, $0 \leqslant \lambda < 1$ therefore form a nondenumerable pairwise different collection of sets. But there is only a denumerable collection of regular events. Therefore there exists a $\lambda$ such that $T(\mathfrak{A}, \lambda)$ is not regular.

The above argument is a pure existence proof. We can, however, present a specific $\lambda$ such that $T(\mathfrak{A}, \lambda)$ is not regular. Namely, let $w_1, w_2, \ldots$ be any enumeration of $\Sigma^*$; then for $\lambda = .w_1 w_2 \cdots$, $T(\mathfrak{A}, \lambda)$ is not regular; we omit the proof.

The above $\lambda$ is irrational. It can in fact be shown that if $\lambda$ is rational, then $T(\mathfrak{A}, \lambda)$ is a regular event.

Let $\mathfrak{A}$ be a p.a. and $0 \leqslant \lambda < 1$. Given a tape $x$ we devise the following probabilistic experiment $E$ to test whether $x \in T(\mathfrak{A}, \lambda)$. We run $x$ through $\mathfrak{A}$ a large number $N$ of times and count the number $m(E)$ of times that $\mathfrak{A}$ ended in a state in $F$. If $\lambda < m(E)/N$ we accept $x$; otherwise we reject it. Because of the probabilistic nature of the experiment, it is of course possible that we sometimes accept $x$, even though $x \notin T(\mathfrak{A}, \lambda)$, or reject it, even though $x \in T(\mathfrak{A}, \lambda)$.

By the law of large numbers, however, there exist for each $x$ such that $p(x) \neq \lambda$ and each $0 < \epsilon$ a number $N(x, \epsilon)$ such that

$$\Pr[E | \lambda < \frac{m(E)}{N} \leftrightarrow x \in T(\mathfrak{A}, \lambda)] \geqslant 1 - \epsilon$$

That is, the probability of obtaining the correct answer by the experiment $E$ [consisting of running $x$ $N(x, \epsilon)$ times through $\mathfrak{A}$ and counting successes] is greater than $1 - \epsilon$.

To perform the above stochastic experiment we must know $N(x, \epsilon)$, which depends on $|p(x) - \lambda|$. Thus we have actually to know $p(x)$ in advance if we want to ascertain whether $x \in T(\mathfrak{A}, \lambda)$ with probability greater than $1 - \epsilon$ of being correct. Once we know $p(x)$, however, the whole experiment $E$ is superfluous.

The way out is to consider values $\lambda$ such that $|p(x) - \lambda|$ is bounded from below for all $x$.

**Definition.** A cut point $\lambda$ is called *isolated* with respect to $\mathfrak{A}$ if there exists a $\delta > 0$ such that

$$\delta \leqslant |p(x) - \lambda| \qquad \text{for all } x \in \Sigma^* \tag{1}$$

It is readily seen that there exists an integral valued function $N(\delta, \epsilon)$ such that for an isolated $\lambda$ and any $x \in \Sigma^*$,

$$\Pr[E | \lambda < \frac{m(E)}{N(\delta, \epsilon)} \leftrightarrow x \in T(\mathfrak{A}, \lambda)] \geqslant 1 - \epsilon$$

Thus the proposed stochastic experiment for determining whether $x \in T(\mathfrak{A}, \lambda)$ can be performed without any *a priori* knowledge of $p(x)$. This fact makes it natural to consider isolated cutpoints.

**Theorem.** Let $\mathfrak{A}$ be a probabilistic automaton and $\lambda$ be an isolated cutpoint satisfying (1). Then there exists a deterministic automaton $\mathfrak{B}$ such that $T(\mathfrak{A}, \lambda) = T(\mathfrak{B})$. If $\mathfrak{A}$ has $n$ states, then $\mathfrak{B}$ can be chosen to have $e$ states, where

$$e \leqslant \left(1 + \frac{1}{\delta}\right)^{n-1}$$

We shall not prove this theorem here (the proof can be found in the paper "Probabilistic automata," *Inform. and Control* 7 (1963); also in the book *Sequential Machines* (E. F. Moore, ed.), Addison-Wesley, Reading, Mass., 1964). The proof again uses the characterization of regular events by means of right-invariant equivalence relations with finite index. The proof also utilizes ideas from the geometry of numbers.

## V. Open Problems

It is impossible to describe in one short lecture the numerous results obtained thus far in this theory of probabilistic automata. Instead we shall conclude with two problems.

The concept of isolated cutpoint plays a fundamental role in the theory of probabilistic automata. Can one devise an algorithm for deciding for every given p.a. $\mathfrak{A}$ [the automaton is given by the matrices $A(\sigma)$, $\sigma \in \Sigma$, and we assume for the sake of simplicity that these matrices have rational coordinates] and every (rational) $\lambda$ whether $\lambda$ is an isolated cutpoint of $\mathfrak{A}$? Another problem is to decide for every given p.a. $\mathfrak{A}$ whether it has *any* isolated cutpoints. Are these problems perhaps recursively unsolvable?

The second problem is the *stability problem.* Given an automaton $\mathfrak{A}$ with matrices $A(\sigma)$, $\sigma \in \Sigma$ and a cutpoint $\lambda$ we are asking for conditions under which we can slightly perturb the transition probabilities of $\mathfrak{A}$ to get an automaton $\mathfrak{A}'$ with matrices $A'(\sigma)$ and still have $T(\mathfrak{A}, \lambda) = T(\mathfrak{A}', \lambda)$; i.e., we want conditions for stability of the set $T(\mathfrak{A}, \lambda)$ under small perturbations of $\mathfrak{A}$. The physical background to this question is obvious. If we have an unreliable circuit we can never know the transition probabilities with absolute accuracy, so that we want to know that even approximate values will lead to a correct description of the circuit's behavior. As of now there are some sufficient conditions for stability, but the general problem is still wide open.

# Sur Certaines Variétés de Monoïdes Finis

M. P. SCHÜTZENBERGER

*Institut Blaise Pascal*
*Paris, France*

Le but de cet exposé est de rassembler un certain nombre d'énoncés de la théorie des monoïdes finis qui semblent pouvoir présenter des applications à l'étude des automates finis et des langages de Kleene.

Nous commencerons par rappeler le résultat suivant de Clifford et de Miller (1956).

**Théorème 1.** *Soit u un élément idempotent d'un monoïde M et soit*

$$G_u = \{m \in Mu \cap uM : u \in Mm \cap mM\} \tag{1}$$

*L'ensemble $G_u$ est un sous groupe de M qui contient tous les sous groupes de M admettant u pour élemént neutre.*

*Démonstration.* Soit $u = u^2 \in M$. Par définition un élément $m \in M$ appartient à $G_u$ si et seulement si il existe $m_1, m_2, m_3, m_4 \in M$ satisfaisant:

$$m = m_1 u = u m_2 \qquad u = m_3 m = m m_4$$

Donc en particulier $u \in G_u$. Les deux premières relations donnent

$$mu = m_1 uu = m_1 u = m \qquad um = uum_2 = um_2 = m$$

Donc $u$ est un élément neutre pour tous les éléments de $G_u$.

Soit $m' = m_1' u = u m_2'$ tel que $u = m_3' m' = m' m_4'$ un autre élément de $G_u$. On a

$$mm' = mm' u = umm' \qquad m_3' m_3 mm' = m_3' um' = m_3' m' = u$$
$$mm' m_4' m_4 = mum_4 = mm_4 = u$$

Donc $G_u$ est un sous ensemble stable de $M$ (c'est à dire $G_u G_u \subset G_u$). Enfin, d'après $u^2 = u = m_3 m$ et $m = um$, on voit que $u = um_3 um$ et il n'y a donc pas de perte de généralité à supposer désormais que $um_3 = m_3 u = m_3$.

Considérons le produit $mm_3$. En utilisant successivement les hypothèses $m_3 = m_3 u$, $u = mm_4$, $m_3 m = u$, $mu = m$, $mm_4 = u$ on obtient:

$$mm_3 = mm_3 u = mm_3 mm_4 = mum_4 = mm_4 = u$$

Nous avons établi que $G_u$ est un sous ensemble stable admettant un élément neutre $u$ et ayant la propriété qu'à tout $m \in G_u$ correspond un élément $m_3 = um_3u$ qui satisfait $u = um_3u.m = mum_3u$.

Ceci montre d'abord que $um_3u \in G_u$ et que l'ensemble $G_u$ muni du produit de $M$ est isomorphe à un groupe puisque chaque élément possède un inverse. Enfin le groupe $G_u$ est maximal car si les éléments $m_5$ et $m_6$ de $M$ sont invariant par multiplication par $u$ et satisfont $u = m_5m_6 = m_6m_5$ ils appartiennent à $G_u$ d'après la définition même de cet ensemble. Ceci terminé la démonstration du théorème.

Rappelons maintenant qu'une famille **V** de groupes (monoïdes) est une *pseudo variété de groupes (monoïdes)* si elle contient tout sous groupe (sous monoïde) tout groupe (monoïde) quotient, et tout produit direct de deux membres quelconques de ses membres.

Par exemple, les groupes (monoïdes) finis forment une variété de même que les groupes (monoïdes) commutatifs; par contre les groupes cycliques ne forment pas une variété puisque le produit direct de deux groupes cycliques n'est plus nécessairement cyclique. On a

**Proposition 1.** *Soit* **V** *une variété de groupes et soit* **V**$'$ *la famille de tous les monoïdes finis dont tout les sous groupes appartiennent à* **V**. **V**$'$ *est une pseudo variété de monoïdes que l'on appelara la pseudo variété de monoïdes finis induite par la variété de groupe* **V**.

*Démonstration.* Soit $M$ un monoïde fini dont tout les sous groupes appartiennent à la variété de group $V$. Si $M'$ est un sous monoïde de $M$ et $G'$ un sous groupe de $M'$, $G'$ contient un et un seul idempotent $u$ et il résulte immédiatement de (1) que $G'$ est contenu dans $M' \cap G_u$. Donc $M'$ appartient à la variété **V**$'$ de monoïde fini induite par **V**.

De même, si $M_1, M_2 \in \mathbf{V}'$, tout sous groupe de produit direct $M_1 \times M_2$ est le produit direct d'un sous groupe de $M_1$ et d'un sous groupe de $M_2$ et par conséquent $M_1 \times M_2 \in \mathbf{V}'$.

Il reste seulement à établir $M' \in V'$ quand $M \in V'$ et quand $M' = \alpha M$ où $\alpha$ est un épimorphisme.

Dans ces conditions soit $u'$ un idempotent de $M'$ et soit $G_{u'}$ le sous groupe maximal de $M'$ qui contient $u'$. Soit $P = \{m \in M : \alpha m \in G_{u'}\}$ d'après $G'_uG'_u = G'_u \neq \phi$ on a $PP \subset P \neq \phi$.

Considérons un élément $m \in P$ tel que l'ensemble $mP \cap Pm$ ait le plus petit nombre possible d'élément. Cette hypothèse a un sens puisque $M$ est fini. Quelque soit $k > 0$ $m^kP \cap Pm^k = mP \cap Pm$ et en vertu de l'hypothèse de minimalité $m^kP \cap Pm^k = mP \cap Pm$.

De plus comme $M$ est fini l'ensemble $m, m^2, m^3, \ldots, m^k, \ldots$ ne contient qu'un nombre fini de termes, donc $m^{k_1} = km^{k_1 k'_1}$ pour au moins une paire $k_1, k'_1$ d'entiers positifs et par consequent toutes les paires $k_2, k'_2$ où $k_2 \geqslant k_1$ et $k'_2 = k_3 k_1$; donc enfin en prenant $k = k_1 k'_1$ on obtient $m^k = m^{2k}$ et l'on peut supposer désormais que $m = u = u^2$ est un idempotent.

Montrons que $uP \cap Pu = G_u$ est bien un sous groupe de $P$ contenant $u$. En effet la relation $m \in uP \cap Pu$ signifie que $m = um_1 = m_2 u$ pour au moins une paire $m_1, m_2 \in M$; par conséquent

$$m \in mP \cap Pm = um_1 P \cap Pm_2 u \subset uP \cap Pu$$

ce qui, d'après l'hypothèse de minimalité, entraine $mP \cap Pm = uP \cap Pu$, donc $u \in mP \cap Pm$ puisque $u \in uP \cap Pu$ d'après (1) ceci établit le résultat cherché.

Maintenant la relation $G_u = uG_u = G_u u$ donne $G_u = uG_u u = u(uP \cap Pu)u = uPu$, donc en prenant les images par $\alpha$ et en rappelant que $\alpha P = G'$ on obtient

$$\alpha G_u = \alpha u . \alpha P . \alpha u = \alpha u . G' . \alpha u = G'$$

et nous avons établi que le sous groupe $G'$ de $M'$ est une image homomorphe du sous groupe $G_u$ de $M$. Ceci termine la preuve de la Proposition 2.

Il y a évidemment bien des manières d'affaiblir la condition de finitude de $M$; il est toutefois impossible de se dispenser entièrement d'hypothèses de ce type puisqu'un sous groupe $G'$ d'un monoïde $M' = \alpha M$ peut, pour $M$ infini, être l'image d'un sous ensemble $P \subset M$ ne contenant aucun sous groupe $G$ tel que $\alpha G = G'$. Ceci est illustré par l'exemple où $M$ est un monoïde libre puisque dans ces conditions $M$ n'a qu'un seul sous groupe—à savoir le sous groupe trivial formé par l'élément neutre de $M$.

On se propose maintenant de définir une opération de composition entre monoïdes. Pour faciliter l'écriture on considère deux monoïdes fixes $M_1$ et $M_2$ et l'on désigne par $R$ la famille de tous les ensembles de paires d'éléments $(m_1, m_2) \in M_1 \times M_2$. Etant donnés des éléments quelconques $r = \{(m_{1,i}, m_{2,i}) : i \in I_r\} \in R$; $m_1 \in M_1$ et $m_2 \in M_2$ on définit les éléments $m_1 r$ et $rm_2$ de $R$ par les relations

$$m_1 r = \{(m_1 m_{1,i}, m_{2,i}) : i \in I_r\} \in R$$
$$rm_2 = \{(m_{1,i}, m_{2,i}, m_2) : i \in I_r\} \in R$$

**Définition 1.** *On appelera produit semi direct, booléen* $M_1 \circledast M_2$ *l'ensemble* $M = M_1 \times R \times M_2$ *muni de la loi de composition qui associe à tout* $m = (m_1, r, m_2)$, $m' = (m'_1, r', m'_2) \in M$ *l'élément*

$$mm' = (m_1 m'_1, m_1 r' \cup rm'_2, m_2 m'_2) \in M$$

Il est facile de voir que l'opération $m \times m' \to mm'$ est associative.

En effect, si $m'' = (m''_1, r'', m''_2) \in M$, on a

$$\begin{aligned}(mm')m'' &= (m_1 m'_1 m''_1, (m_1 m'_1) r'' \cup (m_1 r' \cup r m_2) m''_2, m_2 m'_2 m''_2) \\ &= (m_1 m'_1 m''_1, m_1 m'_1 r'' \cup m_1 r' m''_2 \cup r m_2 m''_2, m_2 m'_2 m''_2) \\ &= m(m' m'')\end{aligned}$$

De plus $M$ a un élément neutre [à savoir $(e_1, \phi, e_2)$ où $e_1$ et $e_2$ sont des éléments neutres de $M_1$ et de $M_2$ et où $\phi \in R$ est l'ensemble vide] et par conséquent $M$ est un monoïde.

**Proposition 2.** *Soit* **V** *une variété de groupe. Si $M_1$ et $M_2$ appartiennent à la pseudo variété de monoïde finis induite par* **V** *il en est de même de leur produit semi-direct booléen $M = M_1 \circledast M_2$.*

*Démonstration.* Soit $u = (u_1, r, u_2) \in M$ un idempotent de $M$ et soit $G_u$ le sous groupe maximal de $M$ qui le contient. Il est clair que $u_1 = u_1^2$, $u_2 = u_2^2$, et que l'application qui envoie tout $g = (r_1, r_g, m_2) \in G_u$ sur la paire $(m_1, m_2) \in M_1 \times M_2$ est un homomorphisme $\gamma$ de $G_u$ dans le produit direct $G_{u_1} \times G_{u_2}$ des sous groupes maximaux $G_{u_1} \in M_1$ et $G_{u_2} \in M_2$. Par construction, le noyeau de $\gamma$ est l'ensemble $N$ des éléments de $M$ de la forme $(u_1, s, u_2)$ qui appartiennent à $G_u$. Donc si nous pouvons prouver que $N$ se réduit à $\{u\}$ nous aurons établi que $\gamma$ est un monomorphisme, c'est à dire que $G_u$ est isomorphe à un sous groupe de $G_{u_1} \times G_{u_2}$. Soit donc $m = (u_1, s, u_2) \in N$. Puisque $m \in G_u$, $m$ possède un inverse $\bar{m}$ (relativement à $u$) c'est à dire qu'il existe un élément $\bar{m} = u\bar{m} = \bar{m}u$ tel que $u = m\bar{m} = \bar{m}m$. Il est clair que $\bar{m}$ a la forme $\bar{m} = (u_1, \bar{s}, u_2)$ pour un certain $\bar{s} \in R$. Nous avons les relations suivantes:

$$r = u_1 r \cup r u_2 \qquad \text{(d'après } u = u^2\text{)}$$

$$r = u_1 \bar{s} \cup s u_2 \qquad \text{(d'après } u = m\bar{m}\text{)}$$

$$s = u_1 r \cup u_1 s u_2 \cup u_2 \qquad \text{(d'après } m = umu\text{)}$$

La première relation montre que $u_1 r \subset r$; par conséquent $u_1 r = u_1 u_1 \bar{s} \cup u_1 s u_2 \subset r$ d'après la seconde relation et, a fortiori $u_1 s u_2 \subset r$. Or la troisième relation s'écrit aussi $s = r \cup u_1 s u_2$ et, par conséquent, on a établi $s = r$, c'est à dire $m = u$ pour tout $m \in N$. Ceci achève la vérification que tous les sous groupes du produit semi direct $M$ appartiennent à **V**.

Afin de rattacher les sonsidérations précédentes à la théorie des langages formels nous considérons maintenant un ensemble fixe $X$ et le monoïde libre $X^*$ engendré par cet ensemble. Les éléments de $X^*$ sont appelés "*mots*" et nous appelerons "*langages formels sur X*" tout sous ensemble de

$X^*$. Enfin étant donnée une *pseudo* variété $\mathbf{V}'$ de monoïdes finis induites par une variété de group $\mathbf{V}$ nous dirons qu'un langage formel $F \subset X^*$ est un $\mathbf{V}'$-langage si et seulement si il existe un monoïde quotient $M \in V'$ et un homomorphisme $\alpha: X^* \to M$ tel que l'ensemble $F$ soit précisèment égal à l'image inverse $\overset{-1}{\alpha}\alpha F$ de son image $\alpha F$ dans $M$ par $\alpha$. Formellement,

$$F = \{f' \in X^* : \exists_F f : \alpha f' = \alpha f\}$$

**Proposition 3.** *Si $F_1$ et $F_2$ sont deux $\mathbf{V}'$-langages sur $X$ il en est de même de leur union $F_1 \cup F_2$, du complément relatif $F_1 \backslash F_2$ et du produit $F_1 F_2$*

$$F_1 F_2 = \{ff' \in X^* : f \in F_1, f' \in F_2\}.$$

*Démonstration.* Soient $\alpha_1 : X^* \to M_1$ et $\alpha_2 : X^* \to M_2$ tels que $M_1, M_2 \in \mathbf{V}'$ $\overset{-1}{\alpha_1}\alpha_1 F_1 = F_1$; $\overset{-1}{\alpha_1}\alpha_2 F_2 = F_2$. Nous considérerons le produit semi-direct $M = M_1 \oplus M_2$ et nous définissons une application $\alpha: X^* \to M$ en posant $\alpha e = (\alpha_1 e, \{(\alpha_1 e, \alpha_2 e)\}, \alpha_2 e)$ et pour tout $f \in X^*$

$$\alpha f = (\alpha_1 f, \{(\alpha_1 f', \alpha_2 f''): f', f'' \in X^*; f'f'' = f\}, \alpha_2 f)$$

Il est clair que $\alpha$ est un homomorphisme de $X^*$ sur un certain sous monoïde $\bar{M}$ de $M$. De plus si $f \in X^*$ on peut savoir en connaissant seulement son image $\alpha f \in \bar{M}$ si $f \in F_1 \cup F_1$ ou $f \in F_1 \backslash F_2$ ou $f \in F_1 F_2$. Donc $\overset{-1}{\alpha}\alpha F = F$ pour $F = F \cup F_1, = F_1 \backslash F_2$ ou $= F_1 F_2$ et la validité l'énoncé résulte de la Proposition 4.

Si la variété de groupe $\mathbf{V}$ est la variété $\mathbf{V}_1$ des groupes triviaux (c'est à dire des groupes réduits à leurs éléments neutres) la famille correspondantes de langage a été étudiée par McNaughton et Trachtenbrot et c'est la plus petite famille fermée par les opérations d'union de complémtement relatif et de produit qui contienne tous les sous ensembles de $X$. On sait aussi que quand $\mathbf{V}$ contient tous les groupes *abeliens* et que $F$ est un $\mathbf{V}$ langage il en est de même du sous monoïde de $X^*$ engendré par le langage $F' = X^* F \backslash X^* F X X^*$ formé de tous les mots de l'idéal $X^* F$ qui n'ont aucun facteur propre gauche dans $X^* F$. Cette deuxième forme de langage a aussi été étudiée par McNaughton (1960). Nous ne reproduirons par les démonstrations ici et nous terminerons en proposant le problème de prouver (ou de refuter) l'hypothèse selon laquelle les opérations d'union, complémentation produits et la formation de sous monoïdes du type qui vient d'être décrit permet d'engendrer tout les $V'_{ab}$-langages (à partir des $X' \subset X$) où $V_{ab}$ est la *pseudo* variété de monoïdes finis induite par la variété des groupes abéliens.

## Bibliographie

McNaughton, R. (1960). Symbolic logic and automata, *Wright Air Development Div. Tech. Note* 60–244, Cincinnati, Ohio.

Miller, D. D., et Clifford, A. H. (1956). Regular D-classes in semigroups, *Trans. Am. Math. Soc.* **82**, 270–280.

Petrone, L., et Schützenberger, M. P. *Sur un problème de McNaughton* (à paraître).

# On a Family of Sets Related to McNaughton's *L*-Language

M. P. SCHÜTZENBERGER

*Institut Blaise Pascal*
*Paris, France*

## I. Introduction

Let $F$ be the free monoid generated by a fixed set $X$ containing at least two elements and let $Q_1$ be the least family $Q$ of subsets of $F$ that satisfies the conditions (K1) and (K2) below where, as always in this paper, $e$ denotes the neutral element of $F$.

(K1). $F \in Q; \{e\} \in Q; X' \in Q$ for any subset $X'$ of $X$.

(K2). If $Q$ contains $A_1$ and $A_2$, it also contains $A_1 \cup A_2$ $A_1 \backslash A_2$ $(= \{f \in F: f \in A_1, f \in A_2\})$ and $A_1 \cdot A_2 \,(= \{ff' \in F: f \in A_1, f' \in A_2\})$.

The study of $Q_1$ is motivated by the fact (discussed in [5]) that $Q_1$ is closely related to the family of the subsets of $F$ that can be described within the "*L*-language" of McNaughton ([3)]. The object of the present paper is to verify the *main property* below, which gives for certain subsets of $F$ the possibility of deciding if they belong to $Q_1$. Finally, as a direct application of Eggan's theory ([1]), we show that for suitable $X$, $Q_1$ contains sets of arbitrarily large "star height."

For each positive natural number $n$, let $M_1(n)$ denote the family of all monoids having at most $n$ elements and admitting only trivial subgroups ([4]); that is, let the monoid $M$ belong to $M_1(n)$ if and only if it has $n' \leqslant n$ elements and if $m^n = m^{n+1}$ for each $m \in M$. Further, for $A \subset F$, let $A \subset Q_1'$ if and only if there exist a monoid $M \in \cup\, M_1(n)$, a subset $M'$ of $M$ and a homomorphism $\gamma$ of $F$ into $M$ that satisfy $A = \{f \in F: \gamma f \in M'\}$. We have

### MAIN PROPERTY

The families $Q_1$ and $Q_1'$ of subsets of $F$ are identical.

As an illustration, let us consider two disjoint subsets $A_1$ and $A_2$ of $F$ and assume that we know three elements $f, f'$, and $f''$ of $F$ for which both $A_1 \cap \{f'f^nf'': n \in N\}$ and $A_2 \cap \{f'f^nf'': n \in N\}$ are infinite sets. Using the relation $Q_1 \subset Q_1'$, we can conclude that it is impossible to find a set $B \in Q_1$ satisfying $A_1 \subset B$ and $A_2 \subset F \setminus B$. Indeed, according to the definition of $Q_1'$, $B \in Q_1'$ would imply the existence of a finite integer $n$ such that the set $\{f'f^{n'}f'' : n' \in N, n' > n\}$ is entirely contained in $B$ or in $F \setminus B$.

## II. Verification of $Q_1 \subset Q_1'$

Since $Q_1$ is defined as the least family which satisfies (K1) and (K2), $Q_1 \subset Q_1'$ follows instantly from the following two remarks from ([5]), which are reproduced here for the sake of completeness.

**Remark 1.** $Q_1'$ satisfies condition (K1).

*Verification.* Let the monoid $M = \{e', x', 0\} \in M_1(3)$ and the map $\gamma : F \to M$ be defined as follows:

$$\gamma e = e' = e'^2 \begin{cases} \text{for each } x \in X', \gamma x = x' = e'x' = x'e' \\ \text{for each } f \in F \setminus (\{e\} \cup X'), \gamma f = 0 = e'0 = 0e' = x'^2 = x'0 \\ \qquad = 0x' = 0^2. \end{cases}$$

Thus $F = \gamma^{-1}M$, $X' = \gamma^{-1}x'$, $\{e\} = \gamma^{-1}e'$. It is clear that $\gamma$ is a homomorphism and Remark 1 is verified.

**Remark 2.** $Q_1'$ satisfies condition (K2).

*Verification.* Let for $j = 1, 2$ the homomorphism $\gamma_j : F \to M_j$, the monoid $M_j$, and the subset $M_j'$ of $M_j$ satisfy $M_j \in M_1(n_j)$ and $A_j = \{f \in F; \gamma_j f \in M_j'\}$.

We consider the family $R$ of all sets of pairs $(m_1, m_2) \in M_1 \times M_2$ and for $m_1 \in M_1$, $m_2 \in M_2$, $r = \{(m_{1,i}, m_{2,i}) : i \in I_r\} \in R$, we let

$$m_1 r = \{(m_1 m_{1,i}, m_{2,i}) : i \in I_r\} \qquad r m_2 = \{(m_{1,i}, m_{2,i} m_2) : i \in I_r\}$$

Further, denoting by $\bar{M}$ the direct product (of sets) $M_1 \times R \times M_2$, we define the product for any two elements $(m_1, r, m_2)$ and $(m_1', r', m_2')$ of $\bar{M}$ by the formula

$$(m_1, r, m_2)(m_1', r', m_2') = (m_1 m_1', m_1 r' \cup r m_2', m_2 m_2') \in \bar{M}$$

Finally for $f \in F$, we let

$$\gamma f = (\gamma_1 f, \{(\gamma_1 f', \gamma_2 f'') : f', f'' \in F; f = f'f''\}, \gamma_2 f) \in \bar{M}$$

The verification that we have defined an associative product and a homomorphism $\gamma$ of $F$ onto a finite monoid $M \subset \bar{M}$ is straightforward and it is omitted. The same applies to the verification that $A_1 \cup A_2$, $A_1 \backslash A_2$, and $A_1 \cdot A_2$ are images by $\gamma^{-1}$ of suitable subsets of $M$. Thus the remark will follow from the fact that any subgroup $G = \{(m_{1,i}, r_i, m_{2,i}) : i \in I_G\}$ of $M$ is isomorphic to a direct product $G_1 \times G_2$, where $G_j$ is a subgroup of $M_j$ $(j = 1, 2)$.

Indeed, by construction, $\{m_{j,i} : i \in I_G\} \subset M_j$ is a homomorphic image of $G$, hence a group $G_j$. Let $e_j$ be its neutral element and let $N$ be the intersection of $G$ with the subset $\{(e_1, r, e_2) : r \in R\}$ of $\bar{M}$; $N$ is a normal subgroup of $G$ and $G/N$ is isomorphic to a submonoid of $G_1 \times G_2$.

Therefore, for verifying $M \in \bigcup_{n>0} M_1(n)$, it suffices to show that $N$ reduces to the neutral element $e'(=(e_1, r, e_2))$ of $G$. To see this, let $g(=(e_1, s, e_2))$ and $\bar{g}(=(e_1, \bar{s}, e_2))$ be inverse elements of $N$. The equation $e' = e'^2$ gives $r = e_1 r \cup r e_2$ and the equation $e' = g\bar{g}$ gives $r = e_1 \bar{s} \cup s e_2$. Therefore, $e_1 r = e_1 \bar{s} \cup e_1 s e_2$ and, since $e_1 r \subset r$, we have $e_1 s e_2 \subset r$. However, the equation $g = e' g e'$ gives $s = e_1 r \cup e_1 s e_2 \cup r e_2$; that is, $s = r \cup e_1 s e_2$ and therefore, $s = r$. This shows that $e' = g$, hence that $N = \{e\}'$, and the verification is concluded.

## III. Verification of $Q_1' \subset Q_1$

For each positive natural number $n$ let $Q_1(n)$ denote the least family of subsets of $F$ that satisfies the conditions (K1) and (K2) and that contains every set of the form $\gamma^{-1} M'$ if $M' \subset \gamma F$ and if $\gamma : F \to \gamma F$ is a homomorphism of $F$ onto a member of $M_1(n)$. Thus $Q_1(1) = Q_1$, since for $M' \subset \gamma F$ and $\gamma F \in M_1(1)$, we have either $\gamma^{-1} M' = \phi$ or $\gamma^{-1} M' = F$. Thus the relation $Q_1' \subset Q_1$ will follow instantly from Remarks 3, 5, and 6, which show that for each $n > 0$ one has $Q_1(n+1) \subset Q_1(n)$ and, therefore, that $Q_1' = \bigcup_{n>0} Q_1(n)$ is a subfamily of $Q_1$. The cores of the arguments below are elementary special cases of well-known theorems of Green ([2]) and of Miller and Clifford ([4]) concerning the $\mathscr{D}$-classes and the $\mathscr{H}$-classes of monoids.

To simplify notations, we assume henceforth that $M = \gamma F \in M_1(n+1)$.

**Remark 3.** To show $\gamma^{-1} M' \in Q_1(n)$ for all subsets $M'$ of $M$, it suffices to verify the same property for $M' = MmM$, $M' = Mm$, and $M' = mM$, where $m$ is an arbitrary element of $M$.

*Verification.* Consider $a_1, a_2, a_3, a_4, b, b' \in M$ and assume that $b = a_1 b' a_2$, $b' = a_3 b$. This implies $b' = a_3 a_1 b' a_2 = (a_3 a_1)^n b' a_2^n$ for all positive $n$. Since $M$ has only trivial subgroups we can take $n$ so large that $a_2^n = a_2^{n+1}$. Then

$b' = (a_3 a_1)^n b' a_2^n = (a_3 a_1)^n b' a_2^{n+1} = b' a_2$. From this we conclude that $b = a_1 b' a_2 = a_1 b'$. Assume further that $b' = ba_4$. By a symmetric argument we obtain $b' = a_1 b'$ (and $b = b' a_2$), showing that $b = b'$ under this supplementary condition.

For any $m \in M$, let $W_m = \{m' \in M : m \in M \setminus Mm'M\}$ and $H_m = (mM \setminus W_m) \cap (Mm \setminus W_m)$. It is clear that $W_m$ is a finite union of sets having the form $Mm''M$ and that $\gamma^{-1} H_m \in Q_1(n)$ if the same is true for $Mm$, $mM$, and $W_m$. We show that in fact $H_m = \{m\}$. Indeed, let $m' \in H_m$. We must have $m = a_1 m' a_2$ (since $m' \notin W_m$), $m' = a_3 m$, and $m' = ma_4$ for some elements $a_i \in M$. The computations made above show that $m = m'$, and Remark 3 is verified.

**Remark 4.** If $m \in M$ is such that $W_m$ has two elements or more, then $A = \gamma^{-1} m$ belongs to $Q_1(n)$.

*Verification.* Let $\beta : M \to \bar{M}$ be a surjection of $M$ onto a set $\bar{M}$ that has the following properties: for each $m' \in W_m$, $\beta m'$ is a distinguished element 0, of $\bar{M}$; the restriction of $\beta$ to $M \setminus W_m$ is a bijection of this set onto $\bar{M} \setminus \{0\}$. Since $M . W_m . M = W_m$, we can define a structure of monoid on $\bar{M}$ by letting $(\beta m')(\beta m'') = \beta(m' m'')$ if $m' m'' \in M \setminus W_m$ and $= 0$ if $m' m'' \in W_m$. It is clear that $\bar{M}$ has only trivial subgroups and $\bar{M} \in M_1(n)$ follows from the hypothesis that $W_m$ has two elements or more. Since $A = \{f \in F : \beta\gamma f = \beta m\}$ the remark is verified.

**Remark 5.** If $m \in M$, $M' = MmM$, and $A = \gamma^{-1} M'$, then $A \in Q_1(n)$.

*Verification.* Since $\gamma e \in M'$ implies $M' = M$ and $A = F$, we can assume $\gamma e \notin M'$. Let $X' = X \cap \gamma^{-1} m$. We have $F . X' . F \subset A$ and $F . X' . F \in Q_1(1)$. Thus, either $\gamma^{-1} m \subset F . X' . F$ and the result is already proved, or there exists at least one $f \subset \gamma^{-1} m \setminus F . X . F$. We consider this last case. The element $f$ admits at least one minimal factor $f''$ such that $M . \gamma f'' . M = MmM$, that is, $f = gxf'x'g'$ $(g, f', g' \in F;\, x, x' \in X;\, f'' = xf'x')$, where letting $m_1 = x$, $m' = f'$, $m_2 = x'$, we have $Mm_1 m' m_2 M = MmM$, $MmM \neq Mm_1 m' M$, $MmM \neq Mm' m_2 M$. Thus $A$ contains $F . X_1 . A' . X_2 . F$, where $X_1 = X \cap \gamma^{-1} m_1$, $A' = \gamma^{-1} m'$, $X_2 = X \cap \gamma^{-1} m_2$, and, since $M$ is finite, it is clear that $A \setminus F . X' . F$ is a finite union of such sets. Therefore, using Remark 4, the result will follow from the verification that $W_m$ contains at least two distinct elements.

To see this, assume for the sake of contradiction that $m_1 m'$ does not belong to $W_{m'}$, that is, assume that $m' = a_1 m_1 m' a_2$ for some $a_1, a_2 \in M$. According to the computations made at the beginning of the verification of

Remark 3, this implies $m' = a_1 m_1 m'$, hence $Mm' m_2 = Ma_1 m_1 m' m_2 M \subset Mm_1 m' m_2 M = MmM$. Since by construction $Mm_1 m' m_2 M \subset Mm' m_2 M$, this relation is excluded by the hypothesis $MmM \neq Mm' m_2 M$. Thus $m_1 m' \subset W_{m'}$, and by a symmetric argument, $m' m_2 \subset W_{m'}$, are proved. This implies $m_1 m' m_2 \subset w_{m'}$. Since it is clear that $m_1 m' m_2 = m_1 m' = m' m_2$ is impossible, the verification is concluded.

**Remark 6.** If $m \in M$, $M' = Mm$ or $= mM$ and $A = \gamma^{-1} M'$, then $A \subset Q_1(n)$.

*Verification.* It suffices to consider the case of $M' = Mm$. Moreover, because of Remark 5, we can assume $Mm \neq MmM$, that is $Mm \neq F$ and $m_0 \subset MmM \setminus Mm$ for at least one $m_0 \in M$.

Let $f \in \gamma^{-1} m$. As above, $f$ has a minimal right factor $f'' = xf' \in A$ ($x \in X$, $f' \in F$), that is, letting $m_1 = \gamma x$, $m' = \gamma f'$, $Mm = Mm_1 m'$ and $Mm \neq Mm'$. We have $F.(X \cap \gamma^{-1} m_1) \,.\gamma^{-1} m' \subset A$ and $A$ is a finite union of such sets. As above, we have only to show that $W_m$ contains at least two elements. That $m \in W_{m'}$ follows from the argument developed in the verification of the last remark, and if $m_0 \in W_m$ we conclude that $W_{m'}$ contains $m$ and $m_0$. If $m_0 \notin W_m$, we have $m \in Mm_0 M$, hence $MmM = Mm_0 M$ (since $m_0 \in MmM$) and therefore also $m_0 \in W_{m'}$. This concludes the verification.

## References

1. L. C. Eggan, Transition graphs and the star-height of regular events, *Mich. Math. J.* **10**, 385–397 (1963).
2. J. A. Green, On the structure of semigroups, *Ann. Math.* **54**, 163–172 (1951).
3. R. McNaughton, Symbolic logic and automata, *Wright Air Development Div. Tech. Rept.* 60–244, Cincinnati, Ohio, 1960.
4. D. D. Miller and A. H. Clifford, Regular D-classes in semigroups, *Trans. Am. Math. Soc.* **82**, 270–280 (1956).
5. L. Petrone and M. P. Schützenberger, *Sur un problème de McNaughton* (submitted for publication).
6. M. Teissier, Sur les équivalences régulières dans les demi-groupes, *Comp. Rend.* **232**, 1987–1989 (1951).

# Pseudo-Variety Separability of Subsets of a Monoid, with Applications to Finite Automata

L. A. M. VERBEEK

*EURATOM–CETIS, Ispra, Italy*

## I. Introduction

In several publications (see [4] and [8]) procedures are given to reduce the number of states of an incompletely specified finite automaton without changing its input-output characteristics insofar as these are specified. These procedures are related to the structure of the monoid of the automaton, that is, the monoid of transformations of the states determined by the transition function. Many authors (see, e.g., [1], [2], [3], and [5]) have studied the structure of monoids of automata, often in relation to the state-reduction problem. These publications, and especially the main property in the paper by Schützenberger [11], led to the formulation of the problem in the algebraic theory of monoids considered in this paper.

Recall that a family **V** of monoids is a pseudo-variety of monoids (cf.[7]) if **V** contains all direct products, all submonoids, and all homomorphic images of all monoids in **V**. A monoid $M$ is said to be of pseudo-variety **V** if $M \in \mathbf{V}$. Some interesting pseudo-varieties of monoids are formed by the set of all finite groups, the set of all finite monoids, the set of all finite monoids whose subgroups are Abelian, and the set of all finite monoids whose subgroups are trivial, that is, consist of a single element.

Let $F$ be a monoid, let $I$ be an index set, and let $\mathbf{R} = \{R_i: i \in I\}$ be a set of disjoint subsets of $F$. Furthermore, let **V** be a given pseudo-variety of monoids. Our problem is to decide whether there exists a homomorphism $\gamma$ mapping $F$ into a monoid $M$ of pseudo-variety **V**, such that $M$ contains a set of disjoint subsets $\mathbf{P} = \{P_i: i \in I\}$ for which $\gamma^{-1}P_i \supseteq R_i$ for each $i \in I$. In case such a homomorphism $\gamma$ exists, we will say that **R** is **V**-separable.

In [9] Petrone and Schützenberger show that a set **R** of disjoint subsets of $F$ is separable by the pseudo-variety of all finite monoids whose subgroups are trivial just in case **R** is an $L$-language as discussed by McNaughton in [6]. An example of this situation is given in Section III.

In Sec. II necessary and sufficient conditions for the pseudo-variety separability of a set of disjoint subsets of a monoid are derived. In Sec. III these conditions are interpreted for the case of incompletely specified finite automata, that is, the case where each $R_i$ is a regular event; then the theorem gives an effective procedure to decide pseudo-variety separability. A simple example of such a procedure concludes the paper.

## II. The Main Property

In this section we first state and prove in Lemma 1 a variation of a property due to Teissier [12]. Then we give Lemma 2, based on a property due to Schützenberger [11]. Finally the main property on pseudo-variety separability is given in the theorem.

**Lemma 1*** (cf. [12]). Let $F$ be a monoid, let $I$ be a fixed set of indices, and let $\mathbf{R} = \{R_i : i \in I\}$ be a collection of disjoint subsets of $F$. Let $\rho_\mathbf{R}$ be the binary relation on $F$ defined for all $f, f' \in F$ by $f \rho_\mathbf{R} f'$ if and only if $f_1 f f_2 \in R_i \Leftrightarrow f_1 f' f_2 \in R_i$ for all $f_1, f_2 \in F$ and all $i \in I$. Then (a) The relation $\rho_\mathbf{R}$ is a congruence on $F$. Hence $\rho_\mathbf{R}$ defines the canonical homomorphism $\alpha_\mathbf{R}$ of $F$ onto the quotient monoid $\alpha_R F$, and we have (b) $\alpha_\mathbf{R}^{-1} \alpha_\mathbf{R} R_i = R_i$ for all $i \in I$. Furthermore, let $\varphi$ be any homomorphism of $F$ onto the quotient monoid $\varphi F$; then (c) $\varphi^{-1} \varphi R_i = R_i$ for all $i \in I$ if and only if there exists a homomorphism $\psi$ such that $\psi \varphi f = \alpha_\mathbf{R} f$ for all $f \in F$. Hence $\alpha_R$ is the unique maximal homomorphism of $F$ for which (b) is satisfied.

*Proof*

(a) From its definition follows immediately that the relation $\rho_\mathbf{R}$ is reflexive, symmetric, and transitive. Also, if $f \rho_\mathbf{R} f'$ and $f_1, f_2 \in F$, then $f'_1 f_1 f f_2 f'_2 \in R_i \Leftrightarrow f'_1 f_1 f' f_2 f'_2 \in R_i$ for all $f'_1, f'_2 \in F$ and all $i \in I$, so that $f_1 f f_2 \rho_\mathbf{R} f_1 f' f_2$. Consequently, $\rho_\mathbf{R}$ is a congruence on $F$.

(b) Let $e$ be the identity element of $F$. From the definition of $\alpha_\mathbf{R}$ follows for $f, f' \in F$ that $\alpha_\mathbf{R} f = \alpha_\mathbf{R} f'$ only if $f = efe \in R_i \Leftrightarrow ef'e = f' \in R_i$ with $i \in I$, hence $\alpha_\mathbf{R}^{-1} \alpha_\mathbf{R} R_i \subseteq R_i$. In general, for any subset $P$ of $F$ and any homomorphism $\alpha: F \to \alpha F$, we have $\alpha^{-1} \alpha P \supseteq P$; consequently $\alpha_\mathbf{R}^{-1} \alpha_\mathbf{R} R_i = R_i$ for all $i \in I$.

* This property is also contained in Section 5 of the paper "Congruences on completely O-simple semigroups" by G. B. Preston, *Proc. London Math. Soc.* **11**, 557-576 (1961).

(c) Assume $\varphi: F \to \varphi F$ is a homomorphism such that $\varphi^{-1}\varphi R_i = R_i$ for all $i \in I$. Let $f, f' \in F$ be such that $\varphi f = \varphi f'$; then, for any $f_1, f_2 \in F$, we have $\varphi f_1 f f_2 = \varphi f_1 f' f_2$, and thus $f_1 f f_2 \in R_i \Leftrightarrow f_1 f' f_2 \in R_i$ with $i \in I$. This implies $\alpha_R f = \alpha_R f'$.

Define the mapping $\psi: \varphi F \to \alpha_{\mathbf{R}} F$ by $\psi(\varphi f) = \alpha_{\mathbf{R}} f$ for all $f \in F$. The mapping $\psi$ clearly is single-valued and $\psi$ is a homomorphism because for any $f_1, f_2 \in F$ we have

$$\psi((\varphi f_1)(\varphi f_2)) = \psi(\varphi f_1 f_2) = \alpha_{\mathbf{R}} f_1 f_2 = (\alpha_{\mathbf{R}} f_1)(\alpha_{\mathbf{R}} f_2) = (\psi(\varphi f_1))(\psi(\varphi f_2))$$

Conversely, assume $\varphi: F \to \varphi F$ is a homomorphism such that there exists a homomorphism $\psi$ which has the property that $\psi\varphi f = \alpha_R f$ for all $f \in F$. Let $f, f' \in F$ be such that $\varphi f = \varphi f'$; then clearly $\alpha_{\mathbf{R}} f = \alpha_{\mathbf{R}} f'$, hence $f \in R_i \Leftrightarrow f' \in R_i$, with $i \in I$, so that $\varphi^{-1}\varphi R_i \subseteq R_i$. Consequently, as in the proof of (b), $\varphi^{-1}\varphi R_i = R_i$ for all $i \in I$.

Note that the homomorphism $\alpha_{\mathbf{R}}$, satisfying the condition $\alpha_{\mathbf{R}}^{-1}\alpha_{\mathbf{R}} R_i = R_i$ for all $i \in I$, is maximal in the sense that no other such homomorphism identifies more elements of $F$ in its image. The monoid $\alpha_{\mathbf{R}} F$ is the minimal quotient monoid of $F$ one can obtain under any homomorphism satisfying the condition. Clearly the set $\mathbf{R}$ may consist of one subset of $F$, as is the case considered in [12]; also $\mathbf{R}$ may be any partition of $F$.

**Lemma 2** (cf. [11]). Let $\alpha$ and $\beta$ be two homomorphisms of a monoid $F$ onto the quotient monoids $A$ and $B$, respectively. Let $\mathbf{Q} = \{Q\}$ be the set of those subsets of $A$ which are images of elements of $B$ under the composite mapping $\alpha\beta^{-1}$. Let $\otimes$ denote the multiplication on $\mathbf{Q}$ defined for all $Q, Q' \in \mathbf{Q}$, where $Q = \alpha\beta^{-1}b$, $Q' = \alpha\beta^{-1}b'$ and $b, b' \in B$, by $Q \otimes Q' = Q''$, where $Q'' = \alpha\beta^{-1}(bb')$. Then

(a) $\cup\{Q: Q \in \mathbf{Q}\} = A$.

(b) $\mathbf{Q}$ is a monoid with respect to the multiplication $\otimes$.

(c) The mappings $\alpha\beta^{-1}: B \to \mathbf{Q}$ and $\gamma = \alpha\beta^{-1}\beta: F \to \mathbf{Q}$ are both homomorphisms onto monoid $\mathbf{Q}$.

*Proof*

(a) Each $Q \in \mathbf{Q}$ is the subset of $A$ determined by an element $b \in B$ by $Q = \alpha\beta^{-1}b$. Since $\beta^{-1}B = F$ and $\alpha\beta^{-1}B = A$ we have $\cup\{Q: Q \in \mathbf{Q}\} = A$.

(b) Since $B$ is a monoid, $bb' \in B$ for all $b, b' \in B$; thus the product $Q \otimes Q'$ is a unique element of $\mathbf{Q}$ for every ordered pair $Q, Q'$ of elements of $\mathbf{Q}$. Moreover, $\otimes$ is associative because the multiplication in monoid $B$ is associative. Let $e_B$ be the identity element of monoid $B$ and let

$Q_e = \alpha\beta^{-1}e_B$. Clearly, $Q_e \otimes Q = Q \otimes Q_e = Q$ for any $Q \in \mathbf{Q}$, hence $Q_e$ is the two-sided identity element of $\mathbf{Q}$. Thus $\mathbf{Q}$ is a monoid with respect to $\otimes$.

(c) By its definition, the mapping $\alpha\beta^{-1}: B \to \mathbf{Q}$ is a single-valued mapping of monoid $B$ onto monoid $\mathbf{Q}$. By definition of $\otimes$ we have $(\alpha\beta^{-1}b) \otimes (\alpha\beta^{-1}b') = \alpha\beta^{-1}(bb')$ for any $b, b' \in B$. Consequently, $\alpha\beta^{-1}$ is a homomorphism of monoid $B$ onto monoid $\mathbf{Q}$. Since the mappings $\beta: F \to B$ and $\alpha\beta^{-1}: B \to \mathbf{Q}$ are both homomorphisms onto, their composition $\gamma = \alpha\beta^{-1}\beta: F \to \mathbf{Q}$ is a homomorphism of monoid $F$ onto monoid $\mathbf{Q}$.

Using Lemmas 1 and 2, the main property concerning pseudo-variety separability can be stated in the following

**Theorem.** Let $F$ be a monoid, let $I$ be a fixed index set, let $\mathbf{R} = \{R_i: i \in I\}$ be a collection of disjoint subsets of $F$, and let $U = \alpha_{\mathbf{R}} F$ be the minimal quotient monoid of $F$ satisfying the condition that $\alpha_{\mathbf{R}}^{-1}\alpha_{\mathbf{R}} R_i = R_i$ for all $i \in I$. Let $\mathbf{V}$ be a pseudo-variety of monoids. Then $\mathbf{R}$ is $\mathbf{V}$-separable if and only if there exists a collection $\mathbf{Q} = \{Q\}$ of subsets of $U$ which satisfies the following conditions:

1. $\cup\{Q: Q \in \mathbf{Q}\} = U$.
2. One can define a multiplication on $\mathbf{Q}$ such that $\mathbf{Q}$ is a monoid of pseudo-variety $\mathbf{V}$, and that there is a homomorphism $\gamma$ of $F$ onto the monoid $\mathbf{Q}$, that is, $\gamma F = \mathbf{Q} \in \mathbf{V}$.
3. Each $Q \in \mathbf{Q}$ has a nonempty intersection with at most one subset of the collection $\{\alpha_{\mathbf{R}} R_i: i \in I\}$ of subsets of $U$.
4. The elements of the collection $\mathbf{R}' = \{R_i' = \gamma^{-1}\gamma R_i: i \in I\}$ of subsets of $F$ are pairwise-disjoint, and $R_i' \supseteq R_i$ for all $i \in I$.

*Proof.* We first prove that the four conditions on $\mathbf{Q}$ are necessary for $\mathbf{R}$ to be $\mathbf{V}$-separable.

Assume $\mathbf{R}$ is $\mathbf{V}$-separable, that is, there is a homomorphism $\beta$ of $F$ onto a monoid $B$ of pseudo-variety $\mathbf{V}$, and a collection of disjoint subsets $\mathbf{P} = \{P_i: i \in I\}$ of $B$ such that $\beta^{-1}P_i \supseteq R_i$ for each $i \in I$.

1. Consider the collection $\mathbf{Q} = \{Q\}$ of subsets of $U$ which are images of the elements of $B$ under the mapping $\alpha_{\mathbf{R}}\beta^{-1}$. From Lemma 2 it follows immediately that $\cup\{Q: Q \in \mathbf{Q}\} = U$.

2. Define the multiplication, denoted by $\otimes$, on $\mathbf{Q}$ for all $Q, Q' \in \mathbf{Q}$, where $Q = \alpha_{\mathbf{R}}\beta^{-1}b$, $Q' = \alpha_{\mathbf{R}}\beta^{-1}b'$ and $b, b' \in B$, by $Q \otimes Q' = Q''$, where $Q'' = \alpha_{\mathbf{R}}\beta^{-1}(bb')$. Lemma 2 ensures that $\mathbf{Q}$ is a monoid with respect to $\otimes$, and that $\alpha_{\mathbf{R}}^{-1}\beta^{-1}: B \to \mathbf{Q}$ is a homomorphism of $B$ onto $\mathbf{Q}$. Since $B$ is of

pseudo-variety $\mathbf{V}$ its quotient monoid $\mathbf{Q}$ is also of pseudo-variety $\mathbf{V}$. From Lemma 2 we know that $\gamma = \alpha_{\mathbf{R}}\beta^{-1}\beta$ is a homomorphism of $F$ onto $\mathbf{Q}$; hence $\gamma F = \mathbf{Q} \in \mathbf{V}$.

3. For any $f \in F$ the subset $\beta^{-1}\beta f$ of $F$ is either contained in one subset $\beta^{-1}P_i$, where $P_i \in \mathbf{P}$, or else $\beta^{-1}\beta f$ has an empty intersection with such subsets. Hence, for any $f \in F$, $\beta^{-1}\beta f$ has a nonempty intersection with at most one subset $R_i \in \mathbf{R}$ of $F$, and the subset $\gamma f = \alpha_{\mathbf{R}}\beta^{-1}\beta f$ of $U$ intersects at most one subset $\alpha_{\mathbf{R}} R_i$ of $U$. In other words, each $Q \in \mathbf{Q}$ has a nonempty intersection with at most one subset $\alpha_{\mathbf{R}} R_i$ of $U$.

4. Let $f_i \in R_i$, and let $\gamma f_i = Q_i$. Then $Q_i \cap \alpha_{\mathbf{R}} R_i \neq \phi$, and from (3) it follows that $\gamma R_i \cap \gamma R_j = \phi$ for any pair $i, j \in I$ such that $i \neq j$. Consequently, $\mathbf{R}' = \{R_i' = \gamma^{-1}\gamma R_i \colon i \in I\}$ is a collection of disjoint subsets of $F$. Clearly, $\gamma^{-1}\gamma R_i \supseteq R_i$; thus $R_i' \supseteq R_i$ for each $i \in I$.

It is a simple matter to prove that the four conditions on $\mathbf{Q}$ are sufficient for $\mathbf{R}$ to be $\mathbf{V}$-separable. Assume $\mathbf{Q}$ satisfies conditions (1) to (4). Then it follows from (2) that there is a homomorphism $\gamma$ of $F$ onto a monoid $\mathbf{Q}$ of pseudo-variety $\mathbf{V}$. Condition (4) ensures that monoid $\mathbf{Q}$ contains a collection of disjoint subsets $\{\gamma R_i \colon i \in I\}$ such that $\gamma^{-1}\gamma R_i = R_i' \supseteq R_i$ for each $i \in I$. Consequently, $\mathbf{R}$ is indeed $\mathbf{V}$-separable. Herewith ends the verification of the theorem.

Notice that conditions (1) to (4) have, somewhat redundantly, been stated such that they may form the basis for an algorithm yielding a monoid of pseudo-variety $\mathbf{V}$ in case $F$, $\mathbf{R}$, and $\mathbf{V}$ are given explicitly. It is interesting that the conditions are predicated on the minimal homomorphic image $\alpha_{\mathbf{R}} F$ and not on $F$ itself.

## III. Application to Finite Automata

A *finite automaton* $A$ is a sextuple: $A = (X, Y, S, s_0, \tau', \omega)$, where $X$, $Y$, and $S$ are finite sets, called the *input alphabet*, the *output alphabet*, and the *states* of $A$, respectively. The element $s_0$ of $S$ is called the *initial state of* $A$. The *transition function* $\tau'$ is a single-valued mapping of the Cartesian product $S \times X$ into $S$, and the *output function* $\omega$ is a single-valued mapping of a subset of $S$ onto $Y$. If $\omega$ is defined for a proper subset of $S$, one calls $A$ an *incompletely specified* finite automaton; if $\omega$ is defined for all elements of $S$, the automaton is *completely specified*. Note that, without loss of generality, $\tau'$ is here supposed to be defined for all pairs $(s, x)$ in $S \times X$. Let $F$ be the free monoid generated by the input alphabet $X$ under the operation of concatenation. The elements of the free input monoid $F$ are called *input words*;

the identity element of $F$ is the empty word $e$. The transition function $\tau'$ is inductively extended to $\tau: S \times F \to S$ by defining, for all $s \in S$, $x \in X$, and $f \in F$, $\tau(s,e) = s$ and $\tau(s,xf) = \tau(\tau'(s,x),f)$.

The operation of a finite automaton $A$ is thus to go, upon receiving an input word $f \in F$, from the initial state $s_0$ to the final state $\tau(s,f)$ and giving $\omega(\tau(s,f))$ as output in case this is defined.

The extended transition function $\tau$ of a finite automaton $A$ associates with each input word $f \in F$ a transformation of the set $S$. Let $\mu: F \to M_A$ be the mapping of $F$ onto the appropriate subset $M_A$ of all transformations of $S$. Thus $\mu$ is defined for all $f \in F$ by $\mu f = m \in M_A$, where $m: S \to S$ is the transformation of $s$ onto $\tau(s,f)$ for each $s \in S$. Take as multiplication in $M_A$ the ordinary composition of transformations. Then $M_A$ is a finite (since $S$ is finite) monoid with the identity transformation as identity element. Now, if $f_1, f_2 \in F$ and $\mu f_1 = m_1$, $\mu f_2 = m_2$, then the definition of $\tau$ implies $\mu(f_1 f_2) = m_1 m_2$. Hence $\mu$ is a homomorphism of $F$ onto $M_A$. $M_A$ is called the *monoid of automaton A*.

Let $Y = \{y_i: i \in I\}$, where $I$ is a fixed finite set of indices. To each output $y_i \in Y$ of a given finite automaton $A$ corresponds a subset $R_i$ of $F$ consisting of all input words which, when received by the automaton in its initial state, yield output $y_i$. Thus automaton $A$ determines a finite collection $\mathbf{R} = \{R_i: i \in I\}$ of disjoint subsets of $F$. Note that if $A$ is completely specified the collection $\mathbf{R}$ forms a partition of $F$. Note also that the collection $\mathbf{R} = \{R_i: i \in I\}$ of disjoint subsets of $F$ for any automaton $A$ is such that their images under $\mu$ in $M_A$ are disjoint, that is, $\mu R_i \cap \mu R_j = \phi$ if $i \neq j$.

The congruence $\rho_{\mathbf{R}}$ on $F$ (see Lemma 1) is such that all words $f$ of $F$ for which $\mu f$ is a given element of the monoid $M_A$ of $A$ are congruent modulo $\rho_{\mathbf{R}}$. Thus $U = \alpha_{\mathbf{R}} F$ is homomorphic to $M_A$. Since $M_A$ is finite, the congruence $\rho_{\mathbf{R}}$ is of finite index (as a matter of fact, $\rho_{\mathbf{R}}$ is the same as the relation $R$ in Theorem 1 of [10]). Hence any collection of subsets of $U$ is finite and conditions (1) to (4) of the theorem can be tested effectively for any pseudo-variety of monoids $\mathbf{V}$ and the collection $\mathbf{R}$ determined by any given finite automaton $A$.

As a simple example of such a procedure consider the following case. Let $X = \{a,b\}$, let $I = \{1,2\}$, and let $R_1 = \{a(ba)^k\}$ and $R_2 = \{(ab)^{2k+1}\}$, where $k = 0, 1, 2, \ldots$. Let $\mathbf{V}$ be the pseudo-variety of all finite monoids whose subgroups are trivial, that is, consist of a single element. The problem is whether $\mathbf{R} = \{R_1, R_2\}$ is $\mathbf{V}$-separable or not.

First, the monoid $U = \alpha_{\mathbf{R}} F$ should be known. Lemma 1 gives the appropriate congruence $\rho_{\mathbf{R}}$ on $F$ by $f \rho_{\mathbf{R}} f'$ if and only if $f_1 f f_2 \in R_i \Leftrightarrow f_1 f' f_2 \in R_i$ for all $f_1, f_2 \in F$ and all $i \in I$. From this definition one derives the ten congruence classes $C_0$–$C_9$ of $F$; $k = 0, 1, 2, \ldots$.

$$\begin{array}{ll}
C_0 = \{e\} & C_5 = \{fa^2f', fb^2f' : f, f' \in F\} \\
C_1 = \{a(ba)^{2k}\} & C_6 = \{a(ba)^{2k+1}\} \\
C_2 = \{b(ab)^{2k}\} & C_7 = \{b(ab)^{2k+1}\} \\
C_3 = \{(ab)^{2k+1}\} & C_8 = \{(ab)^{2k+2}\} \\
C_4 = \{(ba)^{2k+1}\} & C_9 = \{(ba)^{2k+2}\}
\end{array}$$

Note that $R_1 = C_1 \cup C_6$ and $R_2 = C_3$.

The monoid $U = \alpha_{\mathbf{R}} F$ consists of 10 elements $u_n = \alpha_{\mathbf{R}} C_n$, $0 \leqslant n \leqslant 9$, where $u_0$ is the identity element of $U$. Note that the subgroups of $U$ are $\{u_0\}$, $\{u_3, u_8\}$, $\{u_4, u_9\}$, and $\{u_5\}$.

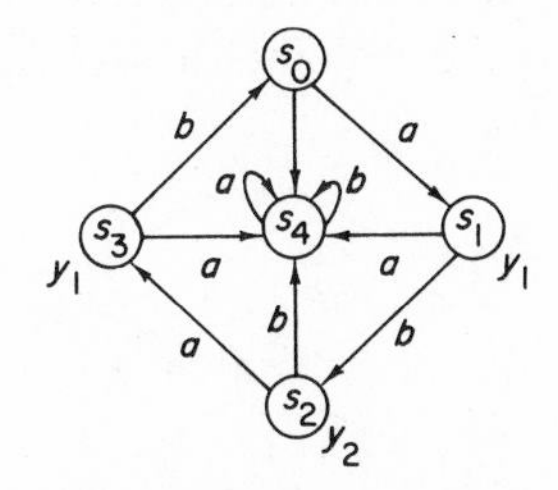


FIG. 1. Transition diagram of the automaton realizing $U = \alpha_{\mathbf{R}} F$.

A finite automaton whose monoid is isomorphic to $U$ is given in Fig. 1 in the form of its transition diagram. The initial state is $s_0$, in states $s_1$ and $s_3$ the output is $y_1$, in state $s_2$ the output is $y_2$, and in states $s_0$ and $s_4$ the ouptut is not defined. Of course we could first have given the automaton of Fig. 1 and derived from it $\mathbf{R} = \{R_1, R_2\}$ and $U = \alpha_{\mathbf{R}} F$.

Now we have to find a set $\mathbf{Q}$ of subsets of $U$, which satisfies conditions (1) to (4) of the theorem. It is easily verified that, for instance, the following set $\mathbf{Q}$ is adequate:

$$\begin{array}{llll}
Q_e = \{u_0\} & Q_2 = \{u_2, u_7\} & Q_4 = \{u_4, u_9\} & Q_6 = \{u_5\} \\
Q_1 = \{u_1\} & Q_3 = \{u_3, u_8\} & Q_5 = \{u_1, u_6\} &
\end{array}$$

The multiplication $\otimes$ on $\mathbf{Q}$ is indicated in the Cayley table, Table 1, where only the indices of the $Q$'s are given. Thus $\mathbf{Q}$ is a monoid with seven elements, the subgroups of $\mathbf{Q}$ are $\{Q_e\}$, $\{Q_3\}$, $\{Q_4\}$, and $\{Q_6\}$.

Figure 2 gives the transition diagram of a finite automaton, the monoid of which is isomorphic to $\mathbf{Q}$. The initial state is $t_0$, in state $t_1$ and $t_6$ the output is $y_1$, in state $t_4$ the output is $y_2$, and in the other states the output is not

TABLE 1

| ⊗ | e | 1 | 2 | 3 | 4 | 5 | 6 |
|---|---|---|---|---|---|---|---|
| e | e | 1 | 2 | 3 | 4 | 5 | 6 |
| 1 | 1 | 6 | 3 | 6 | 5 | 6 | 6 |
| 2 | 2 | 4 | 6 | 2 | 6 | 4 | 6 |
| 3 | 3 | 5 | 6 | 3 | 6 | 5 | 6 |
| 4 | 4 | 6 | 2 | 6 | 4 | 6 | 6 |
| 5 | 5 | 6 | 3 | 6 | 5 | 6 | 6 |
| 6 | 6 | 6 | 6 | 6 | 6 | 6 | 6 |

defined. The subsets of $F$ determined by this automaton are $R_1' = \{a(ba)^k\} = R_1$ and $R_2' = \{(ab)^{k+1}\} \supset R_2$. Consequently, the set $\mathbf{R} = \{R_1, R_2\}$ is indeed $\mathbf{V}$-separable, and Fig. 2 gives a finite automaton whose monoid is of pseudo-variety $\mathbf{V}$ and determines the disjoint subsets $R_1' = R_1$ and $R_2' \supset R_2$ of $F$.

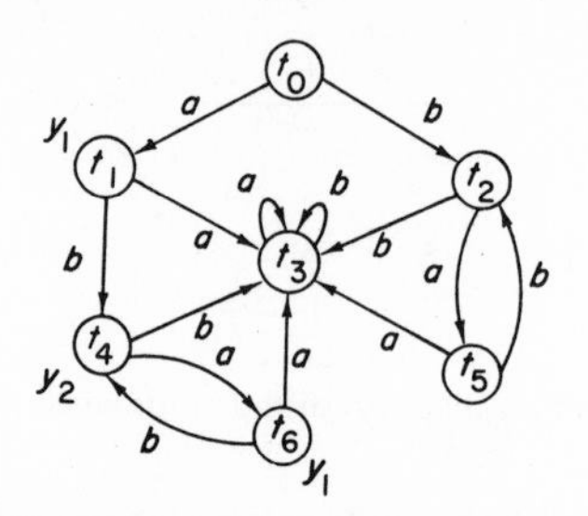


FIG. 2. Transition diagram of the automaton realizing $\mathbf{Q}$.

## ACKNOWLEDGMENT

The author is grateful to Professor M. P. Schützenberger for his proposal to prove the theorem, which forms an extension of the main property given in [11].

## REFERENCES

1. J. Beatty and R. E. Miller, Some theorems for incompletely specified sequential machines with applications to state minimization, *Proc. AIEE 3rd Ann. Symp. on Switching Theory and Logical Design*, Oct. 1962.
2. C. C. Elgot and J. D. Rutledge, Machine properties preserved under state minimization, *Proc. AIEE 3rd Ann. Symp. on Switching Theory and Logical Design*, Oct. 1962.
3. S. Ginsburg, Connective properties preserved in minimal-state machines, *J. Assoc. Comp. Mach.* 7, 311–325 (1960).
4. S. Ginsburg, A technique for the reduction of a given machine to a minimal-state machine, *IRE Trans.* **EC-8**, 346–355 (1959).

5. K. B. Krohn and J. L. Rhodes, Algebraic theory of machines, in *Mathematical Theory of Automata* (J. Fox, ed.) Polytechnic Institute of Brooklyn, Brooklyn, New York, 1963, pp. 341–384.
6. R. McNaughton, Symbolic logic and automata, *Wright Air Develop. Div. Tech. Note* 60–244, Cincinnati, Ohio, 1960.
7. A. I. Malcev, On the general theory of algebraic systems, *Mat. Sb.* [n.s.] **35**(77), 3–20 (1954).
8. M. C. Paull and S. H. Unger, Minimizing the number of states in incompletely specified sequential switching functions, *IRE Trans.* **EC-8**, 356–367 (1959).
9. L. Petrone and M. P. Schützenberger, Sur un problème de McNaughton, *Rapport Euratom* EUR 2292. f. Presses Académiques Européennes, Bruxelles, 1965.
10. M. O. Rabin and D. Scott, Finite automata and their decision problems, *IBM J. Res. Develop.* **3**, 114–125 (1959).
11. M. P. Schützenberger, On an abstract machine property preserved under the satisfaction relation, *IBM Res. Note NC-167*, Nov. 1962.
12. M. Teissier, Sur les équivalences régulières dans les demi-groupes, *Comp. Rend.* **232,** 1987–1989 (1951).

# Author Index

Numbers in parentheses are reference numbers and indicate that an author's work is referred to although his name is not cited in the text. Numbers in italics show the page on which the complete reference is listed.

# Subject Index

C



D



E



F